Vikings in the Playoffs

Vikings in the Playoffs
*The Golden Era Under
Bud Grant, 1968–1977*

RICK BOWMAN

McFarland & Company, Inc., Publishers
Jefferson, North Carolina

All photos courtesy the Minnesota Vikings
and the National Football League.

ISBN (print) 978-1-4766-9762-8
ISBN (ebook) 978-1-4766-5550-5

LIBRARY OF CONGRESS CATALOGING DATA ARE AVAILABLE

Library of Congress Control Number 2025019761

© 2025 Rick Bowman. All rights reserved

No part of this book may be reproduced or transmitted in any form or by any means, electronic or mechanical, including photocopying or recording, or by any information storage and retrieval system, without permission in writing from the publisher.

Front cover image: Minnesota Vikings head coach Bud Grant
(Jerry Coli/Dreamstime)

Printed in the United States of America

*McFarland & Company, Inc., Publishers
Box 611, Jefferson, North Carolina 28640
www.mcfarlandpub.com*

Table of Contents

Acknowledgments vi
Preface 1
Introduction 3

1. Holiday Bliss? 9
2. Ozzie Dives, Carl Sacks 27
3. It's Washington by Air 43
4. The Lost Years 56
5. The Seed and Gillie Show 69
6. Fran's Colossal Catapult 80
7. Nate's Scoop and Score 96
8. Wright's Timely Chase 105
9. Hail Mary Agony 118
10. Sammy's Acrobatics 134
11. Bobby's Big Day 149
12. What Could Have Gone Wrong Did 162
13. One More Time for the Master 175

Epilogue 193
Chapter Notes 201
Bibliography 207
Index 209

Acknowledgments

My brother, Bill, instilled in me my love for football, and his support, along with that of the rest of my family, made this project possible. Special thanks to former Viking tight end Stu Voigt, whose untiring efforts helped me connect with many of his teammates. The book would not have been written without Voigt's dogged determination. Thanks also to former longtime Vikings public relations man Bob Hagan, who helped me reach several key individuals.

Preface

Would the true story ever be told of the Golden Era of the Minnesota Vikings, a run that started in the tumultuous late 1960s and ran throughout the '70s, a stretch that saw the team capture 10 divisional championships and make four Super Bowls in 11 seasons?

With an increasing number of that generation's players and coaches having gone to their long home, including the recent losses of Joe Kapp and head coach Bud Grant, I wondered if that would be the case. Will we ever know what happened behind the scenes? Will these teams be remembered solely for their four devastating Super Bowl losses?

There have been multiple attempts to encapsulate this more-than-a-decade-long journey, one which essentially began on a snow-blanketed Franklin Field in Philadelphia on December 15, 1968, and ended nine years later in a quagmire at Memorial Coliseum in Los Angeles on December 26, 1977, a game famously known as the "Mud Bowl."

None of these efforts fully satisfied me. I didn't believe any of these accounts truly did justice to the team's storied accomplishments. There certainly have been books on the team's grandiose NFL championship season of 1969, volumes that skimmed over the team's history and others that focused on individual players such as Fran Tarkenton, but I wanted more.

How was the team built? What made it click? How did its success endure?

Living in northeast Ohio and falling in love with the Vikings was very challenging, because I never got enough information about the team. Newspaper coverage was sparse during my early years as a fan. There, of course, was no internet, and the only video highlights available were either during halftimes of *Monday Night Football* or on Saturdays during the NFL Films show *This Week in Pro Football*.

Upon becoming a sportswriter after graduating from college, and due to, among other things, my inquisitive nature that loves nuances and intricate details and a background in playing the game myself, as well as a voracious love of history, I believed there may be no individual better suited to dig into what made these teams so great, how they won so many big games and how they picked themselves up after devastating defeats.

With Vikings fans having suffered so long, I believed it best to not focus on the Super Bowl setbacks but on the team's nine glorious playoff wins during this stretch and the players that made them possible. Minnesota's first taste of playoff success came in the NFL Western Conference championship game on December 27, 1969, against the Los Angeles Rams, a postseason opponent they would become uniquely familiar with. The last of the nine playoff wins was a rousing upset over these same Rams in the 1977 Mud Bowl, with veteran backup Bob "The General" Lee, not the injured Tarkenton, starting at quarterback.

Five years later, Minnesota did garner another playoff victory under Grant, on January 9, 1983, over the Atlanta Falcons. By that time the glory days at Metropolitan

Stadium were long over, as this contest was played in the sterile environment of the newly christened Hubert H. Humphrey Metrodome. Also gone were the heroes of the team's Golden Era, players like Carl Eller, Alan Page and Paul Krause, making the Mud Bowl victory truly "One More Time for the Master."

For the sake of chronology, I also included chapters on four years they didn't win a playoff game, the 1970–72 seasons and 1975.

It was a thrill to reach out to these players, the majority of whom had to work a job in the offseason to make ends meet. Virtually all the players of this era had a second career beyond football. Except where noted, all quotations come from my interviews with them.

The first player I interviewed was Bobby Bryant, the cornerback who is second all-time for the Vikings in career interceptions with 51. I wanted to know how Bryant had the wherewithal to leave the man he was guarding on the right side of the field only to drift all the way to the middle of the gridiron to make an improbable, game-saving interception against the Los Angeles Rams during Minnesota's last NFC championship game triumph on December 26, 1976.

I wanted to know what it was like on the team buses leaving historic Franklin Field on the way to the airport after the Vikings clinched their first NFC Central crown with a win over Philadelphia in 1968. I wanted to know how Carl Eller was able to get around the great right tackle Bob Brown to make one of the biggest plays in team history: a sack of Roman Gabriel that went for a safety in the team's first-ever home playoff game.

I wanted to know why an organization that made such great personnel decisions went two seasons—1970 and 1971—without knowing who its starting quarterback was. I wanted to know how, despite having a bum shoulder, Fran Tarkenton could uncork a 55-yard bomb to the speedy John Gilliam in the 1973 NFC championship game. I wanted to know how little guys like safety Jeff Wright could play so big in games like the 1974 NFC championship when he ran down a mercurial receiver similar to Gilliam in the Rams' Harold Jackson, stopping him just short of the go-ahead touchdown.

I wanted to know why Alan Page was off the field on the infamous Hail Mary pass on December 28, 1975. I wanted to know why the Vikings weren't in nickel defense when the season before they often deployed six defensive backs on passing downs.

I wanted to know what made Jim Marshall such a truly great man and the ultimate team player. I wanted to know how the team was built. That's why I was so grateful to interview Jerry Reichow, a bulwark in the organization who oversaw the famous 1967 draft that saw the Vikings nab three players in the first round—Gene Washington, Alan Page and Clinton Jones—who each competed in one of the most historic college football games in history, the fabled 1966 "Game of the Century" between Michigan State and Notre Dame.

I wanted to know all this and I believe Vikings fans across the country did, too.

Without a doubt, there are untold record books, trivia books and anecdotal books concerning this team, but none that present a detailed look at this era of Viking playoff football.

It was a time of outside football at venerable Metropolitan Stadium, a lovable venue that played host to 10 wintertime playoff skirmishes. It was a decade that captivated the hearts and minds of the fans who became the building blocks of the team's current and vast following. A fan base, not unlike Dodgers fans of the 1950s, who have stuck with their team despite glaring disappointment after glaring disappointment.

Introduction

When Roger Kahn wrote the classic 1972 book *Boys of Summer*, he lovingly chronicled the team of his youth, a collection of charismatic ballplayers whose daring acts would become sewn into his life's very fabric.

Having grown up in the shadows of New York's Ebbets Field, Kahn recounted the images indelibly sketched in his mind of the Brooklyn Dodgers, i.e., "Dem Bums," a once ragtag bunch that eventually flourished into perennial National League pennant contenders.

As a grown man in the 1950s, he would cover for the *New York Herald Tribune* the legends of his childhood, a cavalcade of stars led by the likes of Jackie Robinson, "Pee Wee" Reese, Duke Snider and Roy Campanella.

Despite these Hall of Famers, the Dodgers would suffer disappointment after disappointment at the hands of the hated New York Yankees, whom they would fall to six times in Fall Classic play during the '40s and '50s, able to break through just once, in 1955.

In the world of professional football during the late 1960s and throughout the 1970s, there was another team that thoroughly frustrated but at the same time captivated the hearts of fans throughout the greater Midwest, if not the nation, and that was Bud Grant's vaunted Minnesota Vikings, the indubitable "Purple-Clad Boys of Winter."

As if ordained from above, the Vikings from their origin were a captivating, competitive and head-turning team, largely due to the player they selected 29th overall (albeit in the third round) in their initial draft in 1961, a cocksure quarterback destined for greatness out of the University of Georgia, the master improvisator Francis Asbury Tarkenton.

Nabbing breakaway runner Tommy Mason of Tulane with their first-ever draft pick to join Tarkenton in the backfield would prove to be a bedrock selection, but in six short years the long-striding back's trade to the Los Angeles Rams would produce a draft pick that was used to select Notre Dame great Alan Page, one of the final pieces of a marauding, home-spun defense. Arriving the same year from Canada would be Grant, whose stoic leadership would place the Vikings into perpetual Super Bowl contention.

Only two other organizations, those in Dallas and in Pittsburgh, have more wins during the Super Bowl era than the Minnesota Vikings, and setting the pattern of success was no doubt Grant, who captured four Grey Cups while head coach of the Winnipeg Blue Bombers.

"Sometimes you'd look over to him and he'd just give you a signal," said Vikings ironman defensive end Jim Marshall of Grant's calm leadership. "Everyone looked to him, 'What do we do?' Everyone should have been able to experience him as a coach. He wasn't just a coach of football, but a coach of men. He certainly changed my life for the better."[1]

Wintertime playoff games at venerable Metropolitan Stadium in Bloomington became a veritable rite of passage under Grant, who took over the coaching reins from the volatile Norm Van Brocklin.

Bundled up on the sidelines in a turtleneck and camel hair trench coat before the Vikings' December 28, 1975, playoff matchup against the Dallas Cowboys, eloquent CBS Sports commentator Jack Whitaker may have best summarized this sentiment: "The Vikings have added considerably to the tradition of these playoffs," he articulately said. "They're as much a part of Christmas as Santa Claus, Dickens and the holly wreath. We're always in Bloomington at Christmastime."[2]

Minnesota's first true sojourn into NFL prominence began on a frozen Franklin Field grass turf on December 15, 1968. It was the biggest game in franchise history.

The Vikings would make history at the most historic of all football venues, as their 24–17 defeat of the hapless Philadelphia Eagles, combined with a home loss by Chicago to the Green Bay Packers, enabled the wide-eyed club to secure a Central Division crown by one game and a first-ever trip to the playoffs.

Minnesota (8–6) entered the contest tied for first with the Bears (7–7), who held the tiebreaker after beating the Vikings twice in regular season play.

It's fitting that so momentous of an event took place at venerable Franklin Field, the oldest football stadium in the country, a gridiron where the "Galloping Ghost," Red Grange, once traversed, a brick-facade structure that serves as the home field for the University of Pennsylvania Quakers, who have hosted more games than any college football team in any division since opening play at a shallowly built wooden structure in 1895.

It was at Franklin Field, before a crowd of approximately 100,000 onlookers, where President Franklin Delano Roosevelt made his acceptance speech as part of the 1936 Democratic National Convention, which was held at the adjacent Municipal Auditorium.

"There's a mysterious cycle in human events," started Roosevelt, seeking his second presidential term. "To some generations, much is given. Of other generations, much is expected. This generation of Americans has a rendezvous with destiny."[3]

After the Vikings went 3–8–3 in their first year under Grant, this was truly a day of destiny for a coach who was the Eagles' first-round pick in 1950 out of the University of Minnesota.

The night before the game, a substantial snowstorm hit town and left most of the stadium covered in snow. At kickoff, temperatures were in the high teens and wind gusts reached 30 miles per hour. It was Minnesota weather, but that didn't mean Vikings players were by any means comfortable.

"The locker room was tiny, and there was a water leak that made everything just miserable," said Vikings taxi squad quarterback Bob Lee. "I was on the sideline as I'm supposed to be charting plays, but it was virtually impossible to do in those conditions."

"There must have been six to eight inches of snow on the field when we got there so we had to work out indoors at a nearby gym," said safety Dale Hackbart. "The grass was semi-frozen and we all had to change our cleats and it was very cold."

After a scoreless first quarter, the Eagles broke through on Norm Snead's five-yard scoring toss to Gary Ballman in the left corner of the end zone. But the Vikings were able go into the halftime locker room tied at 7–7 thanks to Bill Brown's rousing 57-yard catch-and-run touchdown. Brown, tripped up inside the Eagles' five by Philadelphia safety Nate Ramsey, maintained his balance before sliding backward into the goalpost after crossing into the end zone, a play made possible when Joe Kapp cleverly avoided tackle Gary Pettigrew by moving forward in the pocket before finding the University of Illinois product all alone down the seam.

"We had Kapp trapped for a considerable loss, but he scrambled, found Brown open and hit him for the touchdown," said beleaguered Philadelphia coach Joe Kuharich.[4]

Most of the players entering the locker room at the half had no idea of the scene that was about to unfold on the field.

Perturbed over the team's lackluster season, the home crowd—cantankerous over having to sit on bleachers blanketed with a half-foot of snow—was having none of the yuletide spirit. Kuharich's club started 0–11 but had won its last two, which made things even worse as it knocked the Eagles out of contention for the No. 1 pick, ultimately University of Southern California star O.J. Simpson. The Eagles would settle for the third pick, drafting Purdue running back Leroy Keyes, who played just four seasons with Philadelphia before toiling his final year with Kansas City.

Hell-bent on mayhem, some fans among the half of the 51,000 season ticket holders who showed up wore buttons reading "Joe Must Go." The only suspense was to see if gritty running back Tom Woodeshick would surpass the 1,000-yard mark. Before leaving the game in the third quarter due to a significant laceration over his eye, Woodeshick carried the ball 24 times for 80 yards, finishing 53 yards short of his goal.

"[Defensive tackle] Gary Larsen came back to the bench one time and told me Woodeshick was bleeding everywhere," said Lee. "Against the snow it was just easily seen, but they kept sending him out there and giving him the ball."

A surreal day all around, the contest would come to be known as the "Santa Claus Game," as it would soon be seen that Frank Olivo, like the steely Grant and the Vikings, had a rendezvous with destiny.

Lee had a sense it was not going to be an ordinary afternoon.

"The game goes along and it wasn't packed and you see the fans making snowballs," he said. "They were letting the snowballs sit there so they got hard and icy and someone throws one right at Kuharich's back. It staggers him, but he never looks back. It was going to get ugly."

The storm prevented the Santa Claus the Eagles had booked for the halftime Christmas pageant from arriving at the game. Eagles entertainment director Bill "Moon" Mullen, needing someone to fill in, picked out the 20-year-old Olivo, who was easily and fatefully spotted because he would always dress as Santa for the last home game.

Olivo, alongside Eagles cheerleaders dressed as elves, appeared as a 50-piece band played "Here Comes Santa Claus." He was supposed to be situated on a large Christmas float featuring eight life-sized fiberglass reindeer, but the float got stuck in the mud, so Olivo was forced to appear on foot. In place of carrying a Santa sack, he carried an equipment bag filled with soggy towels.[5]

"It was a bad game, it's a cold game, [the fans] are sitting their rear ends in snow and here comes this lousy, little Santa running down the field," said WTEL (94 WIP-FM) sports talk radio host Glen Macnow.[6]

In other words, a perfect storm was brewing.

Olivo was unceremoniously pelted with snowballs, forever associating Philadelphia fans with heretofore unseen fan wickedness.

Once the snowball carnage had cleared, the Vikings went ahead for good in the third quarter after linebacker Wally Hilgenberg set them up with a fumble recovery on the Philadelphia 40.

Kapp, who led British Columbia to its first Grey Cup title four years earlier, found second-year wide receiver Gene Washington from 30 yards out on an out-and-up route to give the visitors a 14–7 advantage. The play drew vehement protest from Eagles left corner Alvin Haymond, who was ejected after arguing that Washington was at least a step or two out of a shabbily marked end zone.

"They had single coverage on Gene and he made a great adjustment on the ball," said Kapp. "He made a move, had Hammond beat deep and made a fantastic grab."[7]

"I was excited about being able to make the play and hang on to the ball," said Washington, who had three catches for 50 yards. "The ball was thrown perfectly but the wind blew it a little bit to the outside. It was some bad conditions."[8]

Establishing the play as even more a part of team lore was that the graceful Washington made his decisive catch on the awe-inspiring east side of Franklin Field, where the grandiose Weightman Hall could be seen rising out of its mouth in the background. The historic gymnasium's stunning design gave professional football games at Franklin an undeniable college atmosphere.

After a Sam Baker field goal cut the lead to four, Kapp rolled left from two yards out early in the fourth quarter behind a nice block from Brown on Eagles safety Joe Scarpati to make it 21–10, and the Vikings hung on for the win.

A fired-up Page, who prevented a touchdown earlier in the contest by stripping Philadelphia running back Cyril Pinder of the ball inside the Vikings' five, set up Kapp's decisive run by recording a near-safety sack of Snead at the Philadelphia one. Baker's subsequent shanked punt to his own 22 gave Minnesota a short field to work with.

As the happy players and coaches trudged into Franklin Field's archaic locker room after the game, some Vikings players were seen huddled around Page, who held a portable radio. The game broadcast declared the Bears, once down 28–10 to the archrival Packers, had cut the deficit to 28–27, and there was still time for a last-ditch drive.

The Bears, who last qualified for the postseason in their championship year of 1963, moved into Packer territory, where they faced a fourth-and-14 situation. If they opted for a field goal, it would have been from 55 yards. That October, Mac Percival had broken the Vikings' hearts by making a 47-yarder to beat them 26–24 at Wrigley Field. Believing that distance unreachable, Bears quarterback Jack Concannon dropped back to throw and old pro Ray Nitschke picked off the pass, sending the Minnesota locker room into bedlam.

"I guess we'll send the game ball to Ray Nitschke," Grant told the *Minneapolis Star* in the postgame locker room.[9]

"This is the first time I ever rooted for the Green Bay Packers," said Brown, whose all-around talents were on full display against the Eagles as he led all players with 146 total yards (78 rushing, 68 receiving).[10]

Before the news came of Green Bay's win, more than half the players, including Marshall, had already worked their way toward the two team buses. But Marshall, unable to bear the strain, didn't last long outside, as he came back to the locker room to hear the news firsthand.

"We're in the money now," exclaimed Marshall to *Minneapolis Star* reporters. "Let's get Baltimore!"[11]

Grant was the last to leave the clubhouse, approaching the buses with his misleading semi-scowl.

"Smile, Bud, smile," yelled Marshall. The rest of the first busload picked up the chant. When Grant walked up the bus steps, the "Smile, Bud, smile" chant became a roar. The stoic coach obligingly broke into a grin. The accompanying cheer developed into "Hurray for Bud! Hurray for Bud!" as the buses started for the airport.[12]

With the invigorating smell of diesel fumes rising behind them, the buses slowly rolled out of the stadium lot, ironically carrying Grant away from the same town he willingly and opportunistically left as a player, becoming the first NFL player to play out his option.

For these festive and wide-eyed gridiron travelers, this was just the beginning of a larger journey, one that would see the Vikings capture division titles nine of the next 10 seasons, win an NFL title in '69 and thrillingly garner three NFC championships.

But there would be bumps along the way, and they symbolically began that dank winter afternoon in the City of Brotherly Love.

"We were all happy but the bus driver got lost and had to make a U-turn and all that," recalled Lee. "It took us forever to get to the airport. The other bus driver took over and we finally made it."

That misstep, though, did not dim the players' emanating joy.

"You worked so hard during the year and you're in a bus with all your teammates around you and you find out you're division champs and it's like you just got the golden ring," said Marshall.

"Once we found out we clinched, it was very jubilant," said Hackbart. "Everybody was so darned happy. Now we had the opportunity to move on. We all got together and celebrated. We had a lot of players there and it was a great night."

It was a whirlwind, and frustrating, 1968 season for behemoth Vikings right tackle Ron Yary. Despite becoming the first offensive lineman that year to be selected first overall in an NFL draft, the University of Southern California All-American didn't crack the starting lineup until midway through his second year. His personal dissatisfaction didn't take away from the joy of making the playoffs.

"I remember Bob Brown, the Eagles' great right tackle, coming into our locker room after the game," said Yary, who in '67 became the Trojans' first Outland Trophy winner, an honor given to the nation's top interior lineman. "He congratulated us on the win and wished the best for us. I already had the greatest admiration for him, and that just confirmed it."

Little did Yary, Marshall and Co. know this blustery and bodacious day would be the beginning of a 10-year stretch that would see the Vikings play in one big game after another, allowing national television audiences to gain a close acquaintance with Metropolitan Stadium, which, due to the team's categorical success, would go on to host 10 frosty playoff contests.

"You obviously don't know at the time what was ahead, but we knew we were good and we're going to get better," said Lee. "You won the division, that's great, but Bud would not have made a big deal about it because that's just the first step in the second part of the season's journey. He had won championships in Canada, so it wasn't like he was new to winning. But everyone was happy and we got to play the Colts. Despite losing to them in the playoffs [24–14 at Memorial Stadium], we thought we were good. The next year we beat the Colts and Joe threw seven touchdown passes."

It would be during the time that ensued, the winters of my youth in Cuyahoga Falls, Ohio, that the Minnesota Vikings, whom I grew to love, would become a team associated with the joys of the holidays and the trappings and triumphs of the season, and despite the disappointments that would come, the Purple and Gold would be woven into my being as much as Dodger Blue was Kahn's.

1

Holiday Bliss?

NFL playoff wins or losses could make or break the holidays for a young fan from northeast Ohio in the '60s and '70s.

I was certainly in that category.

The season was just 14 games, so the playoffs were always smack-dab in the middle of the Christmas season.

Was it going to be a great holiday season or a depressing one? For me, a lot of it depended on how the Vikings fared.

In today's NFL, one can enjoy the holidays within the safety net of a 17-game regular-season schedule and take their playoff lumps after New Year's.

Making matters worse is my birthday falls on December 28. Why not ruin it along with the holidays?

The Vikings certainly did that on December 28, 1975, the day of the dreaded "Hail Mary game." For the team's long-suffering fans, it was a day that shall live in infamy as Roger Staubach's 50-yard, last-ditch heave to Drew Pearson with 32 seconds left snatched defeat out of the jaws of victory against what Vikings players to a man say was the best team of the Bud Grant era.

"Now, that was a great team," said hulking defensive end Mark Mullaney, a rookie that year out of Colorado State. "That was a game we had won. Still bothers me."

Every Viking player echoes that sentiment.

The Vikings lost 17–14. The next week I didn't even turn on our scratchy black-and-white set that got about four channels to watch the Cowboys rout the Los Angeles Rams in the NFC championship game, 37–7. The Rams should have been playing in Minnesota.

I came by my love for the Vikings and the color purple honestly.

I'm a first-generation Ohioan. My parents didn't move to Akron until 1952, well before I was born. My beloved father, William Donald Bowman, who I was told also shared my affinity for purple, worked as a sheriff's deputy in mountainous Carroll County in southwest Virginia.

Once his beloved Sheriff Jackson left office, despite being a popular choice as Jackson's replacement, Dad opted to "go over the bridge" and head north to Ohio on I-77 like thousands of other men from the South at that time. They came to work at the monstrous Akron rubber plants and the many thriving car manufacturers, like the Ford Stamping Plant in Walton Hills, 30 miles north of Cuyahoga Falls, where my dad spent 35 grueling years.

Raised on a sprawling 100-acre dairy farm during the Great Depression, an era in our nation's history that did not lend itself to trivial pursuits, Dad never really latched onto any big-league team in any sport, although my mom told me he would root for the underdog Dodgers when they played the hated Yanks.

As a result, my brother, Bill, who was born in Virginia, joined me in becoming a fandom free agent. My sisters, Brenda and Bonnie, could only curiously and feebly look on as we proceeded to insufferably live and die with our favorite teams over the trying years ahead.

My attraction to the Vikings was partially due to the fact the NFL blacked out all home games that were not a sellout. Due to playing in cavernous, 80,000-seat Municipal Stadium, which hosted its first event when Max Schmeling met Young Stribling on July 3, 1931, for the heavyweight title, the only time the Cleveland Browns were on television was for away games, the routinely sold-out contests with Pittsburgh and when they were on *Monday Night Football*.

That set the stage for northeast Ohioans getting a large dose of the NFC Central. Known as the Black and Blue Division, it featured the rugged Vikings, Bears, Lions and Packers.

The Vikings were on almost every week, like clockwork, at 1 p.m. Eastern Standard Time. I fell in love with the Norsemen's beautiful uniforms and the cold-weather games, the glistening white snow contrasted with that glorious purple, the steam coming out of the players' face masks. Unforgettable images.

"Teams like the Rams certainly didn't enjoy their trips to Met Stadium," said Vikings star wide receiver Gene Washington.

By the early '70s, the Browns were becoming an unappealing team to follow. They remained in contention each year for the AFC Central, but Leroy Kelly was aging, quarterback Bill Nelsen's knees were shot and, after trading Paul Warfield for the rights to draft Mike Phipps, their only viable receiver was Frank Pitts. Arguably their best remaining running back, Ron Johnson, was traded to the New York Giants, where he almost led them to a playoff appearance in 1970.

When the Pittsburgh Steelers drafted unknown Franco Harris out of Penn State and he promptly led them to the playoffs in 1972, many erstwhile Browns fans started adopting the Black and Gold. The Browns' growing mediocrity—they lost the first 15 games they played at Three Rivers Stadium after it opened in 1970—spawned a generation of Steelers fans from the Buckeye State.

That group included one of our neighborhood buddies, Mark. He was a huge fan of the flamboyant John "Frenchy" Fuqua, who was the Steelers' feature back before Harris's arrival.

Two doors down from us was our friend Lenny, who loved the Cowboys, a team I would come to dread.

Despite the Vikings' excruciating home playoff losses in 1970, 1971 and 1975, I never gave a second thought about jumping to the Browns, whom I followed, but only with passing interest. They were my rooting interest as far as the American Football Conference went, but that's as far as it got.

The lot my brother drew was less propitious. He grew up a St. Louis "Football" Cardinals fan because he was enamored with the deep-ball ability of the team's unheralded quarterback, Big Spring, Texas, native Charley Johnson. Sonny Randle, Billy Gambrell (who played sandlot baseball in Georgia with Fran Tarkenton), Jackie Smith and Bobby Joe Conrad were his favorite targets.

During Minnesota's lean quarterback years of 1970 and 1971, a deal for Johnson, whom Washington played with in Denver during his last year in the NFL in '73, would have been intriguing for the Vikings to have worked out.

"Oh, he was great," said Washington of the 1962 Pro Bowler for St. Louis who threw for 3,000 yards twice in his 14-year career, a number not often reached in those days. "He was the first one who greeted me when I got there. He was very welcoming. He was smooth. When you came out of the break, the ball was right there."

Johnson led the NFL in TD passes in '64 and twice threw six TD passes in a game. No. 12 would have looked good in purple. The Big Red were not nearly as successful as the Vikings but always had talent, especially on the offensive side.

My brother, Mark, Lenny and I were all good in multiple sports and we liked watching talented athletes play football. Mark loved to imitate Fuqua's quick-twitch moves, Bill loved the underrated Johnson and tight end great Smith, Lenny loved Staubach and was also enamored with fabulous Prairie View A&M product Otis Taylor's one-handed stabs and I was captivated by the ferocious pass rushes of the likes of nearby Canton product Alan Page, plus Jim Marshall and Carl Eller.

My birth on December 28 is confirmation that I was divinely predestined to be a lifelong and long-suffering Viking fan in addition to a huge NFL fan in general, as it was on that day in 1958 the Baltimore Colts defeated the New York Giants 23–17 in overtime for the NFL title at fabled Yankee Stadium. It became known as the "Greatest Game Ever Played."

Not surprisingly, my brother's Cardinals' last NFL title, that coming in 1947 at old Comiskey Park, was won, of course, on a December 28 as they toppled the Philadelphia Eagles 28–21 on the strength of great games by backs Elmer Angsman (10 rushes for 159 yards, two 70-yard TD runs) and Georgia All-American Charley Trippi, who scored on a 44-yard run from scrimmage and a 75-yard punt return.

Luckily, I was only 14 in '75 so losses didn't hit as hard. Back then, I could be easily consoled during the rapturous two-week Christmas break by playing electric football in our homey fake-wood-paneled attic with the treasured *Music from National Football League Films* album my mom sent away for me blaring in the background.

The precious vinyl featured many Sam Spence compositions such as "A Golden Boy Again," "March to the Trenches" and "Sunday with Soul," all which I grew familiar with due to my love for NFL Films.

Not a huge fan of school, I lived each week for Saturday's *This Week in Pro Football*, a glorious half-hour NFL Films show hosted by the nattily dressed duo of Pat Summerall and Tom Brookshire. Most of the Minnesota highlights were Page or Eller sacking the quarterback or the stubby Fred Cox kicking a short field goal, but it was well worth the wait.

Years before ESPN, this was the only way I or anyone else outside the Twin Cities could watch Vikings highlights, unless I was lucky enough to have Howard Cosell feature them on his famous "Monday Night Football" halftime highlights segment.

"Cosell, given a bare-boned play sheet, and with no rehearsal, narrated the footage with his own multisyllabic vocabulary and pointed intonations which were in sharp contrast to the empty cadences of a generation of highlights readers," described Michael MacCambridge in his sensational book *America's Game*.[1]

The ultimate outcome was if the Vikings were chosen for the much-anticipated *NFL Game of the Week*, a full half-hour show offered by NFL Films focusing on just one game.

Every winter break I could look forward to sleeping in, Vikings playoff football and electric football—my sports trinity.

The NFL avoided playing championship or playoff games on Christmas Day, so much so the Vince Lombardi Packers' first-ever title game appearance in 1960 against the Philadelphia Eagles at historic Franklin Field was moved from a Sunday to a Monday afternoon to avoid the game being played on December 25. Before a meager crowd for the noon start, the Packers lost and one of the stars of that game, Eagles quarterback Norm Van Brocklin, would give up playing to become the Vikings' first head coach.

Championship games were typically played in mid-December.

The 1943 championship game between the Chicago Bears and Washington Redskins was the first regulation NFL game played after Christmas. It was played on December 26 because of scheduling complications brought on by World War II.

My earliest recollection of the Vikings tainting my holiday season (many of those would follow) was on December 25, 1971.

The day marked the first time in NFL history that a pro football game was played on Christmas Day.

I was just 11 years old.

Fittingly, Minnesota, despite playing in its type of weather at Metropolitan Stadium (12 degrees with wind chill), lost 20–12 that afternoon to Dallas, despite outgaining the Cowboys 311 yards to 183 and having 17 first downs to its 10.

The year before, I was ecstatic after the Vikings squashed the hated Cowboys in regular-season play in October by a 54–13 count. It gave me bragging rights over Lenny for more than a year. It was known as the Ed Sharockman game as the veteran cornerback had a 23-yard blocked punt return and a 34-yard interception runback, both going for touchdowns. Lenny should have been happy, though, because the blowout turned around Dallas's season.

"The Minnesota game was the changing point that season," said Dallas running back Duane Thomas, who had 13 carries for 79 yards in the loss. "I came into the game in the third quarter. I was surprised they put a rookie in at that point. It was like 44–6. I never played in a lopsided game like that. The next week we go to play [reigning NFL champion] Kansas City at Municipal Stadium and we beat them and then we went on a roll."

The Cowboys rolled over the Chiefs 27–16 as Thomas had the biggest game of his career to that point, rushing 20 times for 134 yards and a pair of scores. Dallas would drop only two more games the rest of the way to finish 10–4. Relying on a Doomsday Defense led by Bob Lilly and the running game behind Thomas and fullback Walt Garrison, Dallas defeated Detroit and San Francisco to advance to Super Bowl V, where it suffered a brutal 16–13 defeat to the Colts.

Lenny was cocky, but cool. He had *Sports Illustrated* photos of NFL teams plastered all over his bedroom walls and I followed suit, but only after my dear mom got Bill and me a subscription.

With the NFL only previously seen by me in black and white, I was enthralled with the vibrancy of *SI*'s color photography. I was also enamored with Lenny's dad always ordering carryout pizza on Friday nights. Our family never went out to eat, so playing electric football with greasy fingers from the pizza was big-world stuff for a shy young lad raised by good ol' Southern folk. Dad was from Laurel Fork, Virginia, and my mom, Geraldine, from Humboldt, Tennessee, home of Chicago Bears gargantuan Hall of Fame end Doug Atkins.

My brother, whom we nicknamed "Bowman Gabriel" because he could throw the pigskin with Rams quarterback Roman Gabriel-like authority—slept upstairs with me in the attic. The ceiling was slanted so I made a collage of *SI* photos on the wall. When I went to bed, I could blissfully drift to sleep looking up at those sweet, colorful pictures—great for a kid with no color TV (unless my dad would rent one like he occasionally did for big Browns games).

Lenny was an electric football savant. He would cut open his mom's curlers to use as goalpost nets. He would halt play after each down to not only meticulously set up his players on the fragile aluminum playing field but to also tediously record stats in a small spiral notebook. The greatest instance of his uncanny attention to detail was when he would dutifully paint his teams to match any yearly uniform changes, doing so with brain-surgeon-like precision, using just a toothpick, cotton swab and model paint.

His most difficult task in these undertakings came following the '71 campaign, when second-year Washington coach George Allen revised the Redskins' helmets. In Allen's first year upon arriving from L.A., the 'Skins retained the Lombardi-implemented yellow helmet with a large maroon *R* in a circle, strikingly similar to the Packer logo. The next season Allen boldly went back to the traditional maroon helmet, but the team added a yellow stripe down the middle trimmed by a pair of white stripes with maroon showing in between and a new logo of an American Indian warrior.

A prominent Native American, Walter "Blackie" Wetzel, who approached Allen about replacing the *R*, envisioned the new logo.

Wetzel presented photos of Native Americans in full headdress, including one of former Blackfeet chief John Two Guns White Calf. Allen and the Redskins most admired that image and it was used on Redskins helmets for nearly half a century.[2]

Lenny's work in transitioning those miniature helmets was his true masterpiece, his tour de force, deftly using a steady-handed ability no doubt garnered from hundreds of runs at Hasbro's Operation game, which was basically in every household in the late '60s and '70s.

I used paper route money to pay for my first electric football set in a layaway arrangement with the J.C. Penney department store in 1971. It may have been my crowning childhood achievement. It was a Tudor set and gloriously included three teams—the Vikings, of course, plus Baltimore and Kansas City, all bedrock teams of the '70s.

Placing the tiny numbers on the players' backs was another undertaking that required unwavering hands from the electric football aficionado. You didn't want to look at a crooked No. 10 on the back of your Francis Tarkenton figure for an entire season.

You received one set of numbers with every team. This often created a dilemma. If you ran out of numbers, you were required to become adept in the art of splicing, a skill that came in handy when I went into mass media communications at the University of Akron. One of our classes required us to splice together an audition tape. I had already taken the prerequisite course in my attic when I was 11.

Another annoyance was replacing the limited number of felt footballs they gave you on a sheet with each set. I became adept at taking the cotton from a Q-tip pilfered from the bathroom, solidifying it with Elmer's Glue, then cutting a slit in the makeshift "ball" in order for it to be hurled by the plastic quarterback.

I also became somewhat of a journeyman electrician. Many times, during vigorous usage, the game switch would become slightly disconnected. I learned how to put the switch back together, skills that came in handy when my wife and I bought a house in North Akron that was built in the 1920s and was in a relative state of disrepair.

Electric football was just one source of joy for the young fan of NFL football during my childhood. Another was the gloriously colorful NFL Action '72 sticker album offered by Sunoco.

We were fortunate to have a Sunoco station a few blocks from our home on Oakwood Drive. You could get a 128-page Deluxe Edition for $2.49 that was full of facts on each team and offered a recap of Super Bowl VI between the Cowboys and Dolphins. The more streamlined 56-page Regular Edition, which I had, was just 89 cents. Both albums came with 144 action player stamps. If you were fortunate enough for your dad to get a fill-up—at 36 cents a gallon my dad more often than not did—you got nine stamps for free.

This left room for a lot of bartering at Lincoln Elementary School for the remaining stickers you needed to fill out your stamp-saver album. Mornings before school and lunchtime recesses became like scenes from *Shawshank Redemption*, where desperate snotty-nosed young men, resplendent in their favorite team's colorful beanie cap, would trade just about anything to fill out the 22 stickers they needed to complete each team.

Making this precious book even more appealing was John Gilliam prominently displayed on my album's beautiful watercolor front cover. My brother and I both loved watching the speedster from South Carolina play, and there he was, in a three-point stance common for receivers of the day, sporting that familiar No. 44 in Cardinal Red a year before he was traded to the Vikings.

A world away over in Minnesota, a young lad who would grow up to become the Vikings' public relations director for 32 years was clamoring for another promotional Holy Grail.

"Pizza Hut had a promotion going where they were giving away Vikings laminated place mats," said Bob Hagan, who now serves as a consultant with the Vikings. "Every week or two weeks they would change them up, maybe defense one week, offense the next. I was forcing my family to go to Pizza Hut so I could get those. I still have some of those around. The Vikings were everywhere."

To Bill and me, the attic was like a loft in a country cottage. It was an early version of a man cave. Electric football. Records. Sports photo collages serving as wallpaper. We'd even toss the old spring-challenged mattresses off the beds onto the floor to cushion our makeshift tackle football games with our surprisingly feisty sisters. We tried it before downstairs but we had to stop after my brother tossed me through the drywall, leaving a Looney Tunes–like cutout too difficult to hide from your soon-to-be-seething dad.

The only bad thing about the attic was that there was no central air—did anyone my age have it? We suffocated up there in the summer. Our only respite was to place a box fan in the window on one side of the room and hope it would suction out the stifling air, thus allowing us a few hours of restful sleep.

I was so disillusioned by the Dallas loss in '71 that I refused to watch the four o'clock Eastern game, which turned out to be one of the most entertaining contests in NFL history, let alone playoff history—the Miami Dolphins' 27–24 double-overtime win over the Kansas City Chiefs in the longest game in NFL history at 82 minutes and 40 seconds. It was the "Ed Podolak Game," as the remarkable Chiefs star running back amassed 350 total yards in the contest.

The previous year, 1970, the Vikings lost in the first round, falling 17–14 to the San Francisco 49ers, thus squandering another amazing year out of the defense. It was the first of the three losses Minnesota suffered in 10 playoff games at The Met.

At least the 49ers game missed both Christmas and my birthday, as it was played on December 27 in Bloomington.

I was 10 years old. It was the first playoff loss I can remember and the Vikings' first ever at home. It still stings. I was too young for the 24–14 defeat to the Colts on December 22, 1968, at Memorial Stadium.

• • •

Playing football in the elements was commonplace in the '70s NFL, but those challenges reached a higher plateau at Metropolitan Stadium.

Combining to make it a mystical place was not only its arctic and sometimes storm-tossed weather but also the purple-clad gladiators who slogged away on its turf and the awe-inspiring nature of their play.

"We have a lot of fans from all around the country," said retired Vikings equipment manager Dennis Ryan, who took over for the eccentric Stubby Eason. "People love the Vikings and part of that was the Purple People Eaters and watching the games at frozen Met Stadium and playing in conditions the normal person didn't want to take part in. I think that kind of instilled a little awe."

Marshall said the Vikings had a mystical, innate sense of when the bad weather was to start storming through the stadium in the same manner Hannibal of Carthage's warring elephants advanced over the Alps.

"At Metropolitan Stadium when the sun would drop over the back of the stadium the temperature would fall, 10, 15, sometimes 20 degrees," said Marshall in the 2010 *History of the Vikings* feature by NFL Films. "We would under our breaths start saying, 'Odin, Odin, Odin,' you know, the Viking god of war. The other teams would say, 'What matter of men are these? These dudes are crazy!'"

While Metropolitan Stadium had its nuances, the players enjoyed taking the field there, even receivers like Drew Pearson, who ran his crisp pass routes in the relatively mundane environs of Texas Stadium.

"When we played them there in '75, it was an eerie game," he recalled. "Just everything about the stadium. Both teams on the same sideline. The baseball field still somewhat visible. The overcast skies. They didn't give us a chance to win. We were the wild-card team. Minnesota had the best record. You had Bud Grant going against Tom Landry, two of the top coaches in the NFL, iconic coaches going after each other. There was a lot of intensity in the rivalry."

The origins of what became known as "The Met," which was located 11 miles from downtown Minneapolis, date to the early 1950s when city officials began searching for a site to construct a stadium in hopes of luring a Major League Baseball franchise. In 1955, a 160-acre parcel in Bloomington was purchased for $458,000 to construct a stadium.

Construction began in June 1955 and was completed in just under a year. The stadium originally had a seating capacity of 18,200 that included a towering three-tier grandstand that extended from behind home plate to the first and third base dugouts.

Although the city had yet to lure an MLB franchise, Metropolitan Stadium became home of the Minneapolis Millers, a minor league baseball affiliate of the New York Giants who played in the American Association. On April 24, 1956—barely 10 months after groundbreaking ceremonies—the Millers opened Met Stadium with a game against the Wichita Braves.[3]

With sluggish attendance and an aging Griffith Stadium, Calvin Griffith agreed to move his Washington Senators to Minneapolis after the 1960 season, with the team becoming the Minnesota Twins.

"That worked out great for me," said Tarkenton. "I grew up a huge Washington Senators fan during my childhood in D.C. and I got to see them come to Minnesota."[4]

With the arrival of the Twins in 1961, the first two decks were extended beyond the foul pole in right field, although a similar extension was not done in left field. Bleachers filled the gap down the left-field line beyond the permanent grandstand.

The ballpark had a disjointed, skeletal feel. It was obvious that it had once been a minor league baseball stadium.

"They always said it looked like an erector set because of all the metal and the fact that the light towers were so prominent," said longtime Met Stadium sideline security guard Dick Jonckowski. "It was made for baseball for sure, it always looked unfinished."

One of the most significant components of Met Stadium was not what it had, but what it didn't have, said Stew Thornley of the Society for American Baseball Research.

"[It didn't have] posts to support decks or roofs above. By going to cantilever construction for the overhanging decks, architect Foster Dunwiddie of Thorshov and Cerny, Inc. had found a way to eliminate the posts which often block the view of some fans in other stadiums," said Thornley. "Met Stadium became the first baseball stadium in the country to take advantage of this principle."[5]

The outfield originally consisted of a series of bleachers, interrupted by a batter's eye in center field and in right-center field by the scoreboard, with the bullpens stationed in front.

"The Vikings ship was right there by the batter's eye with the band," said Jonckowski of the team band location. "There really wasn't much seating there, maybe about two thousand. The whole thing was an afterthought. It wasn't ideal seating by any means. In right field it was just bleachers. A lot of people sat out there for baseball but it definitely wasn't a good vantage point for football."

A huge improvement took place in 1965 when the bleachers in left field were replaced by a double-decked grandstand. In exchange for a reduction in rent, the Vikings financed and built the grandstand, increasing the seating capacity to just under 48,000.

"Those [left-field] outfield seats for baseball were also nice for football and the people really liked them," said Jonckowski. "That's because they sat up higher. When the stadium first opened for baseball, those were just bleachers, not a two-deck grandstand. The grandstand on the other side, the first-base side away from the players' sideline in football, some of those seats were pretty close to the ground, plus they were further away from the field."

The spacious new grandstand in left field was primarily for the Vikings, but the Twins also benefited from the extra capacity as they hosted two major events in 1965: the All-Star Game in July, then the World Series in October as Minnesota won the American League pennant. The Twins lost to the Los Angeles Dodgers, with Game 7 drawing 50,596, the only time a baseball crowd exceeded 50,000 at Met Stadium.[6]

The only issue with the new grandstand was there no concourse built to connect it to the rest of the stadium.

"It was completely separate," said Jonckowski. "It was tough to go from that side to the infield stands. Even going from left field to right field was difficult as far as the bleachers were concerned."

1. Holiday Bliss?   17

The gridiron ran from right field toward third base, with barely enough room to squeeze in the playing field and end zones. However, the space between the sidelines and the stands was vast.

Metropolitan Stadium changed little until it closed in '81.

"Met Stadium was a cold stadium," said Ryan. "It was wide open, there was nothing dug in. There were openings on every side of the stadium. There was a huge parking lot and lots of farm fields so there was nothing to break the wind. It was a flat prairie, with an airport nearby. The wind just rushed through there."

Thomas, who died unexpectedly at age 77 in August, 2024, said he enjoyed the times he got to play at Metropolitan Stadium over the course of his five-year career.

"I liked playing there," said Thomas, who would later join Allen's Redskins. "It was the openness of it. It reminded me of my college days playing [at the Buffalo Bowl in Canyon, Texas]. The esoteric aspects. You could see into the far distance. You could see a thunderstorm booming in the distance, on the horizon."

Texas Stadium, which debuted in 1971, had an opening in the roof, but other than that was entirely enclosed. Thomas cared little for the sparkling new ballpark, especially its Tartan Turf playing surface.

"The turf was horrible there," said Thomas, who scored the stadium's first touchdown. "Tore up my legs all the time. Could never understand why the NFL moved in that direction."

An idol of both my brother and me, Jackie Smith shared Thomas's disdain for the wretched playing fields of the '70s.

"The coming in of [artificial] turf was the big thing," he said. "You were always apprehensive about what kind of turf they were going to have. We had baseball infields we had to contend with. I remember one time running over a pitcher's mound and then looking back and seeing they didn't take it all the way down.

"The turf then wasn't that sophisticated," he added. "Underneath it eight or 10 inches down was blacktop. The turf came in huge sheets about 25, 30 feet wide. The grain would be going one way about 15, 20 feet and another way further down the field. The baseball teams didn't care about which way the grain was going. I began wearing soccer cleats with rubber soles because you had to watch if the grain of the turf was going with you or against you. I even began to modify my shoes and get the regular steel cleats and take a file and place grooves on the bottom of the steel cleat in order to get traction. I had about 30 pairs of shoes in my locker."

• • •

Ah, purple. The color of royalty.

I fell in love with the Vikings for many reasons. I loved the classic purple uniforms, especially those with the NFL 50-year anniversary patch on the shoulder. The yellow trim on the pronounced numbers was the perfect complement.

The team's purple-and-gold color scheme was believed to be owing to Bert Rose, Jr., the Vikings' first general manager, a proud University of Washington grad.

"We first had a two-color number [stitched] on the home jerseys," said Ryan. "The gold number on the purple jersey had to be much bigger than the white number that got sewn on top of it, so the numbers were doubly thick and super wide because of that. Those numbers were noticeably big. You even had teams that had three-color numbers; those were really thick. Now they laser-cut those things, so you get one layer."

I was also captivated by the white horns on both sides of the helmet. They were much bigger in those days, much more prominent, and the tips of the horns almost came together as they wrapped around the back of the headgear.

The Rams were the first team to decorate their helmets. Fred Gehrke, a halfback on the team who was a commercial artist in the offseason, painted the original rams horns on the helmets in 1948, setting off a wave of imitation.

When wearing the classic Vikings headgear, the majestically sauntering Washington, who opted for a single-bar face mask, gave the mystical appearance of the Greek god Hermes, who in the *Odyssey* is depicted as messenger to the gods.

Oh, to be young and a Viking. Washington was the epitome of Viking youth, Viking greatness, Viking dominance.

"There's a lot more face mask choices now than when I first started," said Ryan. "I think we had five different masks a guy could choose from. Kapp would wear a single bar, but he was a tough guy. We have guys wearing custom face masks now and it gets expensive.

"Originally the horns were hand-painted," added Ryan, who officially served as the team equipment manager from 1980 to 2023. "A helmet's one of the pieces I still have. I'm not a collector, but I have an old suspension helmet, and some Duke footballs. I also have a Tarkenton jersey around somewhere. Stubby always made sure to order extra Tarkenton jerseys."

The Vikings uniform worked; it resonated with the masses. This despite the constant struggle of matching the purple on the helmet with that on the jerseys.

"For a period of time, you were at the mercy of the manufacturer and what they would determine as a purple," said Ryan. "Sometimes they would change their injection molding. It was tough to match helmet to jersey. The jersey color would change from year to year because they didn't have very much control over the dye lots on the fabric and they allowed variances. You might have a slight variance in the purple from one year to the next. The colors might not be that off, but the television cameras would magnify the difference. Generally, we would start over with new jerseys every year, but you would have blank jerseys which were carried over from year to year and they might not necessarily match with the new dye lot. They often wore them, but in the '60s and early '70s, most of the TV viewing was still in black and white so no one really noticed. Later they just started going to no carryover jerseys."

Ryan said there was never much thought going with purple pants and jerseys at home after the debacle in 1964 that saw both the Lions and the Vikings arrive at Met Stadium with white jerseys. That was the year Minnesota wanted to give its home fans a look at their road getup with the purple pants and white jerseys. Eason scrambled to get the purple jerseys to the stadium and the Vikings ended up in all purple, prompting Coach Van Brocklin to famously say, "We looked like a bunch of Easter eggs out there."

"Anytime purple pants were mentioned that Easter egg comment would come up," Ryan said. "Then everybody just dropped the subject. Everyone liked the clean look of the white pants and the nice purple sock top. It was a nice finish to the uniform, so we never adopted the purple until, I believe, 2006. Of course, [head coach Brad] Childress hated it, so we never wore it."

Some fans have fantasized about an LSU look with yellow pants, but Ryan said don't hold your breath.

"We got some yellow pants as a sample years ago when Bud was still a coach and his immediate response was, 'The Vikings will never wear yellow. That's Green Bay's color.'"

1. Holiday Bliss?

Los Angeles cartoonist Karl Hubenthal designed the Vikings' original helmet, uniforms and Norseman logo in 1961, using the purple and gold colors under instructions from Rose, who knew Hubenthal from his days as the Rams' public relations director.

According to Paul Lukas of ESPN.com, all of that was spelled out in notes and drawings that Hubenthal's family saved after his death in 1997 and then donated to the Vikings in 2016.

"There was no reason to doubt any of this; Hubenthal had been a highly respected professional, and the Vikings themselves thought enough of the donated materials to showcase them in an exhibit at their stadium," said Lukas in his extremely well-researched article "The Untold History of Minnesota's Uniforms."

Rose died in 2001. But his sons, Scott and Stephen Rose, who both now live in Texas, confirmed with Lukas their father had chosen the Vikings' colors at least in part because of his alma mater.

"My father chose purple for two reasons," Stephen Rose told Lukas. "First, there were no other purple teams in the league at the time, so that was an opportunity to come up with a unique look. And No. 2, on a personal level, he was partial to purple and gold because he'd gone to the University of Washington. He told Hubie [Hubenthal] that, but he didn't tell a lot of people. He didn't tell Pete Rozelle, because the NFL wouldn't have liked that. He didn't want a lot of publicity about it. It was mostly something between our family and Hubenthal."[7]

According to Lukas's article, Stephen Rose provided further evidence of how his father had been close to Hubenthal. It turns out that Hubenthal created a second Vikings uniform presentation storyboard identical to the one currently being exhibited by the Vikings. Bert Rose kept it, and Stephen Rose now has it framed on his wall. Stephen Rose also has original Hubenthal artwork with notes from Hubenthal to Bert Rose. All of this lends credence to Hubenthal's note about the color scheme's origin.

There's yet another theory, said Lukas.

"Several Vikings fans pointed out a death notice for a man named John Merritt Aldritt. According to the notice, Aldritt and his family were in the sporting goods business and had supplied the Vikings with their uniforms during the 1960s," said Lukas.

The death notice said this: "In addition to providing the Vikings with their equipment, John also designed one of the most iconic symbols in Minnesota sports, the logo on the Vikings' football helmet. John had a very good relationship with the Vikings' first head coach, Norm Van Brocklin. It was Van Brocklin who asked John to come up with a design for the helmet. The one stipulation was the logo had to be a horn."

Lukas said Hubenthal's daughter, Karen Chappell, who donated her father's old notes and drawings to the Vikings, said she had never heard of Aldritt.

"All I can tell you is that the Vikings gave my dad a helmet, and he had that helmet on the wall of his office, along with the original [uniform] artwork," she told Lukas. "I don't think he ever talked specifically about designing the helmet, as opposed to the rest of the uniform. It was just a given in our house that he designed all of it."[8]

She also provided a helmet drawing from her father's files dated March 1961. Aldritt died in 2016. But his sons, Tom and John Aldritt, still live and work in Minnesota. They provided old news clippings and other materials showing that the Vikings did indeed purchase their uniforms and equipment from Aldritt Athletic Goods. But did their father really design the horn on the team's helmet?[9]

"The Aldritt brothers said the horn story came to light in the mid–1980s, when their parents were preparing to move from Minnesota to Florida," said Lukas. "The family was going through some personal effects and came across an old envelope with 'Viking Horn' written on it. Inside were a horn template and some horn decals."

"We asked my father why he had those things," Tom Aldritt told Lukas. "He said, 'Because I designed it. I designed the horn.' We had never heard that before, but that wasn't surprising. My father didn't like to talk about himself. We had no idea, and if they hadn't moved to Florida, we probably still wouldn't know."

Lucas said the Aldritt brothers were told by their father he had come up with three horn designs.

"Their father said he presented the designs to Vikings management—apparently in early 1961, although the exact time frame is uncertain—at the North American Life and Casualty building, where the team initially had its offices," said Lukas.

Tom Aldritt said team executives apparently couldn't decide on which one to choose, "[at] which point an assistant coach named Stan West said something like, 'Here, let's just go with this one'—the one the team ended up using."[10]

"I don't know what the other two designs were," Aldritt added. "He just said he came up with three designs. It could have been that he positioned the horns in three different places, or he could have come up with three separate horn designs."

According to Lukas, when the Vikings' new stadium was being built in 2015, the Aldritt family purchased a legacy brick. It reads, "John M. Aldritt, Designer of the Original Logo on the Viking Helmet." This means the stadium has two separate origin stories about the team's helmet: the Hubenthal exhibit and the Aldritt brick.

Lukas said the Aldritt brothers noted that shortly after they ordered the brick, they heard back from the brick contractor, an Idaho company called Fund Raisers Sports, and were told that they couldn't purchase the brick unless they verified the claim about their father, so they provided documentation. That information was then forwarded to the Vikings, who approved the brick design.

"After reviewing the information provided by the Aldritt family, we had no reason to question what they sent us, so we approved the brick," said Jeff Anderson, the Vikings' executive director of communications. "At the same time, we're not questioning what the Hubenthal family has told us. Both stories could be true, and we'll be reaching out to the Aldritts to learn more."[11]

The Vikings' helmet logo has always had that little gold ring where the horn is "mounted" to the helmet. Tom Aldritt said his father had nothing to do with that detail. "He told me he didn't design that little gold circle thing. He was just asked to design the horn."[12]

Lukas said both stories could be true. "Maybe Aldritt came up with the horn, and then Hubenthal used that as the basis for the finished helmet design, complete with the gold ring."

That possibility is particularly intriguing in light of a recollection from Scott Rose, one of Bert Rose's sons.

"Hubenthal came up with multiple helmet options," he told Lukas. "In fact, we actually sat around the dinner table one time and dad laid out the drawings and we, as a family, selected the one they ended up using. I would have been in third grade at the time. As I recall, there were three designs. One kind of looked like the Rams' horns: It was a Viking horn, but it was kind of curled up. We all dismissed that, saying it was too much like the Rams. Another one was a short, stubby horn, which we didn't think looked too cool. And incidentally, the drawings for each design showed the side view and back view, and one reason we chose the one that we did—the one they ended up using—was that we liked how the horns wrapped around to the back and almost touched."[13]

Lukas said that matches Aldritts' story about their father coming up with three different horn designs. He said it seems plausible that Aldritt might have come up with the horn and then Hubenthal added the gold ring as part of his larger uniform presentation.

"One thing that is certain, however, is that the three families involved here—the Hubenthals, the Aldritts and the Roses—feel strongly about their respective family legacies," concluded Lukas.

"All sound very sincere; none of them wants to discredit or disparage any of the others; and their stories don't necessarily contradict each other. The hunch here is that all of them are right," he added.

• • •

The Vikings franchise would be eight years old before seeing its first playoff appearance, that coming in 1968 against the eventual NFL champion Baltimore Colts.

But people around the league knew the Vikings were a coming team, largely thanks to the calculated, diplomatic and decisive work done by Jim Finks. A former star quarterback for the Steelers, Finks arrived from Canada to direct the Vikings front office in 1964.

The team's roster soon bore Fink's significant imprint. While Rose and talented Director of Player Personnel Joe Thomas are credited with drafting in 1961 the likes of Tarkenton, Tommy Mason, Rip Hawkins and Sharockman, and adding tackle Grady Alderman and Marshall from the Detroit Lions and Browns, respectively, it was Fink's steady hand that turned the Vikings into perennial Super Bowl contenders.

He was also diplomatic when the emergencies came. After a promising '64 season that saw the Vikings tie Green Bay for second place in the Western Conference behind Baltimore at 8–5–1, the wheels began to fall off the next season.

After a solid start in '65, the Vikings, winners of five of their first eight, watched as Gary Cuozzo, starting for the Colts due to an injury to Johnny Unitas, proceeded to toss five TD passes in a 41–21 loss.

Distraught following the debacle, Van Brocklin announced his resignation the next morning, only to be talked into returning the next day. The damage was done. The team finished 7–7.

Tarkenton, never a fan of The Dutchman, asked for a trade after the abysmal 1966 season, which saw the team sink to 4–9–1. The coup de grace came when Van Brocklin spitefully started Bob Berry over Tarkenton in the Vikings' final home game against the Georgia product's hometown Atlanta Falcons.

Tarkenton was shipped to New York. Van Brocklin would also depart, leaving Finks without both a quarterback and head coach.

Finks, however, didn't look at this as a catastrophe.

"What it could do was give him some building blocks," said Minnesota sportswriter Jim Klobuchar on Finks's contemplation of a possible Tarkenton trade. "He knew the Vikings weren't going to terrorize the NFL in 1967 or the immediate future."[14]

The trade yielded a harvest that would have the Vikings in Super Bowl contention in three years. In addition to getting running back Clinton Jones, offensive tackle Ron Yary, guard Ed White and receiver Bob Grim with draft picks from that trade, Finks also drafted Gene Washington out of Michigan State and the great Page with a pick received from the Los Angeles Rams in a swap for Mason.

"Jim Finks said we're going to get a good package in this [Tarkenton] trade," remembers longtime Vikings scout and former player Jerry Reichow. "His thinking was, 'Trade him, what the hell? We're not kicking anyone's ass anyway.' It was a helluva deal for us. We had a good team but we were a little short because we were still young. We got all those picks and made most of those picks good, and then we get Tarkenton back later, a win-win situation."

Finks was responsible for hiring Grant to replace Van Brocklin, and after a rocky first season in 1967, the Vikings' run of success would commence the next year. They would make the playoffs in 1968 as they won their first Central Division title with an 8–6 mark and go on to three Super Bowl appearances in six years.

"Finks knew me from our being in the Canadian Football League together and I played against him [in the NFL] when he was the quarterback for Pittsburgh and I was with the Eagles," said Grant. "He went up to Calgary for more money. He got hurt then coached for a little bit before finding out he had good managerial skills and eventually became Calgary's GM. For starters, he was a great athlete. He played at Tulsa [University] and he was a tremendous quarterback and baseball player. He also could play basketball. He was a very good athlete and was very competitive. He had the ability to hire the right people and recognize that it always wasn't about what *he knew*, but what *other people* knew when it came to personnel. He made good decisions."[15]

It was an unforgettable time for David Finks, who was just 12 years old when his dad took the Vikings job.

"It was just wonderful. It was so exciting, the team was so exciting," said Finks. "Bud Grant was amazing. My dad brought him down [from Canada] in '67. I remember I spent one summer at Mankato as a ballboy. I was sitting on a football and Coach Grant came over to me and said, 'We don't sit down around here.' I couldn't have gotten up any faster. Bud was always about discipline—no joking around and doing the job right. To be around that at Christmastime for playoff games and getting your snowmobile suits on … it was just wonderful. Cold weather didn't bother us at all. It was just so fun to be there."

Finks, who resigned from the Vikings in 1974 after club owners inexplicably refused to allow him stock in the team, didn't fully get to enjoy the fruits of his labor. However, befitting his calm and steady demeanor, he never complained.

"He never talked about that," said David Finks, who now lives in Arizona and works with Southwest Greens. "He always kept a low profile. He never got too high or too low. By the time he went to Chicago, he was excited to build a new team."

Reichow said losing Finks to Chicago was devasting.

"It killed us. It killed us. He's the smartest football man I've ever been around," he said. "He went to Chicago and New Orleans and built both of those clubs into contenders."

Replacing him was the immensely unpopular Mike Lynn. "A football wannabe," Reichow said of Lynn, who once managed movie theaters in Delaware and Memphis. He is most remembered for the ill-fated Herschel Walker trade in October 1989.

Reichow was another architect whose player personnel decisions became a cornerstone in the Vikings' construction after he joined the front office in 1965 following the departure of Thomas, the organization's first employee. Thomas had hoped to be named

Rose's replacement as the club's second-ever general manager, but Finks was chosen. That prompted him to seek work elsewhere, and he was eventually named the executive assistant to co-owner Joe Robbie of the AFL's Miami franchise, which debuted in 1966.

Thomas told the *Minneapolis Star* that in leaving for Miami he would "receive considerably more" than the $15,000 he was paid as the Vikings' director of player personnel.[16]

"I think in Joe Thomas we have one of the very top people in American professional football," said Robbie.[17]

Thomas stayed with the Dolphins until 1972, helping build Miami teams that reached three Super Bowls in the 1970s, including Super Bowl VIII, in which they topped Minnesota 24–7 in the biggest mismatch of the Vikings' four Super Bowl appearances.

Ably replacing Thomas was Reichow, who, like Finks, was not only an accomplished and decorated collegiate quarterback but also a versatile athlete who knew a gifted ballplayer when he saw one, having played on the Iowa Hawkeyes Final Four–qualifying basketball team in 1955. Reichow's keen eye for targeting the top available athlete would prove vital.

"Van Brocklin had just cut me [from the Vikings]. And they also lost Joe Thomas, the director of scouting," recalled Reichow, now 89 and living with his wife, Carolyn, in Santa Fe, New Mexico. "They brought me in to take his place. I was a player. I didn't know anything about scouting or anything else, but we survived."

Reichow's career timeline touched on a staggering amount of seminal NFL moments. Chosen in the fourth round of the 1956 draft by the Detroit Lions after leaving Iowa as its all-time leader in total offense, Reichow, who sat behind Bobby Layne and former Vikings coach Harry Gilmer during his first year in pro ball, can claim the following distinctions:

He accounted for the final touchdown pass in the last Lions NFL championship game, in 1957, coming in for Tobin Rote to connect with Howard "Hopalong" Cassady on a 16-yard rollout pass to help hand head coach Paul Brown his worst loss with the Browns, 59–14.

Disgruntled with a lack of playing time in Detroit, he was shipped to Philadelphia and was on the field for special teams as the Eagles handed Vince Lombardi his only championship game loss, a 17–13 decision on December 26, 1960, at Franklin Field. Ironically, it would be at this same historic venue where Reichow, in his third year as a scout, would watch from the press box as the Vikings beat the Eagles to capture their first Central Division title.

"In '59, the Lions traded for Earl Morrall. They had Earl, Tobin Rote and myself at quarterback," said Reichow. "Before the opening exhibition game, our coach, George Wilson, said we're going to flip to see who starts and I won the flip. We're going to start the game and coach says, 'You're not starting, we're going with Morrall.' I said after that I'm getting out of here and I was traded the next year to Philadelphia. I played receiver there and they already had guys like Tommy McDonald and Pete Retzlaff."

Reichow played just one year in Philadelphia and was later traded to Washington but never played a down there before being flipped to the Vikings in time for their inaugural season in 1961.

"After 1960, I was done with football," said Reichow. "I just wanted to get back home. I'm from northeast Iowa and Minnesota's 10 miles away. Van Brocklin was our quarterback and he didn't get the head coaching job with the Eagles and he wanted it. So, all the sudden he's the head coach at Minnesota. The Eagles would not talk to him about trading me there, so they traded me to Washington. I'm getting ready to go to their training camp in Palo Alto, and George Preston Marshall called me and said, 'I've traded you to Minnesota.' I'm sure it had something to do with Van Brocklin."

Playing in the first game in franchise history, Reichow caught Tarkenton's second-ever TD pass, that coming in an improbable 37–13 victory over the Chicago Bears on September 17, 1961. Having never taken a snap at receiver until reaching professional football, he remarkably finished the day with three catches for 103 yards.

"I got there on Wednesday or the Thursday before the first league game," recalled Reichow. "Tarkenton and I didn't start. George Shaw started at quarterback and the team didn't know me from Adam. Finally, Van Brocklin said, 'You guys go in,' and we go on to beat the Bears. He throws a touch to me and a couple other balls. We connected up pretty good."

Reichow's 11 touchdown receptions that season stood as a Vikings record for 34 years before being broken by Cris Carter in '95. He also had 50 catches for 859 yards. His previous high for nabs was just 17.

Reichow joined the great Hugh McElhenny in becoming the first Vikings players to make the Pro Bowl. The Hall of Fame back had an illustrious career with the 49ers before playing out his career with Minnesota, New York and Detroit. He showed flashes of his former greatness in Minneapolis, rushing for 570 yards and three scores.

"I was in awe of him," said Reichow, the Hawkeyes' team MVP as a senior. "He was just a pretty runner. It wasn't just boom, boom with him. He could flow into it. One run he made against the 49ers I'll never forget. We're at about the 30-yard line. They give him the ball and he runs left, then he comes back right. About everybody on their team had a shot at him. He struts into the end zone the way he did with his chest out, looking regal. He ran about a half an hour to score a touchdown and we were only 30 yards away. I think I blocked about three different guys. He had a style that was amazing. He was a drifter, a smooth runner that would just glide. He was truly the 'King,' just different than anybody."

Reichow was unable to reclaim the same magic his second year in purple.

"The next year I got hurt with two or three games to go so my numbers dropped," said Reichow, who had three TDs and 39 catches in '62. "We didn't have very many good players. Van Brocklin said, 'I've got 33 stiffs here.' It wasn't hard to stick out in that group."

Reichow first spearheaded the Vikings draft in '67, possibly the best in team annals. He astutely selected not only Jones, Washington and Page in the first round, but also nabbed other eventual starters in the speedy Grim, cornerback Bobby Bryant and tight end John Beasley.

Minnesota would be in the Super Bowl in three years.

"On the face of it, this has to rate even better than 1961 when we got Tommy Mason, Rip Hawkins and Tarkenton," Vikings assistant general manager John Thompson told the *Minneapolis Star* on March 14, 1967, the first day of the draft.

With Finks and Reichow, along with Grant, the Vikings possessed razor-sharp discernment in what it took to build a winning franchise.

The 1967 draft, historic in that it was the first common draft between the NFL and the AFL as part of the AFL-NFL merger agreement in June 1966, was held at the Gotham

Hotel in New York, a city that served as the draft's home for 50 years. Reichow was able to call his selections in.

"Jim Finks was sick that year," said Reichow. "Bud Grant was right there next to me, just the two of us. We sat right there in Minnesota. He didn't say a damn word. He was a different guy. We had a good draft, getting Page, a Hall of Famer, and several other starters. I think overall we had eight guys make the team that year. Bud had just been hired, so he didn't know all the players, so I just had all my charts and stuff there and did the best I could. We did our draft, and I didn't know if he was going to fire me or not, but all those guys made it so he must have liked what I did."

Reichow and Grant were in for quite a journey.

"I had a wife and three kids so I required that if I was going to take the job, we had to join BLESTO [the Bears, Lions, Eagles, Steelers Talent Organization]," said Reichow. "I was our only scout and I couldn't be everywhere at once. I just tried to cover the top guys. I was at the Michigan State-Notre Dame game in '66 where I saw Washington, Page and Jones. I've always been an athlete and a competitor. Those were my two strengths and that's the kind of player I looked for."

Following Vikings football is often synonymous with pain. But much-needed solace can be found in the simple but powerful words written on a piece of paper the diplomatic Finks kept in his wallet.

Jim Finks, Jr., who sadly passed away in 2012 at age 59, read them when presenting his dad at his HOF induction in 1995:

"If we are ever unlucky enough to have it made, then we will be spectators, and not participants in life. It's the journey, not the arrival that counts. Does the road wind uphill all the way? Yes, to the very end."[18]

"In the latter days, we have to not just look at our careers, but our lives and what they meant," said Eller. "I have a son and two daughters and four grandkids. I want to leave a mark that my family would be proud of it. It really is a journey. We owe so much to so many people. I think there's something more than just the mental and the physical, and that's the spiritual. I was blessed. I was blessed to wear the purple. It was a great gift to be a Minnesota Viking."

What has kept me coming back year after year, despite heartbreak upon heartbreak, is the journey. As the brilliant Ralph Waldo Emerson wrote in *Experience*:

"To finish the moment, to find the journey's end in every step of the road, to live the greatest number of good hours is wisdom."

"I am Minnesota Viking and I always will be," added middle linebacker Lonnie Warwick, who played for the Vikings from 1965 to '72 before passing away in October 2024. "I want to see them win a Super Bowl and I'm hoping I'll be around when they win one. That's my ambition. I want to be there to cheer them on. I always enjoy going back to Minnesota."

To Vikings fans, the sense is that the team has never arrived, and in turn, neither have they. The road is truly uphill, as Finks said, but it's the journey, not the arrival, that counts.

"My dad was part of this journey," said David Finks. "But this was a team, not one individual. He wouldn't take the credit. It takes everyone to be a winner, from the players to the coach, to the owners, to the scouts, to the general manager. This team absolutely captured the nation's hearts. I think it was the aura of playing at that stadium, Metropolitan Stadium, seeing your breath in the air. I think the whole country was interested in games like that, instead of in Los Angeles where it's 70 degrees. This was a whole different ball game."

Not to be forgotten in the hardship of four Super Bowl defeats is the realization that from December 1968 to December 1977, the team captured fans' hearts with nine memorable playoff victories, each of which is chronicled here, along with insights from the assorted stalwarts who made the wins possible with their heroic feats.

2

Ozzie Dives, Carl Sacks

Minnesota Vikings 23, Los Angeles Rams 20
December 27, 1969, Metropolitan Stadium
Western Conference Championship

It's ironic that the organization the expansion Minnesota Vikings drew from the most for their early stability was the one on which they would inflict the most playoff pain.

At the recommendation of almost everyone Minnesota's five owners consulted, the club hired as its first general manager the young, intelligent and energetic Bert Rose, Jr., who had been publicity director of the Los Angeles Rams.

"Rose had a deep and thorough knowledge of the operation of a pro football club and he had been trained by one of the ablest executives in the business—Dan Reeves," said Tex Maule in *The Game*. "He had also worked under two exceptional general managers—Tex Schramm and [Pete] Rozelle."[1]

After purchasing the Rams in June 1941 for $100,000, Reeves moved the club from Cleveland to Los Angeles after it defeated Washington 15–14 in the 1945 championship game at chilly Municipal Stadium. (The margin of victory came on a Rams safety after a first-quarter Sammy Baugh pass from the end zone hit the goal post, a rule since abolished.)

Rose moved the club partially because he hated the frigid cold and Lake Erie–effect snow and also that his teams never drew well in Cleveland—just more than 32,000 attended the championship game, resulting in the 80,000-seat stadium looking virtually empty.

He is credited with instituting an exhaustive draft system that set a pattern for the rest of the league's organizations.

To scout college and pro players, the Vikings at the suggestion of Rozelle, who left the Rams to become NFL commissioner, hired Joe Thomas, who had been an assistant coach in both Canada and with the Rams.

Rose, Jr., would select as the team's first head coach former Rams quarterback Norm Van Brocklin, so prolific as a thrower that he still holds the NFL's single-game passing yardage mark with 554 yards.

It was the team Rose, Jr., Thomas and Van Brocklin left that the Vikings would go on to dominate in the playoffs.

It all began on a cold December day in 1969.

Quarterback Joe Kapp's swashbuckling play was once again inspirational, as he went 12 of 19 passing and rushed for the go-ahead touchdown in the fourth quarter, but running back Dave Osborn and defensive end Carl Eller joined him in doing the kind of blue-collar work that so characterized the Vikings.

It all added up to an epic 23–20 come-from-behind Western Conference championship win for the Vikings over the Coastal Division champion Rams, the Vikings' first playoff triumph.

Despite previously struggling in regular-season play against Los Angeles, Minnesota would post four wins in five playoff contests against the Rams under head coach Bud Grant, including a pair of riveting NFC championship game victories at Metropolitan Stadium.

"We were like a band of brothers. We were very close. All we wanted to do is win," said right end Jim Marshall, who notched a sack against colossus All-Pro Rams tackle Charlie Cowan in the historic win.

A man so tough that he once played with a broken neck, Osborn was a player the Vikings would repeatedly turn to during critical moments of the team's first home playoff game, in which he scored on a pair of TD plunges against George Allen's vaunted defense, while Eller, ferocious as ever lining up at left end, notched a pair of sacks, one an end zone game-decider in the fourth quarter.

During his 11 years with the Vikings, Osborn was involved in many milestone moments in team history, and one that will not soon be forgotten was his signature run

Minnesota Vikings running back Dave Osborn (41) is about to bounce outside for a key first-down run behind blocks from guard Jim Vellone (63) and tight end Kent Kramer (89), who seals off Los Angeles Rams linebacker Jack Pardee (32) during the 1969 NFL Western Conference championship game on Dec. 27, 1969, in Bloomington. Looking on from across the field is Rams cornerback Jim Nettles (19). Osborn rushed for two touchdowns as the Vikings defeated the Rams 23–20 at Metropolitan Stadium to advance to the NFL championship game.

for a key first down against the Rams in the fourth quarter, a play that may have been just as big as his two scoring excursions.

Osborn rushed for only 30 yards in this scintillating game, but his four-yard run with the Vikings trailing 20–14 after the Rams tacked on a 27-yard Bruce Gossett field goal following a Kapp fumble may have been the best of his career.

That's because it capsulized everything he did well.

Facing a third-and-two at the Rams' 20, Kapp called for a Vikings staple—an off-tackle run right—behind towering Hall of Fame right tackle Ron Yary, guard and University of Minnesota product Milt Sunde and bruising tight end Kent Kramer, who arrived from New Orleans.

However, enormous Rams left end David "Deacon" Jones and outside linebacker Jack Pardee blew up the play, pushing Kramer back into Osborn. Undaunted, Osborn displayed his trademark balance and power, bouncing off Pardee and getting around safety Richie Petitbon with a deft spin move to the outside before stumbling to the first down.

It was only four yards, but it was very valuable real estate. Those types of runs were classic Osborn.

"I got hit in a pile and just spin out of the arms of a Rams tackler [Merlin Olsen] to make the first down," said the stocky back.[2]

That gaining of precious ground paved the way for Kapp's two-yard TD sweep off left tackle to give the Vikings their first lead of the game at 21–20 with 8:40 remaining. The stouthearted Kapp, who followed a blocking convoy of Osborn, fullback Bill Brown and pulling guard Jim Vellone, was exuberantly mobbed by fans in the corner of the south end zone before heading back to the bench with his fists characteristically pumping, exhorting his defensive teammates to get back the "seed."

"It was wide open and all I had to do was run," said Kapp, who scored twice on the identical play the year before in San Francisco.[3]

"We normally don't like to run our quarterback," added Grant, "but they jammed in there so tough we figured when we get deep down on their goal line that this was one play that would work."[4]

Osborn's whirling dervish antics near the goal line were huge against the marauding Rams, but Eller's fourth-quarter sack belongs on the Mount Rushmore of Vikings playoff moments.

As he stood on the sideline waiting for the kickoff following Kapp's run, John Beasley, the Vikings' big tight end out of the University California, was heard to implore, "Come on, Carl. Do something."[5]

With the Rams taking over at their own 12, the 6-6, 247-pound defensive end answered Beasley's call to action, bursting like a bolt out of his angular three-point stance. His ferocious left-handed slap to the head of Bob Brown allowed him to blow past the man most considered the best right tackle in the game before enveloping a shell-shocked Roman Gabriel in the end zone.

Eller's pillaging takedown of the 6-5, 220-pound Rams quarterback for a safety with eight minutes left whipped into a lather a crowd that was already in a frenzy following Kapp's scoring run.

"Brown is so strong it took Carl some time to set him up," said Vikings defensive line coach Jack Patera. "Eller outplayed him in the second half and Brown even limped off the field a couple times. I think he was beat."[6]

Eller was able to prepare to play against powerhouses like Brown by going against the likes of Yary every day in practice.

"Ron Yary was an All-Pro tackle," said Eller. "He was a lot like me, a big guy. He would always give me good preparation for the game. He would go hard when we were working on our defense. When I would be going against a certain style of player, Ron would duplicate it as much as he could. Ron would accommodate me, which I was thankful for."

Yary's admiration for Eller was unquestioned.

"I first was aware of Carl Eller when I was drafted. They showed a video montage on Carl. He was so active and so big," said Yary, who starred on the defensive line for USC before moving to offense as a junior. "When I was drafted by the Vikings, I thanked God I wasn't going to have to go against him. He was just reaching the best part of his career when I came on. I had a great deal of respect for him. Carl pushed me in practice. He had a great outside pass rush.

"Carl didn't have to worry about the inside because he had Gary Larsen and Alan Page. He could just focus on containment. He had a great up-field rush, extremely fast and strong," added Yary. "He made me a better player. Defensive ends turn the corner on tackles a lot in today's NFL and you can't let them do that. Carl was great at that. Carl would come up field about four yards, then start pushing toward your outside shoulder toward the quarterback. He taught me as a right tackle to keep my right shoulder strong. Keeping an end from turning the corner was probably the best thing he taught me."

The five-time Pro Bowler Brown, a behemoth at 6–4, 280 pounds, was rarely beaten around the edge during his 10-year career.

"Our careers pretty much paralleled each other," said Eller, drafted four spots in the 1964 draft after his longtime friend Brown, picked second overall by the Eagles. "I was able to get to the outside. Gabriel was trying to go outside the pocket and that's where I was."

Eller was remarkably close to becoming an Eagle, but Philadelphia general manager Vince McNally and company opted to draft Brown to provide protection for immobile quarterback Sonny Jurgensen. Four months after the draft, on April 1, 1964, Jurgensen was traded for another pocket passer, Washington's Norm Snead.

"He was probably the best offensive tackle in football, especially right tackle," said Yary of the fellow Hall of Famer Brown, who finished his career with the Oakland Raiders. "That sack wasn't really Bob's fault. Gabriel took a deep drop and gave Carl time. Brown was a great man and a great player."

Rugged middle linebacker Lonnie Warwick, in his fifth year playing in the same starting lineup with Eller, wasn't surprised by Moose's ability to get to the quarterback.

"That guy was unreal," said Warwick, signed as a free agent by the Vikings in 1964, the same year Eller was drafted. "He had the longest reach of any player in the NFL. His arm span was massive and he had the biggest hands you've ever seen. And he had the best head slap that there was. Gabriel was as a helluva quarterback. To be able to even tackle him alone was tough, but for Eller to sack him in the end zone it was just unreal. It was a big game for us."

Defensive tackle Larsen saw it coming.

"It was an outside rush against Gabriel," said Larsen, who started his career with the Rams. "You got to credit the whole defense. Everyone had a job to do. That meant our defensive backs and linebackers were covering the receivers to give us enough time to get to the quarterbacks. That play was a good example of how plays should work. Our primary third-down call was '4–3 Rush.' That meant the back end had to guard, and we had to get to the quarterback anyway we could."

So athletic that earlier in his career he occasionally lined up at tight end on goal-line situations, the man nicknamed "Moose" just missed putting up more points for the Vikings' defense earlier in the contest.

On the Rams' first play from scrimmage following the recovery of a Brown fumble on the Minnesota 45-yard line, left outside linebacker Roy Winston bowled past the startled blockers and was about to tackle Gabriel as he tossed a soft pass right into the arms of the unsuspecting Eller, who ran 46 yards for what would have been a touchdown had Page not been ruled offside.

"All week we've been keyed up and tense and we talked about it," Page told *Sports Illustrated* after the game. "We tried to gear down, but we couldn't. That hurt us in the first half. Especially after I jumped offside and cost us a touchdown."[7]

Page didn't make mistakes often.

"When Alan Page came here that just made our defense," said Warwick. "It was unreal. I'd tell players if you cut me, if you chop me—I had bad knees—that I'd line up Page on them. There wasn't nothing like Alan Page. Nobody could block him."

Eller's sack made it Vikings 23, Rams 20. But the play went much deeper than the cushion it gave the team on the scoreboard.

It was an indelible image in Viking lore, one capturing the cold, the darkening sky, the purple jerseys with the NFL 50-year anniversary patch glowing in the afternoon light against the Rams' staunch white and blue; Alan Page, with that big No. 88 stitched across his chest leaping in jubilation in the background; and the forcefulness of a willful and not-to-be-denied defense that was made for moments like this.

"His teammates call him 'Moose,'" wrote Peter Range of the *New York Times* on the powerful Eller. "His strength is his strength, which is mighty, and his specialty is containment: stopping outside sweeps and botching up the direct run. His position coach Jack Patera said, 'All of our linemen are expected to beat two people. Moose can beat the third one.'"[8]

The heavy lifting was done, with the coup de grace coming later after the Rams, behind short passes from Gabriel, got precariously close to field goal range, driving to the Vikings' 44 with 39 seconds left. But Page, backing off the line into coverage, tipped a Gabriel pass, gathered it in and raced 29 yards down the sideline before being pushed out of bounds at the Los Angeles 26.

"I had to do something to make up for my poor play in the first half," said Page. "I was just coming off the ball trying not to get cut off by Tom Mack. I didn't get a good pass rush, so I was standing behind the line of scrimmage. He threw the ball right at me chest high and I took off for the end zone."[9]

It was a wise read by Page, whose big play allowed Kapp to lie on the ball a few times before the clock expired.

From the grandstand, a banner could be seen that read: "Dec. 27, 1969, The Fall of Roman's Empire." It has been said that Rome's empire fell from within; Gabriel's offensive game plan did from without, and his pillagers, clad in purple, were Eller, Marshall, Page and Larsen.

"It wasn't fair because I would come from one side and Marshall would come from the other and then you get Alan and Gary [Larsen] coming up that middle," said Eller.

"Our slogan was, 'Meet you at the quarterback.' That was a very, very successful format that we had. We could control the offense through our skills and uniqueness and combination of both power, speed, quickness and just really the knowledge of the game and enthusiasm for the game we loved."[10]

On the instruction of offensive coordinator Ray Prochaska, the Rams wisely chose a strategy of dumping the ball off short in front of the Vikings' stingy zone defense, but the tactic backfired on their last-ditch drive thanks to the omnipresent Page. Only three of NFL MVP Gabriel's 22 completions were to a wide receiver (Wendall Tucker).

The approach worked early on as the Rams took a 17–7 lead into the locker room on Gabriel's two-yard bootleg lob to tight end Billy Truax.

"We really thought we were going to win at the half," said Vikings punter and third-string quarterback Bob Lee, who averaged nearly 40 yards a punt that season as a rookie. "We should have played better. We knew what we had in us. But if you look at some of our scores that year, there were some games where we won but didn't play that great or put up a lot of points. I remember the game at Green Bay where we won 9–7 and I had a couple punts inside the seven. We would kind of start slowly sometimes."

Kapp's 41-yard pass to Gene Washington and ensuing piling on penalty on Pardee set up an Osborn dive from the one to pull the Vikings to within three, 17–14, in the third quarter. Osborn had scored in the first quarter on another catapult over the scrimmage line—his specialty—to tie the score at 7–7. Washington's 27-yard reception helped key the 10-play, 75-yard drive.

For Osborn and Co., it all added up to a remarkable and historic comeback against a stout and proud Rams defense, as the Vikings outscored their West Coast visitors 16–3 in the second half.

"We just benefited by recognition and awareness of what they were doing to us in the first half," said Grant after the contest. "We changed no blocking. We just had a chance to run because we had the ball more, so we made some first downs and therefore utilized more of our offense."[11]

Minnesota had the ball more in the second half because of its aroused defense. The Purple People Eaters were like a storm rolling over a Kansas farmhouse: they came from all directions, and all there was to do was to tie everything down and hope they didn't take the roof.

"At our peak, we changed the game," said Marshall. "Rules were passed to help teams adjust to us. The new holding rules, the outlawing of the head slap—that was because of the things we did. We were like a SWAT team, a task force—quick and agile. It got to the point where I knew what the others were going to do the moment they started it. It was just understood."[12]

"We contributed to a lot of the changes that were made during that time and probably are responsible for the game that you see today," said Eller. "I would say that [due to] our front, the 'Purple People Eaters' as they called us—that would include Jim Marshall, Alan Page, Gary Larsen and myself and later Doug Sutherland and occasionally the 'Benchwarmer,' Bob Lurtsema—the pocket was not a safe place to be. When I came into the league, the pocket passer was the thing—you know, the guy that could drop back, stand in the pocket and look around for a receiver. We would demolish the pocket. The safe place for the quarterback was no longer."[13]

Upon the fidgety and masterful Allen taking over the reins in Los Angeles in 1966, the resurgent Rams had the Vikings' number to say the least, winning 21–6 in '66 and crushing them in both '67 and '68 by a combined score of 70–6, the latter loss coming in December at Met Stadium.

The Rams opened the '69 season with an 11-game winning streak, but the Vikings put an end to that with a 20–13 victory at the Coliseum in week 12. Nevertheless, Los Angeles came into the Western Conference championship game confident of a victory. Following the regular-season loss, ferocious left end Deacon Jones said, "There's no way they're going to beat us twice."

Eller thought otherwise, and the Vikings' subsequent win would begin a string of rousing playoff successes under Grant's tutelage against Los Angeles, as Minnesota defeated the Rams in both the '74 and '76 NFC championship games and in the divisional round in '77.

"We really believed we were going to win," said veteran Rams guard Tom Mack of the teams' first playoff matchup. "It was a very, very close game. It was a painful loss. Of course, I had that experience a lot, unfortunately. We would always lose to the damn Vikings. We'd come up with a different way to do it each time."[14]

For the second time in three seasons, Allen and his Rams had failed to advance past the first round of the playoffs, having also dropped a 28–7 decision to the eventual Super Bowl II champ Packers in the '67 Western Conference championship.

"What hurts is that everything was right on the button," Allen told reporters after the loss to the Vikings. "We were mentally and physically prepared for the game. We were sure we'd win."[15]

Six days later, Los Angeles would go on to destroy the Cowboys 31–0 in the meaningless Playoff Bowl in Miami, but that provided little solace for Allen, who in four years would be leading another team into Minnesota for a playoff game, the Washington Redskins.

• • •

Defensive back Dale Hackbart's huge special teams tackle of former Wisconsin teammate Ron Smith pinned the Rams at their own 12 to set up Eller's safety, the biggest play in the history of the franchise to that point.

"I was L-5 on the coverage team, the outside man," said Hackbart, who played five seasons with the Vikings. "Our main focus was to not let anybody knock you down to allow the return man to run around you and go up the sideline. That's what the coaches always said. I ran down and they came out of the end zone a little late, and as I got nearer, around the 20, I just cut in. There was nobody that blocked me. I went right around the wedge and cut right off the back off it and I nailed him. He tried to go inside of me and we just collided. It was a hard-hitting game all the way."

A standout quarterback at Wisconsin, Hackbart led the Badgers to the 1960 Rose Bowl and finished seventh in the Heisman voting behind LSU's Bill Cannon.

In a twist of fate, Hackbart became the first draft choice in the history of the Oakland Raiders. Minnesota was set to join the eight-team AFL and participated in its first draft, where it was awarded Hackbart as a territorial pick. But once Vikings ownership jumped at the NFL's last-minute franchise offer, an effort spearheaded by Chicago's George Halas, all of the team's AFL draft selections, including Hackbart, were awarded to the Raiders.

"Bud Grant came up to me when the Rams game was over and he shook my hand and he said, 'That set it up,'" said Hackbart. "Bud was a quiet man who didn't talk to his players much. He let the coaches communicate with the players, so that meant a lot."

Known by his teammates as "Crazy Crane" due to his angular 6–3 frame and propensity for clothesline tackles and borderline late hits, Hackbart teamed with Karl Kassulke to make up a diabolical, rampaging, head-hunting pair of safeties before the Vikings stole Paul Krause from Washington in a 1968 swap.

"Kassulke, all he wanted to do was hit somebody. That was his gig," laughed Hackbart. "We had to work around Kassulke, because sometimes he was supposed to be deep middle, but he was still taking on the tight end or he was coming up wanting to blast some poor running back when he was supposed to be back deep. The guys used to give him a lot of flak about that. It was fun. That was just the way he played. It worked out well, though, because quarterbacks would drop back, and they'd look at Kassulke and they would never be able to figure out what type of defense we were playing because he was never in his proper spot. But he could cover, and he would hustle and he would hit and he just loved it."

"Dale Hackbart was always one we had to keep quiet in the huddle," said Warwick, who played college ball at both Tennessee and Tennessee Tech. "He'd run around saying, 'Call the play! Call the play!' Of course, Karl Kassulke was always really hyped up, too. All our defensive backs wanted me to get the play call out."

Warwick said Grant was a perfect coach for the likes of Hackbart because he wouldn't put up with freelancing players.

"One of his first meetings, he drew up on the board how many penalties we made [the year before]. He said, 'You can't win like that, boys,'" noted Warwick. "One time he said, 'Hackbart, you see that 15 yards we got penalized on that clothesline? That almost cost us the game! If you do that again you might as well pack your bags!'"

Hackbart was skillful enough at baseball in college that he spent a season playing for the Grand Forks, North Dakota, Chiefs, a Class C minor league team in the Pittsburgh Pirates organization.

The Chiefs played some games in Winnipeg, where Grant was serving as coach of the Blue Bombers of the CFL. Knowing him from his days with his hometown Badgers, Grant sought to convince Hackbart to play for the Bombers. At the end of the baseball season, Hackbart decided to take Grant up on his suggestion.

The problem was Hackbart was also taken in the fifth round of the 1960 NFL draft by Vince Lombardi's Green Bay Packers. Lombardi took umbrage with Grant's perceived tampering and demanded Hackbart be turned over to the Packers. Lombardi subsequently convinced Hackbart to drop baseball and concentrate on a career in the NFL. He was a backup safety in 1960 for the Western Conference champion Packers and served in the same role for two games in '61 before being traded to the Redskins.

"Bud never got along with Lombardi after that," said tight end Stu Voigt, another Wisconsin product who joined the Vikings in 1970. "He never acknowledged Lombardi's accomplishments and it all started with the Hackbart incident."

Hackbart played three years with the Redskins before being picked up by the Vikings in '66. His attacking approach was so contagious it wasn't surprising Eller's big play followed Hackbart's.

Gabriel got a strong taste of the Vikings' defense that afternoon.

"I met Gabriel personally at a function about a year after the game," said Hackbart. "I don't think he knew who I was. They had several athletes there. I walked up to him, and I held out my hand and we shook hands briefly. Then he said, 'Give me your name.' I said, 'Dale Hackbart.' He pulled his hand away and he looked at me and said, 'You're a nasty son of a bitch,' and I don't think he was kidding. In that game I got him on several safety blitzes when he was in a throwing position. He was back and cocked and here I come, and I stick him in the chest. He never forgot that."

The Vikings' defense was known for its great front four, but it also had an accomplished battery of defensive backs. Upon Krause's arrival, Hackbart was regulated to being used as a great weapon off the bench and was a terror on special teams.

"When I came out of Wisconsin, I played both quarterback and defensive back, but I was not a very aggressive player. I never really looked at really rocking someone on defense," said Hackbart, who chalked up six interceptions in nine games with the Redskins in '61 after being traded from Green Bay. "I would make the tackles, but I didn't go around kicking the shit out of people, but that was something that I was going to have to change to make it in the NFL. That was probably why Lombardi let me go because he knew I had a lot to learn, and they didn't have time for it at Green Bay."

Hackbart opened the '64 season as a starter with the Redskins but was later supplanted by Krause. The well-traveled defensive back was then let go by Washington after separating his shoulder.

Hackbart worked hard in rehab and joined the Minnesota Vikings for the 1965 season. He played free safety during exhibitions but was cut before the regular season started. He then went up to Winnipeg, where he finally got to suit up for Grant.

Hackbart started at safety for the Bombers but was released before the playoffs. Because of the difference in schedules between the CFL and NFL, he was able to rejoin the Vikings and finish out the 1965 season under Van Brocklin.

"Van Brocklin was a great strategist," said Hackbart. "He could put in great offenses and defenses that picked the opponents apart. But he was a perfectionist. He couldn't tolerate mental and physical errors. He would really chew you out unmercifully. He was tough on his players. You had to be strong emotionally and mentally to play for him. Grant was just the opposite."

• • •

Osborn may not have had the explosive ability of teammates like Eller and Page, but his steadfastness epitomized the team's mindset.

Just as Jerry West's silhouette inspired the National Basketball Association logo, it could be argued that No. 41's image, along with those of revered icons like the great Marshall, would be similarly etched into any design celebrating the history of the proud Minnesota franchise.

Osborn, who after playing out his last NFL season with the Packers in 1976 was asked by a doctor after a postseason examination, "When did you break your neck?" saw it all during his Vikings career.

"I think I remember the play because my neck kind of went numb a bit," said Osborn, a 13th-round pick in 1965 out of North Dakota who still makes his home in Minnesota. "The NFL makes you go in once you retire to get kind of like an exit examination, and that's when he saw it. It's calcified over, so I guess I'm all right. I don't have much movement there. I basically have to turn my whole body to look to the right or left."

Unlike teammates Marshall, Fran Tarkenton, Ed Sharockman and Grady Alderman, the Cando, North Dakota, native Osborn was not there for the franchise's inception in 1961, but in playing for both Van Brocklin and Grant, he both witnessed and experienced firsthand the team's ascension from a talented, albeit dysfunctional, group to a thriving, disciplined machine that would go on to churn out 10 division titles and four Super Bowl appearances from 1968 to 1978.

"Bud said he didn't need the best players, just guys who weren't going to make a mistake," said Osborn, who played for the Vikings through the '75 season. "We didn't look for bigger, stronger, faster, we just wanted to play good, basic football and let our great defense keep us in the game."

The Vikings were northern tough, with many players on the roster of Hackbart's and Osborn's ilk, like longtime backfield mate Bill "Boom Boom" Brown, a University of Illinois product.

"Bill and I weren't fancy," said Osborn. "We were power runners. Once I got hit, I was always moving forward. I think the only guy I remember stopping me in my tracks was [Bears middle linebacker] Dick Butkus."

On his two TD dives against the Rams, Osborn showcased the uncanny ability to propel himself over the line, becoming one of the early NFL players to successfully deploy this method of contortion, his stocky body wedging through a torrent of arms, legs and helmets at the storm-laden goal line.

While he could break a long run occasionally—he had a 73-yarder against the Browns in '67 where he was stopped just short of the goal—most of his 29 career TDs came on dive plays.

"We'd call them 'Flyover Left or Flyover Right,'" recalled Osborn, who, like most of the players of his day, didn't lift weights and credited his strength to throwing hay bales. "You'd go off guard right or left and you'd jump into the air. Brown would lead block and the linemen would try to lower the pile and you'd just fly over. You'd roll over and stumble backwards into the end zone."

For those who watched him play, the image indelibly sketched in their minds of Osborn, who finished his career with 4,336 yards rushing, is that of a sturdy figure with a white-and-gold No. 41 stitched on the back of a purple jersey once again leaping over a tempestuous line of scrimmage.

Enabling Osborn on these launches was his leaping ability.

"I played high school basketball, and although I'm barely six feet tall, I could dunk," he said. "I was the biggest guy on the team. Having spring in your legs is very important. A lot of it, too, was the linemen weren't as tall back then and they couldn't move as well as they do today. You'd attack the pile and roll over the top. I always felt like I could get into the end zone or get a couple yards."

Osborn, a 1970 Pro Bowler, said there was never a doubt what the Vikings had in Grant, who captured four Grey Cups in 10 years at the helm of the Winnipeg Bombers.

"I always felt Bud was a winner," said Osborn, who became a full-time starter Grant's first year, gaining a then team-record 972 yards and chipping in an additional 272 yards receiving. "You could see things were happening.

"Those coaches [Van Brocklin and Grant] were like night and day," added Osborn, a member of the North Dakota Sports Hall of Fame who had his jersey number retired by the university. "Van Brocklin was a tough coach, but I didn't know anything different. I just thought this was the way it was going to be in pro ball. When Grant came along, we all thought we died and went to heaven.

"Although I must say," he continued, "that I'm forever thankful that Van Brocklin gave me a chance. I was just a green kid who played for a small school up in North

Dakota. He saw something in me. I'm sure a lot of teams ruled me out. I think he liked my toughness. He seemed to like to draft tough farm boys."

The playoff win over the Rams was the team's coming-out party. Under the Dutchman's six-year watch, the Vikings showed just tempting flashes, going 8–5–1 in '64.

"It seems like every year we split with the Packers when they had Lombardi," said Osborn. "Beating the Rams was special."

Osborn also played a key role the next week as the team secured its only NFL championship with a 27-7 victory the over the Eastern Conference champion Cleveland Browns. In a game played January 4, 1970—a contest that marked the last NFL championship game before the merger—Osborn in his best-ever playoff outing, and one of the top games of his career, carried 18 times for 108 yards, including a 20-yard TD rush in the second quarter that put the game out of reach at 24–0.

The Vikings would go on to lose Super Bowl IV to the Kansas City Chiefs, but once again, Osborn became a part of team lore as he scored the team's first-ever Super Bowl touchdown on a four-yard scamper in a 23–7 setback.

Fans watching may have noticed when Osborn scored there was no name on his back as he characteristically twisted and churned into the end zone.

"That jersey was historic as it was the last season, as a matter of fact, the last game in which an NFL team didn't have the players' names on the back," said Paul Lukas of Uni-Watch.com. "That was the last game before the merger. The AFL had been putting players' names on their jerseys from day one because they were trying to market themselves and the individuality of their players. When the merger happened, the NFL got on board with that. The Vikings were the last team to not wear names on the back of the jersey."

Undoubtedly, if there was ever a player equipped to play in Minnesota at the old Met Stadium, it was Osborn. Despite being fairly sizable at 6–0 and 208, he played with an extremely low center of gravity and with sure and steady feet.

"I loved playing there," he beamed. "I didn't mind the conditions. On game day when I looked outside and saw that it was bad out there, I'd think, 'I'm going to have a day.' My best game was in '67 in the snow at home against the Packers when I had 155 yards. I didn't mind being cold and dirty. I was a mudder for sure.

"I mean this was a baseball field where we played football," Osborn added of the home the Vikings shared with the Twins, "and the sod they used to cover the infield dirt with would be flying all over the place when you ran. I believed I always had the edge over the defender because I knew where I was going, and they didn't."

Osborn had a solid year in 1970, gaining nearly 1,000 yards from scrimmage as he made his only Pro Bowl. He rushed for 681 yards and five TDs, while adding 23 catches for 202 yards and another score. But due to slipshod quarterback play following Kapp's untimely departure after the fabled '69 season, the Vikings would not get back to the Super Bowl until after the 1973 campaign.

It was then that Chuck Foreman arrived in town after being drafted in the first round. With the Miami of Florida star carrying most of the load during a fabulous Rookie of the Year campaign, the 30-year-old Osborn was limited to just 42 carries, his least since the '68 season, which saw him start just two games due to knee surgery.

The team player that he was, Osborn accepted his situation very favorably and had no qualms playing a mentoring role with the talented Foreman.

"I saw the potential he had. I took him under my wing," said Osborn. "Pro ball was a big adjustment for Chuck because he played a lot of positions in college. But I saw he was a guy who was going to help us win and I was glad to help him out. Chuck was and still is a good friend."

The Vikings earned their second Super Bowl trip after that season, falling to the powerful Dolphins 24–7. With Oscar Reed getting most of the work opposite Foreman, Osborn toted the ball only four times during their three-game postseason run, which included a 27–20 win over Washington and a 27–10 rout of Dallas in the title game.

The next year saw the return to prominence for Osborn, as he ran for 514 yards on 131 carries and four TDs as the Vikings again advanced to the Super Bowl.

He was a major contributor during that playoff surge, especially in the 30–14 divisional-round victory at home versus the St. Louis Cardinals, accounting for more than 100 yards from scrimmage (67 yards rushing, 36 yards receiving). He then scored a key touchdown in the fourth quarter of the NFC championship game against the Rams as he had another one of his signature one-yard TD runs to give the Vikings some breathing room at 14–3. Minnesota held on for a 14–10 victory to earn a trip to play the Steelers in Super Bowl IX.

Osborn and Foreman were stuffed by the Steel Curtain in a 16–6 loss, a game in which Minnesota trailed just 9–6 with 11 minutes remaining following Terry Brown's end-zone recovery of a Matt Blair block of a Bobby Walden punt.

Losing three Super Bowls during his career does not haunt Osborn. But one game he and most Vikings may feel bad about is the 17–14 "Hail Mary" playoff-game loss to the Cowboys in sadly Osborn's final game with the Vikings, on December 28, 1975.

"That was a tough one. No way we lose that game. That may have been our best team, but we had a great run," said Osborn. "For 10 to 12 years, we had the same team, and we were like a family. Coach Grant did a great job preparing us and whether we were playing the Lions or the Rams, we went in with a solid game plan."

• • •

Unquestionably, the Vikings had an accomplished running back room to go with Brown and Osborn, one that included change-of-pace backs in Reed and the speedy Clinton Jones.

Seemingly ordained to be blessed with multiply gifted skill position players was a Minnesota club that was voted for approval at the same January 1960 session Rozelle was elected as NFL commissioner and the Dallas Cowboys were granted a franchise.

Rose, Jr., Thomas and Van Brocklin selected from other clubs such backs as Hugh McElhenny, the incomparable former 49ers star who had grown old but not elderly, and Mel Triplett, a powerful runner and fine blocker at fullback with the New York Giants.

The team's first draft pick was a big, quick halfback from Tulane who looked every bit like a young McElhenny—Tommy Mason.

With McElhenny and Mason both gone, Minnesota hoped drafting Jones would bring the team a new-age, game-breaking element to their otherwise plodding attack.

Jones, who rushed for 241 yards in 1969, was drafted second overall by the Vikings in '67 out of Michigan State over Syracuse's Floyd Little, who was selected four picks later by the AFL's Denver Broncos. Little would go on to rush for 6,323 yards and 43 touchdowns and earn a spot in the Hall of Fame.

"We liked Floyd Little, but he had a knee [injury]," said Vikings scout Jerry Reichow. "Turned out to be a helluva player. Clinton was clean. That was the only reason we took him over the other guy. Clinton was a good, solid player. We had no regrets over taking him."

The prolific college runner had only had 13 carries his rookie season, but that didn't seem to matter much to Jones, a graduate of Cathedral Latin High School in Cleveland who was overlooked by Ohio State coach Woody Hayes, at least until it was too late to grab him away from legendary MSU coach Duffy Daugherty.

"Woody Hayes wasn't interested in me until he saw me run in the state track meet in the Horseshoe at Ohio State University and I broke the national record in the high and low hurdles. I was six feet, weighed 196 pounds. Once he saw that, then he became interested," laughed the speedy Jones. "I had no intentions of going to Ohio State, I wanted to get out of the state of Ohio as well as East Cleveland. I wound up taking a trip to [the University of] Detroit and I wanted to go there, but my coach said, 'I don't think that's a good place for you to go. I want you to take a trip to Michigan State.' When I saw that beautiful campus, I fell in love with it and for me it was the best choice. I know truly my life was synchronized with that university and campus."

His early years in football ingrained in Jones the value of team play, and he would need that mindset in Minnesota as he had to bide time behind holdovers Brown and Osborn.

"One thing I learned very early is when the team wins everyone wins," added Jones. "This value creation started in high school and continued through my time at Michigan State. Sure, I wanted to play more, and I had a problem with them trying to tell me how to run the ball. But it was ingrained in me team comes first. Even Buddy Young [the former star All-American Football Conference and NFL running back who was director of player relations for the NFL], who mentored me early on, told me not to worry about playing time at first. It turned out Minnesota was the perfect place for me."

Young was the man NFL commissioner Pete Rozelle used to keep Black players from jumping to the AFL, which held its own draft before the merger. Many top-notch players were lured away.

"Buddy Young started 'babysitting' me after the '65 season after the AFL went after Bubba Smith," recalled Jones. "But I never really wanted to go to the AFL. I was raised on the NFL back in the day, Y.A. Tittle, Sam Huff, Jim Brown, et al. I followed the Browns. They had more Black players than anybody. I grew up with that blue-collar, running-the-football style. I grew up idolizing Jim Brown. He was a man amongst men. I watched him play so much he became a part of my subconscious when I was running the ball. The way he presented himself. He did his pregame warmups separately, doing his own stretches. The way he walked, it was like watching the *Lion King*. The way he was built. He looked like he was poured into his uniform. If you looked, he was very neat. Tight uniform. No sagginess in his uniform at all. Almost a Greek god."

Considering his love for Brown, one would have assumed Jones would have asked to wear No. 32 for the Spartans.

"The equipment man gave me No. 26 because of Herb Adderley," said Jones of the former Packers and Cowboys great, an All-American halfback at Michigan State before being moved to cornerback by Lombardi, who already had the steady Paul Hornung and Jim Taylor in the backfield.

It was a rough first year under Grant as the Vikings went 3–8–3 in 1967. But Jones, who ran back a kickoff for a TD that year against the New York Giants, knew a turnaround was on the horizon.

"I knew that we had something," said Jones, "because of the ['67] draft that we had. And we had very solid leadership in terms of Jim Marshall and Grady Alderman. The Vikings were in transition. They brought in a coach from Canada [Grant], a quarterback from Canada [Kapp] and Jim Marshall played a year in Canada [with Saskatchewan] after leaving Ohio State early before going to the Browns. Marshall was an iconic man."

Lee's voice started breaking up with the thought of Marshall, whose health did not permit him to attend the Vikings' 50 anniversary celebration of the '73 Super Bowl team.

"He is a special man. He did something for me that first camp I will never forget," said Lee, still choked up. "He was like that with everyone, encouraging everyone. Calming people down who needed to be calmed down. He was Bud's coach among the players. We had more parties at his house than anyone else. And we were always welcome. They weren't wild events, just the kind you'd like to be at with all your friends. The veterans' committee should vote him into the Hall of Fame. It's a shame, a shame."

Jones said few people know the true story behind why Marshall landed in Minnesota. The widespread narrative was that he couldn't get along with Paul Brown. Then there was the belief Marshall's bout with encephalitis, which resulted in significant weight loss and near death, prompted the Browns to move on.

It was neither of those, said Jones.

"He and Jim Brown got into an argument," Jones said emphatically. "Marshall decked him. That's why Paul Brown got rid of him. This is what I heard from Jim. Paul Brown couldn't send him to Canada, so he sent him to the next-closest place. I was never aware of a beef between Jim Marshall and Paul Brown. Jim Brown could be very intimidating ... but not to Jim Marshall. I was familiar with this situation. We all lived in the same neighborhood, the Mount Pleasant neighborhood in East Cleveland. Jim Brown, when he was playing for Cleveland, lived two blocks from my grandparents. A lot of Browns players lived there, including Ernie Davis."

"We did get into an altercation, and I did get the best of him," said Marshall on his encounter with a player many consider the best running back in NFL history. "But it wasn't the reason the Browns didn't protect me. That really wasn't me. There were other factors. They did not protect me because I was a rookie. They protected all the veteran players they expected to come back and make contributions to the team. They certainly didn't want to protect an unproven player over a veteran who might get picked up right away."

Marshall didn't come to the Vikings via the expansion draft, but by trade. Minnesota sent its second and 11th pick in the 1962 draft to the Browns for six players, among those Marshall and Paul Dickson, who became a starter at defensive tackle until the arrival of Page.

Jones got more opportunities in '68 due to a knee injury to Osborn as he rushed for 536 yards and a TD in addition to posting a solid 4.2 yards per carry, thus showing the burst that made him a college All-American. In doing so, the former high school state hurdles champ helped the Vikings to their first division title.

Osborn's return from injury saw Jones's carries go from 128 to just 54 in '69, but he still thrived on special teams, averaging 26.1 yards per kickoff return, good for seventh in the league. The vocal team leader didn't mind taking a back seat, even against the Rams.

"My only attitude was if I wasn't playing, I was going to be a cheerleader," said Jones, repeatedly captured during the game by NFL Films vociferously supporting his teammates on the sideline. "It's static. That's what players live for, to win those kinds of games. We just knew that there was something really dynamic happening. That was the main thing. It was like hitting the lotto. You play the game to be champions."

At the epicenter of it all was Grant.

"The thing about Bud Grant, he was very unusual and very unlike your traditional coaches," said Jones, whose best season came in 1971 when he led the team in rushing with 675 yards. "He played professional football, he played professional basketball, he was in the navy, where he was influenced by Paul Brown. He was a stoic person and his personality and style kind of all fit in with the times."

Grant enlisted in the navy after high school in 1945 during World War II. His first duty station was Treasure Island Naval Station in California, where he trained as a crewmember for a landing ship. Before he could get his first taste of combat, the war ended. He was then assigned to the Great Lakes Naval Training Center in Illinois, where he played on the Bluejacket, the base football team.

The team was coached by Brown, a World War II veteran. Brown later became cofounder and the first coach of the Cleveland Browns, the team that bore his name.

Grant, a native of Superior, Wisconsin, and homesick from a year and a half away from his beloved Midwest, opted to use his GI Bill funds to attend the University of Minnesota since it was only 150 miles from home compared with the 350 miles required to make the trip to the University of Wisconsin.

At Minnesota, he became one of its top all-time athletes, playing football, basketball and baseball. After graduation, he was selected in the first round of the 1950 NFL draft by the Philadelphia Eagles and was the fourth-round selection for the Minneapolis Lakers in the National Basketball Association draft that same year. He also drew interest from the Chicago White Sox.

"They wanted me to sign but I wanted the guarantee that I would go straight to the major leagues," said Grant. "If I played basketball, I'd go straight to a world championship club; if I go to football, I go straight to a championship club. If I played baseball, I didn't want to be sent to a Mobile or a Little Rock, I wanted to go right to Chicago or New York. They wouldn't do that, so I went to the Lakers."[16]

Minnesota, led by George Mikan, was coming off winning the NBA title in the 1949–50 season, while the Eagles, spearheaded by Steve Van Buren's 196 yards rushing, had captured the NFL crown with a 14–0 win over the Rams at the Los Angeles Coliseum in '49.

Having familiarity with Grant from his time with the Gophers was not only Lakers owner Max Winter, who would go on to become part of the Vikings' first ownership group, but his friend Sid Hartman, the team's general manager.

"The Lakers had a player get hurt and my GI Bill money had run out, so I went to the NBA as a hardship case," said Grant. "I never played my senior year of basketball at Minnesota."[17]

"I used to watch him very closely," said Jones of Grant. "He was very consistent. We were very basic. Football was like his life—all about consistency. He let the coaches do the coaching. I hardly ever saw him lose his temper and you would never see him argue with the coaches, especially in front of the players. He was very loyal, and his mantra was 'consistency wins.' The other thing was football was not everything to him. He was a naturist. He loved nature, he loved hunting. He loved his family, his kids. Bud was not interested in flash. It was a way to make a living for him. All of it came together: a spiritual experience that manifested into physicality."

It was during Jones's third season with the Vikings that all the winning elements came into place, a remarkable convergence of time, space, gifted players and undoubted leadership.

"I knew nothing about the Vikings," said Jones, who played on two national championship teams at Michigan State. "The Vikings were never on my radar when I was growing up. But it was one of those things where in time, everything kind of comes together. I call it the right energy. I call it vibrational matchups. Everything clicks. You have [coming together] the old and the new. You had the rock-'em, sock-'em grind-it-out ground game of the '50s and early '60s, then you bring in some new talent and speed: Gene and I, Alan Page, Bobby Bryant, John Beasley, Bobby Grim. Then in the following years you get more of the same: Ron Yary ['68 overall top pick], Ed White ['69 second-round pick], then also you bring in guys like Paul Krause [in a '68 trade with the Redskins for linebacker Marlin McKeever and a draft pick]. No one will ever break his [interception] record."

In a remarkable sequence, it was the Vikings' selecting Jones second behind Bubba Smith in the '67 draft that enabled them the flexibility to trade Mason on draft day to the Rams for the pick they used to nab Page, who was shrewdly moved to tackle by Grant.

"He [Page] could be that overpowering guy you need on the inside who can make the defensive ends so much more effective," a prophetic Grant told the *Minneapolis Star* on draft day.[18]

"When you look at my career, it couldn't have been any better. It worked out for me," added Jones, who resides in California. "I have no regrets, from Michigan State to the Vikings. I don't think they really took advantage of my abilities, but again if the team wins everybody wins. When we won against the Rams, I wasn't in the game, but I played it on the sidelines. My energy helped the team. I was going to be in the game one way or another."

No doubt the energy at Met Stadium that afternoon was palpable.

"The environment was great," said Eller. "They were always behind us, and they didn't mind the cold. It was hard to turn the fans off. They knew when to cheer, they knew when we had the momentum. The fans were just a part of our game."

Although many fans were situated far from the field due to the stadium being designed for baseball, Eller said their presence was felt.

"You could still feel them," he said. "We had to come on and off the field via the [first-base] dugout and there were always a lot of fans swarming there. They were very much a part of our success. There was kinship with the fans. They knew the import of the game to our franchise. They were very supportive. There was nothing but encouragement from them."

"The fans were outstanding," added Hackbart. "We had more sellouts during that time than any other NFL team. And even though the fans were pretty far away from the field, we could still hear them screaming and hollering."

And these hordes would be back at it the next week against Cleveland.

3

It's Washington by Air

Minnesota Vikings 27, Cleveland Browns 7
January 4, 1970, Metropolitan Stadium
NFL Championship Game

Predominately undetected by the myriads of NFL fans born after the "Gipper" administration is the realization the Minnesota Vikings had a smooth and rangy flycatcher who proudly and with aplomb wore No. 84 before Randy Moss.

Like Moss, he was an elite athlete.

Like George "The Gipper" Gipp, portrayed in the 1940 film *Knute Rockne, All American* by the man he became synonymous with, former president Ronald Reagan, he was a legendary collegiate athlete for a historically great program.

He suited up six years with Minnesota, playing in consecutive Pro Bowls and winning a National Football League title.

He was 6–3, 208 pounds and could both run and jump like a mountain gazelle, winning the 1965 NCAA indoor title in the 60-yard-high hurdles and six Big Ten championships, three indoor and three outdoor, in hurdles.

He ran with a gait rarely seen during his career.

He wasn't allowed to play college football in his home state.

He was confused for a contemporary who shared his name and starred at the same position for the San Francisco 49ers.

His name? Gene Washington. His time with the Vikings, who captured the NFL Central Division crown in '69 with a 12–2 mark, while relatively short, was nevertheless impactful.

He had only three catches in the last NFL championship game before the merger, but they went for 120 yards and a score in the Vikings' dominating 27–7 win over the beleaguered Cleveland Browns at a raucous Metropolitan Stadium.

"They outplayed us in every phase of the game," said Browns coach Blanton Collier, who led the team to the NFL title in 1964. "I'm on record prior to this season that Minnesota just possibly had the best team in the NFL. Minnesota has fine material. I hate to be a prophet. I'd like to have proven myself wrong."[1]

Collier's seer-like prognostication was right on the money, and a lot of it was due to his team's inability to contain Washington.

The Michigan State star was the Vikings' first true gamebreaker at wide receiver, setting the precedent for other great ones to come. While other teams produced great linebackers or offensive linemen, Minnesota would become a club known for its seemingly limitless number of star receivers.

Every standout Viking receiver that followed Washington seemingly drew from his immense talents, drank from the cistern of his bountiful skill set, shared in his glory and esteem.

Through the ensuing decades it was seen. John Gilliam had his speed and grace, Anthony Carter his uncanny balance and jumping ability, Cris Carter his hands, Sammy White his downfield burst, Ahmad Rashad his sturdiness, Moss his explosiveness, Adam Thielen, Stefon Diggs and Jordan Addison his sharp cuts and Justin Jefferson his flair.

"It could be said I was a blend of all of them," said Washington, who went to Michigan State upon the recommendation of his friend, high school rival and later college teammate, the top overall selection in the '67 NFL draft, enormous defensive lineman Bubba Smith. "It's hard to compare because the game is so different.

"When I played, if the ball was in the air, they could do whatever they wanted to keep you from getting downfield. If you were looking the wrong direction, you were in trouble," said Washington on a practice that changed with the implementation of the illegal contact rule for the 1978 regular season.

The 1960s version of Randy Moss harbors no resentment for Vikings fans' amnesia regarding his accomplishments.

"I never looked at it that way, but I've thought about it," said Washington, who went to the Vikings eighth overall in the 1967 draft. "I just recognized we are just here for the moment, so to speak, and time moves on. I was just very glad, and proud of the career I had."

Washington was Joe Kapp's favorite target—a perfect fit for a quarterback who needed a flanker with not only the acumen for catching off-target, wobbly throws, but also one who could aptly track high-trajectory, wafting deep balls, both Kapp staples.

On this frigid, eight-degree day in Bloomington, the Cleveland Browns had no answer for Washington, as each of his three catches resulted in scores in what was the most monumental win in team history.

"I always felt if I had a one-on-one matchup, if the corner wasn't getting help over the top, it would be to my advantage," said Washington. "But even if you have the edge, one thing you always had to worry about when you played at The Met was the footing. It was horrible, particularly in that game."

Each of Washington's three receptions came in the first quarter. And each showcased a certain Washington elite trait.

Trait one: rare body control.

On the Vikings' first offensive series, Washington split left on a first-and-10 play from his own 43-yard line. Lining up against him in a brutal mismatch was Browns rookie cornerback Walt Sumner.

The La Porte, Texas, native started downfield and took a subtle step to the inside, then turned his shoulders and raced past Sumner down the left sideline. Kapp's throw, not purposedly underthrown, forced the thoroughbred Washington to make a sensational back-shoulder catch as he fell out of bounds.

It was a back-shoulder catch before back-shoulder catches became the norm, as Washington's effort was truly ahead of its time.

The lunging, acrobatic reception of 33 yards set up Kapp's seven-yard run for the game's first score.

"I played basketball four years in high school," said Washington, who could easily

3. It's Washington by Air

Minnesota Vikings wide receiver Gene Washington (84) is about to gather in a back-shoulder catch as he falls backward in the first quarter of the NFL championship game on Jan. 4, 1970, at Metropolitan Stadium. Cleveland Browns cornerback Walt Sumner (29) stumbles down, while safety Mike Howell (34) looks on. The play set up the Vikings' first touchdown, a seven-yard run by quarterback Joe Kapp. Washington finished the day with 120 yards receiving and a TD as the Vikings routed the Browns 27–7 to advance to their first Super Bowl.

dunk with two hands off just one step. "Having the ability to adjust, and the fact I was 6–3, helped me make catches like that. I was able to jump over a lot of guys. Very seldom did you have a corner taller than six foot [Sumner was listed at 6–1]."

Trait two: straight-ahead speed.

On the team's next series, facing a third-and-nine from his 25, Kapp sent Washington wide right. This time he lined up against Erich Barnes, a six-time Pro Bowler who played the final seven of his 14 years in the NFL with the Browns, who finished 10–3–1 to place first in the Century Division well ahead of the Giants, his former club.

After the snap, Washington leaned to the outside, then broke inside the hashmarks as Kapp pump-faked off a deep drop from his own 18. The third-year receiver, despite taking a double-forearm smash across the face from Barnes, was able to work his way free.

Barnes slipped on the icy turf at the Browns' 45, allowing Washington to catch the ball all by himself. The trot-in score made it Vikings 14, Browns 0.

Washington nearly had a broken nose, but the rout was on.

"It was a bad field, but they had to play on it, too," said Barnes.[2]

Many of the Browns switched to rubber-soled sneakers early in the second quarter, but the damage had already been done.

"There were some frozen spots, but we were able to work around them," said Kapp. "Our coaches felt we would be able to throw deep on Cleveland. Cleveland uses some double coverage and that results in leaving some people open."[3]

"On the sidelines we said the next time we get the ball we're going to run the 'Banana Go' pattern," said Washington, a graduate of George Washington High School in Baytown, Texas, who was not recruited to play college ball in his home state due to segregation. "Joe called it, we wanted to go at Erich. On the pattern, I would start toward the defender's outside shoulder, then break to the post and Barnes fell down. I always thought Joe could never overthrow me. I loved that deep post pattern, especially when the free safety's off."

A solitary man at the Browns' 40, Washington said his biggest concern was simply gathering the ball in.

"I'm running full speed and the ... hardest thing about that type of play is there is no competition because you know the guy has fallen down," he said. "The field was frozen. All these things are going through my mind. I'm running, it's cold and I'm hoping that my hands are not too frozen. I also didn't want to overrun the ball. I ended up catching the ball over my shoulder."

"He was a hurdler so he had a bigger stride," said backup quarterback and punter Bob Lee. "He wasn't one of these quick-twitch guys. When he got rolling, from like seven or eight yards out, and moving to a point of 40, 50 yards out, that's an awful tough cover for anybody. Plus, he was 6–3. Gene struck fear into a lot of people."

With his footing secure, Washington, who will hold the MSU record for the 120 high hurdles for perpetuity at 13.6 seconds, caught the ball, then calmly strode the rest of the distance into the end zone while holding the ball above his helmet with one massive right hand.

"After I graduated, they changed to meters. Now it's the 110 high hurdles," said Washington, who won the Big Ten hurdles championship three straight years. "That record won't be broken."

Trait three: great hands.

Late in the first, Kapp faced a second-and-10 from the Browns' 30. Washington lined up right and ran a 10-yard turn-in. Kapp, in one of the tightest passes of his Vikings career, stuck the throw. Posting up like a great basketball big man, Washington made a claw-like catch with linebacker Dale Lindsey and Barnes smothering him.

The catch set up a Fred Cox field goal to make it 17–0.

Soon after, it was all over but the shouting as Dave Osborn, getting a great block from pulling guard Milt Sunde, scored on a 20-yard run on the ensuing series to give Minnesota a 24–0 halftime bulge.

All told, Minnesota's unheralded offensive line, a group that included free agent acquisitions Mick Tingelhoff and Jim Vellone, a 20th-round draft pick in Sunde, original Viking Grady Alderman and its only headliner, right tackle Ron Yary, paved the way to 222 yards rushing.

Doing the rest was a defense that held the Browns to 97 yards on the ground and without a touchdown until the fourth quarter. But it was the big-play ability of Washington that was the key.

"We got behind early and we had to play a different game," said Pro Bowl running back Leroy Kelly, who led the Browns with 80 yards rushing. "We couldn't mix it up. It's pretty hard to play catchup against a good team."[4]

The Browns earned the trip to Minnesota by routing the Dallas Cowboys 38–14 the previous Sunday in the Eastern Conference championship game at the Cotton Bowl as Kelly rushed for 66 yards and a TD.

"A good team can play two good games in a row against good opponents," added Kelly. "We aren't that kind of team."⁵

Blessed with huge hands, Washington rarely dropped a ball despite not enjoying the advantages players have today.

"We didn't use gloves. I've been amazed when I go into locker rooms after games today and see these. I say, 'Damn, I would have never missed a ball,'" he laughed. "The guys are still talented, I'm not taking anything away, but the game is so different now."

Injuries shortened Washington's career, leaving one to wonder how great he could have been. He finished his career with the Denver Broncos in 1973 as a third receiver, catching just 10 balls.

Speaking to the man's character, Washington has no ill will toward the Vikings organization for sending him to the Broncos for wide receiver Rod Sherman and a fifth-round pick.

"I had the ankle injury and I eventually had to get it fused," noted Washington. "It was a painful injury. I had fragments of bones causing biting pain. As a wide receiver it was just a difficult injury to deal with. Bud [Grant] was even-keel. The whole Vikings family showed a lot of love to me even after I left. Everyone was treated the same. I was very disappointed I couldn't stay, but this is the place I wanted to raise our family. The players recognize that in the Twin Cities area the fans love the Vikings and that's very important. The whole sports community and the fan base of this community is just excellent, and the Vikings take great leadership in that."

Washington is not bitter concerning his limited usage in his first year with the Vikings. His rookie year he finished with just 13 catches. Ironically, that was the same amount of carries Clinton Jones, his Michigan State teammate, had as a rookie. Jones was drafted second overall in '67, completing a watershed Minnesota draft that also included the selection of Alan Page with the 15th pick overall and nabbing Bob Grim in the second round, Bobby Bryant in the seventh and John Beasley in the eighth.

"The 13 balls were disappointing, for sure," said Washington, "but what was really tough is that we went 3–8–3. You have to remember at Michigan State we didn't lose a game my last two years. We were undefeated and national champions two years in a row. All of a sudden, you're playing on a team that isn't winning and not starting. I knew for a fact I was the fastest player on the team. I felt like I had the ability, but you have to go with the flow of the team."

Washington knew when he went to Minnesota that he wasn't going to an aerial circus like the one Sid Gilliam had in San Diego.

"It was a different era," said Washington. "We had a great defense. We were able to get a lot of turnovers and we got the ball in good shape, close to the end zone. Along with that, we had an outstanding running game, so you could really be more conservative. We didn't have the wide-open offense that you see today. I always figured if I got thrown five or six passes that was a good game. We were not going to fill the air up with footballs."

Even with his rare skills, Washington, who retired from Minnesota-based 3M after working there throughout his playing days, would most likely have never played in the NFL had it not been for Duffy Daugherty.

Knowing as a Black man he would not be offered any football scholarships in his home state of Texas, Washington took his talents to East Lansing, where he was part of one of the premier collegiate football teams of all time—the 1966 Michigan State

Spartans coached by the great Daugherty, a man ahead of his time when it came to integrating his football program.

That '66 team, which was 9–0 heading into a showdown with Page-led Notre Dame in the season finale labeled as the "Game of the Century," also featured stars like Smith, George Webster and Jones. It was not only one of the greatest teams in NCAA history, but also one that hailed in a new era of college football desegregation, one chronicled in Gene's daughter Maya Washington's remarkable and poignant 2014 documentary, *Through the Banks of the Red Cedar.*

The contest with the Irish game ended in a tie as the Spartans would finish the season ranked second in the country.

A two-time All-American under Daugherty's tutelage, Washington, inducted into the College Football Hall of Fame in 2011, was highly sought after entering the 1967 NFL draft.

Thanks to trades that sent Fran Tarkenton to the New York Giants and Tommy Mason to the Rams, the Vikings had three first-round picks in 1967. Vikings general manager Jim Finks used them to nab Jones, Washington and Page.

"What a lot of people don't know is that Bud took some flak for that," said Washington. "Some people would say, 'The Vikings don't do that, select three Black players in one draft.' But Bud didn't care. He just wanted good players."

Washington immediately became an impact player, averaging 29.5 yards a catch as a rookie, then snaring 46 catches for 756 yards in 1968 before his breakthrough season in 1969.

Firmly established as one of the league's premier deep threats, he finished the '69 season with 821 yards and nine touchdowns, earning All-Pro honors. His last standout season was in 1970, when he caught 44 balls for 702 yards and four TDs.

"It was humbling and exciting," said Washington of his career in purple. "I just had excellent teammates. It was a family atmosphere. We enjoyed that at Michigan State, and it carried on to my pro career. I was fortunate to have some outstanding coaches. Bud was just an excellent coach to play for. He showed a lot of love and commitment to the players. It was a wonderful situation. Even when I look back on that first year, I wasn't playing and we weren't winning, but everything worked out pretty well. Bud Grant was the one who provided the leadership."

• • •

The Vikings came into the championship contest brimming with confidence, having already defeated the Browns in an exhibition game at the Akron Rubber Bowl as well as trouncing them 51–3 in week-eight play.

"When we played Cleveland, when I watched the film, I didn't see any way in the world that they would beat us," said middle linebacker Lonnie Warwick, who suffered a sprained ankle during the game. "Our defense was just so good against their offense. I couldn't even see them scoring on us."

"We were worried about the championship game, not nervous, because how do you beat a good team three times?" questioned Lee. "But we thought we would win, but there's that unknown."

Vikings captain Jim Marshall played a key role, rocking Browns quarterback Bill Nelsen with a hit early on that severely limited the veteran quarterback.

"On a pass rush Marshall hit me on the head," Nelsen told the *Minneapolis Star.*

"The nerves in my arm went dead. I could grip the ball but I didn't have a good feel for my throws. Right after that I had Gary Collins wide open but I couldn't get him the ball."[6]

Nelsen had 17 completions on 33 attempts, good for 181 yards and a TD, that coming on a three-yard toss to Collins in the final quarter to close the scoring. The Vikings sacked him only twice, but the sore-kneed Nelsen was often under duress.

"We couldn't really get to him so we had to stop him some other way," said Page. "We pressured him and kept our hands up, so he had to throw over us. I think a key was when I knocked a pass down early. That made him aware."[7]

The NFL championship for the defensive end Marshall made the hard knocks of his first eight years with the Vikings more palatable. It was clear now the team, under his and Grant's unwavering and unquestioned leadership, had cut for itself a clear course, a clear direction.

"We had a job to do each time we went out on the field. Everything was laid out for you," said Marshall. "A winning system was set up. All you had to do was execute and go on to win the game. Before Bud came, we were a team that committed a great deal of penalties. It didn't work out so well. We'd score a touchdown and get called for holding and so on. Bud just knew how to take a player and understand what and where would be his best contribution to the team. He put you on that train to where that's what you were working for every day you came to practice, every time you played a game. He had the skill to see these things."

"Bud came in and he was a totally different person as far as his approach to penalties goes," said backup quarterback Gary Cuozzo. "Norm Van Brocklin gave out a 'Golden Jock' award for the hardest hit, whether it was in bounds or not. I was there for Bud's second year and he told the refs ahead of time that we were going to try to cut back on penalties. We went from being the highest-penalized team to one of the lowest. Bud was a highly disciplined coach. I'm not sure how much he knew about offense and defense but he always delegated to smart coaches. He spent most of his time with special teams. He was a tremendous leader and caller of situational plays, but he never really got involved in X's and O's."

Grant coaching Minnesota was seemingly ordained before the franchise even debuted. He attended Superior Central High School, where the football team was called the Vikings and wore purple and white.

There's growing belief, said Paul Lukas of ESPN.com, the team received its colors—and perhaps its name—from Grant's fellow Superior Central High School graduate Ole Haugsrud, a colorful character from the NFL's early days.

Haugsrud originally owned the Duluth Eskimos and later became one of the Vikings' founding owners, holding a 10 percent stake in the team. Haugsrud, as the story went, made sure his alma mater's colors and name were used for his new NFL team.

"Ole was only a 10 percent owner, and he was really a silent owner," Stephen Rose, son of original Vikings GM Bert Rose, told Lukas. "Choosing the colors and the name and all that, that was part of my father's job description. I'm sure Ole agreed to it, but did Ole generate the idea? No."[8]

Haugsrud died in 1976. Superior Central High School no longer exists. But Lukas said Ray Kosey, activities director for the town's current high school, confirmed that Haugsrud had attended the old high school and that the football team's colors had been purple and white. But did that provide a chromatic connection to the Vikings?

"That's always been the story around here," Ken Olson, sports editor of the *Superior Telegram*, told Lukas. "You know, Packers fans up here like to say that the Vikings got their colors from Wisconsin. But I don't know if it's actually true."[9]

"Haugsrud reportedly insisted that the team adopt the colors purple and white, which were, ironically, the same colors of his native Superior Central High School football team," said Ross Bernstein, author of *Pigskin Pride: Celebrating a Century of Minnesota Football*. "I've heard it from many people, and especially from Bud Grant. He told me that many times."[10]

Chuck Frederick, editorial page editor of the *Duluth News Tribune* and author of the book *Leatherheads of the North: The True Story of Ernie Nevers and the Duluth Eskimos*, agreed: "It was something Ole himself said several times. As far as documentation, I don't know how you'd prove that sort of thing. I once asked Bud Grant about it, and he said that's how he had always heard it."

By 1969, everyone knew Grant was the perfect coach at the perfect time for the Minnesota Vikings. Having won four Grey Cups as a coach (1958, '59, '61 and '62), Grant knew how to win, and so did Marshall, having led Ohio State to a national championship in 1957 and a rousing win over Oregon in the Rose Bowl.

Marshall also knew what it meant and what it took to be great as a player, having rubbed shoulders as a youth with fellow Columbus East High School grad Bill Willis, a cat-quick, all-time Cleveland Browns great who showed that one can excel on an NFL defensive line despite his relatively smallish 6–2, 210-pound frame.

"I lived right around the corner from his house. It was a thrill for me as a kid to have this real famous person be right near us," said Marshall, a running back in high school. "I didn't get to see him play on TV, you didn't have the video productions you have today, but I knew the kind of player he was. He would come by when the kids were playing outside and always talk to us about keeping out of trouble. Just the closeness of someone with his greatness gave us hope that we could somehow duplicate the feats he had."

Marshall earned All-American honors in '58 under Woody Hayes's tutelage but opted the next year to play ball in Canada for Saskatchewan, where his one-year stint there overlapped with Grant's coaching career with Winnipeg.

Chosen by the Browns in the fourth round of the 1960 draft, he departed Canada for the opportunity to play for his hometown team, where he played right end for a year opposite Paul Wiggin, who would later become a successful defensive line coach for the Vikings, overseeing such players as Henry Thomas and Hall of Famer Chris Doleman before becoming a fixture in the front office.

Marshall, despite wearing No. 76 with the Buckeyes and No. 80 for the Browns, interestingly asked for No. 70 when he arrived for his first Vikings training camp in Bemidji, Minnesota, after being unceremoniously traded from Cleveland.

"I always liked the number 7," said Marshall of, fittingly, the number for perfection. "And 70 is a number defensive linemen could wear."

Upon Grant taking over the helm, he immediately installed Marshall as defensive captain, and Marshall held that role until his retirement in 1979.

"If you put a face on the Vikings, it would be Jim Marshall," said Grant without hesitation. "He's the best player, the best representative, the Vikings have ever had."[11]

"Everything was clear and clean with him, and you knew what the purpose of your job was, no matter the position you played," Marshall said of Grant, who once said there would be no Minnesota Vikings if it weren't for Jim Marshall. "He talked realistically about techniques that we could perfect to make us successful.

"He and Van Brocklin each were coaches that wanted to win and had been with winners," added Marshall. "Norm's system was a system of passing, that's what he knew. Bud was able to take us to the next level. The foundation we had was to win every game we played and that would lead to championships. We got laughed at a lot in the early stages because we were a ragtag group. The thing that we looked for was the absolute truth that we were no longer losers and that every time we went on the field, we were a potential winner."

• • •

The fluid Washington's capable sidekick at wide receiver, nearly his mirror image, was No. 80 out of the University of Michigan, 6–3, 195-pound John Henderson.

In today's new era, the likes of Jefferson and Jordan Addison roam the outer ranges for the Minnesota Vikings, but years gone by, when Vikings games were played in the vulnerable outside, in the snow, wind and rain, and on the dirt, it was the classy, fluid duo of Washington and Henderson who ushered in the heroics of youth.

Henderson caught two passes for 17 yards in the win over the Browns and had a key block on strong safety Ernie Kellerman on Osborn's game-clinching TD scamper.

"I got a great block from John Henderson on the Cleveland cornerman," said Osborn. "That gave me the opportunity to make a good move and break into the open."[12]

It was in the 23–7 Super Bowl loss to the Chiefs where Henderson really shined, as he snared seven catches for 111 yards.

"It was good, but it would have been better had we won. They were double-teaming Gene so I was open," said the self-effacing Henderson of the loss to Kansas City. "If you look at our game footage from any ball game, I was often open. A lot of guys would complain about not getting the ball, but that wasn't my way.

"We were fairly similar," added Henderson on his running mate. "Gene and I competed against each other [in college] in track in the high hurdles. He had good hands, great speed and a good work ethic, a really good guy. Our skills were comparable. Teams sometimes got us confused because we were about the same size and had the same gait. Gene was faster than I was, but in my opinion, I was quicker."

Henderson arrived in Minnesota from Detroit in 1968 by way of a trade. Coming over the same year was his Lions teammate Wally Hilgenberg, who played college ball at Iowa. After starting just 10 games in three seasons in Detroit, Hilgenberg became a fixture at linebacker along with Roy "Moonie" Winston and Lonnie Warwick.

"We were so close it was unreal," said Warwick of the vaunted linebacking crew, which from left to right wore Nos. 60, 59 and 58. "Everywhere we went we'd line up that way. It was the way we sat, whether we ate or were sitting in the car, anything. We did everything together. We ate together, we hunted and fished together. We did everything together."

The final piece was Hilgenberg, who had a pick versus Cleveland.

"Wally was so talented," said Warwick. "He didn't know the game at first as well as me and Roy did, but once he learned our defense, it clicked. He was the final cog to our linebacking corps. He could run, cover, what have you. He could run well. Wally sometimes would forget the coverage but boy, he was a good player."

Warwick said few knew the true value of the 5–11, 225-pound Winston, a fourth-round draft pick out of LSU in 1962.

"The No. 1 thing that made Roy so good was that he knew the game," said Warwick. "As soon as he'd see them line up, he knew what they were going to run. He was just a master of the defense. He'd see a formation and he knew what to do. He was so smart it was unreal. All the years I played with Roy Winston, he never made any mistakes and he did his job. We had a grading system and Roy Winston was always the highest-graded defensive player."

With the additions of Hilgenberg and Henderson, the Vikings were ready to make a move in '68.

"That's when Minnesota started winning, and we took credit for that," joked Henderson, a product of Roosevelt High School in Dayton, Ohio, who learned of the trade in late August.

"I remember coach [Joe] Schmidt walking over to me during training camp and saying, 'John, John. We just made a deal to send you to Minnesota.' That was a surprise to me. I thought I was good there in Detroit. But it's a business."

Henderson started six games for Detroit in '67, snaring 13 passes for 144 yards. The Lions went 5-7-2 and didn't exactly light it up on offense with Karl Sweetan and Milt Plum at quarterback.

No doubt football meant a lot to Henderson, but it wasn't his life, making news like that delivered by Schmidt easier to consume.

"I was better in football than I was enthusiastic about it," said Henderson, MVP of the prestigious Ohio North-South All-Star Game in 1961. "After hearing of the trade, I had several options to consider. I was possibly going to go into my family business in printing. Or I could go to the military. I didn't want that as a career, but I knew that was a possibility because there was a war.

"I didn't even go to Minnesota for at least 10 days. They were calling me trying to find out where I was. Going to Minnesota wouldn't have been my first choice. I went to Minnesota during college as a player for Michigan. I saw all the grain silos and we stayed in the Curtis Hotel and there was nothing around for miles. That's why I thought about my other options."

Michigan connections on the Vikings coaching staff played a key role in the team's willingness to wait patiently for Henderson.

"They had Jocko Nelson [ends coach at Michigan] as a defensive assistant, and also Bob Hollway, who was defensive coordinator at Michigan [same role with Vikings]. There were two former coaches of mine that apparently had a lot of say in the Vikings remaining patient while I weighed my options," he recalled. "At receiver they had Art Powell, who Bud brought down from Canada, Paul Flatley [who was eventually traded to Atlanta] and Gene Washington, who I knew of from his days at Michigan State."

Henderson wasn't sure what to expect with the Vikings.

"I didn't know much about them. I didn't study their roster. But I know once I got there, they had a much healthier climate than Detroit," he noted. "I tell people Bud Grant treated us all the same, like dogs. [Packers star tackle Henry Jordan used the same line in regard to Vince Lombardi.] He was also a guy you could talk to. You wouldn't think you could, but you'd go in private and have a discussion and he'd be pretty straight with you, and I liked that. There were a bunch of cliques in Detroit and that wasn't healthy."

"Everybody got along with Grant," said Yary. "Fran Tarkenton said this once, that if you couldn't play football for Bud Grant you couldn't play for anyone."

Once Henderson got to Minnesota, offensive coach Jerry Burns quickly realized he had a nice complement to Washington. Blessed with blazing speed, Washington specialized on the deep posts and the go routes, while Henderson mastered intermediate patterns.

"My coaches always celebrated my ability to run the 'Z Out' [pattern]," Henderson said. "You make a hard move to give the appearance that your final move was to go to the inside on a post pattern. They would bite on that, and I would cut it off and do the Z Out. That was very effective, and they had to play me honest."

Henderson was drafted 63rd overall in 1965 by the Philadelphia Eagles but could not work out a contract in negotiations with head coach Joe Kuharich. Consequently, he was traded to Detroit, which was coming off a 7–5–2 campaign under coach George Wilson.

Henderson played not only with Hilgenberg at Detroit but also with former University of Michigan stars Terry Barr and Ron Kramer, the multitalented ex–Packer who had a huge game to help Vince Lombardi to his first NFL championship, snagging four catches for 80 yards and a pair of scores in the team's 37–0 rout of the New York Giants on New Year's Day 1961.

Due to his late arrival to Minnesota, Henderson didn't have much of an impact in his first year, but he burst out in 1969, posting career bests in receptions (34), yardage (553) and TDs (five). He played well in the 23–20 playoff win over the Los Angeles Rams, snaring four balls for 68 yards in a game the Vikings trailed 17–7 at the half.

"Carl Eller gave a very animated halftime talk. I remember that vividly. He was fired up and he spoke up," said Henderson. "We were cold. We didn't take advantage of the weather in the first half. But in the second half, we used the weather to our advantage. Those guys were ready to go home. They wanted out of the cold."

The Vikings quickly took control in the second half, as a big Washington catch from Kapp and a spearing penalty on Jack Pardee set up Osborn's one-yard scoring plunge to make it 17–14. After a Bruce Gossett field goal made it 20–14, Kapp walked into the end zone untouched on a rollout left to give the Vikings their first-ever playoff lead, one they would not relinquish.

Henderson played with an assorted group of quarterbacks with the Vikings after Kapp's departure to Boston, including Cuozzo, Lee, Norm Snead and Fran Tarkenton. And while Kapp didn't throw a great ball, his leadership skills weren't lost on the rangy receiver.

"It was a challenge," he said of hauling in Kapp's non-spirals. "But he was a leader. You would see him come to the huddle, all scarred and broken up. He would have just tried to run the ball and gotten clobbered. But he would pull himself up, barely able to walk. But then he would look you in the eye and say, 'I'm coming to you on this play.' You didn't want to let him down. Those were the characteristics that he brought to the team. If you wanted a guy to drop in the foxhole with you, he'd be the No. 1 person."

Henderson has fond memories of Grant.

"He told me years later that I was one of his favorites," beamed Henderson. "That meant a lot. I'm not sure how many people he said the same thing to, but it surely meant a lot to me."

Some players, though, could not fit into a new Minnesota way that was ushered in by the stickler Grant upon his arrival.

"It didn't take long for him to earn my respect," said Warwick. "Once we came in late for a meeting after me, Roy and Wally went hunting. He said, 'Let me tell you,

Lonnie, if you ever do that again, you better be finding yourself another team.' Normally they would let us come in a little late on Mondays, but not with Bud. We knew it was just a matter of time before we started winning. He didn't take crap. He was just instilling discipline. We could see it working."

With injuries to both Washington and Henderson in 1971, the Vikings brought in rangy Al Denson, a two-time Pro Bowler out of Florida A&M with the Denver Broncos. The 6–2 Denson had 11 touchdown receptions in 1967 and 10 in '69 for head coach Lou Saban, but he was never comfortable with the Vikings.

"I think by then he had some knee problems," Henderson said of Denson, who had 32 TD catches with the Broncos and made two Pro Bowls. "But I don't think he felt comfortable there. I had a locker next to him. Some guys keep quiet about things but he kind of let people know he wasn't happy. It was unfortunate but it just didn't work out as the Vikings released him."

Denson played only seven games in Minnesota with no TD catches. The fit just wasn't right, and he quickly found out.

With the arrival of John Gilliam and with injuries catching up, Henderson retired after the 1972 season.

"I went out on my own terms, and that was important," said Henderson. "I played eight years, and it was time to go. I played football, but that was not who I am."

Going out on their own terms was surprisingly rare for a Vikings player under Grant. Washington finished in Denver, Jones in San Diego, Eller in Seattle, Page in Chicago, Osborn in Green Bay, Kapp in Boston, Chuck Foreman in New England and so on.

"I believe that was due to Bud not wanting his veterans to get comfortable," said the astute Henderson. "It was different with Jim Marshall [who after being traded from the Browns played his final 19 years with Minnesota]. He was Bud's bell cow. Jim earned that because he was a real leader. He was clearly, clearly a leader on the team. Bud relied on Jim to lead the team."

"Jim Marshall was so precious it was unreal," added Warwick, who has two children, one a son who played football at Tennessee Tech. "Jim Marshall was our captain. He could settle anybody down. He settled me down many a times. I can still hear him say, 'Come on, Lonnie, call the play! Lonnie, call the play!' Of all the people I met while I was in football, Jim Marshall was the No. 1 man on my list. There is no one else that could compare to him."

Yary felt the same way about Marshall.

"He was a leader by both performance and personality on the team. He made everybody feel good about themselves," said Yary. "He was a very demonstrative, happy team leader. He never had a bad thing to say about anybody or any situation. Jim was just a guy you didn't want to let down because he was such a strong personality. I didn't want to let Jim down, I didn't want to let Carl [Eller] down, I didn't want to let the defense down. That was my motivation. You liked those guys so much, they were such great guys, I just never wanted to let them down. All great teams had that quality where they played for each other because they had such respect for one another."

Page didn't get the same treatment as Marshall at the end of his Vikings career due to a dispute with Grant over his weight.

"Alan had lost a certain amount of weight and Bud thought he was too small to play that [tackle] position. His stats maybe indicated that," said Henderson. "Alan was a tremendous individual, a strong-willed individual, and he became a good football player because of his will to succeed. His wife was a marathon runner, and he would spend time running with her and his weight was down. He eventually went to Chicago and performed very well at that weight [40 sacks in 58 games with the Bears]. Alan didn't believe his weight would be a detriment to the team. He was a classy guy and he went on to be a great Minnesota Supreme Court justice."

Henderson, who worked for 27 years with Honeywell prior to retiring in the '90s, said he never regretted leaving football despite the fact Minnesota advanced to the Super Bowl the next two seasons.

"We had a house in Michigan, but we ended up moving to Minnesota," he added. "I told my wife it was a great place to raise a family. Every offseason I had a job. I needed to because we didn't make much money then. I called Bud and told him I was going to retire [after the '72 season]. That was it. The big concern that I had was would I regret it. I didn't want to leave just due to emotions. It never happened though. I was at peace.

"Looking back, we had a lot of local pride surrounding our team. We were a team to be reckoned with. The team got on the map in 1968 and that was my first year. It was an honor to be a part of it."

"It was exhilarating," Yary added. "You knew you were always going to be in a game we could win. We were never really outgunned; we believed if we played our best, we could win. The fans were the best in America. It was one of the best cities to live in—a great place to raise your family. It was a happy and clean city. Not a lot of social issues. I couldn't have found a better place to have a football career than Minneapolis-St. Paul. I don't think I could have been in a better place. The fans, the culture, the people were civil. They called it 'Minnesota nice.' It was probably the most serene time of my life."

For the Vikings, their serenity would soon dissipate as the team would go on to lose Super Bowl IV to Kansas City, then commence a three-year stretch that would see them lose an unfathomable two straight home playoff games and fail to make the postseason the third year despite reacquiring Francis Tarkenton.

4

The Lost Years

When one begins to fully understand the magnitude of time squandered, the 1970 and 1971 seasons for the Minnesota Vikings, not to mention the '72 campaign that saw the team fail to even make the playoffs, could be truly remembered as the organization's lost years.

Minnesota fielded historically amazing defenses the first two years of that stretch, leading the NFL in touchdowns allowed both in '70 and '71 with a meager 12 each season.

The Purple People Eaters were also tops in the NFL in points allowed both seasons with 133 and 139 in '70 and '71, respectively. Both of these seasons saw the Vikings capture the Central Division, with the most wins in football both years at 12–2 and 11–3 (tied with Dallas) in 1970 and '71, respectively.

Guided by defensive coordinators Bud Hollway and Neil Armstrong, who took over when Hollway left to become the head coach of the St. Louis Cardinals in 1971, the Vikings allowed under 3.5 yards a play in 1970. That's still the best in the NFL during the Super Bowl era. In addition, the Vikings didn't allow a team to score more than 20 points against them the entire 1970 season. That is also the best in the Super Bowl era.

In '70, the Vikings also led the NFL in yards allowed (2,720) and first downs allowed (158). In '71, they were second in the NFL (to the Baltimore Colts) and first in the NFC defensively in yards allowed (3,406), yards per play (3.9) and first downs (194).

The defense was so dominating that a 30–12 road loss to the San Diego Chargers on December 5, 1971, broke a string of 42 straight games—stretching all the way back to the second week of the 1969 season—where Minnesota held a team to fewer than three TDs. The next best in the Super Bowl era? *Seventeen* games.

What was the missing link? Most would say quarterbacking. Or at minimum, the organization's slipshod handling of the key position.

Without either Joe Kapp or Fran Tarkenton at the quarterback position, the Vikings, following their 23–7 Super Bowl IV loss to Kansas City, lost two straight postseason games at home, contests that saw them notch utterly abysmal play on offense.

Norm Van Brocklin's toxic relationship with Francis Asbury Tarkenton led to the unconventional March 7, 1967, trade that sent the quarterback to the New York Giants. An original Viking, Tarkenton had been with the team for six seasons. He was just 26.

The NFL, as part of the merger agreement with the AFL and with Joe Namath stealing the hearts of football fans in Gotham City after leading the Jets to a 16–7 upset win over the Colts in Super Bowl III, had given the Giants two options in the 1967 draft. They could have the first overall pick in either the 1967 or 1968 draft for the purpose of drafting a quarterback, or the right to trade that selection for a quarterback. The two signal callers expected to go first in '67 were Florida's Steve Spurrier and Purdue's Bob Griese.

A stalwart on the team's prolific defense, Minnesota Vikings defensive end Carl Eller (81) pressures San Francisco 49ers quarterback John Brodie (12) during the 1970 NFC divisional round playoff game on Dec. 27, 1970, in Bloomington. Led by Brodie, the 49ers defeated the Vikings 17–14, handing Minnesota its first-ever home playoff loss. The loss would start a string of three straight seasons in which the Vikings would not win a postseason game.

Coming off a dismal 1966 season that saw it go 1–12–1 under Allie Sherman, New York, with Earl Morrall (recovering from a broken right wrist), Tom Kennedy and Bob Post as its only options at QB, chose the second option—to make a trade. The Giants' previous starter, Gary Wood, was taken by the New Orleans franchise in the expansion draft.

The Giants apparently decided they didn't have time to wait on the development of either Spurrier or Griese. Before he went on to a fabled career as football coach at the University of Florida, Spurrier had a decent career with the San Francisco 49ers but was known more as a punter, while Griese would go on to lead the Dolphins to a pair of Super Bowl championships.

In trading Tarkenton, Minnesota had two options to choose from as a return. As one option, the Vikings could have the first overall pick in the '67 draft, the Giants' second-rounder that year and their first-round pick in '68. The Vikings chose the second option, which was New York's first- and second-round picks in '67, the first overall choice in the 1968 draft (used to select massive USC tackle Ron Yary) and a second-round pick in '69.

In Tarkenton's absence, the indomitable Kapp led the Vikings to the playoffs in '68 and an NFL championship in '69, leaving one to wonder how far the Vikings would have gone in '70 and '71 had Kapp or Tarkenton been at the helm instead of the ill-fated rotation of Gary Cuozzo, Bob Lee and Norm Snead.

It's easily conceivable, given the team's historically stout defense, that the Vikings would have won a Super Bowl one of those seasons. Baltimore was an aging team in '70 and the Dolphins were not quite ready in '71. More than likely, the Vikings would've gotten past either San Francisco or Dallas in the playoffs to advance to the Super Bowl and subsequently may have won at least one.

The picks received from the Tarkenton trade established the right side of the offensive line for the next decade, as they tabbed Yary and Ed White (second-round selection in '69). Top-end speed was added with the first- and second-rounders gained in the '67 draft in running back Clinton Jones and wide receiver Bob Grim.

The Vikings' astute general manager of 10 years, Jim Finks, a former star quarterback with the Pittsburgh Steelers in the 1950s before leaving to play in Canada, was brilliant in so many ways but he didn't believe in constructing a team around a quarterback.

"Our success has never been built around Joe Kapp," Finks told the *Chicago Tribune* on August 9, 1970.

That statement made sense in an era where NFL teams largely centered their offenses on the running game. That's why the Vikings over the years stockpiled a gaggle of talented running backs, such as Hugh McElhenny, Tommy Mason, Bill Brown, Dave Osborn, Oscar Reed, Jones, Jim Lindsey, Robert Miller, Ed Marinaro, Brent McClanahan and, finally, Chuck Foreman.

But these standout running backs could not overcome the lack of a quarterback who could stick a throw when you had to have a completion.

"We missed our leader," said Gene Washington, drafted eighth overall in '67 out of Michigan State. "For everything people say about Joe Kapp, he could throw the football and he was our leader."

"He wanted too much money," said longtime scout and player personnel director Jerry Reichow. "Finks was not interested in that. I don't think it was a mistake. He wanted $100,000. We couldn't do that. He was tough leader guy but he wasn't a great quarterback.

"We were looking for quarterbacks," Reichow added. "Kapp was a linebacker playing quarterback. He was a tough son of a bitch and a great leader. [Linebacker] Lonnie Warwick and he would go at each every day. They would get in a fight about every day and it helped our team. We had good group of tough players then."

Not known for tight spirals, Kapp had not only the intangibles of a hard-tack winner but also what Vikings offensive coordinator Jerry Burns described as "the ability to throw the best deep ball I've seen."

"Am I a classic quarterback? Classics are for the Greeks," Kapp told the *Minneapolis Tribune* following the Vikings' 27–7 NFL championship game win over the Cleveland Browns. "I think I can pass the ball when necessary, and I can probably do a little more."[1]

George Halas, Jr., president of the Chicago Bears, was in Minnesota when the Vikings played the Browns for the NFL title. That afternoon, he made what would prove to be a haunting statement to *Minneapolis Tribune* columnist Sid Hartman.

"They're going to be a power for a long time," said Halas, Jr. "Kapp is a real winner."[2]

Unable to come to an accord on a contract, Kapp was free to move on to the New England Patriots after the '69 campaign. Due to the Rozelle Rule, the Vikings received in compensation a first-round draft pick used to select Jeff Siemon. The middle linebacker out of Stanford made four Pro Bowls, but Kapp's absence was felt.

There was one school of thought after Kapp left that the Vikings may very well have had the quarterback they desired in their very midst. A player who was by no means a superstar, but one who proved solid and effective when given the opportunity to start more than a few games in a row.

When given a chance to play unfettered for a full season, Robert Melville Lee, i.e., "The General," displayed rare arm strength, in-game leadership and the ability to lead his troops, as he so admirably did when he started in place of an injured Tarkenton to lead the Vikings to a 14–7 win in the fabled Mud Bowl game against the Rams in Los Angeles in '77.

A 17th-round pick in '68 out of the University of Pacific, Lee once launched a ball 76 yards in the air and first attracted the Vikings' attention when Reichow saw him throw on the sidelines during the East-West Shrine Game. Lee was there as a punter.

"We didn't know who he was," said Reichow. "We get out there and I'm walking around and I say, 'Who the hell is that guy?' He was a really good punter. But watching him throw the ball, I go, 'Damn, he's also got a good arm.' We did some work on him and drafted him. A smart guy and good player. It wasn't a risk since we took him so late and he was just such a good punter. He worked hard and took advantage of his opportunities."

Traded along with linebacker Lonnie Warwick in '73 to Atlanta for Bob Berry and a first-round pick in '74 that the Vikings used to select UCLA linebacker Fred McNeill, Lee started 10 games for Van Brocklin's Falcons and won eight as the team went 9–5, the best record in franchise history to that point.

"I don't know why the Vikings didn't have more confidence in Lee," said Warwick. "He was a winner. He made mistakes with the Vikings because he was young. Eventually he would come back and make a play. We almost came out on top [in the West Division] in Atlanta because of him. Cuozzo couldn't take a punch. Once he got hit it was over. He was fragile. Lee could play."

One of Atlanta's nine victories in '73 was a famous 20–14 triumph on *Monday Night Football* over the Vikings, who entered the contest 9–0. Lee was 11 of 23 for 171 yards and a pair of TDs. One of them went down as one of the craziest scoring plays in prime-time history, as Lee, fantastically avoiding both Jim Marshall and Carl Eller, lit out on a wild and wooly scramble toward a bonkers Minnesota bench before gathering himself and flinging a deep toss down the right sideline to unsuspecting Falcons running back Eddie Ray, who scored to send the Atlanta-Fulton County Stadium crowd into a frenzy.

In the middle of Minnesota's quarterback quandary for four years was Cuozzo, who had one of the most bizarre careers in NFL history.

He signed with the Colts in '63 as an undrafted free agent out of the University Virginia upon the recommendation of Don Shula, who coached the Cavalier defensive backs in 1958 before leaving for Kentucky to become an assistant under Blanton Collier. Shula became the Colts' head coach in '63 after the team fired Weeb Ewbank, whom he played for both in Cleveland and Baltimore.

Cuozzo was a solid backup to Johnny Unitas for four years, with his claim to fame being his five-touchdown, zero-interception game in a 41–21 win at Minnesota on November 14, 1965.

Cuozzo, poised and smooth in clean pockets all day long, was at his best that day, completing a steady 16 of 26 passes for 208 yards. His first scoring pass didn't come until under a minute left in the first half when, with Baltimore down 7–3 at the Vikings' 43, he uncorked a deep throw along the right sideline to the wily Jimmy Orr, who turned around rookie Earsell Mackbee on a stop-and-go.

Letting a receiver get behind him with seconds left in the half was the start of a brutal day for Mackbee, who was again victimized for a TD by Orr in the third quarter, this time on a 22-yard post pattern.

Cuozzo next picked on Warwick, starting at Sam linebacker, whom running back Lenny Moore easily beat on a circle route out of the backfield, steaming down the right sideline past a player better accustomed to playing inside to set Baltimore on its way to a blowout win.

Cuozzo's fourth TD, making a total of three for the third quarter, came on a sneaky rollout left and six-yard pass to the great Raymond Berry. Cuozzo's final paydirt effort—one where he displayed nice bounce in the pocket—came on a strong-armed slant pass to Willie Richardson, who beat the beleaguered Mackbee inside from 14 yards.

The record-setting effort, one where he displayed a strong arm, good decision-making and the ability to get the ball out quickly, helped advance Cuozzo in the minds of NFL general managers to the point that in three separate transactions over the next seven years he would be traded for no less than a No. 1 overall pick, two first-round selections, a Pro Bowl receiver and a second-rounder.

That first overall pick came from the expansion New Orleans Saints in 1967, who thought enough of Cuozzo to forfeit a pick used by the Colts to select the mammoth Spartans great Bubba Smith.

"I think it had a lot to do with it," said the New Jersey native on his rise in status following the game in '65 in Bloomington. "That was when Norm Van Brocklin was the coach. He actually quit [only to later change his mind and come back] the next day."

It was a struggle for Cuozzo with the first-year Saints, who went 3–7 with him under center. He accounted for a then-solid 51 percent completion rate but also tossed just seven touchdown passes and threw for 12 interceptions. With no offensive line to speak of, he was sacked 33 times and dreadfully pressured better than 11 percent of his drop-backs, by far the worst in the NFL.

"I had some good sub games with the Colts and played well in exhibition games," recalled Cuozzo, who now resides in Florida. "I asked Don Shula to trade me after my fourth year with them, but I didn't know they'd trade me to an expansion team.

"I didn't really fit in New Orleans with the line we had. I wasn't a running type of guy," added Cuozzo. "When Archie [Manning] went down there, it was a better fit because he was such a great runner and thrower. We had a decent year for an expansion team but I wasn't an Archie Manning, so it was better for me to get out of there."

Cuozzo is the poster child for a quarterback who understands the value of a quarterback landing with the right organization.

"It has to be a good match," he said. "If you get a guy in the right situation at the right time, he'll most likely do well. Like Bart [Starr] in Green Bay. He had Boyd Dowler, Carroll [Dale], [Ron] Kramer and [Paul] Hornung and [Jim] Taylor. And it was a simple offense suited for him. In Baltimore, Johnny had receivers like Ray Berry, Jimmy Orr, Lenny Moore and John Mackey. When you have those type of players it really helps. I had those guys in that game I subbed for John in Minnesota."

Over in Minnesota, the Vikings' passing attack struggled mightily in Grant's first season, as it was second worst in TDs (11) and third worst in yards. Kapp and backups Ron Vander Kelen and Berry threw for fewer than 2,000 yards and a dismal 44.6 passer rating.

Those bleak numbers prompted Finks to acquire Cuozzo in '68. He gave up a king's ransom, sending New Orleans a pair of first-round picks in '68 and '69.

"Cuozzo was a very smart kid," Reichow said. "Probably not a starter type guy, but he played well when he was in there. He wasn't going to last long; he wasn't a big strong guy. He was a smart football player, which I liked as much as anything. There may have been better guys, but we liked his smarts. Did we give up too much for him? Probably, but you didn't know at the time. There was a lot of guesswork. We had one scout and that was me. It wasn't until seven years later we added another guy and that was Frank Gilliam."

There was one caveat to the trade.

"[Saints head coach] Tom Fears told me they'd try to get me back in a couple of years if the Vikings wanted to send me back because we'd probably have a better offensive line by then," said Cuozzo, referring to a rare agreement woven into the trade.

The Vikings essentially made a rental agreement with the Saints that said if things didn't work out over the next two seasons, Cuozzo could be sent back to New Orleans for its *first pick* in the '70 draft.

"I had heard it was between Bill Munson of the Rams and myself in regard to who the Vikings considered trading for. Jim Finks called me when I was down in Memphis at dental school and he said they planned on keeping me," said Cuozzo.

Cuozzo had no idea what the Vikings had planned for him when he sat down in a quarterback room that already included the uber-competitive Kapp and taxi squad rookie Lee.

"They didn't tell me anything. I saw Bud at an offseason event and he didn't even talk to me, I don't remember having a conversation," said Cuozzo. "He was a very different kind of guy. I heard a story about Bud going to the bank when he first got the job. The guy at the bank was all excited about the team and getting Bud and the players and this and that, and he had a lot of questions. The next week Bud goes back to the bank and the guy starts in again, and Bud says, 'Are we going to do this every time I come in?'"

After seeing action in just four games in '68, Cuozzo had consecutive stellar outings relieving Kapp the following season. In a 9–7 win over the Packers November 16, he went 11 of 16 passing for 105 yards and a score, then in a 52–14 victory against Pittsburgh the next week, he was 12 for 19 for 142 yards and two TDs.

"I finished consecutive games and Finks told me if I had stepped under center [during practice] I would have been the starter the next week but that just wasn't my personality," he said. "I was the kind of guy who was waiting for the coach to tell me I was going to start that week. Joe came back and we went on a roll and that was it."

Despite both limited opportunities and success, the Vikings passed on sending Cuozzo back to the Saints for their first pick in '70. That decision initially looked to be an extremely difficult one for Finks and Co. as the Saints started 0–6 in '69 and appeared a sure bet to land the consensus No. 1 prospect in Terry Bradshaw. However, New Orleans rebounded to win five of its last eight and ended up with the 10th pick, which it used to draft receiver Ken Burrough.

That left Minnesota with just its own first-rounder in '70, which it used to draft lineman John Ward out of Oklahoma State. He started in 14 games in five years as a defensive tackle and guard.

With Kapp's departure, Cuozzo was the Vikings' primary starter in 1970, the long-armed Lee's third year in the league. The offseason dentist would get the nod for most of the next two seasons.

"I don't know what all went into the front office not bringing Kapp back," said Lee. "That was above my pay grade. But they did have a lot invested in Cuozzo, so he was going to start."

Lee spent his rookie season in anonymity on the Vikings' taxi squad, charting plays on the sideline as the emergency quarterback. He then punted admirably for the '69 team, which won the NFL championship, including averaging 47 yards on six punts in a November 16 win over the Green Bay Packers.

Lee got some opportunities in 1970. He started two late-season games due to Cuozzo spraining his ankle against the Jets, the most intriguing of which was a December 13 start against Kapp and the Patriots at antiquated Harvard Stadium, a rickety, tiny venue that seated under 30,000. All he did in the snow and ice that day was throw for 268 yards and a pair of scores on 18 of 25 passing in a 35–14 win.

"It was a memorable game for a lot of reasons," said Lee. "It was going to be the last game played at old Harvard Stadium. [Former Golden Gophers and Patriots great] Gino Cappelletti had a hotel where the team stayed and we had a nice breakfast there. We got to the stadium for a walkthrough the day before the game and they're expecting a snowstorm. Before we go out the next day for the game, we're dressing in a crappy locker room, the kind that has like the PE classrooms right next to it. We're about 100 yards to where we go into the stadium, so Bud says, 'Don't put on our cleats yet, just bring them with you. Put your artificial turf shoes on.'

"We come out," continued Lee, "the fans are getting all over us because they were so close to everything, we look like a high school team coming out with our shoes thrown over our shoulders and the field is an utter mess, turf torn up, ice all over the field. Bud had with him two pairs of broomball shoes from Canada. I don't know anything about broomball but these shoes are good on ice. Bud wanted Gene [Washington] and John [Henderson] to have a pair and [Paul] Krause wanted them, too. It all worked out, we win the game, both Gene and John caught TD passes and it was just another example of Bud thinking ahead. After the game they were burning up the bleachers."

Battered all day long, Kapp didn't fare as well as Lee, throwing three interceptions in 29 attempts and getting sacked twice. He would play in one more league game, throwing two picks in a 45–7 loss to the Cincinnati Bengals in the season's final week.

4. The Lost Years

Warwick remembers well facing his tempestuous former quarterback, whom he once got into a fistfight with over which unit, the offense or the defense, was more to blame for a Vikings loss.

"I lined up for our first defensive series and the first words that came out of Kapp's mouth were: 'Yellow, 59! Yellow, 59!' They ran the play and I just stood there," laughed Warwick [who wore jersey No. 59] on Kapp joking about his intestinal fortitude when giving the pre-snap cadence. "I came off the field and my coach said, 'Lonnie, what are you doing just standing there?' I'll never forget that.

"We hated it when he left. If we would have had Joe Kapp, we could have won a Super Bowl with him," added Warwick, who enjoyed his retirement years in his native West Virginia. "He wasn't a real flashy quarterback, but he was a winner. He was the hardest-working guy on the team. He liked to play off the field, but he was a great teammate. They knew we had a good defense and that we could win with the defense, but when it came down to the nitty-gritty, Joe Kapp got the job done. We'd win a lot of low-scoring games because he never gave the game away."

Lee was just five of 12 for 92 yards in a less noteworthy game the previous week, a 16–13 Central Division–clinching win over the Bears. Throwing the ball was a challenge as it was brutally cold (below-zero wind chill), but in a game now forgotten, a Dick Butkus story lives on.

"It's still one of the coldest games in the history of the Vikings," said Lee. "I hit Henderson on an out and up for the score that basically clinched it. It was so cold. You'd go on a 40-yard drive, and it felt like you were out there for an hour. We go ahead by 10 and it seemed safe, but then Cecil Turner out of Cal Poly, a great small-college program, runs back the kickoff 98 yards [to make it 16–13]. We're basically just going to run quarterback sneaks to run out the clock. Then Butkus calls time-out. Leroy Caffey had been traded from the Packers and he's now with the Bears playing linebacker. He was every bit as big as Butkus. I notice they started yelling at each other. Caffey says, 'You stupid son of a bitch! You stupid son of a bitch!' Butkus turns to Caffey and says, 'Why? Why?' Caffey said, 'Look at the f-ing scoreboard!' Butkus looks up and sees there's like five seconds to play and says, 'Leroy, I'm sorry, I'm sorry,' and then he hugs him. Butkus loved that story."

Still severely limited with his high ankle injury, Cuozzo returned as the starter in week 14 in Atlanta and went 13 of 20 for 175 yards with a TD and interception. Lee came off the bench and followed up his strong performance in the snow against Boston by going six of 10 for 103 yards with a TD and interception in a 37–7 Vikings rout. Lee presented a strong case the last three games of the '70 season, going 29 of 47 for 463 yards and four TDs.

A week later, Cuozzo started in a first-round playoff game against the heavily underdog NFC West Division champion San Francisco 49ers (10–3–1) at Metropolitan Stadium and went an atrocious nine of 27 for 146 yards and two interceptions as the Vikings lost 17–14 for their first-ever home playoff defeat.

John Brodie was solid, if not spectacular, in the face of the Vikings' ferocious pass rush, going 16 of 32 for 201 yards and a TD. The game marked the third straight postseason where Minnesota faced a quarterback who would garner NFL MVP honors. In 1968 it was Morrall, '69 Gabriel and '70 Brodie.

"Brodie walked up to me on the field after the game and said, 'All I can say is we're really glad you didn't start,'" said Lee, whose son Zac became a starting quarterback at

Nebraska. "I wish I had played that game, but the thing is Bud only had three samples of my playing that year. You have to see it from a coaching perspective."

Cuozzo said his poor game against the 49ers precipitated the Vikings trading for Wake Forest product Snead in the offseason.

"I had a terrible game against them with the sprained ankle," he admitted. "It was a high ankle sprain, which you never heard of at the time. I played in the Falcons game the last game of the season to get some work in. I could play, but I couldn't play. I couldn't move at all. I was in terrible, terrible pain. I regret it, but it was a playoff game and I wanted to be out there. I thought I could pull it off."

After a promising opening drive against the 49ers aided by a deep ball to Henderson got the Vikings inside the San Francisco 10, a poorly thrown Cuozzo pass intended for Clint Jones in the left flat was picked off at the San Francisco five by linebacker Jim Sniadecki. The offense never recovered, going a dismal one of 11 on third-down chances the rest of the way.

It started as another day where the defense was going to be the team's offense as Minnesota got on the board first when Paul Krause picked up a fumble by 49ers fullback Ken Willard (game-high 85 yards rushing) and ran untouched 22 yards to paydirt to make it 7–0 in the first quarter.

In what would prove to be a theme for the contest, Bruce Taylor's 30-yard punt return later in the first paved the way for a Brodie-to-Dick Witcher TD pass from 24 yards to tie the game.

Osborn uncharacteristically fumbled in the second quarter to set up a 40-yard Bruce Gossett FG to give the 49ers a 10–7 halftime lead.

Following a scoreless third quarter, the Vikings, who had dramatically come from behind to beat another West Coast team the previous year in the playoffs, the Los Angeles Rams, looked to be in great shape to do it once again when Krause came up with his second big play of the contest, returning a Wally Hilgenberg–forced fumble 12 yards to the 49ers' 32 in the fourth quarter. But Tommy Hart took the wind from the Vikings' sails as he sacked Cuozzo for a six-yard loss on a third-and-eight play from the 30 and Cox's ensuing FG attempt came up short.

Later in the fourth, Taylor ripped off his second huge special teams play as he returned a punt 23 yards to the Vikings' 14 to set up a one-yard QB sneak by Brodie for a 17–7 lead, which seemed more like a hundred.

Cuozzo connected with Washington for a 24-yard TD pass with a second left to make the game seem closer than it was.

"The Vikings never have been noted for the spectacular play to win," wrote Bill Hengen of the *Minneapolis Star*. "They work at it like an ordinary menu—meat and potatoes. The defense gets the ball back, the offense grinds out the footage. Finally, they score. It was a meatless day for the offense."[3]

Changes were on the horizon.

"After the game, I met with Bud and I told him I was contemplating taking a year off," said Cuozzo. "I was playing football six months and going to dental school six months and it was getting difficult. He told me, 'We're going to get you some help.' And they trade for Norm Snead. I didn't think that was going to be the type of help they were going to get.

"I mean we had a good year in '70. We went 12–2 and opened the year by routing Kansas City [27–10]. Our offense was not going to be what was winning the game. The idea was not to make mistakes and let the defense take over the game. We weren't going to be throwing 30 passes. We were third and eight a whole lot. I remember Jerry Burns once said, 'They're going to put that on my tomb.' I still believe if we hadn't lost that play-off game to San Francisco, I don't think Grant trades for Norm Snead."

With Grant not fully trusting in either Cuozzo's or Lee's ability, the Vikings acquired Snead from the Philadelphia Eagles for Steve Smith and a pair of draft picks. While Snead went on to make the Pro Bowl in 1972 (2,307 yards passing, 17 TDs, 60.3 percentage) after being traded to the Giants for Tarkenton, it never worked out for the ex–Redskins star in his one year with the Vikings despite his winning both of his starts (versus the Eagles and Bills).

"We thought Bob should have been our quarterback," said Warwick. "Cuozzo wasn't strong enough and Norm Snead was pretty much over the hill by then. If they would have stuck with Bob Lee, he could have done the job."

Grant went back and forth during the 1971 season among incumbent Cuozzo, Lee and Snead.

"We'd go the whole week and we'd not know who was going to start the game," said Cuozzo of the quarterback chaos. "We had three guys—myself, Norm and Bob—alternating at practice. You never had any input into what type of plays were in the game plan. It was hard to lead a team under those circumstances. It was close to the day before when you'd find out who was going to start. If they hadn't traded for Snead, it would have been completely different. Now, Norm was a really good quarterback, a great thrower, but it was a bad circumstance to be in. You never felt like you were the guy. If they would have just come out and said to one of us you're the guy, it would have been much better."

Grant finally settled on Lee, who started four of the last five games, winning all but one.

One of the victories was a 24–7 week-11 win against Van Brocklin's Falcons. Lee completed only 10 passes, but he particularly recalls a pass caught by the fullback Brown, who rushed for 85 yards and a pair of scores.

"Bud Grant had always said that Bill Brown was the best player he ever coached, because he could do anything," said Lee. "He could run, catch, block, play special teams and he could even throw the ball. I never in my life ever heard Brownie say a bad word about anyone on our team. Against the Falcons, I throw him a ball in the flat and he's coming back to the huddle but on the way back he's jawing with Van Brocklin, saying, 'Dutch this, Dutch that,' because he had played for him five or six years after [George] Halas traded him here from Chicago. I grab Brownie and say, 'Come on, Brownie, you can have your love affair with Van Brocklin later!' Van Brocklin says, 'Yeah, Brownie, get back in the huddle!'"

The General would end up in Atlanta two years later.

Lee's top outing down the stretch in '71 was the season finale against the Bears, where he went 13 of 22 for 271 yards and two TDs as the Vikings finished 11–3.

Lee got the start in the infamous Christmas Day playoff game against NFC East Division winner Dallas (11–3) at Metropolitan Stadium and made a couple of key mistakes, throwing a pair of interceptions, one each to Chuck Howley and Cliff Harris.

The Vikings were again a dominating, pulverizing defense, posting three shutouts in 14 games and allowing a 40.4 passing rating, but even the Purple People Eaters could not overcome the team's five turnovers to the Cowboys' zero as the Vikings would go on to disappointedly lose their second straight home playoff game, 20–12.

Lee and Cuozzo, who came on in relief, combined to go 19 of 38 passing for 210 yards and four interceptions.

Lee's best ball came in the first quarter on a signature maneuver, a semi-roll right where he threw a dart off his back leg 45 yards downfield to Grim. With the game tied at 3–3, the Vikings, deep in Dallas territory, had a chance to go ahead, but Howley picked off a screen pass intended for Osborn, who had fumbled (a play the Vikings protested) to set up Dallas's first score. Instead of the Vikings taking the lead, the pick set up a go-ahead FG for the Cowboys from 44 yards out by Mike Clark.

The play looked a lot like Cuozzo's early-game interception in the red zone against the 49ers.

"[George] Andrie was Dallas's right defensive end, and Howley kind of slipped in behind him on a delayed blitz," said Lee. "I looked right, then back left. I threw it when I saw Grady [Alderman] cut Andrie. I threw the ball to get it out in a hurry and there's Chuck Howley right there. He made the same kind of play against Brodie [in the NFC championship game] the next week against San Francisco at Kezar Stadium. I was already home and watched that game."

After a start-and-stop, 61-yard kickoff return by Jones nearly went the distance, the Vikings missed a chance to knot the game before halftime when Fred Cox missed a 42-yarder.

Duane Thomas, Dallas's second-year running back out of West Texas State, rushed for 66 yards on 21 carries and scored on a 13-yard run to put the Vikings behind 13–3 in the third quarter. A 10-point lead was virtually insurmountable given the Vikings' offensive woes.

Roger Staubach hit Bob Hayes with a nine-yard scoring toss in the third to make it 20–3. Defensive tackle Alan Page sacked the Dallas quarterback in the end zone for a safety and Stu Voigt caught a six-yard TD pass late from Cuozzo to conclude the scoring.

"Dallas was a good team," said Lee. "They went on to win the Super Bowl that year. Bud Grant said he wishes he would have started me earlier, but I had a back injury from a pinched nerve, which caused me to have a bad practice, and that gave Bud some hesitation about going with me earlier. We would have had a good shot against the Dolphins. Our last game exhibition game, which I started [he completed 10 of 17 for 103 yards], we shut out the Dolphins 24–0. They went to the next three Super Bowls."

Thomas had great respect for Grant's ballclub.

"The Vikings had an excellent defense," he said. "And I loved their camaraderie. They were a true team. Dallas was not really a team. They were a collection of players. Guys on a tour of duty. [Vikings running back] Clint [Jones] told me the Black and White players socialized more in Minnesota. That makes a difference when you hit the field. You can correct problems on the field when things are good off the field. There were a lot of politics in Dallas, especially with a quarterback controversy [between Craig Morton and Staubach], which should never happen during the season. There was also a lot of what some people would call prejudice."

Foreman, who would come on the scene two years later when the Vikings providentially drafted him 12th overall out of the University of Miami, said Thomas would have loved wearing purple.

"He would have excelled up here," said Foreman, who still lives in Minnesota. "I don't think Dallas was the right place for him. It seemed like the coach there [Tom

Landry] wasn't a good fit for him. I don't think they treated him with the kind of respect he deserved."

The loss to Dallas resulted in the Vikings squandering yet another great defensive season, this one spearheaded by the cat-quick and lionhearted Page, who became the first defensive player in history to garner the NFL's Most Valuable Player Award.

It was the kind of season Grant had envisioned for Page when he and Reichow selected him in their initial draft together.

"We drafted Page with the 15th pick [in the '67 draft]. If we would have known he was going to be quite so good we would have drafted him earlier," Grant said with a smile. "We had a few picks before him. He was a defensive end in college and we moved him inside and he was great there. Alan was able to be involved in more plays on the inside. He had great instincts and fit with the others in that group. You would normally play the outside shoulder of the guard but he would make a play inside the blocker and he'd be right there to get the ball carrier. You'd ask him how he did it and he wouldn't know. It was just his great instincts. He was dominating."[4]

"You see him take offensive linemen weighing 260 and 280 and stand 'em up and bend 'em over and sometimes knock 'em down," said Peter Range of the *New York Times* describing Page. "And you know he shouldn't be able to do that at all."[5]

• • •

The defeat to the Cowboys recast Grant's thinking as the team began to consider bringing in another signal caller.

Tarkenton, now north of age 30 and having spent five years with the Giants, was ready to play for a legitimate contender.

"Grant told Finks he is the one quarterback in football I want for this team," said Jim Klobuchar.[6]

It became a reality on January 27, 1972, as the Vikings shipped Snead, running back Vince Clements, a No. 1 pick in '72 and a No. 2 in '73 to reacquire Tarkenton, who turned 32 less than a week later. (Minnesota still had a No. 1 pick in '72, awarded to them from New England as part of Kapp leaving as a free agent.)

An Associated Press report in the *Reporter Dispatch* cleverly stated: "'Don't worry,' one defensive lineman said to another after Fran Tarkenton had eluded him in a wild behind-the-line-of-scrimmage chase. 'He'll be back in a moment.' And so Tarkenton, who turned the once-desperate act of scrambling into a fine art in the National Football League, is indeed, returning from whence he came."[7]

"The trade abolished the three-quarterback, starter-announced-Friday system of 1971," wrote Dick Gordon. "Tarkenton is No. 1—just as he has been in his 12 years in the National Football League."[8]

Upon the Vikings making the trade, Grant had no hesitation in working his previously subdued offensive scheme around Tarkenton's rare skills.

"We will use his play mobility," he said. "There may be more running plays to the outside, bootleg plays and spin outs."[9]

The trade marked a rare occurrence where a general manager both trades and reacquires a player while serving with the same team.

"This was a totally different type of deal," an ecstatic Finks told the *Minneapolis Tribune*. "In 1967 we gave up a proven quarterback for four intangibles, for four draft choices. In 1967 we were selling. We were at a disadvantage because Tarkenton said he wanted to leave our club. This time New York was doing the selling. They called us. This was the type of deal we couldn't afford to make two or three years ago. It was the type of a deal only a contender can make."[10]

Tarkenton was more than thrilled about coming home.

"This is exotic," he said. "What a break to get with a club like the Vikings, a club that has the best defense in football, a club that gives the offense a chance to handle the ball."[11]

Heavy favorites along with Dallas to grab the NFC crown, the Vikings finished 3–3 in exhibition play. In its final exhibition game September 10 at home, in an era where most teams played their starters in the preseason, Minnesota led Miami 19–14 late in the game only to see Jim Lindsey fumble at the Dolphins' 19. Mercury Morris would cap a 10-play, 81-yard drive with a six-yard TD run with under a minute left to give the eventual Super Bowl champs a 21–19 win.

It was a harbinger of things to come as a team with its franchise quarterback back in tow would drop five games by three points or less, including a near mirror-image 16–14 loss to the Dolphins in week-three play at Minnesota on Jim Mandich's last-second TD catch. Buoyed by that win, Miami would run the table the rest of the way, defeating George Allen's Redskins 14–7 in Super Bowl VII. The Vikings finished the campaign a shocking 7–7.

A slipping defense, injuries and the normally steady Cox would play a key role in the team's demise.

Cox missed two field goals, one from 22 yards and another from 44, in a devastating 24–21 home loss to Washington in a much-ballyhooed season opener on *Monday Night Football*. The 34-year-old former running back for the University of Pittsburgh also missed a 26-yarder that would have beaten the Cardinals the week after the Miami loss, and a 27-yarder two weeks later that would have salvaged a tie with the Bears. In the final week, he was off the mark from 42 yards away in a last-second 20–17 loss to San Francisco.

Green Bay, buoyed by the running of John Brockington and MacArthur Lane, clinched the Central Division championship with a 23–7 thrashing of the host Vikings in the next-to-last week of the campaign. Brockington carried 25 times for 119 yards and Lane 19 for 99. The Packers finished 10–4 and traveled two weeks later to Washington for an opening-round playoff game that they lost 16–3 to the eventual NFC champions.

The Vikings will forever look back at the ill-fated '70 and '71 seasons in terms of what could have been. Had they gotten by a pair of first-round road playoff underdogs to advance to NFC championship games, they would have played for the opportunity to face the Colts and the Dolphins, respectively, in the Super Bowl, teams they matched up with better than the 1969–70 Chiefs, 1973–74 Dolphins, 1974–75 Steelers and 1976–77 Raiders. With either Kapp or Tarkenton at the helm, they likely would have been able to hurdle at least one.

The '72 campaign, with all the narrow losses, also left a sting, but not one as sharp as the ones endured the previous two years.

The tide would dramatically turn in the team's favor the next year, as riding the back of the versatile rookie Foreman, a flashy and electric running back out of the University of Miami, Minnesota would open the '73 season by reeling off nine straight victories and easily go on to capture its fifth Central Division championship.

5

The Seed and Gillie Show

Minnesota Vikings 27, Washington Redskins 20
December 22, 1973, Metropolitan Stadium
Divisional-Round Playoff

On the initial series of Fran Tarkenton's first playoff appearance against a veteran and swashbuckling Washington Redskins club, he opted to throw deep.

His wont was to catch the opposition off guard.

It wasn't to Homer Jones this time, but a man known as "Gillie."

John Gilliam, whom the Vikings had stolen in a trade from the St. Louis Cardinals the previous offseason, could stretch defenses like no receiver Tarkenton had enjoyed since teaming up with the explosive Jones for three years in Gotham City.

Tarkenton had waited 13 seasons for an opportunity like this and he wasn't going to be timid. Facing third and one from his own 20, he made a nifty play-action fake to halfback Oscar Reed and looked deep for the mercurial Gilliam, also seeing his first postseason action.

Lined up wide right against the diminutive but great Washington cornerback Pat Fischer, Gilliam came out of his three-point stance and casually slanted toward the right hashmark to give the appearance he was interested in blocking down on Redskins free safety Brig Owens.

Gilliam caught Owens unawares by swiftly breaking downfield, but Tarkenton's near 50-yard heave barely missed connecting, sailing just through the silky-smooth receiver's outstretched hands.

Gilliam blamed himself, saying, "I should have caught it," but in reality, had the ball been thrown more toward his inside shoulder, it would have been a statement-making, jump-starting touchdown.

Nevertheless, the Tarkenton-Gilliam duo would not be denied versus the wild-card entry Washington—the two rarely were during their brief, but illustrious, time together. For it would be the great glider Gilliam as well as the elusive and slippery Reed, the unheralded back from Colorado State, who would prove to be the Redskins' undoing, as the Vikings prevailed 27–20 to snap a two-game home playoff losing streak and advance to their second championship game.

"I was so tense I didn't know what I was doing out there," said Gilliam after the win over the reigning NFC champs. "On that long pass I missed, I was a little late getting off the ball. I was one step away from it all the way, and then at the last second it tailed off a bit to my right. The ball went right through my hands. If I had caught it, I'd have been home free."[1]

Vikings quarterback Fran Tarkenton (10) hands off to Oscar Reed (32) as guard Ed White (62) leads the way during an NFC divisional round playoff game on Dec. 23, 1973, in Bloomington, Minnesota. Tarkenton passed for 222 yards and threw two touchdown passes while Reed accounted for 171 total yards to lead the Vikings to a 27–20 win over Washington.

With their team trailing 13–10 on Curt Knight's 42-yard field goal to open the fourth quarter, Tarkenton and Gilliam would connect for two scores in less than two minutes to give the Vikings a 24–13 lead.

"They can't say we went out there and sat on the ball," said Tarkenton, who nearly led the Giants to the playoffs in '70 when the team finished 9–5, good for second in the NFC East. "We came out throwing at the start and we were throwing at the finish. I have been called a loser and I have been called a scrambler. But the only thing I want to be known as is a winner."[2]

The Central Division champs got a huge game from Reed, who posted a career-best 171 total yards, including 95 yards rushing on 17 carries.

The Vikings went ahead for good when Tarkenton hit Gilliam down the right sideline off a play-action fake from 28 yards out to make it 17–13. Having the misfortune of trying to guard Gilliam on that play was Washington left corner Leslie "Speedy" Duncan, a player better known for his kickoff return prowess. Duncan went for the play fake and the South Carolina State product ran right by him.

Duncan, seeing his first action at corner in four years, entered the game in the second quarter when Fischer left with cracked ribs after tackling Reed. Nebraska product Ted Vactor, a special teams maven and Fischer's normal backup, was on injured reserve, thus forcing into action Duncan, to that point used sparingly in George Allen's vaunted nickel defenses.

"Much better, much easier," Gilliam said of going against Duncan instead of

5. The Seed and Gillie Show

Fischer. "Of all the defensive backs I faced, Pat Fischer was the toughest to go against. He was smart. He knew the pass routes. He was only about 165 pounds and 5–10, but he should be in the Hall of Fame. He was a smart defensive back."

Tarkenton said he doesn't remember picking on Duncan, but it's hard to imagine he would fail to notice the drop-off in coverage ability.

"I never remember in my 18 years ever picking on a defensive back. It all depended on the coverages and how they were playing us," said Tarkenton. "I was disappointed after Gilliam left because he had elite speed. He probably had more speed than Ahmad [Rashad] or Sammy White. He was an elite receiver. When he played for us, we didn't have Ahmad or Sammy yet, so he was easily our best receiver. When Sammy and Ahmad played together, they both drew attention and that helped both get open."

Always a presence in playoff games, Vikings left corner Nate Wright, a rookie in St. Louis in '69, the same year Gilliam arrived there in a trade from New Orleans, then picked off Billy Kilmer's next pass and returned it inside the Redskins' 10, setting up Gilliam's second TD.

"I got Nate to come in," said Gilliam on the unsung Wright, who went on to have a sensational 10-year career with Minnesota. "They didn't want him in St. Louis after they got Roger Wehrli. I told Bud [Grant] there's a good cornerback down there in St. Louis. I said, 'I ran against him.' Bud said, 'If you ran against him, I'll bring him in and give him a shot.'"

Two plays after Wright's pick, Tarkenton semi-rolled to his right, then darted left looking for Chuck Foreman, who was covered in the back of the end zone. He doubled back to his right, and then fanned out toward the sideline, ala Joe Montana on his famous toss to Dwight Clark. This drifting movement gave Gilliam time to work his way back to the right corner of the end zone, where Tarkenton got the ball to him near the end line before Owens could recover.

Vikings 24, Redskins 13.

"All that was instinct," said Tarkenton on his ability to go off-script. "I played all the sports. I just played the way I think I should play. I didn't think that was unusual. I really was never called a scrambler in high school and college. I didn't even realize I was doing those things then until I looked back at film. It was just my instinct. No one taught me to throw, no one taught me to run, no one taught me to scramble. Even calling plays. I called plays in high school, college and the pros because that's what you did then. No one sent in plays. I never had the luxury of someone sending in plays from the press box and telling me what the defense was doing. When I came to pro football, no one ran. Unitas, Y.A. Tittle were pocket passers."

"Fran was some player," said running back Dave Osborn, who played in both of Tarkenton's stints with the Vikings. "He had eyes in the back of his head. He was still just as quick when we got him back in '72. He was also such a smart quarterback. He knew the game. He called his own plays. He was his own boss out there."

The right corner of the north end zone where Gilliam caught his second TD ball was the scene of many key Vikings moments. It was as close as any Met Stadium fan would get to the playing field.

As was the case for most multiuse stadiums in the '70s, The Met was often considered less than ideal for football. The gridiron ran from around third base to right field (north to south), with barely enough room to fit the playing field and end zones.

"[That north] end zone was only a few feet from the permanent stands," wrote Pat

Duncan in his book, *The Last Kings of the Old NFL*. "In the baseball set-up, this unforgiving short corner was a little past third base, just to the foul side of the left field line over which Harmon Killebrew boomed home runs and Gene Washington and other receivers slammed without mercy into the fence."[3]

"It was tough on that side because it was so tight and the fence so close, but that was the flattest part of the football field," said Gilliam. "I caught them going both ways, but that was *my* end zone. I liked that end zone, both sides of it. That was the best side of the field to run patterns. If you ran a fly the other way [toward the scoreboard], you were going downhill. It was hard to judge the ball."

Stu Voigt, who became ensconced in the Minnesota lineup in '71 following an injury to John Beasley, wasn't in the end zone as much as Gilliam during his 11-year Vikings career (17 TDs), but he was certainly aware of the stadium's quirks.

"It was pretty tight down there," said Voigt. "It was certainly not a stadium made for football. We played many a league game with the baseball infield still in [on that side]. When the Twins were done, they would cover it with sod and it didn't take too well. We definitely had a home-field advantage because we knew all of the foibles. At that end, it was glorified dirt painted green."

Voigt said it was akin to the advantages the great Boston Celtics championship teams of the Bob Cousy era enjoyed by knowing every dead spot on The Garden's fabled parquet floor.

Gilliam, who played two years in New Orleans and three in St. Louis before heading up north, was no stranger to finding the end zone. He even practiced that way.

"Every ball I caught in practice I would run it all the way down," said Gilliam, a member of the South Carolina Athletic Hall of Fame. "A lot of guys wouldn't do that. I practiced expecting to score."

His home-run ability was no more evident than when he caught three touchdown passes from Charley Johnson in a game against the Browns at Municipal Stadium on October 26, 1969. His final TD came with less than 30 seconds left when he caught a sideline pass at the Browns' 10-yard line and broke a tackle by corner Walt Sumner to enable the Cards to come away with a 21–21 tie.

The Cardinals repeatedly gave the Browns fits with their plethora of crackerjack skill position players, including Cleveland's title-winning year in '64 when St. Louis battled Blanton Collier's club to a tie at Municipal Stadium and won 28–19 at home. The man Gilliam played for his first two years in St. Louis, Weeb Ewbank's son-in-law, Charley Winner, took over for Wally Lemm in '66.

"My favorite uncle had died. He was to be buried that Sunday at 3:00 p.m.," he recalled. "He was from my hometown, Greenwood, South Carolina. I asked Winner if I could go but the Cardinals wouldn't let me. But I had a job to do, and I just took care of my business and played my normal game. I flew out after the game to sit with my auntie and stayed there until Monday and flew back to St. Louis."

Gilliam's other two scores against Cleveland came on his signature pattern—the sharp-cutting slant route, the first for 85 yards lined up to the right and the other from 74 yards split to Johnson's left.

Gilliam ran this route as well as Jerry Rice. He had good teachers.

"Herb Adderley and Willie Wood taught me how to run that pattern," he said. "I was with New Orleans in my first year. We got to Green Bay for a game and they call a slant. Adderley was about six yards off me and guarding me to the outside, toward the

5. The Seed and Gillie Show 73

sideline. Adderley let me get inside and he was just setting me up. Willie Wood was right there, and [when he hit me] I thought I was in hell. The ball went one way, and I went the other.

"After the game they came to me and said, 'Man, you're going to be a good receiver, a good athlete in this league.' They told me if I see a guy sitting outside you have to square him up. From that point on I would run right at a guy's numbers so he'd have to get through me to get to the ball."

Watching the Vikings play the Redskins from his Missouri home was Hall of Fame tight end Jackie Smith, a teammate of Gilliam's in St. Louis who was amazed at the wideout's unique ability to set up defenders.

"Guys like Gilliam could run full speed right at you and then, boom, he'd be right out there," said Smith. "He didn't give the defensive back any time to react. He was a helluva player and a good guy. Some guys had the ability to just run straight at a guy and all of sudden be going immediately at an angle. It would really catch the defender off guard because they would do it so abruptly. One step or a half a step means a lot on those type of timing patterns. He had the ability to get that step. That's a huge thing."

Smith preferred a more squared-off route.

"I liked the crossing pattern," said the star tight end. "The guys on the other side would come through and clear things off, then you'd be man-for-man and you could go flying across the field. You should catch the ball then almost immediately you get a lot of speed up and momentum toward the sideline. We also had an option pattern, where you would read the tight safety. If he went outside, you went inside, and vice versa. It would be either a flag or a corner. That's how I got a lot of yardage."

Undaunted by Allen's stingy defense, Tarkenton rebounded from his near miss to Gilliam on the game's first series to complete 16 of 28 passes for 222 yards. He was at his best when it mattered the most against the Redskins as he connected on eight of 10 throws in the second half and threw for both of his TDs.

"We did miss a touchdown pass to Gilliam early in the game and one to Carroll Dale a little bit later," said Tarkenton. "But if you are punching enough, you are going to get some blows in."[4]

Smith wasn't surprised Tarkenton was able to pull off his second TD pass, a play that lasted what seemed like a minute.

"It's always been amazing to me watching different quarterbacks and see how they got the ball out," said Smith. "I got to observe that during my times at the Pro Bowl. I would have liked to play with some of these different quarterbacks to watch how they saw things differently. Guys like Tarkenton. He could sure throw the ball—he was out there. He moved around pretty much, too. But he had the ability to really anticipate who was going to be open and the ball would be there. It would have been nice to play with him. It was nice to see what these guys could do."

Another team that made the '73 playoffs was the NFC West Division champion Los Angeles Rams. Their star left defensive end Jack Youngblood, who played against the Vikings four times in the playoffs, including twice in grueling championship games, said he grew weary of chasing around the likes of Tarkenton and Dallas quarterback Roger Staubach, whose Cowboys would defeat the Rams in divisional-round play one day later.

"Tarkenton was a pain in the ass," laughed Youngblood. "He remained a great athlete into his 30s. He was very smart, very agile and athletic. He studied what we were doing. He wasn't that big of a guy. He wasn't 6–4, but he played smart. Staubach was a very nice guy, unless he was trying to throw the ball. Tarkenton was a little cocky. He thought he could get into your head, that he could do something to make you hesitate. You'd get pissed off, and you'd lose thought of what you're supposed to be doing."

Youngblood said Tarkenton did just that in the Rams' last playoff encounter against Sir Francis in the '78 divisional round.

"We're playing at home against the Vikings and they get the ball deep in our territory at about our 20-, 25-yard line," said Youngblood. "I'm going, 'Boys, we have to tighten up right here now.' We line up and Tarkenton came up to the line of scrimmage on first down, and he was talking to his guys back and forth. I got [Ron] Yary and the tight end [Stu Voigt] on my side; it's a right-handed formation. I'm listening to what he is saying and I'm getting intense before the ball is snapped, and he turns my way and says, 'Hey, Jack! What do you think?' I turn my head and look at him and bam, they snap the dang ball. Yary knocked the shit out of me. Yary and I started laughing. I started walking up toward Tarkenton and Yary started walking up with me because he knew I was going to kick Tarkenton's ass."

Not to be lost in the star power of Tarkenton to Gilliam against the helpless Redskins was the play of Reed, who by 1973 had finally worked himself into a place of prominence in the Vikings' backfield.

Nicknamed the "Seed" due to his propensity to slip by would-be tacklers, Reed displayed that moniker to the utmost in this game, undoubtedly his most prolific in seven years in purple.

"I don't remember who gave me the nickname, but it was pretty descriptive," laughed Reed, who still resides in Minnesota. "You know when seeds are fresh, and they first get taken from the fruit they just slip out of your finger? That's kind of what I did."

With the game scoreless in the first, the Vikings faced a third-and-seven from their own 36. Reed, stationed in a split backfield with Foreman, streaked straight down the right hash ahead of former Green Bay star linebacker Dave Robinson. Tarkenton hit Reed in stride at the Redskins' 42, and after breaking a high-tackle attempt by Hall of Famer Ken Houston, he sojourned to the Redskins' 14.

It was a 50-yard completion. The Vikings settled for a Fred Cox field goal to make it 3–0.

Ironically, the man they called the Seed trained by running on furrows, trenches where the seed went.

"I used to work out during the spring and summers on my grandfather's farm in Mississippi," said the lovable Reed, who attended Booker T. Washington High School in Memphis after moving from Mississippi when he was in grade school. "He used to have me run in the freshly plowed fields prepared for the seed.

"I would also follow his car running on the dirt roads," added Reed. "In Mississippi, the roads would turn to sand, and running was really difficult. All that helped me. I knew the harder I worked, the better I would be. I trusted him on that. My grandfather was only 45 minutes away [from Memphis], but once I went to play pro ball it was a little too far away to train there."

The Redskins took a 7–3 lead into halftime on a three-yard TD run by the hard-charging Larry Brown.

"Our team was so keyed up in the first half," Tarkenton told the *Minneapolis*

5. The Seed and Gillie Show

Tribune. "I've never seen a team more ready to play than this team. The Vikings had been disappointed in two playoff games before and I think we were too intense in the first half."[5]

Undaunted, Reed, a seventh-round pick in '69 (167th overall), kick-started the Vikings' offense at the opening of the second half on a play that, given its import, would go down as one of the top runs in the team's illustrious history.

Facing a third-and-two from the Washington 48, Tarkenton handed off to Reed, slanting right. Getting a good seal block from Charles Goodrum, who was in the game for short yardage plays, Reed started wide, then cut hard inside Robinson, who had outside leverage. Reed then somehow deftly spun away from Owens, who had a good bead on him coming up hastily from his safety position.

It got crazier from there.

With the tumult of the line of scrimmage in his wake, Reed stormed downfield, where he was eventually surrounded inside the 10 by no fewer than four doggedly pursuing Redskin defenders. With tackle Ron Yary and Voigt steaming downfield to offer interference, Reed was finally toppled at the Redskins' two by the hustling Robinson, the same man he had so masterfully outmaneuvered at the line of scrimmage.

"We had all of our big guys in there since it was a short yardage situation," said Reed. "Francis called an outside play for the fullback. Chuck knocked the cornerback out and I cut back inside Chuck's block. One guy had a hand on me, but I got loose."[6]

Chicago Bears great Gale Sayers famously told NFL Films, "Give me 18 inches of daylight, that's all I need."[7]

Slippery as a seed, Reed also didn't need gaping holes to get free in the secondary. "I was told I was quicker than most backs and I could get through tackles," he said. "I felt I could be successful any chance I was given the ball. We'd get in the huddle, and they'd say, 'Give it to Seed; give it to Seed.'"

Reed didn't remember the "Beast Quake," Marshawn Lynch's stadium-shaking, 67-yard, four-broken tackles touchdown run against the visiting New Orleans Saints in a 2010 NFC wild-card playoff game with the Seattle Seahawks, but his 46-yard effort was similar, and it propelled Minnesota on another Super Bowl run.

Following Reed's stunning jaunt, the bruising and bow-legged Bill Brown, who once had 11 rushing TDs in a season, took it in from there, giving the Vikings a 10–7 advantage 3:30 into the half.

"I had been with the Vikings six years and played in the playoffs for five years," said Reed. "I figured it was about time to do something big. They wouldn't concentrate on me. I wasn't the world's greatest runner or pass catcher, but given a little room, I'd use what I had. I had good blockers in front of me and I wanted to take advantage of them as much as I could. For instance, Ed White. That guy could lift a building and I always could depend on that."

The Vikings' lead looked safe after Gilliam's second score gave them a 11-point bulge, but two possessions later, the Redskins blocked a Mike Eischeid punt and recovered at the Minnesota 25. They quickly scored on Roy Jefferson's 25-yard circus catch—one that saw the former Colts star secure the ball between his legs with Nate Wright smothering him—to pull within 24–20 with just more than five minutes left, plenty of time to wreck the Vikings' hopes.

But the Vikings answered with a Cox field goal with 1:36 remaining, and when Kilmer's fourth-down pass from near midfield fell incomplete on the Redskins' last drive with 10 seconds left, Tarkenton and Co. had secured the Vikings' first playoff win since 1969.

"It was one of those games that sold pro football all over again," said Grant. "We knew Washington would be tough. They gave us nothing in the first half, but as is often the case, things happened later to turn it around."[8]

Reed had no inclination the Vikings were interested in him as the 1968 draft approached. "I had no clue. I never heard from them. There was one team that kept in contact with me every month, but not the Vikings, so I was really surprised they drafted me. When I got there—just like my experiences in high school and college—the guys really embraced me and were there for me. There was no rookie hazing or anything like that. The Vikings didn't do that.

"I worried at first because I came in late to training camp because I played in an all-star game [North-South]," said Reed. "But they never held that against me."

Vikings scout Jerry Reichow remembered how he stumbled onto the sturdy and dependable runner.

"First of all, I liked to go to the mountains," he said. "A lot of coaches weren't happy with you coming [to their schools]. The Colorado State coach [Mike Lude] couldn't be nicer. He gave us all the information we needed about anyone, even guys on other teams. Oscar wasn't tall, about 5–9 or 5–10 at the most, but he was stocky. He had good eyes and could feel the run. We also got [defensive end Mark] Mullaney out of there. They just couldn't do enough for you."

Reed logged 83 carries for 393 yards and a score in '69, but his breakthrough season came in 1972. In a frustrating campaign for the Vikings, who went just 7–7 after reacquiring Tarkenton, Reed had career highs in carries (151), yards (639) and TDs (three).

Reed's favorite running back growing up was the great Jim Brown, so it's no surprise he wore No. 32 for the Vikings.

"I wanted to wear it in college, but I had to wear 30 because an older player had that number," he said. "I loved watching Jim play."

Reed almost ended up at Memphis State.

"I would have been the first Black athlete at Memphis State," he recalled. "I met Martin Luther King when I was in high school, and he wanted me to go there. He wanted me to be the first [Black man] to play there. It was a difficult time, and our family got threats about it. Some of my family members wanted me to stay close to home so they could watch me play. But I decided I didn't want to play in the South, so I looked at other schools. This was during the Civil Rights Movement. My mom was really impressed with [Colorado State coach Mike] Lude, so I decided to go there."

At Booker T. Washington High School in Memphis, Tennessee, Reed earned the nickname "Golden Shoes" after spray-painting his cleats gold following a record-breaking season.

"We wore green and gold," recalled Reed. "That's why I painted my shoes that color."

He didn't choose Colorado State because his shoes matched.

"It was quite an experience," he said. "In Memphis, I couldn't ride on the same buses, go to the same restrooms or eat in the same restaurants as White people. It wasn't like that in Colorado."

Reed chewed up more yards than any post–World War II back to that date for CSU. As a sophomore in 1965, he broke the school record for yards rushing in a season with 725 and backed it up his junior year with 946 yards.

5. The Seed and Gillie Show

After carrying for 910 yards as a senior, Reed finished his CSU career with 2,581 yards rushing. He held the school record for most career rushing yards until 1971. Reed received national recognition in 1966 when he toted for 194 yards against West Texas State and *Sports Illustrated* recognized him with the National Back of the Week Award for his accomplishment.

Reed harbors no resentment over having to constantly battle for playing time with the likes of Dave Osborn, Brown, Clinton Jones, Ed Marinaro and Foreman. "I didn't question a thing from Coach Grant," said Reed. "That's the way I was. I had a lot of trust in him, and he had trust in me."

• • •

There is a legend surrounding the game involving a blackboard and an imposing Vikings defensive end.

Entering the contest, the Vikings had dropped three postseason games in row and Eller was not having any more of it. The Super Bowl IV loss to Kansas City and the subsequent home playoff losses to San Francisco ('70) and Dallas ('71) were certainly weighing on Eller's mind when he walked to the halftime locker room with the Vikings down 7–3 on Brown's scoring run.

Game reports said Eller gave an inspiring speech and laid a blackboard to waste. The observant Voigt saw it a different way.

"I'm not saying it didn't happen, but it wasn't on the grand scale they made it out to be at the time," he said. "The locker room wasn't that big at The Met. We shared it with the Twins. They had some 25 players and we had 40. It was jammed in there and there was a coaches' room off to the side. I know the offensive players would be on one side and the defense the other. There was a little bedlam at halftime of any game: guys getting taped, using the bathroom and so on. It was organized confusion. But it wasn't like the guys on our side of the room stopped and said, 'What the hell just happened?' We won the game, so I think that myth just grew. I'm sure it happened, but to what extent I'm not sure."

Eller, smiling, discussed the scene.

"That's probably true," said a coy Eller of the blackboard incident. "We were playing the Redskins, and it was a game I felt we could win, and I let the team know it. We weren't playing our hardest and that was unusual for our team. Maybe that gave us confidence since we went on to win the game."

Vikings safety Terry Brown validated the story.

"It happened," said Brown. "He broke the chalkboard. He wasn't happy and it got us charged up."

There were certainly tight quarters in the locker room at The Met, but Midway Stadium in Saint Paul, where the team practiced for at least a month every year until the Twins' season ended, was even cozier.

"When I started working with Stubby [Eason] in '75, we were over at Midway," said retired Vikings equipment manager Dennis Ryan. "We moved when the Twins were done but we had no storage, so we kept everything at Midway."

Spartan in its accommodations, Midway Stadium was the home of the Saint Paul Saints of the American Association from 1957 to 1960. It was located at 1000 North Snelling Avenue, on the east side of that street. It was built with just a small uncovered and presumably expandable grandstand.

"The locker room and everything was on a much smaller scale in those days, both at Met Stadium and at Midway," said Ryan, who was actually given the moniker "Midway" by Voigt because every time someone was looking for him, he was over at Midway searching out a piece of equipment. "Both of those stadiums were built for baseball teams and only meant for a 25-man roster and not really a coaching staff like football had. They just used makeshift rooms, the offense in one and defense the other. They would use the visitors' locker room for the meeting room.

"Our weights consisted of what the players purchased themselves. They would use them on a dirt basement at Midway," Ryan recalled. "They ended up welding the weights on the bench press barbell. They also did this with the curl bar; this was so the city employees wouldn't steal the weights. Everyone was stuck lifting the same weight, regardless of who you were. Of course, a lot of guys didn't lift weights back then and Bud sure didn't promote it. He thought that would tighten everyone up and take their athleticism away. A lot of people believed that in those days."

Midway was intended to compete with Metropolitan Stadium for attracting a Major League Baseball team, but the already-larger capacity of The Met doomed Midway Stadium. Used as a Minnesota Vikings practice field for the next 20 years following the Twins' arrival, it was demolished in '81.

"It was meager," chuckled Voigt. "You hung your pants in a little locker with a hook on the wall. There was no real weight room. Me and [guard] Milt Sunde worked out there some and there was all of about 100 pounds worth of weights down there."

• • •

It was ironic Tarkenton's first playoff game came against the Washington Redskins, a team he once loved.

His family moved from Richmond, Virginia, to Washington, D.C., when he was five years old. It was there, in a nearby alley, where he learned to operate in tight spaces, dodging trash cans and clotheslines before delivering the ball to his athletic older brother Dallas, named after his father, a Methodist minister.

"I really believe that our football games in that narrow, confined alley contributed a tremendous amount to my career," Tarkenton said. "To move in that alley, and to dodge or get off a pass, demanded quickness and a critical sense of direction. When I started becoming a more polished player in high school and college, I brought these vital instincts with me."[9]

As a child, he became captivated by University of Maryland quarterback Jack Scarbath, whose playing style prompted Tarkenton to wear No. 10 for his high school, college and pro careers.

"He was my hero," said Tarkenton in *Every Day Is Game Day*. "The only problem is that Scarbath did not wear No. 10 at the University of Maryland—he wore No. 62."[10]

Tarkenton mistook a picture of Scarbath wearing No. 10 for his collegiate jersey, but it was what he wore in high school.

"I must have seen the high school picture of him somewhere," said Tarkenton of Scarbath, who started at quarterback in the 1953 College All-Star Game against the defending NFL champion Detroit Lions at Soldier Field in Chicago but played only three years in the pros for Washington and Pittsburgh. "There were few televisions in the early '50s and even fewer college football broadcasts. I never actually saw him in a Maryland uniform, but I thought I had."[11]

5. The Seed and Gillie Show

Tarkenton was also enamored with the great "Slinging" Sammy Baugh, who arrived in Washington, D.C., eight years before his dad accepted a pastorate there. The revolutionary quarterback, drafted sixth overall in '37 out of Texas Christian, led the Skins to a pair of NFL crowns and preceded Tarkenton into the Hall of Fame. That's why it was such a disappointment for Tarkenton that the Redskins, holding the second overall pick in the 1961 draft, opted to select the bigger and stronger-armed Wake Forest QB Norm Snead, whom the Vikings ironically sent to the New York Giants to get Tarkenton back in 1972.

"I was assuming he would be picked in the first round," said Tarkenton, who became a friend with Snead at the Blue-Gray game. "I wanted Washington to draft me. I was deflated. Just smothered. I then waited for the news report or the telephone call that would identify the NFL team that had drafted Tarkenton in the first round. Nothing showed. I thought the wires must be down."[12]

The second signal caller taken was Billy Kilmer out of UCLA, whom the 49ers nabbed with the 11th pick of the first round. Tarkenton was the third quarterback selected, chosen by the Vikings with the first pick of the third round (29th overall). The Boston Patriots chose him in the fifth round of the AFL draft, but the Georgia signal caller never gave any thought toward playing in the new league, telling Boston GM Ed McKeever, "The National Football League was my idea of the zenith in athletics."[13]

While Snead and Kilmer would have solid careers, neither were in Tarkenton's category. Snead played 17 years and threw for 30,297 yards and 196 TDs, while Kilmer, who spent a lot of time at running back early on, passed for 20,495 yards and 152 scores.

The inability of scouts and NFL front office personnel to properly vet and evaluate quarterback prospects still thoroughly frustrates Tarkenton, who led the Georgia Bulldogs to an SEC title during his junior year in 1958 and a 14–0 win over Dan Devine's Missouri team in the Orange Bowl.

"They have no idea about the quarterback position. None. Zero," he said. "Why did what many consider the best football coach in history in Bill Belichick not start [Tom] Brady until his second year and not draft him until the sixth round [199th overall in the 2000 draft]? That's because he didn't think he could play. Coaches don't have any clue as to what a successful quarterback looks like. They go to the combine and they see how far they can throw it, they see high how he can jump, they give him some intelligence test. All that stuff and they don't understand that doesn't make a player. Everybody can throw the football, everybody has a brain, but what they don't know is if a guy is going to shit his pants in an NFL game at a loud stadium. Johnny Unitas was a ninth-round pick by the Steelers and they cut him. The Colts picked him up and he won championships and was great. Joe Montana was taken in the third round. If they miss Tom Brady in this age of sophistication we are in, that's about a bad of miss as you can have. This has gone on for the history of pro football. I read somewhere that about 10 percent make it. Dan Marino was drafted late in the first round [27th overall in '83]. It just amazes me how they continue to miss year after year."

The unflappable Tarkenton narrowly missed connecting on his first-ever deep launch in postseason play, but his Vikings were still able to end a two-game playoff losing streak thanks to the mercurial wideout they called "Gillie" and an unsung back known as "The Seed."

6

Fran's Colossal Catapult

Minnesota Vikings 27, Dallas Cowboys 10
December 30, 1973, Texas Stadium
NFC Championship Game

For more than 30 glorious minutes, it had the appearances of a rare stress-free playoff excursion for Bud Grant's Vikings.

But as President Theodore Roosevelt once famously said, "*Nothing worth having comes easy.*"

Following Dallas wide receiver Golden Richards's scintillating 63-yard punt return for a touchdown, the hosts, after being thoroughly dominated and shut out in the first half by an intent-on-mayhem Minnesota Vikings squad, suddenly trailed by just three early in the third quarter of the NFC championship game at gleaming, three-year-old Texas Stadium.

Thomas Paine once wrote of the trials and hardships of the American Revolution, "*These are the times that try men's souls.*"[1]

Richards's dash down the left sideline to make it a 10–7 game was a sign the metallic-silver-and-white-clad Cowboys, not the Redcoats, were coming.

Paine continued, "*Tyranny, like hell, is not easily conquered.*" Nor were the Dallas Cowboys, as the Vikings found out the hard way in a divisional-round playoff game that ruined their Christmas in 1971.

Answering Richards's volley would be an unbroken and insouciant Francis Asbury Tarkenton, who, despite playing in his first NFC championship game, proceeded to reach back for a little something extra, an unexpected salvo.

With the crowd of 60,272 in full throat after Richards's TD, the former University of Georgia and Athens (Georgia) High School star answered Dallas's score with the kind of prodigious heave that may even have impressed the impetuous former Minnesota head man Norm Van Brocklin, who would often grizzle over his former pupil's "suspect" arm strength.

Three plays after Richards's dash, Tarkenton called for a deep post to John Gilliam, stalked like a fugitive most of the day by Dallas star corner Mel Renfro.

Stepping into the throw from his own 40, Tarkenton who, after separating his shoulder his junior year in high school football never quite had the same arm, launched a ball likely farther or at least equal to any of his career. Getting every ounce out of his 6–0, 190-pound frame, he heaved the ball 55 yards in the air.

Cleanly beating the Hall of Famer Renfro, Gilliam caught the projectile somewhat in stride at the Dallas five. Cornell Green, late arriving from his safety position, could only look on as Gilliam, sporting a white No. 42 on his purple mesh Vikings jersey, jubilantly crossed the goal line to give Minnesota back its 10-point cushion.

"That's as far as Fran Tarkenton can throw a ball," a smiling Tarkenton told the *Minneapolis Tribune* in the postgame locker room.²

"It was a rainbow pattern," said Grant. "I mean the trajectory and what was on the end of it. He threw it that far. I thought the ball would never come down."³

"That was the most critical play," said Dallas coach Tom Landry. "We were only down 10–7, the crowd was catching fire and then the long pass took everything away."⁴

"Man, it was beautiful coming down. No way I was going to drop that one like in the Washington game," said Gilliam of his near miss of a Tarkenton deep ball on the Vikings' third play from scrimmage in the first-round win over the Redskins. "I gave another burst and there it was."⁵

Despite the Purple People Eaters limiting Roger Staubach to the worst effort of his career (10 of 21 passing for 89 yards, four interceptions, three sacks), the NFC East Division champs would later pull within seven points, but the Vikings enjoyed full control the rest of the way, easily winning 27–10 to earn their second trip to the Super Bowl.

*"Yet we have this consolation with us, that the harder the conflict, the more glorious the triumph."*⁶

Tarkenton led his Athens High School football team to a state title in 1955, trouncing perennial national power Valdosta 41–20 in the championship game at Sanford Stadium. During their undefeated season—"that had to be the best high school football team in history," said Tarkenton—the indomitable junior separated his throwing shoulder. Unable to throw the ball over 10 yards, he threw only one pass in the title game, which dropped incomplete.

"I could easily throw the ball 75 yards when I was 15 years old," he said. "The injury modified my ability to do many of the things I would like to have done. I played with that bad shoulder for the rest of my career. Fifty-five yards became my maximum.

"When I got out of football, after my 18th year, three years later I had shoulder replacement," added Tarkenton, who at 84 still goes into the office every day at Tarkenton Financial in Atlanta. "I've never heard of a quarterback—and I've asked a lot of them—if they ever had to have their shoulder replaced. Never heard of one who had. I did that as a junior, then I hurt my elbow during the spring in baseball. I could really throw it—we didn't have [radar] guns back then but the Detroit Tigers drafted me—but I couldn't throw a baseball at all after that. I never pitched an inning past my junior year. I played second because I couldn't throw. It would have called for Tommy John surgery but they didn't have that back then. Luckily that didn't hurt my throwing the football but the shoulder separation did."

In a testimony to his raw, unbridled determination, Tarkenton, despite his throwing abilities being hampered from that point on, was still able to walk away from his pro career the NFL all-time leader in passing yards (47,003) and touchdown passes (342).

"Sometimes, reflecting back on many games and key plays brings me painful memories," he said. "I just could not make every throw necessary to make the play successful. I never threw with the same intensity after that injury.⁷

"I go through college with it and my first 10 years in pro football the farthest I could throw it was 55 yards," Tarkenton added. "My last three years I could only throw it 40 yards. My last year [1978] I still led the league in passing yards [3,468 and tied for third in touchdowns with 25]. I did that when I couldn't throw it over 40 yards. When I went to New York, they would shoot me up on Friday with the stuff you shoot up horses with [Butazolidin]. They did that for the last two or three years of my Giants career and I was still able to throw for 47,003 yards, a record which held up nearly 20 years. I beat Unitas's record [40,239 yards] and he was terrific. How I threw for that many touchdowns and that many yards in pro football with that shoulder I'll never know."

Jerry Reichow, the former star Iowa quarterback who later become the team's only scout, caught 19 touchdown passes during his four-year career with the Vikings, the majority from Tarkenton.

"I could throw the ball left-handed further than him," laughed Reichow. "But Tarkenton and Van Brocklin both had that touch. Fran would throw it before you looked and it was right there. It was floated in. I once threw it 80 yards in a passing competition, but Fran knew where it was going. I didn't know where mine might end up. I never had a quarterback coach in high school, college or the pros, so I'm just throwing the ball hard. I didn't know how to take anything off. He was great at that, and great at moving around."

Another what legends-are-made-of event in Tarkenton's career occurred 15 years earlier in Austin, Texas.

Its unfolding was so extraordinary that, without its occurrence, Tarkenton may never have played a single down in pro football, let alone go on to bedazzle defensive linemen such as the Rams' Deacon Jones and Merlin Olsen, players he wore out by scrambling for a breathtaking 12 seconds before finding Reichow for a 57-yard scoring pass down the right sideline in a 27–24 loss to the Rams at the Los Angeles Coliseum on October 10, 1963.

"It took about an hour, it seemed like," laughed Reichow. "The guy that was covering me was exhausted from chasing me. I just got up in the air enough, and got my hand in there against the defender, and after I caught it there was no one there [behind me]. He was something else, Tarkenton. He knew when to throw it, and if you weren't there you were in trouble. I remember we were playing the Colts, and their great end [Gino] Marchetti grabbed me once when Tarkenton was scrambling and he said, 'Tell that little son of a bitch to quit running around. It's hotter than hell and I'm tired.'"

After leading the frosh team to an undefeated season during an era where freshmen could not play varsity, Tarkenton entered his sophomore year at the University of Georgia with high hopes. However, strong-willed head coach Wally Butts's full intention was to "redshirt" Tarkenton.

Knowing Butts's disdain for utilizing underclassmen on varsity, it wasn't surprising when Georgia opened the 1958 season at No. 11 Texas that "[my] name didn't appear on the depth chart, nor was I announced by the public address announcer or listed in the program," Tarkenton recalled.[8]

By late in the third quarter none of that would matter because a frantic offensive series that began after a Longhorn punt was downed at the Bulldogs' five served to truly launch Tarkenton's career.

A fidgety Tarkenton, who until then was desperately pacing the Georgia sideline as his team trailed 7–0 and had yet to record a first down with a scuffling Charlie Britt running the team, tells two versions of what happened next.

In *No Time for Losing*, written in 1967, Tarkenton, technically the third-stringer behind Britt and Tommy Lewis, said he yelled to Butts, "Let me go in now! Let me go in now!"[9]

Forty years later, in *Every Day Is Game Day*, he said, "I noticed that Charlie is still sitting on the bench, slow to get up and back onto the field. When I saw that, something just clicked inside me and I went in! I entered the huddle and everybody was confused, asking what was going on. I said, 'Let's go. We're going down the field!'"[10]

Tarkenton's racing onto the field landed him full face in the limelight, and what followed was evidence of the heart of the man.

What Tarkenton initiated may not have been the longest scoring drive in the history of college football, but there was likely no other series of downs that more displayed, more manifested or more broadcast the will, the drive and the moxie of the unassailable man who piloted it.

Picking a lifeless offense up from its bootstraps, Tarkenton escorted Georgia on an ineffable 21-play, 95-yard scoring march that fully displayed all the abilities he would put on stage during an NFL career that saw him make the Pro Bowl nine times.

Not the possessor of great speed, he ran eight times, three times for clutch first downs.

On his first collegiate carry, on a third-and-three, he tripped behind the line of scrimmage but terrifically collected himself and stumbled around right end for the needed yards. The second first-down effort was to the same side, a dash he finished off by running out of bounds before leaping over some pads and into a crowd of players near the Bulldogs bench. Gathering him up after the five-yard run that advanced the ball to the Georgia 39, his teammates must have wondered, "What type of man is this?"

Not the possessor of a big arm, he connected on three of four passes, each of which came from different angles and foot placement.

On his first throw on the Bulldog varsity, coming from his own 45 on third and two, a Texas linebacker came clean on a blitz and forcefully corralled him by the jersey near the shoulder pads, only to see Tarkenton determinedly balloon a completely flat-footed lob pass to the left flat that George Whitton caught for a first down.

Operating out of Georgia's full-house backfield, he on numerous times caught Texas off-balance with his masterful ball-handling and creative play-calling skills, twice calling for draw plays to fullback Theron Sapp, the second going for nine yards on a key third-and-seven call from the Texas 14 following his only incompletion.

Three plays later, facing a third-and-two at the Texas two, the right-handed Tarkenton rolled left, was quickly chased down by two defenders, but threw *from behind his body* to the back of the end zone to Jimmy Vickers, who made a leaping catch. Eschewing the point after, he then rolled right before throwing *across his body* back to Whitton for the go-ahead two-point conversion to give the unbelieving Bulldogs an 8–7 lead.

Both tosses came off one foot, as Tarkenton offered an early glimpse into his innate ability to make off-schedule throws from not only different arm slots but varied feet placements, rare traits seen in modern-day playmakers such Patrick Mahomes.

"In compensating for my shoulder injury, I learned how to protect the ball and become comfortable running the bootleg," said Tarkenton. "I adapted by throwing the short pass, running the ball. And keeping control of the football."[11]

Butts, who inexplicably had Tarkenton back on the bench for Georgia's next series, was nevertheless impressed.

"I never saw a more beautifully conducted drive than the one Tarkenton guided to a touchdown. He mixed the plays to perfection."[12]

Texas immediately answered Georgia's TD to go up 14–8, and with five minutes left Britt reentered the contest.

"With the eyes of Texas upon him, the 182-pound Athens lad put the bite into the Bulldogs who had been doing nothing but barking at the moon against the University of Texas Longhorns," said *Columbus Ledger* columnist Cecil Darby.[13]

"His best assets are his desire and enthusiasm," said Georgia quarterback coach Johnny Rauch. "His spirit seems to overflow the whole squad."[14]

"I created that [drive] in my heart and soul. I think about my life, if I don't force myself onto the field and have that sense of desperation that night, I may have never played college football again, let alone pro football," said Tarkenton, who 15 years later, in the same state, displayed the same dogged determination against not the Texas Longhorns but the Dallas Cowboys.

• • •

For the Vikings, the win over despised Dallas, a team they thoroughly resented due to its "America's Team" moniker, was truly a glorious triumph. By all accounts, it may have been a Grant squad's best overall playoff performance.

Gilliam, a student of the game, noticed a Dallas tendency on defense the Vikings could use to their advantage.

"I called that play," said Gilliam of the long-scoring toss from Tarkenton that turned the tide. "They couldn't get me open because they were double-teaming me. They'd roll the zone to my side and Mel Renfro would come up in the bump and run. I told Francis on the sideline, 'Put me in the slot and run the 35 pitch to Chuck [Foreman].' They were being very aggressive. They knew they had to take me and Foreman out of the game. I noticed on that pitch play that they'd run right by me. I told Fran run the pitch and don't tell Foreman you're going to throw. I ran right by the safety.

"They didn't even look at me," he said with a smile. "Fran told me to go deep and cut inside Renfro. Green came over but he was a second too late. I had to wait on the ball. I was acting like I was going to block and just took off. Francis threw a great pass. I beat the ball like 20 yards. By the time the ball got there, they were waving at the ball. On deep balls I told Francis, 'Throw the ball at 10 yards.' If he waited till 20 yards, it was too late."[15]

Tarkenton had a different version of his game-changing heave.

"I don't know where John Gilliam came up with that," laughed Tarkenton. "He had great speed and he ran a post route down the middle of the field and was pretty much open. John Gilliam never came back to me in the four years he was with me and say, 'I can get open on this pattern or that pattern.'

"I remember that play like it was yesterday," Tarkenton continued. "We really had great talent on that team. Back in those days, Tom Landry ran both the offense and defense. He'd play four down linemen and if you'd split your running backs, he'd adjust to that and if you had a fullback behind you, he'd adjust and so on. As great as a defensive mind that he was, I was able to figure out what he was going to do by my formation. That enabled me to have an edge on him when I was going to throw it and when I was going to run it and where. He was a very scientific. He would stagger his ends, with one off the line and one on it. By formation I could buy a little more time to throw it and be able to run it a little better, too. The thing about Landry that was so great was he never changed how he ran the defense. I thought that gave me an advantage. I called the plays, Jerry Burns put in the offensive game plan, but I'd put in the pass offense. It just shows planning helps you to execute better."

Minnesota opened the game at its own 25 and proceeded to go on a beautifully

6. Fran's Colossal Catapult

conceived drive lasting nearly nine minutes. The result was only a 44-yard Fred Cox field goal after Oscar Reed's eight-yard TD run was called back due to a holding penalty on right tackle Ron Yary.

Minnesota easily controlled both sides of the football throughout the game, having no issues either running the ball—All-Pro Bob Lilly was out due to an injury—or shutting down a Dallas running attack without the services of leading rusher Calvin Hill, who dislocated his elbow late in his team's 27–16 divisional-round playoff win over the Rams. The franchise's first 1,000-yard rusher, Hill totaled 1,142 yards rushing and six TDs in '73. His replacement was Robert Newhouse, who finished the contest with just 50 yards on 14 carries.

Another long Vikings drive followed the Cowboys' second straight three-and-out to start the game. This time Minnesota cashed in, scoring on a five-yard run around right end by Foreman behind key blocks from Yary, guard Ed White and tight end Stu Voigt to make it 10–0. This march lasted just more than six minutes.

The running game was dominant. Foreman, who had 70 yards rushing by halftime, finished with 76 yards, while Reed tallied 75.

"Oscar was a good mentor, and he was a very smooth runner," said Foreman. "He was always ready to play despite being rotated with Bill Brown and Dave Osborn. He was

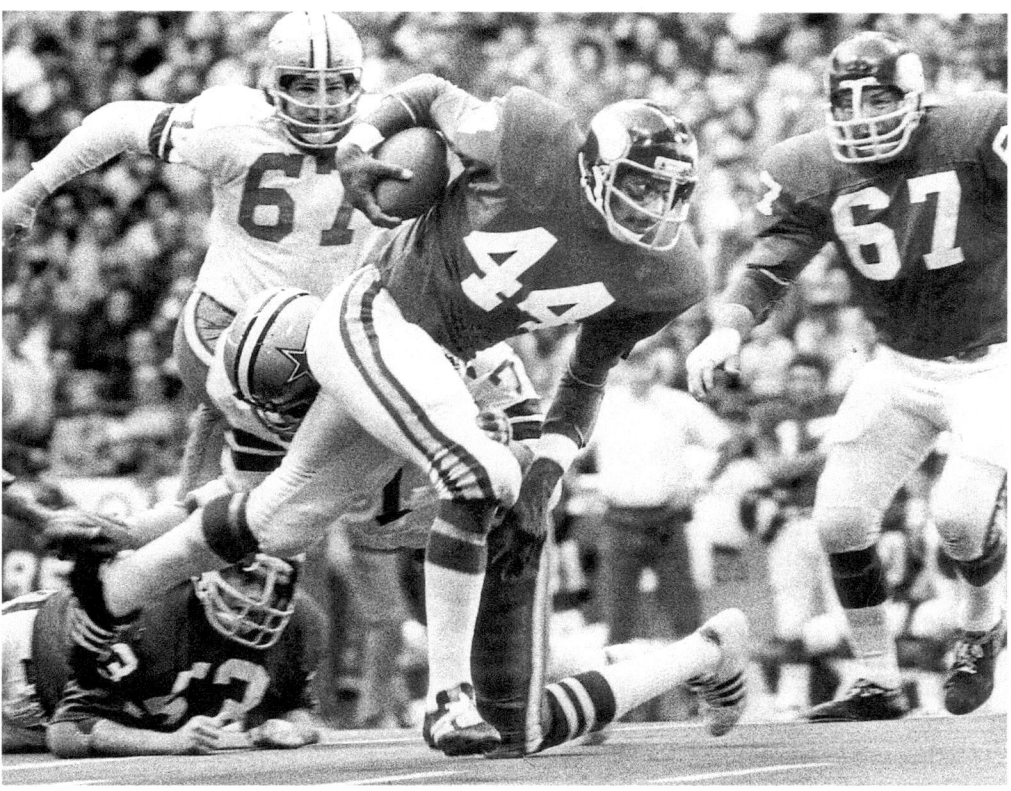

Minnesota Vikings running back Chuck Foreman (44) breaks through the line on a carry as left tackle Grady Alderman (67) looks on during a 27–10 win over the Dallas Cowboys in the NFC championship game on December 30, 1973, at Texas Stadium in Irving, Texas. A Pro Bowl selection as a rookie, Foreman finished the regular season with 801 yards rushing.

a very even-tempered kind of guy. Kind of a guy that settled me down a bit because I was kind of like the Energizer Bunny most of the time."

Foreman and Reed, taking advantage of newly installed misdirection plays by offensive coordinator Jerry Burns, helped Minnesota amass 205 yards rushing on 47 carries, while Dallas had just 90 on 25 carries. Advancing to its first Super Bowl in three years, Minnesota doubled up the Cowboys in yardage, 306 to 153.

"I know they used the flex defense, so it gave us the opportunity to do some different things," Foreman added. "And you got Ron Yary out there and he and Ed White doing what they do. It was a run-dominant game at that time. It was about clock management; that's the way we played the game. Having near 100 yards was a big deal."

"It was the first time we saw some of those traps and some of that kind of blocking," said a beleaguered Dallas tackle Jethro Pugh. "They were pulling people in front of us and sending them the other way, and then coming back at us with the backs. Other teams had done it, but nobody as well as the Vikings."[16]

All told, it was a masterful game plan by Burns.

"He gave the Cowboys first-down passes, play-action passes, rollouts, misdirection plays and double fakes," wrote veteran *Minneapolis Star* reporter Jim Klobuchar. "He went early to Carroll Dale, Stu Voigt and Chuck Foreman to remind the Dallas defense he had more than Gilliam to shoot for."[17]

With the Vikings up 10–0 in the third, Dallas threatened but Bobby Bryant intercepted a pass at his own two. That was good and bad as Minnesota, unable to drive out of the shadow of its own goalposts, had to call on Eischeid to punt from his own end line and Richards returned the punt for a TD to make it 10–7.

"Mike just out-kicked the coverage," said Grant. "We couldn't get anyone down there quick enough."[18]

That set the stage for Tarkenton's all-he-could-give heave to Gilliam to give the Vikings back their 10-point cushion.

After Dallas cut the lead to 17–10 in the third quarter on a Toni Fritsch FG, Bryant deftly jumped a sideline route intended for Bob Hayes and took the interception back 63 yards to give the Vikings a 24–10 bulge.

Jeff Wright's interception later in the quarter set up Cox's 34-yarder to make it 27–10. The closest Dallas came to scoring again was after it recovered a fumbled punt by Bryant inside the 20. The Cowboys drove to the Vikings' five only to have Walt Garrison fumble and tackle Gary Larsen gather in the recovery. The Vikings proceeded to grind out the final five minutes.

Extricated out of their '72 doldrums by the likes of the rookie Foreman, the jubilant Vikings were headed to another Super Bowl.

"Chuck Foreman had that extra move you don't teach—you have to be born with it," said Miami head coach Fran Curci of the 1986 inductee into the Hurricane HOF. During his time at Miami from 1970 to 1972, Foreman was used at cornerback, tight end, wide receiver and running back.

"I could have been a Pro Bowler in the NFL at all those positions," said Foreman. "My commitment to being the best was up there. I worked hard at it."

"Before he became star running back of the Minnesota Vikings, Chuck Foreman hardly did any running of all," wrote *New York Daily News* columnist Dick Young before the Vikings met Miami in Super Bowl VIII. "He was a defensive lineman and tight end in high school. Of his three years of varsity ball at U. of Miami, only his junior year was spent at running back. As a soph he was a cornerman on defense; as a senior a wide receiver. If football were played like baseball, Foreman could do what Bert Campaneris did (on Sept. 8, 1965 vs. the California Angels); play an inning at each position."[19]

It's not difficult to envision Foreman being a brutish corner, ala Mel Blount; a rangy, shorter version of Kellen Winslow at tight end; and a sturdy but fluid wideout, like his teammate of four years, the talented Ahmad Rashad.

Curci took over as head coach at Miami for the 1971 season and switched Foreman to running back. That season, Foreman combined with teammate Tom Sullivan to form a running back tandem nicknamed the "Gold Dust Twins" due to their running abilities. It was Foreman's finest statistical season as a ballcarrier, as he rushed 191 times for 951 yards. He also caught seven passes for 72 yards and was named a first-team All-American by the *Sporting News*.

Foreman transitioned to wide receiver his senior season, learning techniques that would help him become a remarkable multipurpose back in Minnesota. That year he had 484 yards on 107 carries, and 557 yards on 37 receptions.

After starring in the backfield in several All-Star games following his senior year, there was no doubt Foreman would eventually land at running back in the NFL. But it was a little shaky at first, he recalled.

"I got comfortable playing the running back position in those all-star games I played in," he said. "Then I get to Minnesota and I'm getting ready to line up in the two-back [set]—we called it two back and three back—two back being running back, three back being fullback. And I'm finding myself as the three back or fullback and I'm upset. Oscar Reed came to talk to me; he was the guy who could kind of calm me down. It got back to Bud that I wasn't too happy about the fact that he moved me to fullback. But I realized that the fullback position was where they could pretty much create an offense to suit my talents. He called me in there and said, 'If you come in here and do what you're capable of doing, you'll be really special.' I get up and I'm feeling good about it and he said, 'And, oh, nobody will recognize it because they'll just recognize your running stats.' He and Burns created the position 'runner-receiver.' That's what I played."

Foreman was the AP Offensive Rookie of the Year in '73, a major reason Minnesota earned the title-game trip to meet the Cowboys.

• • •

A game-breaking receiver in the similitude of Gene Washington whose time in purple was also shorter than Vikings fans would have liked, Gilliam came to the team during the 1972 offseason in a trade involving quarterback Gary Cuozzo. It may have been the most lopsided trade favoring the Vikings in team history as Gilliam made the Pro Bowl each of his four years in Minnesota.

During the '73 season, he averaged 21.6 yards on 42 receptions, good for 907 yards and eight TDs. He gave the team a virtually unparalleled combination at the skills positions when the multifaceted Foreman arrived out of the University of Miami in that year's draft.

Drafted in the second round in '67 by New Orleans, Gilliam will be forever remembered as the man who ran back the first opening kickoff in Saints history 94 yards for a TD. But, as destiny would have it, his time was short-lived in New Orleans, spanning just two years before he was traded away in 1969 to the St. Louis Cardinals for end Dave Long and a second-round draft pick.

"This was the '60s. Remember, this was during the Civil Rights Movement. They didn't want to wait on us," said Gilliam. "They had me at flanker and a good tight end named Jim Hester [out of North Dakota]. Later they had split end [1970 first-round pick from Texas Southern] Ken Burrough—now he could run a fly. We just didn't have a quarterback. We had Gary Cuozzo, Billy Kilmer and Gary Wood. The first ball I touched for them I ran back for a touchdown. They thought I would be bigger than the team and a problem in the locker room because I became famous so quick.

"They just had some bad actors, some bad talent scouts that were working for the Saints," Gilliam added. "[Team owner] John Mecom, Jr., was just a young guy, about 27 years old. His dad bought the team for him. He had no idea how to run a team or anything. They just brought a lot of bums in, from the GM down. They spent too much money on veteran guys like Paul Hornung [retired before playing with the Saints] and Jim Taylor, who only stayed for a year, instead of building around [young] guys."

As great as Gilliam was, he's widely ignored in the recounting of NFL history despite his four Pro Bowl appearances. The disrespect was even evidenced on draft day in 1967 as Gilliam wasn't chosen by the Saints until 52nd overall.

Not surprisingly, Washington, whom Gilliam played with one year with the Vikings, was the first wide receiver taken in that '67 draft, going eighth overall. On paper, the two could have been a dynamic duo in '72 but it never materialized as Washington was plagued by injury most of Gilliam's first season in Minnesota.

Head scratching was the fact that also selected ahead of the 6–1, 195-pounder were the University of Washington's Dave Williams (16th overall by St. Louis), Oregon State's Bob Grim (second round, 28th overall by Minnesota), San Diego State's Bob Jones (second round, 36th by Chicago) and Duke's Dave Dunaway (second round, 41st by Green Bay). Without doubt, Williams and Grim both had solid careers but neither changed games in the same fashion as Gilliam, who finished his 12-year career with 7,056 yards receiving and 50 TDs, two of those as a kick returner. His 48 TD receptions are the same amount Drew Pearson posted during his HOF career.

One of the reasons Gilliam went reasonably low in the draft is he didn't start playing football until his senior year at Brewer High School in Greenwood, South Carolina. He then joined head coach Willie Jeffries at South Carolina State, a school that produced the likes of Deacon Jones, Harry Carson, Donnie Shell and Marion Motley.

Gilliam started just six games in two seasons with the Saints, posting 46 catches before being traded to the Cardinals.

"The second-round pick they got for me [from the Cards] they used to get Richard Neal, a good defensive end out of Southern," said Gilliam. "They ran him off, too." Neal, drafted 45th overall by the Saints in 1969, was shipped to the New York Jets four years later. He had a solid career, starting 96 games over 10 seasons.

It was in St. Louis in '69 where Gilliam's career took flight as quarterbacks Charley Johnson and Jim Hart were not shy about throwing the deep ball. He had a career-best nine TDs catches that first year, with a whopping 997 yards receiving and 19.2 yards per catch.

With Hart taking over full-time in 1970, Gilliam totaled 952 yards receiving and five scores. His 21.2 YPC was the best of his time with the Big Red, who gained national attention that season by walloping the eventual NFC champion Dallas Cowboys 38–0 on *Monday Night Football*.

"He threw a sweet ball," said Gilliam of Johnson. "He was one of the greatest quarterbacks I played with. And Jim Hart could also throw the ball well. Francis threw a good ball, too, a catchable ball. I give him credit. Charley had a good career, but he wasn't really into football. He was trying to be a major in the military. He'd spend Monday through Wednesday with the military, come back Thursday and play on Sunday. When Jim Hart took over, they sent Charley to Houston [in 1970]."

That trade sent backup quarterback Pete Beathard and cornerback Miller Farr to the Cards as Johnson reunited with his old coach Wally Lemm, who had returned to the Houston franchise he piloted to the American Football League championship in 1961.

The Vikings once had significant interest in Hart, who had a prolific career at Southern Illinois.

"He wasn't even drafted," said Reichow, shaking his head. "I went to Southern Illinois and I talked to the coach [Don Shroyer], and I said, 'Who's that quarterback?' He said, 'He throws the ball pretty well but he can't play.' There were three or four other scouts there. That's why he wasn't drafted because he told everyone else that, too. I guess we were all wrong."

Hart set the school passing record with 3,779 yards and played 18 seasons for the Cardinals. He was selected to the Pro Bowl four times (1974–77) and was named NFC Player of the Year in 1974.

The *MNF* win over the Cowboys marked the team's third-straight shutout as the Cardinals looked like a sure bet to capture the NFC East when they ventured to Municipal Stadium to play the reigning NFL champion Kansas City Chiefs. The Big Red played the Chiefs toe-to-toe, coming away with a 6–6 tie to move to 7–2–1.

But Charlie Winner's crew collapsed down the stretch, dropping its final three games. The Cowboys, who fell twice to the Cardinals by a combined score of 58–7, won the divisional crown with a 10–4 mark, while the Cardinals had to settle for third place behind Tarkenton's upstart Giants, finishing a disappointing 8–5–1.

"As far as offensive talent, we had more in St. Louis then we had in Minnesota," said Gilliam, who now lives in Atlanta. "We had a great offensive line, guys like Irv Goode and Ernie McMillan, and all the running backs ... we were loaded. We had MacArthur Lane, Johnny Roland, Cid Edwards, Roy Shivers ... then they go out and draft Mel Gray [in 1971]. We didn't need any receivers. We already had Dave Williams, he was like 6–5 and could run the fly and Jackie Smith was a great player. We'd score so fast we'd put the defense right back on the field. We needed some linebackers and defensive ends. We couldn't stop nobody. We had Larry Wilson, Miller Farr, Larry Stallings and Roger Wehrli, who was a rookie that year, and pretty much nobody else. My wife could outrun our linebackers."

Safety Terry Brown, who played with Gilliam all four years in Minnesota, was the Cardinals' third-round draft pick in 1969 out of Oklahoma State.

"St. Louis had some really good talent but the difference in Minnesota is you had 40 guys pulling the same direction. There was nobody that was going the other direction. It's not all about talent," said Brown, who scored the Vikings' only TD in Super Bowl IX against Pittsburgh when he recovered a punt blocked by Matt Blair in the end zone. "No one cared who got the publicity. It was just win. Some of the guys in Minnesota were not great athletes but they just played like they were. You take guys like Grady Alderman and Roy Winston; they were just 6-foot. My gosh, these guys today are 6–6. It was just an attitude that the other team was going to eventually make a mistake. Some of it was about age. We were a veteran team. I mean these guys saw it all and knew how to handle things."

St. Louis' shocking late-season collapse led to the dismissal of Winner, who was replaced by Bob Hollway. A respected defensive coordinator under Grant with the Vikings, Hollway was a disastrous head coach, going 4–9–1 his two seasons in St. Louis.

Nevertheless, Hollway's being in St. Louis worked out extremely well for the Vikings. Needing another quarterback due to an injury to Hart, he helped precipitate the ill-fated Gilliam-for-Cuozzo trade.

"He's the one who shipped me out," said Gilliam of the former University of Michigan player and assistant coach. "First, when he got there, he tried to be Bud Grant and he couldn't. Wear our socks like Minnesota, the haircuts, the way we stood at the national anthem, the whole thing. The guys just didn't buy in."

Hollway's connection to Minnesota led to other Cardinals arriving in the Land of 10,000 Lakes. Was Grant allowing Hollway to go to St. Louis the ultimate chess move?

"Hollway was the reason I went to the Vikings," said Brown, who along with Gilliam was preceded in going to Minnesota by cornerback Nate Wright. "Karl Kassulke got hurt in '72 and they got me up there [off waivers] and I didn't even have to learn the playbook. It was the same. Hollway liked Grant, he liked the Vikings and Bud was in a bind. Hollway didn't seem to mind helping them out."

The great tight end Jackie Smith said the Cardinals were wondering what was up with Hollway sending players to his old club.

"We were surprised," said Smith on receiving mate Gilliam being shipped to Minnesota. "I remember when Hollway came, we were thinking is that guy a plant? Was he just working undercover as a Cardinals coach? It was different."

Gilliam almost didn't agree to go to the Vikings.

"I didn't want to go to Minnesota," said Gilliam. "It's too cold. When I was coming out of college I said, 'Please, don't let me get drafted by one of those teams in the Black and Blue Division,' Minnesota, Detroit, Chicago, Green Bay. I done watched them playing with smoke coming out of their mouths and I'd say, 'I can't play in this cold weather.'"

Gilliam remembers how the trade went down.

"I was at the barber getting a haircut and I come back home and my wife said, 'Coach Bud Grant called you.' I said, 'Minnesota? What did he want?'

"I called him and said, 'This is John Gilliam.' He said, 'Welcome to the Vikings, we traded for you.' I said, 'Hey, Coach, I'm not coming. It's too cold. I don't play in cold weather. Plus, there ain't no Black people up there. I don't see no Black folks in the stands when you-all play.' I kept trying to call the Cardinals to tell them I didn't want to go, and they never picked up the phone."

Two of Grant's greatest traits were straightforwardness and honesty. These were both displayed in his dealings with Gilliam.

"Bud was a great guy once I got to know him," Gilliam noted. "He said, 'Do me a favor—let me line you up for the weekend and let you see the city.'"

Gilliam agreed to make the trip and was greeted by a contingent of Black players from the Vikings, including Jim Marshall, Oscar Reed, Charlie West and Clint Jones, as well as University of Minnesota star quarterback Sandy Stephens, the first Black quarterback in college football to be named first-team All-American.

"They pick me up at the hotel and guess where they take me? To Saint Paul—that's where all the Black people are," he said with a smile. "They take me to a club. It was all up in there. 'This is not bad,' I thought. We had a good time. They took me to another club and I'm liking this. I said, 'I didn't know you had so many Blacks up here.' We got back at about 1:30. Bud calls me the next morning and asked me how it went. I said, 'I'll give it a shot.' They made me feel at home. I spent another four or five days there."

The rest, as they say, is history.

The best season of Gilliam's career came in his first year with the Vikings. He had 47 catches for a career-best 1,035 yards and led the league with 22.0 yards per catch. The team finished just 7–7 that year as it was not until Foreman's arrival that Burns had all the necessary pieces for greatness.

Gilliam's numbers with the Vikings dipped in '74, down to 26 catches for 578 yards and just five TDs, but he posted the best yards per catch of his career at 22.2 and helped the team to its second straight NFC championship and a trip to Tulane to play the Steelers in the Super Bowl.

He left after that season to play for the Chicago Wind of the World Football League, but his departure was short-lived.

"I had an option year, so I told Bud, 'I'm going to go get my money.' I told him I'd be back,'" said Gilliam. "Bud knew it [the WFL] wouldn't last. A lot of guys left the NFL, Jim Kiick, Paul Warfield, Larry Csonka … the WFL folded after five games, and I came back. When I came back, I signed just a one-year deal."

He made the Pro Bowl again in '75 after hauling in 50 receptions for 777 yards and seven TDs, but his career with Minnesota would end after the fateful December 28 Hail Mary loss to Dallas.

In a contract squabble with the notoriously spendthrift Vikings and General Manager Mike Lynn, Gilliam opted to join hometown Atlanta in 1976 and split the '77 season with Chicago and New Orleans, having come full circle.

"After the '75 season, I met with Lynn and he looked me right in the eye and said, 'I'm not going to give you another dime,'" Gilliam recalled. "I left right then to go home to Atlanta. I had a lot of teams interested in me, including the Rams and Detroit, but I signed with Atlanta because I had a shoe store there and I could do both."

Gilliam said he would have remained in Minnesota had the universally respected Jim Finks not left as Vikings GM following the '73 season.

"When I got to Minnesota, I met with Jim and he was a good man, down-to-earth. I said this is a good organization. This'll be a good spot for me. Jim was my man," said Gilliam. "I never leave the Vikings if he stays there. I retire as a Viking. He took a chance on me. I didn't want to let him down. When I left Atlanta, he brought me into Chicago [after Finks took the Bears job]. I was there two weeks and Jack Pardee said two words to me. I didn't like Pardee. I couldn't play for a coach I can't talk to. Bud had spoiled me."

• • •

The Purple People Eaters defense that picked off four Staubach passes and sacked him three times would have never come to full realization without a decision made by Jack Snow.

A native of Rock Springs, Wyoming, the glue-fingered receiver was an All-American for Notre Dame in 1964. The 6–2, 210-pounder finished second in the nation in receptions with 60 and fifth in the voting for the Heisman Trophy, won by his teammate John Huarte. The quarterback-receiver duo teamed to lead Notre Dame to a national title.

Snow was drafted eighth overall by the Vikings in '65 and in the seventh round by San Diego of the AFL. Snow grew up in California, where he played for Saint Anthony's Boy School in Long Beach. He told Finks his desire was to play in the NFL but specifically on the West Coast, preferably with the Los Angeles Rams.

The Apostle Paul said, "*All things work together for the good*," and it did in this case as the Vikings traded Snow to the Rams for veteran wide receiver Red Phillips and Larsen. Larsen, a 10th-round draft pick of the Rams in 1964, ended up a fixture in Minnesota, playing a steady 149 games for the Vikings over 10 seasons, while Snow had a great career in Los Angeles.

Larsen wreaked havoc on the interior line against the Cowboys, recovering two fumbles and jamming up the running lanes for Newhouse.

"That win over Dallas was right up there for me," said the 6–5, 265-pound Larsen. "But the games in our division stood out, too. We had to win our division first. You didn't need much incentive in wanting to beat Dallas though, with everyone talking about them as America's Team. I didn't think they were America's Team. I know no one on the Vikings thought that. I think the game in '71 was on the back of everyone's mind. You don't forget losses like that."

The trade to the Vikings was a dream come true for Larsen, who hails from north Minnesota, where he played football and basketball at tiny Concordia College. The Snow trade was not as favorable for his wife, Wende, a Los Angeles native Larsen met during his stint in the marines.

"They [the Rams] didn't ask me about [the trade], they just did it on their own," said Larsen. "It worked out great for me, but my wife wasn't too happy about it. Most of the time when I was growing up, the Chicago Bears were on TV in our area. When I got to the marines and played football for them, that's when the Minnesota franchise came into existence. I was playing for the El Toro Marines and when they announced Minnesota had a franchise, I said, 'That's great, I can play for them.' All my teammates with the marines poked fun at me for even thinking such a dumb thing. When it turned out I got to play for the Vikings, I got a letter from my football coach in the marines and he congratulated me. He said, 'I guess you lived up to your expectations.'"

Phillips, who joined Paul Flatley at wide receiver, played three seasons in Minnesota, accounting for 1,091 yards and seven TDs on his 68 receptions.

The Vikings had high hopes Flatley's sidekick would be Snow, who played 11 seasons in the NFL, all with the Rams. He finished his career with 340 receptions, 6,012 yards and 45 touchdowns.

Two selections after Snow, the Vikings drafted another nifty receiver who didn't finish his career with the team, Oklahoma's versatile 9.9 sprinter Lance Rentzel. Originally drafted as a running back, the 6–2, 210-pound Rentzel was traded to the Cowboys due to off-the-field issues two years later. Ironically, his last NFL appearance was the '74 NFC title game at Minnesota when he suited up for Snow's Los Angeles Rams.

The Vikings learned their lesson from the Snow draft snafu when it came time to make the first overall selection in the 1968 draft.

"The day of the draft, Bud Grant called me at seven in the morning," recalled Yary. "He said, 'Ron, we're thinking about drafting you with the first pick. We need to find out if we draft you, do you want to play for the Vikings?' I said yes. It was an honor, but it was also a statement for me to do well. I didn't want to let people down. It was a statement of expectation."

Yary was joined by White the next season, giving the Vikings two players who brought a defense-like mentality to the offensive side of the football. Their skills were honed each day in practice as they faced a defensive line group that now had all the requisite pieces.

At nearly 6–6, Larsen added to a formidable front as Carl Eller and Marshall were already in the fold upon his arrival in '65. Alan Page would come onto the scene two years later via another Vikings-Rams trade. Los Angeles sent its 15th pick in the '67 draft and Marlin McKeever to the Vikings for Tommy Mason, Hal Bledsoe and a '67 second-round pick (Willie Ellison). The Vikings used the 15th pick to select Page.

"I fit in pretty well," said Larsen, who laughed about the idea that he gained his prodigious strength from throwing hay bales on trucks while growing up on his grandfather's farm in neighboring North Dakota. "Eller was 6–6, and Page and Marshall both about 6–4. We were all about the same height. When Page came in you didn't know for sure how things would turn out because there's a big difference from college to pro ball, but we kind of crossed our fingers that it would work out and it surely did."

Despite the Purple People Eaters coming from diverse backgrounds—Eller from North Carolina, Marshall and Page from Ohio and Larsen from Minnesota—it was a close-knit unit.

"I think I can speak for the other guys and say it was never Black and White, it was purple," he added. "It was a team. It wouldn't have worked without Page. It wouldn't have worked without Eller or Marshall, and I guess you could say it wouldn't have worked without me. As a unit we knew how to play together and how to cover for each other."

"The mindset in that Vikings huddle was somebody has got to make a play," added Brown, who never played safety full-time before coming to the NFL. "It didn't matter who it was, just somebody. We felt that every time they called the defense that somebody was going to make a big play to stop the drive. I don't know if I ever saw a fight or anything the years I was with the Vikings. Everybody just wanted one thing—to win."

Larsen came close to landing in Kansas City.

"After I was drafted by the Rams, Hank Stram called me and wanted me to play for the Chiefs," he said. "Stram said he would beat anything they paid me. If it weren't for my wife, I probably would have gone there."

Larsen was named to the Pro Bowl in 1969 and 1970. In '70, the entire Western Conference Pro Bowl front four was Vikings.

"I was an injury replacement for Merlin Olsen," said Larsen. "It was an honor to play. I remember hearing the public address announcer at the Coliseum saying, 'Now playing the front line [for the Western squad] are the Purple People Eaters.' That was a thrill."

Pulling everything together was the job of defensive line coach Jack Patera, who also coached Larsen with the Rams. "We loved playing for him," said Larsen. "He had a way of coaching us that the players loved.

"I always thought the other guys were faster than me, so I was kind of left behind," added Larsen, known as the line's "policeman" due to his willingness to sit back for screens and draws. "That's why they called me that. But I was never asked to 'spy' a player like [Roger] Staubach. It just worked out that way with our four guys."

Larsen said he had no concerns about the Vikings after they finished just 3–8–3 in Grant's first year.

"It just took some time for his system to get into place," said Larsen. "He was completely different than Van Brocklin. You had to do things a certain way under Grant. That didn't bother me having served three years in the marines. Once we got everyone going with the new system, it was great to see."

Foreman agreed.

"Bud Grant was the best coach to play for at that time," said Foreman. "I don't know if he was ahead of his time or not, but he treated people the way they were supposed to be treated as far as the football field goes. Everybody was equal."

"Bud kept everything on an even keel," added Larsen. "He didn't get really, really high if we won or really, really down if we lost. He kept a happy medium, which played off on the team. It's a hard game. If you win, great. If you lose, you just must realize you gave it your best. That was our mindset."

• • •

An interesting anomaly in the Cowboys game saw the Vikings for the first time in their playoff history wear purple mesh jerseys with no trim on the white numbers and no sleeve stripes. However, a few of the starters (Larsen, Jeff Siemon and Page) somehow managed to sport the mesh versions during the previous week's win over Washington.

Dennis Ryan replaced Stubby Eason as Minnesota's equipment manager in 1980 and stayed in the role for nearly 50 years. He got to know the team jersey better than anyone alive.

"What happened against Washington [players wearing nonmatching jerseys] would never happen today—they'd be all over you in social media," said Ryan, who started working for the Vikings part-time in 1975 as a junior in high school. "The reason there was no sleeve stripe on the jersey we wore against Dallas was that it was a mesh fabric. The home jersey was cloth, a heavier fabric which didn't breathe as much. It was a nylon durene, a knit fabric [that consisted of two fabrics plaited together: an outer nylon or rayon and an inner layer of cotton]. When they first came out with the mesh fabric, they couldn't weave our jersey stripe on it, which at home was a Northwestern stripe and the road a UCLA stripe. It was based on the uniform design of the college team."

Paul Lukas said players wearing mismatched jerseys wasn't so rare during this less-structured era of the NFL.

"In the late '60s and early '70s, NFL teams would have two sets of jerseys. One was a lighter weight for use normally in warmer weather or just the player preferred the lighter-weight jersey," said Lukas, host of the popular website uni-watch.com. "Those lighter-weight jerseys tended not to have the full graphics. They might not have sleeve stripes, they might not have shoulder stripes, the name on the back might be in a more simplistic font. That all varied by team. There just wasn't as much uniformity in those days. If you look at game footage, you would see a lot of teams had this kind of thing going on, especially early in the season and the preseason when it was warmer and the players would want to wear those lighter-weight jerseys. Not only because it was warmer, but because some teams wanted to save the wear and tear on their regular jerseys. Sometimes they wouldn't even put their helmet decals or logo decals on the side of the helmets during the preseason to save this wear and tear."

6. Fran's Colossal Catapult

Ryan said it took a while for teams to figure out how to best use the mesh jerseys.

"They sewed the numbers on the cloth jerseys but screen printed them on the mesh ones," he said. "It took a couple years for them to figure out you could screen print the sleeve stripe just like you did the number. That's when the cotton jerseys started going away."

Osborn loved the lighter-weight jersey, but he said nothing could beat the heavier versions the team wore earlier in his career.

"Stubby was a piece of work," laughed Osborn. "What happened [in the playoff game] against the Redskins isn't that surprising. Those older jerseys were great. I still have about two or three of them, including one with the NFL 50th anniversary patch. They were heavy—no one was going to tear one of those. They were like putting on a darned jacket. The mesh ones were like a breath of fresh air, but in the winter, you couldn't beat the other ones."

"Nylon durene could be kind of heavy," agreed Lukas. "When it was wet it didn't dry very easily. It didn't breathe very much. It was kind of stretchy, which was good for pulling over shoulder pads. There was one great picture of Joe Kapp in Super Bowl IV where a Kansas City defender had his jersey stretched out what seemed like three feet. The durene wasn't exactly athletic-performance fabric so you started seeing a lot of teams go to a mesh jersey in the '70s. They even quit sewing the numbers on and having them screen printed."

With the Vikings dressed to kill in their purple mesh jerseys and helmets sparkling from the afternoon sun streaming through Texas Stadium's gaudy roof, it was truly a game for the ages against a team with a much-resented nickname, and it was Francis Asbury Tarkenton, pulling from resources deep within, who found a streaking Gilliam for a scoring play that beat back the Vikings' perennial playoff bully.

> *"I love the man that smiles at trouble: that can gather strength from distress, and grow brave by reflection."*
> —Thomas Paine.[20]

7

Nate's Scoop and Score

Minnesota Vikings 30, St. Louis Cardinals 14
December 21, 1974, Metropolitan Stadium
Divisional-Round Playoff

Minnesota Vikings fans should know their Bibles well. For these long-suffering saints, the Book of Job would be a good place to start.

Offering the most comfort during the most difficult day of Nate Wright's 13-year National Football League career as well as the lowest point in team history—December 28, 1975—was a man who knew about painful moments.

In his 20-year NFL career, Jim Marshall started 270 straight games and appeared in 292 consecutive contests—both still records for defensive players. Like the standout left cornerback Wright, he understood what it was like to have a lengthy career whittled down to a single play.

In a sloppy October 25, 1964, game against the San Francisco 49ers at Kezar Stadium, Marshall scooped up a fumble by 49ers running back Billy Kilmer (the former Saints and Redskins quarterback) and sprinted toward daylight. Despite Fran Tarkenton desperately trying to get his attention from the sideline, Marshall proceeded untouched to the wrong end zone, where he tossed the ball away and scored two points for the 49ers.

History's postscript was that the Vikings won that game.

Most have forgotten.

Marshall was consoling the Vikings defensive back because he had just been involved in one of the NFL's epochal plays—the 50-yard Hail Mary pass from Roger Staubach to Drew Pearson with 32 seconds left that went for a score to beat what many consider the best Vikings team of the Bud Grant era in a National Football Conference divisional-round playoff game at Metropolitan Stadium.

Offering encouragement was something that came gracefully and naturally to the well-spoken Marshall, a characteristic that easily made him one of the most beloved teammates who ever lived.

"If you're there and you can put your hand on someone's shoulder, you do that," said Marshall matter-of-factly. "Who doesn't want someone to encourage them and say you did the best you could do? You encourage them to go on."

Wright did not shy away from being around the ball when the big moments came. This was evidenced in playoff action the year before.

In a 1974 divisional-round showdown against Wright's college coach at San Diego State, Don Coryell and his high-flying Cardinals, the sturdy corner scooped up a Terry

Metcalf fumble in the early stages of the third quarter and raced 20 yards down the left sideline to help break open a 10–7 game.

Thanks to Wright's touchdown, the game was no contest from there on as the Vikings, now up by 10, cruised to a 30–14 win over the Cardinals to advance to a second straight NFC title game. It was a much easier contest for the Vikings than their week-nine nail-biter at St. Louis on *Monday Night Football.* Jim Hart tossed for a career-best 353 yards and had the Cardinals knocking on the door of the end zone when the game ended with Minnesota ahead 28–24.

"[Carl] Eller made a great hit and Alan [Page] came in to clean up," said Wright, who played two years in St. Louis before coming to Minnesota. "The ball bounced off to the side. I picked it off and ran it in for the score."[1]

For the great Metcalf, it was his 15th fumble of the season. He set an NFL record with his 14 regular-season mishandles.

"I got upfield and cut Metcalf off," said Eller. "I got a hand on the ball and sort of joggled it loose. Then Alan hit him again and knocked the ball loose."[2]

The loss marked the end of a magical season for the Cardinals and Coryell, who was named the United Press International's NFC Coach of the Year after leading the club to its first playoff appearance in 26 years and first since the team moved to St. Louis in 1960. The team earned the nickname the Cardiac Cards as 11 of their 14 games came down to the wire. He joined the Cardinals in 1973 following a tremendous 12-year career at San Diego State, where he led the Aztecs to a 127–24 mark.

Wright's playoff career with the Vikings saw him play in 12 games and snare three interceptions. In his playoff debut against the Washington Redskins in 1973, he swiped a Kilmer pass in Redskins territory and raced inside the 10. That set up a Tarkenton-to-John Gilliam TD pass to put the Vikings up 24–13.

"I'm identified with the Hail Mary, which I guess is not a good thing," said Wright, who had six interceptions in '74. "If they want to talk about the game, I don't mind. But I tell them that was only one play."

One play does not a career make.

"I didn't let a mistake like that hijack the rest of my life," said Marshall, who so graciously dealt with his unfortunate event that in January 1965 he accepted an invitation to fly to Texas to receive the Bonehead Club of Dallas's "Bonehead of the Year" award. He missed his flight, ending up getting rerouted to Chicago, but he continued to Dallas, accepting the "award" good-humoredly.

After signing as an undrafted free agent in 1969 with the Atlanta Falcons, Wright played three games before being cut by Norm Van Brocklin. He was picked up by the Cardinals and played the last 10 games of the season with the Big Red. "The Cardinals were having some difficulties with their secondary and so they signed me after the DB coach in Atlanta gave them a call," said Wright, who spent the '70 season as a backup.

A week before the opening of the 1971 season, he was traded to the Vikings for defensive tackle Mike McGill, head-hunting safety Dale Hackbart and a 1972 fourth-round pick. In addition to acquiring Wright, the Vikings also received tight end Bob Brown, a move precipitated by the loss of John Beasley to a season-ending knee injury in the team's last exhibition game.

The man who set up the trade? Bob Hollway.

Hollway was recruited by Grant to join his first staff in 1967 and would serve admirably during two separate stints as his defensive coordinator. But some of his best

Minnesota Vikings defensive tackle Alan Page (88) and defensive end Carl Eller (81) team up to force a Terry Metcalf fumble in the third quarter with linebacker Wally Hilgenberg (back) ready to lend a hand during a 1974 divisional round playoff game with St. Louis. Nate Wright would pick up the loose ball and return it for a key touchdown as the Vikings recorded a 30–14 win to advance to play Los Angeles in the NFC championship game.

contributions for the Vikings came when he became coach of the stumbling Cardinals in 1971.

"Hollway was very loyal to Bud," said Wright, who was selected as a Pro Bowl alternate in '74 and '76. "He thought I could help the Vikings so he traded me."

A year later, Hollway, whose teams went 4–9–1 both his years in St. Louis, would send Gilliam, a 1973 second-round pick (Jackie Wallace) and fourth-round selection (John Lohmeyer) to the Vikings for Gary Cuozzo, possibly the biggest heist in Vikings history.

Wright and the perennial Pro Bowler Gilliam would become cornerstone players on two NFC championship teams and play key roles in the victory over the Redbirds, who, like the Vikings, entered the game with a 10–4 mark and a divisional title in tow.

After a scoreless first quarter, the Cards took a 7–0 lead on a 13-yard pass from Jim Hart to Earl Thomas. The Vikings tied it on a 16-yard aerial from a rolling Tarkenton to Gilliam, who had just two catches, but both went for scores. The Cardinals had a chance to take the lead with seconds left in the opening half, but the normally reliable Jim Bakken missed a 23-yard field goal, sending the teams into the locker room tied 7–7.

"They had the edge in the first half," said Grant. "We were glad to settle for a 7–7 score at halftime. Missing the field goal, well, it let us come in at half and feel good. It also let us forget that they had moved right down the field against us [on a 56-yard drive to end the half]. Then we got some early Christmas presents—an interception and a fumble."[3]

Bruising St. Louis fullback Jim Otis, held to 35 yards on eight carries, said Bakken's missed FG was not a game changer.

"One play doesn't hurt you," said the former Ohio State star who was drafted by the New Orleans Saints in the ninth round of the 1970 draft. "If you're any kind of football player, one play or one mistake isn't going to take you out of a game."[4]

The Vikings would take control in the second half, grabbing a 10-point advantage in the first five minutes and not allowing the Cardinals a first down until the final minute of the third quarter.

"For a defensive line, it's sometimes hard to get started right off," said Eller. "The offense has got you where they want you when things start and the Cardinals played a helluva game. We were lucky enough to come up with some big plays. After that we got our five-man front going and then you can go get 'em."[5]

Three plays into the second half, Vikings strong safety Jeff Wright made a great diving interception near the sideline on an off-target, low throw from Hart and ran it back 18 yards to the Cardinals' 44. Gilliam then took a reverse—as he so often did when he was thriving in St. Louis—for 16 yards to set up a 37-yard Fred Cox FG.

Cox's boot gave the Vikings a 10–7 lead and set the stage for Wright's timely scoop and score on the Cardinals' next possession.

"I had control of the ball and all of a sudden it squirted out," said Metcalf, a Pro Bowler who had more than 1,000 yards from scrimmage and seven scores in '74 and added 963 yards and a TD on punt and kick returns. "That Alan Page hit me real hard. They took after us in the second half."[6]

After Wright's big play, the Vikings put the game out of reach when Tarkenton found Gilliam deep from 38 yards out. His speed flowing easily, Gilliam raced down the right sideline past the Cardinals' best cornerback, Norm Thompson, and proceeded untouched into his favorite end zone, the north.

"The first TD was just a crossing pattern," said Gilliam. "We had everybody going to the left. I went underneath about seven or eight yards and I came open on that [other] side. On the second one, I just ran by their cornerback. I have a lot of confidence in myself. I was sure that this was going to be my day. A cornerback is a cornerback, and there's not a cornerback in the league I can't beat one-on-one. We knew we could go deep anytime. We saw that in the first half, but we just kept waiting to see if they would make any adjustments. We kept running and running and bringing their safety up closer, and like I said, one-on-one."[7]

Gilliam's second score made it 23–7 as Cox missed the extra point, but the rout was on against the young Cardinals.

"In the playoffs you go for the kill," said Tarkenton after the game. "These guys could come back and destroy you. People call Bud Grant and the Vikings conservative. We must have 200 plays. We run reverses, we throw the ball from the 1-yard line and we do anything anybody can do and maybe some things a lot of 'em can't."[8]

Chuck Foreman, who had 23 rushes for 114 yards and 54 more yards on five receptions, added a four-yard TD run in the final quarter to build the lead to 30–7. The Vikings held the explosive Metcalf to just 55 yards rushing and 43 receiving, due partially to Wright's ability to force the run.

"I think our grass bothered him," said Grant. "He [Metcalf] plays on their artificial turf, which is suited for his stop-and-go style. There's nothing wrong with our turf, but you can't accelerate the same way. Besides, he's pretty small and he was doing a lot more running than he usually does. Every time a guy that small gets hit, it's got to take something out of him."[9]

A steadying presence on the left side of the defense, the 5-11, 180-pound Wright started from 1973 to 1978 opposite Bobby Bryant. He grabbed 34 interceptions in 156 games, playing against standouts like Charley Taylor, whom he said was his most difficult receiver to guard.

"He was big and physical, and he could run," said Wright. "He was a former running back so he knew what to do with the ball once he caught it."

The Vikings, who won eight division titles during Wright's 11 years in Minnesota, were *"a body jointly fitted together"* as scriptures say, with all the pieces coming together in beautiful synchrony.

"I think we were just hungry," said Wright, who moved from Georgia to California after his mom died when he was 15. "I was undrafted and [strong safety] Jeff Wright wasn't drafted so we had chips on our shoulders. Bobby was injured off and on but when we were all together, we played positions most suited for us and it just worked, especially having [Paul] Krause back there."

The Monterey (California) High School product played the defensive strong side next to Eller and set the edge well with his reliable tackling. On pass plays he played with good feet and hip swivel, despite being unnoticed by pro personnel men coming out of college.

"They didn't think I could play but I was good in one-on-one coverage. We played zone but I played man within it," he said.

Undrafted out of college, Wright was bowed but not broken by the "Hail Mary" play, as he grabbed a career-best seven interceptions in 1976 to lead the team. That total was good for third in the NFC behind Los Angeles's Monte Jackson (10) and Joe Lavender and Rod Perry (eight) of the Redskins and Rams, respectively.

"It was devastating," Wright said of the Dallas game. "You never really get over it. But I had a whole offseason to get over it and I came back to have a nice season."

History shows Wright came up with a huge play late in the '76 championship game versus the Rams. The Vikings went up 17–0 after their first possession of the second half on a one-yard run by Foreman.

But Los Angeles scratched its way to within 17–13 and had it first and 10 at the Vikings' 39 with 2:50 left. Would a playoff collapse happen two years in a row, only this time against the Rams?

Rams quarterback Pat Haden went for the kill, sending speedy wide receiver Harold Jackson down the right sideline on a go pattern. But the faithful Wright was again right there, running step for step with Jackson before breaking up the pass in the end zone and nearly making a stupendous interception. Bryant then completely snuffed out the drive a few plays later when he made a great interception on a pass intended for Ron Jessie.

"Defensive backs have to have real short memories," said Bryant. "That's true of football players in general. You may have a terrible game, but good players have a way of using that to play better. You don't forget it completely, but you put it out of your mind."

Wright teammate tight end Stu Voigt said the Vikings' team makeup would not allow for a letdown, even after a bitter disappointment. After the Dallas loss, Minnesota would go on to play in NFC championship games the next two seasons.

"We were a veteran team and we never got too high or too low," said Voigt. "We just knew that there were going to be games like that in football and you had to keep looking ahead."

Attributable to his 4.5 speed in the 40, Wright said one of his best skills as a cornerback was that "he could recover." Meaning, if he bit on a route—like he did when he thought Jessie was going to run an out, only to break wide open on a post pattern before Bryant made his huge interception in the '76 championship game—that he could quickly make up ground.

"I was sure thankful for the play Bobby made," said an appreciative Wright, smiling as he thought about the play.

• • •

The Vikings limited Hart to just 18 completions in 40 attempts, with just one of them going to the great Jackie Smith, who spent part of his day trying to contain Eller.

"You had to gear yourself up going against him," said Smith. "I tried to hit him as low as I could. Nothing up too high. I'd try to hit a guy around the belt loops. I was always concerned about injuring another player's knees. As a tight end, you just try to get in their way. You just try to shield them one second or two and then the back would be by there."

Trailing Smith throughout the day was Jeff Wright, who was part of a Vikings defense that would sometimes deploy five linemen and six defensive backs against the high-powered Cardinals.

"We took away a lot of good things Hart likes," said Wright. "They had been throwing a great deal to Smith, a big-play guy for them. He only caught one pass, that in the final minutes. We never saw some of their big-play patterns. Our defensive scheme was that good."[10]

Grant had the upmost respect for the Hall of Fame Cardinals tight end, having essentially played the same position with aplomb for a year with the Philadelphia Eagles. After reluctantly playing left defensive end on Philadelphia's five-man front his first year and leading the team in sacks, Grant petitioned Coach Jim Trimble to play offense in '52.

"They said that we have Pete Pihos [35 catches in '51] and Bobby Walston [31] already there but I told them I was better than both of them," said Grant.[11]

The rangy Grant was correct, as he finished second in the NFL in both receiving yards (997) and catches (56) in 1952. He did all of that in just 12 contests as the NFL didn't move to a 14-game slate until '61. The nine-letter winner at the University of Minnesota also became the first Eagles receiver to surpass 200 yards receiving in a game when he had 11 catches for 203 yards on December 7 against the Dallas Texans, who won just one game (in week 10 in Akron over the Bears) and were out of the league the next season.

"After running a few plays, I told our quarterback I can get open on any pattern you want to throw," said Grant, who wore No. 86 with the Eagles. "Their left corner couldn't guard my grandmother."[12]

Both players could run, with Smith posting an unheard-of 21.5 yards per catch in 1967, a single-year total better than any HOF tight end, while Grant posted 17.8 yards per catch and seven TDs in '52.

The play that epitomized Smith's determined running ability greater than any other was his 19-yard scoring reception for a TD from Hart in the Cardinals' scintillating 31–28 win over the Dallas Cowboys in week-five play, a game that set the tone for the team's tremendous run to its first East Division title. Smith broke about five tackles, starting with his shaking free of Cliff Harris.

"The funny thing about that game is that I had been open several times," recalled Smith. "I really got mad at Jim. I said, 'Dammit! Throw me the ball!' When he dropped back to throw, I wasn't really open. But he must have thought, 'Smith's a little nuts, so I better throw him the ball,' so he just went ahead and threw the damn thing. I caught it and then I thought, 'Well, now that I have the ball, I better not make an ass of myself.' That was my mindset: that I better to do something with it. Every time I see Cliff, he reminds me of that. He's a great guy. He's just a wonderful guy and a tremendous athlete and I get a lot of static from him."

A pioneer as a player and coach, Grant is believed to be the first player in NFL history to play out his option, leaving the Eagles after his remarkable second season to head north to play in the CFL with Winnipeg.

"Money was the reason. I was making $7,000 a year and I asked for a raise and the Eagles offered me $8,000," recalled Grant. "Winnipeg was going to give me $10,000. In those days that was a big deal. A lot of NFL players, like great Browns receiver Mac Speedie [who led the league in receptions in '52 with 62], were leaving for Canada because this was well before the league had TV money. Living in Philadelphia was not the Garden of Eden. I was a Midwestern guy and that's not where I really wanted to put my roots down. I just got married and had a young family."[13]

A decade after Grant was tearing up defensive backfields prior to leaving for Canada, where he led the league in receiving three of his four years as a player with Winnipeg, Smith was debuting with the Cardinals after being drafted on a flyer in the 10th round out of Northwestern (Louisiana) State in 1963. Taking over at tight end after an injury to Taz Anderson, Smith didn't take long to prove his worth, as in week-two play he had 212 yards receiving on nine receptions in a 24–23 win over the Pittsburgh Steelers.

"Mainly for me was whenever I caught the ball I wanted to do as much with it as I could. I wanted to get as far downfield as I could," said Smith. "A lot of guys, they catch the ball and they get the yardage, they get the first down and that was it. There's not much effort put into it. I was so surprised to make the team, to even be there that I always had that mentality that I don't want to be done with the game and look back when I was 80 and say, 'You could have done this or could have done that.' I had this feeling about me. I held myself accountable for all that."

Smith wasn't surprised with his fast start in the NFL.

"It was something that was normal for me," said the Kentwood, Louisiana, product. "I was just doing what I was supposed to be doing. I didn't think about it too much. I was just being myself. I heard Knute Rockne say the game is played with arms and legs but mostly from the neck up. I always remembered that."

At age 34, while still averaging an impressive 16.5 yards a catch, Smith walked onto the treacherous Met Stadium field that cold December afternoon to compete in the Cardinals' first playoff game since the December 19, 1948, NFL championship contest at Philadelphia's Shibe Park. Hall of Fame back Steve Van Buren trudged in from the five to give the Eagles a 7–0 victory in blizzard conditions.

The previous year, the Cardinals, then based in Chicago, captured their last NFL title on December 28 against the same Eagles, triumphing 28–21 at Comiskey Park thanks to a pair of long scoring runs by a versatile athlete who preceded Tarkenton at the University of Georgia—1968 HOF inductee Charley Trippi.

As he prepared to walk on the field, Smith caught Grant's steely eyes.

"Absolutely respected him," said Smith, who still lives near St. Louis. "I remember going out to play them. We were all gathered together to go on the field. He looked over at me and was pointing his finger at me and laughing. He and I had conversations before. And we talked about the different types of pass patterns and playing tight end. He didn't say a lot but he was still a real charismatic guy. You did things because he was so confident in what he was saying. He didn't say much but when he did, you really listened. I remember being in Pro Bowl games with him. He was a great guy."

Smith could well relate to his former Cardinals teammate Wright, as well as to Marshall, concerning being a star player who is tied to one unfortunate and fateful play. They all understood redemption.

Smith was vilified for not coming up with an end zone pass from Staubach against the Steelers in Super Bowl XIII with the Cowboys down 21–14 with just under three minutes left in the third quarter. They went on to lose 35–31. Untold fans treated Smith as an anathema, but his teammates knew that it was anything but an easy play to make as the ball was thrown low and behind him.

"Roger apologized. He told me he never expected me to be that open," said Smith, who finished his career with 7,918 yards receiving and 40 TDs and, along with John Mackey, revolutionized the position upon both of their NFL arrivals following the '63 draft. "I had to block, then wait for a bit before getting downfield. When he threw the ball, he said he took a lot off because I was so wide open. He wanted to make sure he got the ball to me. There's no way to judge the speed of the ball. You have to see the motion of the arm. The ball didn't have much speed on it so I had to slow down and that's when my feet slipped out from under me."

The fan outcry that arose against Smith bothered his teammates more than the Cowboys missing out on a TD.

"The ball was behind him because Roger took a little off the ball. That threw the timing off with Jackie," said Pearson, who had 489 career receptions and 48 TDs. "That was a tough situation. A touchdown there would have been nice, but we probably felt worse for Jackie Smith than anything else. What a great guy. He only played with us one season and he learned coach Landry's complex offense. What a great teammate for a short period of time. We normally didn't bring guys in. Jackie Smith and Preston Pearson [from the Steelers] were like the only two guys we brought in that way."

What threw the timing of the play off was the Cowboys designed it to be run at the goal line. Dallas snapped the ball from the 10.

"We had that play in our game plan for weeks," said Pearson. "Coach Landry would do that. He would put plays in that we weren't going to use for that week, but just so we could practice them that week. Everything worked to perfection. The formation, the motion, the way it opened up. Just not the completion."

Landry had coaxed Smith out of retirement in '78 after an injury to tight end Jay Saldi. The offer was alluring for a player who toiled for Cardinals teams that always came up short.

"We were right on the edge so many times," said Smith, a 9.8 man in the 100 who could still run a 4.6 40 at age 38 when he was signed by Dallas. "We were just about there. We needed either a little more on defense or a little more on offense and it would have been over the hump. That goes to show just how critical it is to have the right guys and the right coach and how hard it is to have everything working together at the same time. That defense Minnesota had, though, we all wanted."

It was a pillaging defense that on a chilly day held Smith's Cardinals to 284 yards of total offense and forced two key turnovers in addition to sacking the normally untouchable Hart twice.

To be young and a Viking in the 1970s meant that even in moments of despair, a teammate like a Marshall or a Bryant was always right there, offering both comfort and reprieve. And despite that dark day against the Cowboys so many years ago, Wright was always able to recover, both mentally and physically, and was undoubtedly a fixture on teams that he said "didn't know anything but winning."

8

Wright's Timely Chase

Minnesota Vikings 14, Los Angeles Rams 10
December 29, 1974, Metropolitan Stadium
NFC Championship Game

The average NFL historian may be able to name the 1970s Minnesota Vikings starters on defense, save one.

Listening closely enough, one can still hear CBS play-by-play man Ray Scott setting the defensive starters in his trademark staccato fashion: *"The Vikings starters across the front ... you know the names, Carl Eller, Doug Sutherland, Alan Page and Jim Marshall. The fabled Purple People Eaters.*

"Behind them," he continues, *"are the linebackers, Roy Winston, Wally and Jeff Siemon. Then the secondary, Bobby Bryant, and Nate Wright at the corners, with Paul Krause at free safety and..."*

The name most often overlooked? Strong safety Jeff Wright.

It's a tidy and simple name. Stout in its utterance, but not flamboyant.

Wright may have been the best athlete his high school ever produced, but that's a boast shared by many an NFL player. But when it came to the titans of professional football, he was just another of the many who admirably toiled in relative anonymity.

That is, until December 29, 1974.

It was on this afternoon that Wright, in an NFC title game showdown with the Los Angeles Rams at storied Metropolitan Stadium, would make a play that would be emblazoned among the heroic playoff moments of the past, most of those chronicled featuring names such as Eller, Page, Marshall or Krause.

Minnesota easily handled Don Coryell's Cardiac Cardinals 30–14 in opening-round playoff action, leaving only Chuck Knox's Rams in the way of a second-straight Super Bowl trip.

The 1974 title game was a sloppy and physical affair as the teams combined for eight fumbles and three interceptions under perfect playing conditions given it was December in Minnesota.

"Most of the time fumbles result from hard hitting and strong defensive play," said Bud Grant, whose team finished 10–4 to win its sixth NFC Central crown. "There were just enough turnovers in the game to keep the tide constantly turning."[1]

"In my 14 years of professional football, I've never been in a harder-hitting game," chimed in Fran Tarkenton. "The Rams were crazy psyched up. I can't remember ever seeing a team mentally ready like the Rams were. They just hit and hit from the word go."[2]

The clash of division winners went scoreless in the first quarter before Tarkenton,

Minnesota Vikings quarterback Fran Tarkenton (10) drops back to pass in the 1974 NFC championship game against the Los Angeles Rams in Bloomington. Tarkenton opened the scoring in the second quarter with a 29-yard touchdown pass to Jim Lash, and the Vikings held on to win 14–10 thanks to a key defensive play in the third quarter by strong safety Jeff Wright.

throwing into a tight window, perfectly placed a 29-yard touchdown pass down the left sideline to Jim Lash in the second quarter. It marked the first career TD catch for the former Northwestern Wildcat, a third-round pick by the Vikings in '73 who played in obscurity opposite John Gilliam.

The score capped a 60-yard, seven-play drive that also saw Lash snag a pass for 11 yards. Not accustomed to media attention, the angular receiver described how the play unfolded.

"Fran put Gillie [John Gilliam] and me on the same side," said Lash, a product of (Akron) Garfield High School along with classmate Steve Craig, the Vikings' backup tight end who followed him to Northwestern. "He told Gillie to run a short post and for me to run a fly. I did a fake post on [Rams corner Al] Clark and got around him. Fran had the ball right where it was supposed to be."[3]

The Rams cut the score to 7–3 on a 27-yard field goal by David Ray right before halftime, but early in the third, the NFC West Division champs, who featured a defense led by the likes of former Tarkenton teammate Fred Dryer at one end and Jack Youngblood at the other, were on the verge of taking the lead.

It was then that Wright made what he considers "the biggest play of my career," one that truly epitomized the player's dogged spirit.

Gaining some rhythm and confidence after a solid four-of-six passing effort on the team's final drive of the first half, Rams QB James Harris dug his team out from its own two after a Mike Eischeid coffin corner punt. He started the drive with a good gain on a sneak, then bruising fullback Jim Bertelsen burst up the middle for 10 yards.

With some breathing room established, Harris, selected out of Grambling State in the eighth round of the 1969 draft by the Buffalo Bills (along with O.J. Simpson), dropped back to pass from his own 25. Uncharacteristically, the Vikings called for a blitz—"We only played three or four defenses and rarely blitzed," said Wright—and the stocky Winston burst unscathed through the middle.

The angular 6–4 Harris somehow pivoted away from the rock-solid Winston, as well as tackle attempts from the hard-charging trio of Eller, Siemon and Hilgenberg. Just as he was being two-hand clobbered to the ground by the fast-pursuing Page, Harris stepped up to find wide receiver Harold Jackson running free at the Rams 42.

A second wild sequence would follow, one that would prove to be one of the most unforgettable in team history.

Catching the ball moving right to left, the quicksilver Jackson stopped hard to elude Nate Wright, then cut back to his right, away from the pursuit. Forced to do so by the presence of teammate John Cappelletti, Jackson reversed his field at the Vikings' 35. In the process, the former Eagles star blew by rookie Jackie Wallace down the left sideline and had nothing but the flag in front of him. Dogged in determination, Wright came from nowhere, "all the way from the other side of the field," to push Jackson out of bounds at the Vikings' two, saving a touchdown and, as it turned out, the game.

"I was going as fast as my little legs could take me," Wright said with a laugh. "If Jackson would have stopped, my momentum would have taken me right by him and he would have walked in. I had a good angle, thank the Good Lord."

One could call him "Right Place Wright."

The play made all the difference, as facing a third-and-goal from the Vikings' two following a procedure call on Tom Mack (it was tight end Pat Curran who flinched), Harris rolled wearily to his right before having his pass tipped by Wallace and the ball fortuitously landed into the waiting hands of Hilgenberg in the end zone.

"Jackie should get all the credit for that one," Hilgenberg said. "He popped it up there and it came right to me. I would say I never had a more important interception in my career."[4]

The lead, and eventually, the game, was preserved.

"I don't know if Jeff Wright has made bigger plays," said Grant. "All I know about this one is that it probably won us a shot at the Super Bowl."[5]

"I was running a sideline pattern," said Jackson, acquired by the Rams the previous year from the Eagles in a package that included Roman Gabriel. "And then when I saw [James Harris] was scrambling, I cut back toward the middle. I should have gone all the way, but it turned out [Jeff] Wright had a better angle on me than I thought he had. I should have cut back and I would have made it."[6]

The magnitude of the play wasn't lost on Wright's safety running mate, Krause, who was in the center of the action for 19 playoff games with Minnesota after arriving from the Redskins in 1968.

"Jeff knew football and he would go as far as he could to make a play," said Krause, who had two interceptions in '74. "I loved playing with him because he just didn't make mental mistakes. He played his position perfectly. He just did everything perfectly. I would always want to have a player like Jeff Wright on my team."

The Vikings tallied what proved to be the decisive score on the ensuing series, which saw them travel 80 yards over 11 tension-filled plays. Veteran back Dave Osborn, once again a fixture in the lineup after starting just one game the year before due to injury, characteristically dived in from the one-yard line on a fourth-down play with 12 minutes left in the fourth quarter to make it 14–3.

Tarkenton, who connected with Gilliam and Stu Voigt for a pair of key completions during the drive, exalted following Osborn's determined touchdown effort, leaping with both arms thrown into the air, figuring there was no way a sluggish Rams offense could score twice in the final 12 minutes.

"We called the play a 'Double Fly,'" said Osborn of his scoring leap. "Chuck [Foreman] flies over the top first. He tries to pick off one of the Ram linebackers. I then fly over the top. Nobody stopped us on that play all year."[7]

"You got to try to win the ball game somewhere," offered Grant on taking the fourth-down gamble. "That seemed like as good as place as any to do so. A field goal would put us up by seven. A touchdown would mean the Rams need two scores. They came right back and scored a touchdown, so the one we got from Osborn was the critical one."[8]

Another important play on the scoring drive was a controversial offside call on a third-and-four play from the Rams' 16. Dryer burst around the right side for an apparent sack of Tarkenton, but instead of forcing an FG attempt, the Vikings, after the fortuitous five-yard march-off, scored a TD four plays later.

"I was watching Tarkenton," said Dryer. "When he moved, I moved. I was going with him. When I saw the flag, all I knew was that it couldn't be me. When they said it was, I couldn't believe it."[9]

On the next series, Harris rebounded from his interception to find Jackson again running free and the sprinter was not about to get caught from behind this time. His 44-yard catch-and-run TD down the right side just five plays after Osborn's scoring play cut the deficit to four.

With the help of a holding penalty against the Vikings that erased a third-down pass to Chuck Foreman for a first down, the Rams got the ball back with seven minutes left at the Minnesota 45.

Enter the Purple People Eaters.

Utilizing a five-man front that was the brainchild of defensive line coach Jack Patera, the Vikings burst through the vaunted Rams offensive line on a second-down play. The result was a sack for a loss of 12 by the fifth lineman, the unheralded Bob Lurtsema.

Then, on third and 20, Lurtsema roommate Doug Sutherland exploded through to sack Harris to make it fourth and 37.

"Jack was a brilliant coach," said Lurtsema of Patera, who coached with the Rams and the Giants before joining the Vikings in 1969. "He was my line coach with the Giants. He coached me for most of my 12 years in the league. He knew who to put out there and when based on formations and matchups."

Patera was a fixture with the club for seven years before leaving to become the first-ever coach of the Seattle Seahawks.

"Jack worked us hard," said Marshall. "We were in the best shape of any front line in the league. He drove us to excel."

With Patera spinning the dials, the Vikings' front wall became a symphony of terror for the opposition. This game they dropped Harris only two times, but he was under constant duress.

"With Marshall and Eller, no one got outside," said Lurtsema. "They played off each other even from that distance. We had our own calls so we could get out of a defense. Marshall and Eller took great pride in their areas. Most guys are chasing the ball around. They locked in. They had outside responsibility, and nobody got outside. You force them inside where you have Larsen, Sutherland and Page waiting. There was no Black and White on the Vikings. They just wanted you to perform and Marshall was the boss. He controlled the line. Everything went through Marshall and coach Patera had no problem with that. Marshall was a 'steady Eddy.' He was only about 225 but everything ran through him."

"We were all very close and we depended on each other," added Marshall. "You develop a sense of trust and where these people are on any given play. You learn where you're going to have help and it's all familiar to you."

Harris had gotten the better of the Vikings in regular-season play, throwing for 249 yards on 24-of-37 passing and a late score to wide receiver Jack Snow in the Rams' 20–17 win at home in week-11 play. In the title game, he threw for 248 yards but tossed two interceptions, was sacked twice and completed just 13 of 23 attempts.

"On those sacks," said Harris, "they just plain beat us."[10]

In the regular-season matchup, Harris was not sacked nor did he throw an interception against a Vikings team that allowed an NFL-low eight touchdown passes. "In Los Angeles, his passing beat us. We were healthier this time," said Grant. "We wanted to force them into passing situations and we had to control the running game to do that. They gained some [the Rams had 121 yards rushing], but we kept the pressure on Harris with Page, Sutherland, Marshall and Eller. A few times we blitzed and we got hurt on that 73-yard play where Harris did a great job getting the ball to Jackson. But there again, Jeff Wright stayed with it and forced him out on the two."[11]

Clinging to a four-point lead following Sutherland's big sack on the befuddled Harris, the Vikings kept the ball for the final 5:37 of the game to seal the win and earn their third trip to the Super Bowl.

Minnesota was able to grind out 164 yards rushing, with Foreman, despite fumbling three times, posting a game-best 80 yards on 22 carries and Osborn 76 yards on 20 totes.

Foreman spoke highly after the game of Rams linebacker Ken Geddes, who he said was "the best linebacker I have played against—bar none."[12]

Sadly, Geddes learned after the game his father had passed away. Nearly a year later to the day, Tarkenton would lose his father, Dallas, during a playoff game with the Cowboys.

Another defensive look the Vikings gave the Rams was using additional defensive backs. Picking up the slack left by an injured Bryant and showing the Vikings' depth in the secondary were both Terry Brown and a 12th-round draft pick who played just one year in Minnesota, Stanford product Randy Poltl, who grabbed an interception and returned it 16 yards against the visitors.

"We used a defense that we called the 46," said Brown. "I would go in for Winston and actually line up at linebacker on passing situations. Neill Armstrong devised that. In pro ball today you see a lot of defensive backs in there because they have wide receivers all over the place. It was just kind of ahead of its time."

"One of the reasons we used the extra defensive backs was because our front four was getting a little older and sometimes we were undersized," said Poltl, who had 10 tackles in Stanford's 13–12 win over fourth-ranked Michigan in the 1972 Rose Bowl. "Alan Page had taken up running and lost a lot of weight and it was just something we could do to help us match up better on passing downs. We'd use a 12-man huddle and wait until the last second to run a man off the field so the offense never knew what type of personnel we'd be in. The NFL later outlawed that."

Grant had another trick up his sleeve against the Rams.

"The rule in the NFL was if you were going to use the field the day before the game for practice, you had to let the other team use it," said Brown. "But they always had the field covered so it wouldn't freeze. That meant the other team never got to work out the day before the game. When they got out on the field they were trying to guess which shoes to wear. It was a psychological battle. Grant tried to make them second-guess themselves, so we never practiced on Saturdays when it was icy because that way they couldn't either.

"I think that affected the Rams," Brown added. "They were changing their shoes during the game. They were totally psyched out. It was cold that day. I remember them questioning each other about which shoes to wear."

Brown, like Wright, was unheralded. He had a knack for big plays as well, grabbing two interceptions in '74. With Wright out much the next year with a knee injury suffered during the preseason, Brown started 12 games.

"I had a great year in '75," said Brown. "I thought I was good enough for All-Pro that year. When I came back to camp, I was listed as second team behind Jeff. Now, Jeff's a great player. Bud's rule was always that you didn't lose your job with injury. I just told Bud I wanted to play. If I'm not going to play, I'd rather you trade me. It was the biggest mistake I made. He later traded me."

Brown ended up with the Cleveland Browns, who finished a surprising 9–5 in '76, but he said playing for head coach Forrest Gregg was a disaster compared with the leadership he enjoyed in Minnesota.

"Probably the biggest mistake I've made," he said. "The players were great in Cleveland, but I wasn't happy with the coach. My biggest memory with the Vikings was scoring the TD in the Super Bowl [against Pittsburgh]. The opportunity to play in that game was unbelievable. My best friend in St. Louis was Roger Wehrli and he played 15 years and never got in one. It was a great thrill."

Making big plays on defense was commonplace for this team. Wright said the Vikings' calm play in pressure games and tenuous moments was truly a reflection of Coach Grant.

"There is no doubt what made the team go was Bud Grant," commented Wright. "He was a great manager of people. He allowed both his coaches and his players to perform their jobs. He assembled a great coaching staff, but it was Grant's single-handed impact which made the organization successful."

Minnesota and Los Angeles had similar coaches. Known as "Ground Chuck" due to his affinity for the running game, Knox was adored by the Rams as much as the Viking players loved Grant. So successful were the two that from 1973 to 1977, Grant and Knox crafted 54–15–1 regular-season records (.783 winning percentage), best in the NFL during that stretch.

"Once you knew who this guy was and what his background was, you had a whole lot of respect for him," said Youngblood of the son of a steelworker Knox, who would later leave Los Angeles for Buffalo, where he turned the Bills into a playoff contender. "He was like our father and he loved all of us like we were his children. We had so much faith in him and his crew, and his coaches."

Lurtsema was no fan of Allie Sherman during his days with the Giants, but he adored his replacement, Alex Webster. When Lurtsema came north, he quickly learned Grant meant business.

"Webster was a players' coach," noted Lurtsema, who made the *Sporting News* All-Pro team in 1968, his second year with the team. "He played the game. We could go up to him and tell him what we were seeing, and he'd make the adjustments. He was a very, very good coach. With Bud, it was the discipline he demanded of his players. He was very, very strict. You were in awe of what he told you to do whether it was on the field or off the field. If you were off that just one iota, the next day you would be traded. That's how tough he was. A no-nonsense guy. If you made mental mistakes with Bud, that was it. He wanted predictability with his players. He didn't want to guess which Bob Lurtsema was going to show up on a play."

Drafted as a cornerback out of the University of Minnesota in 1971, Wright was a three-sport standout at Edina (Minnesota), where he was considered the best all-around athlete in school history.

He played special teams as a rookie, then was a backup to Karl Kassulke at strong safety his second year, starting eight games.

It was anything but an eye-catching start to his career, but little did the self-effacing Wright know that beginning his third year, he would prove to be an unheralded—albeit key—cog on three Vikings Super Bowl teams over the next five years.

"He fit in very well because he never made mistakes," said Krause, who was in his 10th year in the league when Wright joined him as a full-time starter. "He could go up and make hits like Kassulke but he wasn't that big. Neither was Kassulke, but I would rate Jeff right up there as a strong safety."

"I was very fortunate to be a part of those teams," said Wright, who started all 14 games in 1973 and grabbed three interceptions. "Bud Grant was a great coach. Each player had a job to do, and we just did it. I didn't ever think about being the unheralded guy. I was just glad to be mentioned along with greats like the Purple People Eaters."

That meant being on the field in the late-afternoon shadows at Metropolitan

Stadium, crunch-time moments when a play had to made, as was the case with Lurtsema and Sutherland bum-rushing Harris on consecutive downs.

"It was a memorable atmosphere," said Wright of playoff football at Met Stadium. "It was a baseball stadium, but we could still feel the fans even though the seats were far away. They just loved the team and the whole environment with all the tailgating. We used to love when West Coast teams like the Rams came here."

"We hated to go there," said Youngblood, a Florida native. "We wanted to stay on our grass. The LA Coliseum [sod] was like your backyard. They did a great job with the turf. It was California. It was perfect. They didn't have any grass over there. You did not want to fall. Because when you fell on that [infield] clay, it was like having knee surgery. It was that hard. It seemed like we were always spending more time on the clay than on the outfield [side]. Maybe that was by design. They tried to sod over the baseball infield, but it wasn't growing in December."

• • •

When the weather-leery Rams first came to Minnesota for a playoff game in December 1969, Vikings All-Pro right tackle Ron Yary squared off against the great David "Deacon" Jones. The '74 championship game marked the first of his four playoff matchups against the equally talented Youngblood.

"I thought Jack Youngblood was the best defensive end I ever played against," said Yary, who couldn't prevent the University of Florida star from posting a sack in the title game but did help block the Vikings to a significant 164–121 advantage on the ground. "I played against [Green Bay star] Willie Davis in the College All-Star game in Chicago, but that was his next-to-last year. It wouldn't be fair to compare Davis at that age to Jack in his prime. I also saw Deacon Jones at the end of his career. But he and Willie were both just as good at age 35, 36 as some of the guys just coming into the NFL. Deacon was a great leader, the leader of the Players' Association.

"Jack was a hard worker and aggressive," added Yary. "He worked hard on every play. He didn't let up. There are times when defensive ends won't put out as much as they can on every play. Jack was intense, quick and strong."

"Preparing to play against Yary, I would watch film going back six ball games to find out what he's doing, what they were running," said the 6-4, 247-pound fellow Hall of Famer Youngblood, a first-round pick by the Rams in '71. "That's typical of how we prepared. [Defensive coordinator and later head coach Ray] Malavasi was just a wonderful coach. He taught us how to prepare for what's coming up. It was as much intelligence as it was physical ability. Yary was athletic. He was tall, strong and healthy. He didn't have bad knees or bad shoulders at that point. He was one of the top three right tackles in the NFL, not just the NFC."

Youngblood has drawn favorable comparisons to another great left end, Baltimore's colossal Gino Marchetti, who, after breaking his leg on his team's final defensive series, gallantly refused to be removed from the sideline so he could watch the final moments of the fabled 1958 NFL championship game versus the Giants, won in overtime by the Colts. Twenty-two years later, Youngblood became the personification of toughness after leading Los Angeles to the Super Bowl in 1980 despite suffering a broken tibia in a first-round win over Dallas. He said the Rams had great respect for the Vikings.

"We were on the same level. From the head coaches all the way down. We respected them and at the same time we hated them," Youngblood chuckled. "We knew that when we saw the schedule and they were on it, that's a full day. That's a full day's work. You'd have your hands full that day. We respected Coach Grant. We assumed that we were respected from that standpoint, too."

The veritable John Wayne of pro football, Youngblood hated losing, but he said he rooted for the Vikings in the Super Bowl.

"There's two sides to that," he said. "One, you hated to get your ass beat. And two, it's 'Go NFC.' They're our cousins. We did a whole lot of stuff in the offseason together in those days and we were all together so long that it created relationships."

Youngblood, who spent each of his 14 years in the NFL with the Rams, making the Pro Bowl seven straight years, drew from the knowledge of line greats Jones and Merlin Olsen.

"I followed Deacon around like a child," said Youngblood. "I had two fathers, and they were Merlin and Deke. They traded Deke [to the Chargers in '72] and I'm like, he's the best defensive end in the NFL and you're trading his ass? What is going on here? Merlin came to me and said, 'All right, big boy ... it's up to you.' I learned how to get upfield from following Deke. I tried to do exactly what he did. They stopped us from using the head slap [Jones's signature pass-rush move]. It was never used to hurt someone; it was to get them to turn their head or close their eyes. With Yary, I'd fake him a lot. He was a pretty good [hand] fighter; he'd block it a lot. Deke also got me to think about the situation I was facing on the field on every play. He never took off a play and I tried to emulate that."

Yary was a teammate of Youngblood's his last year in the NFL when he joined the Rams in 1982 after a 14-year stay in Minnesota. It was an abysmal season as the Rams finished fourth in the NFC West Division at 2–7 under Malavasi in a strike-shortened year.

"Going to the Rams was one of the good moves I made because I realized how good I had it in Minnesota," said Yary. "That Rams team had great players, but they were nothing but individuals. They were a fractured team. Nobody played *for* the Rams. It wasn't a team. I told Jack if he ever played on the Vikings, he'd be the greatest defensive end to ever play the game. You can't play this game for yourself. I didn't see that with the Rams."

It was all about teamwork and winning in Minnesota. That's why Wright, who helped Edina to consecutive undefeated state football championship seasons, didn't expect the Vikings to miss the playoffs in '72, especially after the team made a pair of blockbuster offseason moves.

The top defensive team in the National Football Conference had the two previous seasons suffered through devastating division-round playoff losses with Gary Cuozzo and Bob Lee at quarterback.

Making the losses in 1970 and '71 to the San Francisco 49ers and Dallas Cowboys, respectively, even more egregious was both came at Metropolitan Stadium, a place where the team didn't believe it could lose, especially on the frozen tundra in December.

The quarterback position, in disarray after Joe Kapp's departure in 1970, had to be fixed or this great defense would go to waste.

"Big mistake. Major mistake letting Kapp go," said Yary. "His leadership was unmatched. I was shocked. It wasn't over a lot of money. I really liked Joe. I wasn't going to let him down. He brought that team together. Joe got 110 percent out of every player. Joe got us all to be the best we could be. That was seen in the huddle. Coaches couldn't see that. He'd say, 'Ron, we're going to run 35. Can you block that?' What are you going to say, 'No'? You know darned well you're going to put out. He would talk that way to the offensive linemen. You just don't see that all the time."

The winds of change came a month after the Vikings' dismal '71 playoff loss to the Cowboys.

Back in the fold after a wintertime trade with the New York Giants—which saw general manager Jim Finks swap his 1972 first-round pick and a second-rounder in '73 along with three veterans to include Norm Snead (the third member of the quarterback carousel in '71)—was none other than Francis Asbury Tarkenton.

And after the St. Louis Cardinals a few months later gifted the Vikings with one of the best deep threats in the game in John Gilliam, a return trip to the Super Bowl was certainly in order.

"Nobody could match Joe Kapp as a leader, but Fran was a great quarterback," said Yary. "We needed someone to replace Joe and he stepped in and did the job. He brought the Vikings back from oblivion. Kapp had more intimacy with the players than Tarkenton. It was more personal with him. He taught us how to win. But Tarkenton was able to get us back on the right track."

The much-anticipated '72 season would open in Minnesota versus the Washington Redskins on *Monday Night Football.*

It would be glorious. Howard Cosell, Frank Gifford and Don Meredith would gush over this formidable collection of talent.

But when Eischeid's first punt of the game was blocked by Redskins special teams ace Bill Malinchak and returned for a touchdown—the Vikings' first blocked punt in 11 years—it proved to be a portent of things to come.

Shockingly, beleaguered by injuries and tough breaks, Grant's team started 1–3—the losses came by a total of seven points. Green Bay, on the strength of a great running attack led by John Brockington and MacArthur Lane, captured the Central Division title as the Vikings finished with just a 7–7 mark and failed to make the playoffs for the first time since 1967, Grant's first year.

"We had the bad year in '72 but we felt like we could contend for the title every year," recalled Wright. "That's the belief we had, and Grant instilled that."

In a sign of bigger things to come, Wright started eight games that year and nabbed three of his 12 career interceptions, but he did not suit up for the final contest of the disappointing season versus the 49ers at Candlestick Park due to an injury suffered during practice.

The 49ers needed a win to make the playoffs but the Vikings, already out of contention due to the previous week's devastating loss to Dan Devine's Green Bay squad at Met Stadium, built a 17–6 lead after Gilliam snatched a 31-yard TD pass from Tarkenton.

Head coach Dick Nolan opted to pull starter Steve Spurrier after three miserable interceptions, bringing off the bench veteran John Brodie, who was unseated at starter earlier in the campaign.

Brodie didn't fare much better, throwing two interceptions himself, but recovered in time to toss a 24-yard scoring pass in the fourth quarter to Gene Washington. Now trailing 17–13, the 49ers defense got Brodie the ball back with a minute and a half left and 66 yards away from the winning score.

Aided by a pass interference penalty on Siemon, Brodie marched the team downfield and faced third down and goal at the Vikings' two with 11 seconds left. Brodie, who had consecutive passes batted away by Marshall, wisely rolled away from him to his right and found tight end Dick Witcher all alone for the winning score.

"In my seven years with the Vikings, I only saw Coach Grant lose his cool one time and it was after that game," recalled Wright. "He was so upset. He said there would be changes coming after the season and that there would be some players gone if they didn't wake up. He even called out some guys individually, which he didn't do."

It would be a seminal moment in Vikings lore.

Wright believes that rare locker room tirade at Candlestick Park gave Vikings players the impetus needed to go on to qualify for three Super Bowls over the next four seasons.

"All of us took that to heart," said Wright, a standout shoulder tackler who rarely missed a stop around the line of scrimmage.

Earlier in the '72 season, the Vikings suffered another tough loss, this one to Pittsburgh and rookie sensation Franco Harris at Three Rivers. Wright remembers an interesting interaction with Harris.

"I tackled him for a loss of about three yards one play and he said, 'Great play ... but it won't happen again.'"

In 1973, with the wise draft addition of Foreman, the Vikings started their great run, pushing out of memory that miserable loss to the 49ers. Wright would start every game and notch three more interceptions, including one off Roger Staubach in the 27–10 win over the Cowboys in the NFC championship game.

Not bad for a player who didn't even give professional football consideration until he was invited to play in both the East-West Shrine Bowl and Hula Bowl following his senior year at Minnesota.

"I didn't give a pro career much thought," said Wright, who resides in Phoenix with his wife of more than 50 years, Jayne. "Those opportunities had me start thinking about the possibility."

Wright, who made All-Big Ten in 1970, caught the attention of NFL scouts in the Shrine Bowl as he picked off a Dan Pastorini pass at his own four and went the distance.

"It's still a Shrine Bowl record," said Wright of the 96-yard return. "There were a lot of great players in that game, and it gave me the confidence that maybe I could play at the next level. It didn't hurt that Bud played at the University of Minnesota and that they were able to see me play a lot.

"I'm sure Bud drafted me not knowing how good I could be. He probably did it more or less as a favor to Sid Hartman," said Wright, who also credits the longtime local reporter for steering him away from accepting an offer at Colorado to instead play for the hometown Gophers.

Wright had to spend part of the Shrine game guarding mercurial receivers like University of Missouri speedster Mel Gray, who went on to star for the St. Louis Cardinals, as well as Kansas City Chiefs standout Elmo Wright, out of the University of Houston.

"It was a big game for me, and I eventually got a call from Jerry Reichow to tell me I got drafted in the 15th round by the Vikings [368th overall]," said Wright. "I didn't even know who Jerry was."

In drafting Wright, the Vikings garnered a sensational overall athlete—who at 5-11 could dunk the basketball—that just happened to be good at football.

"Jeff was a good cover guy," said Brown, "better than me. We just wanted to make plays."

Wright, twice all-state in basketball, played guard on two state championship teams ('66 and '67) that were part of the school's record 69–0 run. He was also the starting shortstop in baseball. In football, he was more known as a two-time all-state halfback.

The guy could play, but thanks to both divine providence and Wright's strong self-evaluation skills, the Vikings plugged him into the right spot. A cornerback in college, Wright knew his best chance at NFL success would come at safety.

"Once I got to the Vikings, I told Neill Armstrong, our defensive back coach, that I could help this team, but it would be at strong safety," said the insightful Wright.

The Vikings were already strong at corner, with Bobby Bryant on the right side and Charlie West on the left. Hall of Famer Krause, he of the NFL-best 81 career interceptions, was at free safety. Kassulke, a ferocious blitzer, was the incumbent at strong safety.

"It really worked out well, the timing of it," said Wright. "We played zone defense. We weren't a bump-and-run team, and that best fit my talents. I always considered myself a smart football player. I always knew where my help was coming from. Minus the no-contact-with-receivers-after-five-yards rule they have now, we used to force receivers into our great linebackers—guys like Roy Winston, Siemon and Wally Hilgenberg—and we used to beat the heck out of them."

Grant and Co. lost Super Bowl VIII 24–7 to the Miami Dolphins—hands down the best Vikings' Super Bowl opponent, according to team members—but Wright was poised for another big year in '74.

Entering his second full year as a starter, Wright, the Golden Gophers team captain in 1970 and a member of the university's sports Hall of Fame, posted a career-best four interceptions, including one off Jim Hart in the playoff win over the Cardinals.

Wright played only three games in '75 due to a knee injury—he was in the press box during the fateful Hail Mary playoff game—but came back to start all 14 games both in '76 and '77, helping the Vikings grab their fourth and last trip to the Super Bowl following the 24–13 win over those same Rams in the '76 championship game.

"Looking back at my career, I pinch myself and say, 'You really did that? You really played on those teams?'" asked Wright. "It was very special playing with those men. We got along so well, and everyone knew each other so well because we played together so long. We had the great defensive line and linebackers and in the secondary Nate, Bobby, Paul and I knew what each other was going to do. We had all of those great players and it all blended together around the culture that Bud built."

Bryant enjoyed having Wright as a teammate.

"Jeff was a very smart player. He was a good athlete and very smart. He always knew his assignments," Bryant said. "He was physically a very tough tackler. He was a good part of our solid defenses for all of those years. Once Kassulke got hurt, he became a fixture on the Vikings' defense. He was strong enough to guard tight ends and take on fullbacks at the line of scrimmage."

Declining due to age and some subpar drafts following the departure of the brilliant Finks to the Chicago Bears after the '73 campaign, the Vikings were still a playoff-caliber unit heading into Tarkenton's last season in '78. Tarkenton missed that January's 23–6 NFC title game loss to the eventual Super Bowl champion Cowboys due to a broken leg. His last game would be December 31, 1978, at the Los Angeles Coliseum in a 34–10 playoff loss to the Rams.

That season proved to be Wright's last as a player as well. Having missed the entire campaign heading into November, he had a decision to make.

"Bud said to me, 'We've been watching you in practice and we think you look ready to be activated,'" said Wright. "But I just didn't think I could play at a level where I wouldn't hurt the team."

As a result, Wright rounded out his Vikings career on the coaching staff before retiring to work in the commercial cleaning supplies business. Proud grandfather of two girls, Wright has lived in Phoenix the last 20 years.

"We love it here," concluded Wright. "I don't miss the winters, but we make it back to Minnesota each year for alumni events."

As Andy Williams sang, "*Try to remember, the kind of September,*" when the likes of No. 43 (Nate Wright), No. 22 (Krause), No. 20 (Bryant) and No. 23—the last piece of the puzzle, Jeff Wright—roamed the secondary for the '70s Vikings.

9

Hail Mary Agony

Dallas 17, Minnesota Vikings 14
December 28, 1975, Metropolitan Stadium
Divisional-Round Playoff

Jimmy Carr wasn't Minnesota's defensive backfield coach in 1975, but if he was, those who knew him say the Vikings' divisional-round game with Dallas would have simply been a continuance of the team's season-long tour de force.

Instead, an anticipated successful step on the road to another NFC title became a "Hail Mary" disaster that still sickens Vikings players 50 years later.

Carr, affectionately known as "Gummy," was a pioneer in the NFL's usage of complex defensive backfield configurations, leaving an indelible mark on players he tutored during his 24 years as an assistant coach with the Chicago Bears, Philadelphia Eagles, Detroit Lions, Buffalo Bills, New England Patriots, Atlanta Falcons and Minnesota, where he first coached in 1966.

When Roger Staubach took the field for Dallas's final drive with under two minutes left and his team trailing 14–10 in the now-famous playoff game on December 28, 1975, at Metropolitan Stadium, it didn't take long to notice the Vikings were using four defensive backs.

By 1975, Jimmy Carr had made three other coaching stops after leaving the Vikings to become the Bears' defensive coordinator in 1969. But if he was in Minnesota, there's no telling how many defensive backs he would have thrown at the Cowboys, who scored with 32 seconds left on Staubach's 50-yard pass to Drew Pearson to gain a 17–14 come-from-behind victory.

Assistant coach Neill Armstrong, who took over as the Vikings' defensive coordinator when Bob Hollway left in 1971 to accept the head coaching job in St. Louis, kept Minnesota in a standard base defense the entire nine-play drive, one that called for four linemen, three linebackers and four defensive backs.

Given Carr's history, undoubtedly one of the team's three linebackers—Matt Blair, Jeff Siemon and Wally Hilgenberg—would have been off the field replaced by a defensive back, particularly since Dallas deployed what amounted to a third receiver in the backfield in former Steeler Preston Pearson.

"Gummy was a very innovative coach," said safety Dale Hackbart, who joined the Vikings in Carr's first year with the club. "He knew the game because he played in the NFL. He knew teams, he knew coaches. He'd come up with so many defenses, with six, seven defensive backs and three down linemen. He had a great sense for changing up defenses to confuse the opponent. Against a running team like Cleveland, which had

Jim Brown, he'd use five defensive linemen; against a team that threw the ball a lot, like the Colts with Johnny Unitas, he'd use five or six defensive backs."

It was under Carr's teaching wizardry that the Vikings rose out of their expansion ashes to forge an ingenious and omnipresent pass defense that would finish in the top three in yards allowed in each of his three years before he left for Chicago, and thus set the standard for the team's history-making defensive units to come.

In the years following Carr's departure, his inventiveness still trickled into the Vikings' defensive playbook. Armstrong mirrored Carr's cutting-edge approach when he effectively used five down linemen and six defensive backs during the team's postseason run in 1974, often subbing in on passing downs Bob Lurtsema, Terry Brown and Randy Poltl, an unheralded defensive back from Stanford who had an interception in the NFC championship game win over the Los Angeles Rams. Armstrong was unable to duplicate that look in '75, as Poltl was let go on the last cut and signed with the Denver Broncos after one year in Minnesota and Brown was being used as a starter for the injured Jeff Wright.

"I didn't play well in the last exhibition game and I guess they decided to go with Autry Beamon," said Poltl of the Vikings' 12th-round pick that season out of Texas A&M-Commerce. "My first training camp with the Vikings, the veterans were out due to the strike. We played our opening exhibition game at Denver and I picked up a fumble at the four and ran it back 96 yards for a touchdown. That was a lot of fun. I guess I made an impression."

Poltl suffered a significant ankle sprain and didn't get his first taste of regular-season action until late in the season. It was then that Armstrong saw enough in his coverage ability to use him as a third safety along with Paul Krause and Brown. His interception in the championship game against the Rams came after James Harris lofted a pass toward the right sideline intended for former Viking Lance Rentzel. Drifting over to help cornerback Nate Wright, Poltl picked off the pass at the Vikings' 20 and ran it back 16 yards.

"Denver used me in much of the same way, coming in on passing downs," said Poltl, who played three seasons with the Broncos, including their AFC championship season in '77. During his four NFL seasons, he played in two Super Bowls "and a Rose Bowl in college as well," said Poltl with a smile.

Carr, a good ol' boy from East Bank, West Virginia, played nine years in the NFL, the first two with the hapless Chicago Cardinals before being acquiring by the Eagles in 1959. It was in Philadelphia where Carr studied under backfield coach Jerry Williams, who many credit for the earliest utilization in the NFL of "nickel" defensive alignments, where five defensive backs are deployed. George Allen later became one of its main practitioners, most notably during his highly successful seven-year stint with the Washington Redskins.

Carr, starting at left corner opposite Tom Brookshire, was part of the nickel deployment Williams used to help the Eagles become the only team to defeat Vince Lombardi's Green Bay Packers in a championship game. Philadelphia won 17–13 on December 26, 1960, at Franklin Field, limiting quarterback Bart Starr to 21 of 34 passing for 178 yards.

The quarterback of that Eagles team was Norm Van Brocklin, who quickly nabbed Carr for his Minnesota defensive staff after the University of Charleston grad played out the final two years of his career as a linebacker with Washington.

"He was a brilliant defensive backfield strategist," said Jerry Reichow, who was in his second year as the Vikings' lone scout when Carr arrived from Washington. "He knew more than our defensive coordinators knew. He knew the game and how to set people up. He could have been the defensive coordinator but he wasn't. He was way ahead of those other coaches. They just didn't understand the things he knew. Gummy Carr was smarter than all of them. Neill was quiet. He was good, but he was more of a 'do your thing' kind of guy. Gummy knew every part of the defense."

Cornerback Bobby Bryant, who was on the other side of the field guarding wide receiver Golden Richards on the Hail Mary play, said there were many times when Carr would pull a linebacker like Lonnie Warwick and have him in at middle linebacker.

"I remember when we played Baltimore in the playoff game [in '68 at Memorial Stadium]. Gummy had me in for Lonnie as an extra defensive back, and I'm lined up at the middle linebacker spot. I'm just praying they don't run the football," laughed the smallish but rangy Bryant, who played at around 170 pounds.

The NFL's all-time leader with 81 career interceptions, Krause credits Carr with changing the course of his career. Upon being drafted by the Redskins in 1964, he played alongside the then-linebacker Carr for two years. Krause believes it was that connection that eventually brought him to the Vikings.

"Gummy was so smart and we had a lot of interchangeable guys playing defensive back on the Vikings that he took advantage of, like Dale Hackbart, who was also with me in Washington," said Krause, who had seven interceptions with Carr as his defensive backfield coach in '68, the second most in his 12 years in purple.

Hackbart became a key player off the bench for Carr.

"Carr was one of the first to implement the fifth defensive back," said Hackbart, used by Carr at all three linebacker spots on passing downs. "We called that the 'Hack Defense,' named after me. They'd take out a Roy Winston or a Hilgenberg and they'd put me in. We'd use four linemen and seven defensive backs. With our defensive front, we didn't have to cover long. [Alan] Page was a holy terror."

Warwick, who started at middle linebacker from 1965 to '72 before being replaced by Siemon, was enamored with Carr, who served a second stint with the Vikings from 1979 to 1981.

"Really the key to our defense was Jimmy Carr," said Warwick. "He knew defenses in and out. Most assistant coaches only know their position. But Gummy knew what everybody on the defense had to do. He was one of the best coaches I have been around. He was so far ahead of everybody. He was brilliant. He didn't mind taking a defensive lineman out and putting a defensive back in. He was so knowledgeable about situations. He would turn to me and say, 'From watching film, what do you think they're going to do here from the formation they're in?' That really helped me figure things out."

By 1975, Carr was defensive coordinator for the NFC Central Division rival Detroit Lions. His pupils remaining on Minnesota's league-leading pass defense, which allowed just 1,621 yards and 93 first downs, were Bryant at right corner and Krause at free safety.

Underdogs despite leading the NFC in total offense, Dallas came into the contest having finished second in the NFC East behind 11–3 St. Louis, but its 10–4 mark was good enough for a wild-card spot. Seen as a team in decline going into the campaign, the Cowboys lost to retirement or defection to the World Football League key players such as Bob Lilly, Walt Garrison, Cornell Green, Bob Hayes, Dave Manders, John Niland and Calvin Hill.

What saved the Cowboys was a historically magnificent draft, one that saw 12 rookies, tabbed the "Dirty Dozen," make the roster, including Randy White, Thomas

"Hollywood" Henderson, Bob Breunig, Burton Lawless, Pat Donovan and Herbert Scott.

Coming off another Super Bowl appearance, Minnesota ripped off 10 straight wins to open the season and was on track to duplicate Miami's 1972–73 season before falling by one point in a nationally televised game to Allen's Redskins on November 30 at RFK Stadium.

The Vikings finished 12–2, led by MVP Fran Tarkenton and back Chuck Foreman, who came within six yards of pulling off an NFC Triple Crown (yards rushing, receptions and touchdowns). He led the NFL with 73 catches and was tied with O.J. Simpson in TDs (22). His 1,070 yards rushing were second in the NFC to Jim Otis (1,076).

On Staubach's deep ball, Vikings left cornerback Nate Wright, as normally was the case with receivers he guarded, was stride for stride with Pearson, but the ball was fortuitously underthrown by Staubach, giving the star Dallas receiver leverage he needed to make possible an inconceivable off-the-hip reception. To the shock of the fans in the right centerfield bleachers, he walked in from the four-yard line.

"I thought I had an interception," said Wright. "The ball was thrown short, and I went to jump for it and Pearson pushed me, and my feet went out from under me."

Drew Pearson, nearly 50 years later, denies there was any shove.

"The ball was underthrown because Roger made a big pump fake," said Pearson, who signed with the Cowboys as an undrafted free agent out of Tulsa in '73. "By the time Roger made the throw, I was way downfield. Receivers are taught if we are going to get inside position on a defensive back, we must use our outside arm to get to the ball. Nate was right there. There was contact, but there was not a deliberate push. He turned to look at the ball and he went down."

Starting along with Krause at safety in a Vikings secondary that led the NFC with 28 interceptions was the Oklahoma State product Brown.

"I had the flat on the Hail Mary play. We were in a zone defense," recalled Brown. "Everybody was deep. It was just one of those things. Pearson pushed Nate for sure. They didn't have instant replay back then. That's the way it is, we were out of luck."

Had Wright kept his feet, he might have made his first interception of the year. He had six picks in his sensational '74 campaign, but "people just weren't throwing my way in '75," he said.

"Absolutely respected Nate," added Pearson. "We were just going after him due to the way he played within their defense. We knew their corners would cover you man once you got in their zone. Nate would do that. On the left side Bobby Bryant would do the same thing, but he's not looking at you. Counter routes didn't work against Bryant. We knew that. I only caught one pass on his side."

Chuck Foreman still contends the legality of the play.

"What the hell, Nate had the coverage, but the guy pushes you down," said Foreman, who gave the Vikings a 7–0 lead with 11:49 left in the second quarter three plays after the special teams set them up at the Dallas four after a punt hit Donovan's foot. "You've got to make that call. If they had instant replay at the time that would have been called back. All the stuff with the Cowboys it was just fluke plays. They didn't beat us; they just gave it to them."

Seconds after the contact was made, a fan threw an orange onto the field, giving all appearances of a penalty flag.

"I saw something go by me," said Pearson. "I thought that maybe it was a flag, but once I saw it rolling, I knew we were all right."

"I thought it was [a flag]," said Wright, only to see field judge Armen Terzian not reach for his whistle. "Pearson will never admit it. He wanted to get in the Hall of Fame and that's his play."

Pearson was inducted in 2021.

"If you're going to catch a Hail Mary pass, you didn't want to do it against Nate Wright," said Pearson. "Solid player. Great guy. Didn't talk on the field, just did his job. Much respect for Nate."

Wright surprisingly didn't get much help on the play from Krause, who had a whopping league-leading 201 return yards on 10 interceptions in '75. He was a step and a half late getting there after biting on Staubach's pronounced pump fake to his right.

"Krause anticipated he was going to Richards," said Nate Wright of the fleet receiver who was limited to a pair of catches for 20 yards by Bryant. "He was their speed guy and they liked to go to him deep."

That's exactly what the Cowboys did on their first series of the fourth quarter, a play that still had to be on Krause's mind. Dallas took a 10–7 lead on the first play of the fourth quarter on a 25-yard field goal by Toni Fritsch. After a three-and-out by Minnesota, the Cowboys faced a third and long at their own 20. Richards ran past Bryant down the left sideline, but Staubach's throw, a little short but very catchable, went off the receiver's hands.

Had Richards hauled in the over-the-shoulder catch, it would have been 17–7 Dallas. Instead, Minnesota got the ball back and marched down for the go-ahead score.

"It was a pretty dramatic pump fake," said Pearson, who played in 22 career playoff games. "Roger told Golden to run a good post route to hold Paul Krause so I could be man-to-man on Nate Wright. We knew Paul Krause and what he could do. We understood also that most of his interceptions were on overthrows. He's playing so deep so he's going to make those plays, so we needed to hold him to the left side of the field."

A little-known aspect of the play was that Alan Page was not on the field at the time. On the front four along with Marshall, Carl Eller and rookie Mark Mullaney was Lurtsema, affectionately known as "Benchwarmer Bob."

"The decision came from the coaching staff," Page told Alex Rubenstein, who along with Jon Bois produced the remarkable *History of the Minnesota Vikings* documentary in 2023 for Secret Base, an offshoot of sports website SBNation. "It had nothing to do with cramps or an injury."

The Cowboys, who dominated statistically, with 356 total yards to Minnesota's 215, started their final desperate drive at their own 15 following Richards's fair catch of a Vikings punt. To this point in the contest, Drew Pearson had yet to make a reception.

Dallas had two time-outs left. The nine-play sequence that followed will go down in NFL lore:

First down and 10 at Dallas 15 (1:51 left)—Sideline completion right to Drew Pearson, nine yards.

Second and one at Dallas 24 (1:45 left)—Low snap by center John Fitzgerald; pass intended for Richards deftly broken up by Bryant.

Third and one at Dallas 24 (1:40 left)—Completion left to Drew Pearson for seven yards.

First and 10 at Dallas 31 (1:24 left)—Another low snap by Fitzgerald and Staubach falls on ball at his own 24.

Second and 17 at Dallas 24 (58 seconds left)—Incomplete on left sideline to tight end Jean Fugett.

Third and 17 at Dallas 24 (52 seconds left)—Lurtsema in at right end for Marshall. Incomplete to Fugett. Lurtsema, with fresh legs, had a quarterback pressure on the play.

"I was in on that play and I didn't get held, I got tackled [by Fitzgerald]," said Lurtsema. "They came out in a split formation, and we ran a deal. I swung inside and Page went outside. In a split formation I would go first and it kind of surprised them. I got literally tackled. They did that the whole game."

Fourth and 17 at Dallas 24 (44 seconds left)—Rookie Kyle Davis in at center for Dallas. Lurtsema still in for Marshall. No stunt this time. Staubach completes a controversial pass on the right sideline to Drew Pearson. Game video shows Page was tackled by Dallas guard Burton Lawless. No call.

Both linebacker Blair and safety Brown had a great look at the play. Brown raced over to express his disapproval.

"I think he was out of bounds. I'm sure of it," said Brown. "I protested but it didn't do any good."

A year later in the championship game against the Rams, Armstrong, maybe with the Dallas play on his mind, dialed up a blitz on a key fourth-down play that resulted in a Bryant interception.

Vikings running back Ed Marinaro, who had his best year in four years with the Vikings in '75, was an eyewitness.

"It was surreal," he said. "Robert Miller was one of the guys I played with. It was fourth and 17 and we're up 14–10 and I look at Robert and say, 'Robert, you're going to see what it looks like to go to the Super Bowl.' The next play … and it was like, 'Oh, my gosh, did I jinx myself?' I would have been the starting running back in the Super Bowl. I played in the Miami one and not much in the Pittsburgh one, but this would have been my chance. I would have been introduced with the starting lineup in the Super Bowl. It was emotionally draining. It was like, 'What the hell just happened?'"

Two plays later, the season was all but over.

"It was miserable," said Miller. "Eddie and I were talking, and the defense was on the field. The defense was incredible the whole year. We saw the pass and your emotions hit rock bottom because that was the season. The season ended on one pass, one throw. It was very quiet. No one said anything. That's the first time I had experienced anything like that. You ask yourself what you could have done differently. That's what my focus was during the offseason, to correct any mistakes I made as a rookie."

After the fourth-down play, Page, looking fatigued, is bent at the waist with his right hand leaning on his right thigh. In the Dallas huddle, Staubach asks Drew Pearson if he can run the same pattern, only deeper. He says, "No man. I'm tired, wait awhile."

First and 10 at 50 (37 seconds left)—Marshall is back in for Lurtsema. Pass incomplete on left flat to Preston Pearson.

On the play, Page can't get by Lawless, so he wisely drops off the line and nearly slaps down the pass. It was eerily like his game-sealing play in the '69 Western Conference championship against the Rams, when he dropped off the line, then tipped and intercepted a Roman Gabriel pass intended for Larry Smith to secure the Vikings' first home playoff win.

Second and 10 at 50 (32 seconds left)—Lurtsema in for Page. In the Dallas huddle, Staubach asks Drew Pearson if he had recovered. He said, "Yeah, I'm ready." Staubach closes his eyes and says a Hail Mary. Viking fans know what happened next.

"The Vikings hurt themselves on that drive," said Drew Pearson. "They're playing a prevent defense. But if you come into their area, they're going to be pick-you-up man. We ran the counter routes on Nate Wright's side because of his style of play."

Why was Page out?

It may be that beloved Vikings line coach Jack Patera subbed for Page for two, possibly three reasons. First, because Page may have been tired—although upon further analysis, the 1971 MVP was often seen bent at the waist with his right hand resting on his right thigh in between snaps. It was just something he often did.

Secondly, Patera had a lot of confidence in Lurtsema, who in 1968 was named to the All-NFL team by *Sporting News*.

"I was the only guy on our team that could play all five positions. They had confidence in me that there wouldn't be too much of a drop-off," he said. "We had a rotation and there would be times when Page was out. Sometimes we did it to give them a different look. Sudsie [Doug Sutherland] was more of a power rusher."

Thirdly, Patera had no way of knowing that it would be his team's final defensive snap. Dallas had time-outs remaining. The Cowboys were still at midfield and it took them eight thumb-biting plays to get there. He didn't expect them to cover it all in one play.

The fourth member of the line on the Hail Mary play along with Marshall, Eller and Lurtsema was Mullaney, a strapping 6-6, 250-pounder drafted 23rd in the first round out of Colorado State. Normally an end, Mullaney was in at tackle for Sutherland.

"It's a demanding position. Nobody knew that it was going to be the last [defensive] play of the game," said Mullaney. "I had never played tackle before, but it was just all about having fresh legs in the game. Offensive linemen are getting tired at that point and when you put fresh legs in the game you got a better chance. Patera was in the press box and all the substitutions I believe went through Bud. That '75 team was the best I've played on. We thought we had the game won. Maybe everybody was a little overconfident."

Eller and Marshall were at end, with Mullaney and Lurtsema playing inside. The two tackles ran a stunt and Mullaney, moving left to right, bull-rushed Dallas guard Blaine Nye, pushing him back several yards. But the wily Nye, in his ninth season out of Stanford, grabbed Mullaney as he was encroaching upon Staubach.

"I thought I was tackled," said Mullaney. "Bob was, too, earlier on the drive. It was unfortunate."

Eller still shakes his head over the loss.

"I just think we didn't have any luck against them," said Eller, who had a monster game with three sacks. "Things kind of went against us. We had to play extra hard to overcome the obstacles. Not just the Cowboys, but other obstacles [officiating]. They were a worthy opponent. Rayfield Wright was a good tackle. We should have beat that team in all the [playoff] games, but we didn't."

Eller said the devastating loss to Dallas shouldn't take away from the team's great success.

"We had the kind of team that everyone took pride in their positions. Everyone could play, from the defensive backs to the linebackers and, of course, our front four," he said. "Our responsibility was to keep them out of the end zone, and that's the attitude we took. The fans supported us, so no matter what the situation, we played to win, even after a tough loss. We were committed to ourselves and to the fans to be the best we could be."

• • •

According to a pair of eyewitnesses, the Pearson-Staubach miracle probably should have never happened.

The Vikings took a 14–10 lead with just over five minutes left on a second-effort Brent McClanahan TD dive. After the teams swapped possessions, Dallas set up for the fateful fourth-and-17 play.

Make a stop here and move on to play the Rams at home in the title game for the second straight season.

Starting out of the shotgun formation that Dallas brought back into vogue that season, Staubach from his own 15 threw a deep, high-arching sideline pass to Pearson. It was the kind of throw only a few QBs would have even thought to attempt, given the length of time the ball had to be in the air. The ball was not only thrown a seemingly forever 35 yards in the air, but also well before Pearson made his cut from inside the right hash toward the sideline.

Nate Wright, again, was right there to seal off the sideline.

Pearson went up for the catch, and as he was nearing the boundary, Wright, known for his strong tackling skills, two-handed him out of bounds.

Head linesman Jerry Bergman ruled that it was a completion, believing that Pearson would have landed in bounds had Wright not shoved him out. The rule, which was changed in 2008, allowed the official to rule a completion in case he believed a "force-out" prevented a receiver from getting both feet down in bounds.

"The rule on the Pearson pass caught on the sidelines is a judgment call," said Jack Reader, assistant supervisor of officials. "In this case, the official thought that Pearson would have come down inside the line with both feet had he not been shoved out of bounds."[1]

"I'm not sure what the call was, but I believe it was a catch either way," said Pearson. "I would have had my feet in if they didn't hit me and force me out. The force-out rule was in effect then. It was a great throw. Roger made it from the far hashmark. He's going to me all the way on the play."

"There's no way he would have been able to get both feet in bounds," said backup quarterback Bob Lee.

The 6-0, 184-pound Pearson, a quarterback for parts of both his high school and college careers, said he and Staubach adjusted on the fly for the entire final drive.

"That whole drive, Coach Landry did not call one play," said Pearson. "Roger took over that drive and pretty much every time we huddled up, he said, 'Drew, what do you got?' I gave him information as to how I could get open. He knew it was solid stuff and that it wasn't based on emotion. It was based on what was happening right then. The [fourth-down] play call was 'Ray 16.' Ray means protection to the right, 16 is the route. Normally that's a route where I run about 15, 16 yards, then break it into the middle of the defense. But Roger said instead of running a 16 route, run a post-corner. The last thing Roger said when we broke the huddle was, 'Make sure you get enough for the first down.'

"Normally on a post corner you would go about seven, eight yards before you break to the outside, but given the distance, I had to run a deeper route," he added. "I took it about 12, 13 yards, then broke it back to the corner. When I made my move and saw the ball, it was humming. I almost needed a catcher's mitt."

Three of Pearson's four catches came on the right side. He said it wasn't due to a lack of ability on Wright's part but a result of the way he played within the Vikings' zone defensive scheme.

"Bobby Bryant on the other side was what we called 'a cluer,'" said Pearson. "That's a defensive back who no matter what route you run is looking through you to the quarterback. When he sees the quarterback throw the ball, he jumps the route. He did that against us in '73 [in the NFC championship game] at Texas Stadium. Nate was more of a corner who followed the receiver. That made him more susceptible to counter routes."

In hindsight, it would have been better if Wright let the play go undefended, as replays showed Pearson, as Lee indicated, had a minimal chance to get both feet in bounds. But since Wright laid hands on him, Bergman made the call that, as providence would have it, set up the Hail Mary two plays later.

"You don't have time to think about that because you're trying to make a play," noted Wright. "I don't remember the play that well, I just know that it was a bad call. I have never watched the replay. I was just reacting and that's all you can do."

The Vikings, mimicking Grant's stoic persona, were not known for blatant shows of emotion, but they displayed vehement dissent over Bergman's call, especially Blair and Brown, both of whom came racing over from their positions with their hands raised.

Even closer to the forgotten lead-up play to the Hail Mary pass was sideline security guard Dick Jonckowski.

Dick Jonckowski?

Jonckowski was 19 years old when he worked his first Vikings game at The Met for Sims Security in 1961. Fourteen years later, he's watching as Pearson is running directly toward him.

"I always anticipated where the ball was going so I could be on camera," laughed Jonckowski, who approximated that he nabbed 112 field goals during his time roaming the field, including each of Garo Yepremian's six against the Vikings for the Detroit Lions in 1966. "They pretty much let me roam around. Since both teams were stationed on the other sideline—we were the last team to do so—I was pretty much free to do some of the crazy things I did on the other sideline. I got away with a lot of things, did a lot of showboating. I would always figure out where the camera would be. Bob Lurtsema once said, 'This guy is always in our films.'"

Drew Pearson is now a few feet from Jonckowski. "He's running too fast to get both feet down," Jonckowski thought.

Jonckowski would go on to become a legendary figure in Minnesota sports circles, serving as a longtime PA announcer for the Minnesota Golden Gophers. One wonders what he would have blurted from the microphone had he called this play.

"There is no way his feet would have landed in bounds," said Jonckowski, who once even tried to break up a Fran Tarkenton fight with New England cornerback Ron Bolton in 1974. "I still believe that to this day. He came down out of bounds."

Jonckowski said confirming his view of the play was the nattily dressed man standing next to him on the sideline that afternoon, none other than CBS broadcasting legend Jack Whitaker.

"Jack looked right at me and said, 'Pearson was out,'" recalled Jonckowski, who was so frustrated by the call that he kicked Pearson while he was lying on the ground after the catch. Once this was found out by the NFL, he was subsequently suspended from working the Vikings sideline for two years.

"I did it out of frustration," he said. "It was nothing personal. It was just instinctive. It was a 'sissy' kick."

Nearly 50 years later, NFL Films Presents documented Pearson visiting Jonckowski at his Shakopee, Minnesota, home. The two hit it off.

"I consider Drew Pearson a pretty good friend right now," he said. "There were no hard feelings. He accepted my apology. It was something I'm not proud of."

Ironically, it would be on another December 28—albeit 28 years later, in 2003—that the dreaded force-out rule would again come back to haunt the Vikings. Cardinals receiver Nathan Poole's infamous TD catch in the right-hand corner of the end zone as time expired cost Randy Moss and Co. the North Division title and the playoffs in an 18–17 loss. He was pushed out of bounds by defensive backs Brian Russell and Denard Walker and a force-out was called.

Jonckowski also had a great look at the Hail Mary play.

"I was three yards from that catch," he said. "With all respect to Drew, I still say he pushed off, but he won't admit it. It was an unbelievable throw, but he did push off on Nate Wright."

Staubach asked Pearson to make another adjustment to the 16 route, his signature pattern, on the Hail Mary play.

"He wanted me to run it, but instead of staying inside, break up field," he said. "That route, the 16, was my best route, my bread and butter, where I ran into the middle of the defense. It's more rounded off than a post pattern and it's effective against a zone. Usually that's the route we'd run on third and eight and longer. Roger had confidence in me to get open on that route.

"When I got into the league, I had to be noticed for something. I went undrafted," he said. "I decided I was going to be the guy who went over the middle fearlessly to make those catches. That's what I prided myself on. Not the Hail Mary and all that but making those third-down catches and keeping the offense on the field. I'm from New Jersey. I grew up watching Johnny Sample and Erich Barnes. Those guys made you pay when you caught the football. I wanted to be a guy who could make those tough catches. Roger could really bring that ball. It got to me quick, so a lot of times I had the chance to catch the ball, brace myself and spin for more yards."

• • •

Minnesota had grittily taken a 14–10 lead on a gut-check of all gut-check drives—an 11-play, 70-yard sojourn that gobbled up better than six minutes of the clock and culminated in a signature broken-tackle scoring effort by the unsung McClanahan. The one-yard foray over the goal line came with 5:11 remaining.

Looking shell-shocked on the ensuing possession, Dallas went three and out largely due to a pair of errant shotgun snaps by Fitzgerald, one leading to a combined sack by Page and Marshall. Making matters worse for the Cowboys, a poor punt by Mitch Hoopes allowed the Vikings to take over at their own 45 with just under four minutes left.

Now was the time to finish things off and the Vikings had just the personnel to do it. A crafty MVP quarterback who had just called a great scoring drive, gifted runners in the multitalented Foreman and McClanahan, a gamebreaker in John Gilliam at wide receiver and a steady, glue-handed tight end in Stu Voigt.

Foreman, who throughout the contest had trouble getting traction, was finally heating up after struggling early, with 22 of his 56 yards coming on the go-ahead drive. He ripped off runs of seven, 10 and five yards and had a pair of big catches for 28 yards as the Dallas front wall of Ed "Too Tall" Jones, Jethro Pugh, Larry Cole and Harvey Martin slowly started to show signs of fatigue.

But with Dallas keying on Foreman, the Vikings put the game into the hands of McClanahan, who had carried the ball only twice to that point, the first coming on a reverse where he took a handoff from Foreman and raced 13 yards to the Dallas 16, setting up his second-effort TD run three plays later.

A four-point lead was favorable, thought Tarkenton, but it could have easily been a double-digit advantage had he and Gilliam connected on one of the three near misses on deep balls thrown in second-year starter Mark Washington's direction in the first half. Then there was veteran Fred Cox missing a field goal from 45 yards out after Marinaro beat linebacker D.D. Lewis for 40 yards on an out and up to the Dallas 35 on the team's first second-half possession when already leading 7–0.

As he stepped to the scrimmage line to take the snap from center Mick Tingelhoff, Tarkenton was determined to end it right here and start preparing for another championship game with the Rams.

McClanahan for four yards.

McClanahan for four yards.

Now third and two at the Cowboys' 47 with 2:20 remaining.

Although the Cowboys had all three time-outs and the two-minute warning upcoming, the Vikings strongly believed they could sew up the game with a first down.

Dallas called a time-out.

Tarkenton recalled the sequence in the book *Every Day Is Game Day* with Jim Bruton.

"I went over to the sideline to talk to Jerry Burns, our offensive coordinator," said Tarkenton, who was sacked four times by the Cowboys. "We needed to come up with a play to keep the ball and control the ending of the game. Burnsie felt that a running play was our best chance to keep possession. I was convinced we try a rollout to the right side and that I could run for the first down, or at the very least have a great opportunity to toss a short pass to Chuck Foreman for the necessary yardage. My self-assurance was enough to convince Jerry, and I went back into the game, confident that we had made the right play call, and that the play would work."[2]

There were two reasons why Tarkenton believed the play would work. First, he had made a living on rollouts right. No quarterback did it better than Sir Francis until a guy named Joe Montana came around. Secondly, it had worked earlier in the game.

On their go-ahead drive, the Vikings faced a huge third-and-two situation at the Dallas 48. They came out in a split formation, with Ed Marinaro in the backfield to Foreman's left. Charles Goodrum was in as an extra lineman and Steve Craig as the extra tight end on the same side as Voigt but a yard off the line of scrimmage.

Marinaro went in motion right and broke toward the flat as Tarkenton semi-rolled that way. The play was designed for Craig to move to his left to pick or rub off Cowboys safety Charlie Waters and for Voigt to crisscross him from left to right. The play worked like a charm and Marinaro was wide open for the first down.

Backup running back Robert Miller didn't believe the call originated out of the playbook.

"We rarely used motion," he said. "But playing with Francis, he would make up things like that. As a rookie I'm playing in my first game in San Diego. It was back when we played six exhibition games. Fran said, 'Robert, I want you to line up a couple steps closer to me. When you get the ball, the hole is going to be so wide open your eyes are going to pop.' The play was our 23, a straight dive, and when I hit that hole, a Mack truck could have driven through it. He would make up plays at different times and they would work. He would see things and that's probably why he sent Ed in motion."

As wide open as Marinaro was, it's no wonder Tarkenton wanted to go back to the same play when he huddled with Burns.

What Tarkenton didn't realize was Dallas coach Tom Landry, while conferring with Waters on the same sideline, may possibly have gotten insight on what the Vikings were going to do by taking into consideration a play he himself called during the NFL championship game on New Year's Day 1967 at the Cotton Bowl.

Playing in its first championship game, Dallas, down 34–27 to the Green Bay Packers, had time for one more drive.

A pass interference penalty on Green Bay safety Tom Brown gave the Cowboys a first down at the Packers' two-yard line with under two minutes remaining.

Dan Reeves gained a yard on first down. Then, a crucial false start by Jim Boeke penalized the Cowboys back to the Green Bay six.

Reeves dropped a pass in the flat on second down. Meredith then had tight end Pettis Norman wide open on third down near the right flag, but his pass was low, a critical error as Norman had to go to his knees to make the catch and was touched down at the two.

The Packers under Lombardi, one of Fordham's fabled "Seven Blocks of Granite" line of the late 1930s, would have opted to power the ball in with Jim Taylor. With the high-tech Cowboys being more disguise and finesse driven, it came as no surprise to the Packers what Dallas's mindset would be on this critical play. And that was for Meredith to roll out right, giving him a run-pass option.

Green Bay left linebacker Dave Robinson knew this and blew past Bob Hayes, who was mistakenly deployed in the Dallas goal line offense instead of Frank Clarke. Robinson easily brushed Hayes aside and forced Meredith into throwing a wobbler that was easily intercepted by Brown near the end line.

"I saw Hayes on the field and was wondering what they were doing," recalled the Hall of Famer Robinson, who played 10 years with the Packers before being acquired by Washington to finish out his last two seasons with the fabled "Over the Hill Gang."

"There was no way he was going to block me and I got to Meredith. I was a little to the inside and if Meredith had any speed at all he could have easily got around me to the pylon."

The ball-hawking Waters, like Robinson, understood tendencies. Whenever the Vikings needed a big play on third down, the preponderance of evidence pointed to a Tarkenton rollout right.

Tarkenton trotted back to the huddle, knowing a successful play would eventually force the Cowboys to use their remaining time-outs. He sent McClanahan, still in for Marinaro, in motion to his right.

Craig, again in as a second tight end to the right of the formation, came off the line but was ignored by Waters, who without hesitation stormed into the backfield. Foreman couldn't get over in time to get a piece of him and Waters easily lassoed Tarkenton to the ground.

"It was almost as though they had been a part of the sideline discussion," said a disgusted Tarkenton.[3]

The Vikings didn't change formations often, but they routinely deployed two tight ends in short-yardage situations.

"It was pretty much a blasé offense, no motion," added Craig. "Pretty much old-time football. We did the same thing year after year. It probably wasn't too hard to scout the Vikings."

Viewed as a much-disciplined team, it was rare for the Vikings to be caught off guard on a short-yardage play like they were against Dallas. Consistent, repetitive situational work at practice was a key.

"It wasn't so much on teaching us techniques—you should know how to block when you're at that level—but more to take it to a professional level," said Craig. "To be consistent and to handle your assignments every time. On defense, one person can make a play and make a stop for the defense. But on offense, everyone has to handle their assignments for a play to work. That's one thing they really stressed in Minnesota. We were normally strong in short yardage."

On this critical play, Dallas was certainly ready.

"You can't go to the well too often," said Foreman. "They saw it coming. You can out-think yourself, and that's what happened."

Dallas got the ball back and went down to score. It was a huge lost opportunity for a team that would have more than likely gone on to meet the Steelers in the Super Bowl for a second-straight season.

In Tarkenton's defense, most teams knew the Vikings often used the rollout in those situations, but they still couldn't stop them. Nevertheless, the play still eats at a man whose father, Dallas, tragically died of a heart attack while watching the game in Georgia.

"There is absolutely no doubt in my mind the decision cost us the game," Tarkenton said. "I should have gone with Burnsie's running play. It hurts to relive it."[4]

It's believed the Cowboys did not officially become "America's Team" until NFL Films produced a documentary by that name detailing the club's '78 season, which saw them appear in their third Super Bowl in four campaigns, losing twice to the Steelers.

"I never liked Dallas," said Foreman. "Thomas Henderson would talk the whole game, but he always got beat by me. We beat them on several occasions. A lot of those guys were trash talkers. That was our greatest team and we had to lose on crap like that."

• • •

The player who tied Dallas's Preston Pearson for most receptions in the game with five was Ed Marinaro, who was having his best year with the Vikings.

Selected by Minnesota in the second round of the '72 draft, Marinaro was a prolific back at Cornell, where he was a three-time All-American, setting over 16 NCAA records. He was the first in NCAA history to run for 4,000 career yards and led the nation in rushing in 1971. He was runner-up to Pat Sullivan for the Heisman Trophy that season, the highest finish for an Ivy League player since the league deemphasized football in the mid–1950s.

Lightly used as a runner with Minnesota, the most carries he had in his Vikings career was 101 in 1975. He played 58 games with Minnesota and had just 306 carries and 1,007 yards rushing. In his three years at Cornell, Marinaro had 918 carries for nearly 5,000 yards.

"To this day, I'd love to know their reasoning behind drafting me," he wondered. "I did not fit the Viking running back mode at that point, head down, tough runners, guys like Dave Osborn, Bill Brown, Oscar Reed. I was just a different kind of guy. Probably my greatest accomplishment as an athlete was learning how to block in the NFL. It's not easy. I knew I could catch the ball. I played basketball and had basketball scholarships to college, but the blocking part was challenging."

He was forced to reinvent himself as a receiver out of the backfield in the NFL, so much so that his 54 catches in '75 were good for sixth overall in the NFL and third in the NFC.

"We took a flyer on Ed coming out of an Ivy League school and it worked out pretty darn well," said Reichow. "Now, he could catch the ball. We drafted him more as an athlete. We had a good team and Bud didn't like rookies."

"They saw the value in me as a receiver," said Marinaro, who went on to have a lengthy acting career. "I probably could have played tight end. I was about 225 and strong and I could get open. All told, I probably played in about half of the games I was active in Minnesota. Ironically, two things I never did in college were catch the ball and block, and that's what they had me doing."

When he did get to start, Marinaro proved to be productive.

"I started 15 games the last year I was there and had a pretty good season," he said. "They just kind of didn't think I could run the ball, but statistics showed that every time they gave me the ball more than five times, I got good games. The first game I ever started was my rookie year in Lambeau against the Packers, and it was the seventh game of the season, and I had 19 carries for 80 yards, the most any Viking player had rushed for us all season to that point. I was not the three-yards-and-a-cloud-of-dust type guy. That wasn't my style. Coming out of college, I would go where I saw daylight. With the Vikings, it was a very structured offense and you had to run to the hole. That game I was running all over the place and they were yelling at me, 'Follow your block, you got to go there!' I didn't run where I didn't see a hole. When they looked at the films the next day, they were chewing my ass out about not running to the hole. I still wonder why they drafted me. I never got down into a three-point stance my whole time in college."

Upon coming to Minnesota, Marinaro was asked by Gilliam to be his roommate. Little did he know the speedy wide receiver had an ulterior motive.

"Even though I was a rookie, he asked if I wanted to be his roommate on the road," recalled Marinaro. "When we traveled, we doubled up. I was flattered that this veteran, All-Pro guy wanted to be my roommate. We stayed roommates our four years in Minnesota. I asked him one time, 'Why did you choose me?' He said, 'I thought you were going to get cut and I would get my own room.' John's a great guy, we stayed friends."

Marinaro wore No. 44 at Cornell, but the number wasn't available when he arrived in Minnesota, so he switched to No. 49.

"When I came to Minnesota to sign my contract, they asked me what number I wanted. They had a guy named Leo Hayden, drafted No. 1 the year before [24th overall in '71] out of Ohio State, who wore 44, so I asked for 42," Marinaro recalled. "My girlfriend had a key chain made, 'Fast Eddie 42.' I get to training camp, and I go to my locker at camp and see No. 49 hanging there. During the offseason they traded for Gilliam. John was No. 44 in St. Louis. That was taken. He had precedent so he took 42, so they gave me 49. Which wasn't bad because ironically that was my high school number.

"We had a lot of running backs—Dave Osborn, Bill Brown, Oscar Reed, Clinton Jones, Jim Lindsey, and there were a couple other rookie running backs—and they were only going to keep six," Marinaro added. "I had to beat Leo out to make the team. He had hands of stone. And in our offense, you had to catch the ball out of the backfield. Leo could not catch the ball. I tried to help him, but the ball would go in and hit him in the face. When they cut Leo, they came to John and asked him if he wanted 44. He said, 'No way, that's an unlucky number.' I didn't take it either."

The next player who wore No. 44 was Chuck Foreman.

A standout on the great Ohio State teams of the late '60s, which included quarterback Rex Kern and fullback Jim Otis in the same backfield, Hayden turned out to be one of the Vikings' worst draft busts.

"At Iowa, I played in the East-West Shrine Game for Woody Hayes," said Reichow. "He and I got along great. I get down to Ohio State and get to watch Hayden play against someone and I thought he was a good little running back and we drafted him first. It turned out later he had all kinds of off-the-field problems, which Woody never mentioned. Nobody knew about it. BLESTO didn't know about it. You just couldn't get that kind of information back then."

When Marinaro arrived at Mankato that first year, he was given an unflattering nickname—Avis. No. 1 in the car rental world in the '70s was Hertz. His needling teammates couldn't resist Marinaro was the "Avis" of the Heisman race to Sullivan's "Hertz."

"We try harder, Avis," laughed Marinaro, whose challenging nickname was featured on an NFL Films segment his rookie year titled *The World of the NFL: Trial and Triumph*. "I finished second in the Heisman. I wish I would have worked that for a big contract with Avis."

He arrived in Mankato driving a purple Porsche. The color he wanted was not available at his local dealership in New Jersey, so he settled for a hue that certainly caught the attention of his veteran teammates.

"One day during training camp, I drove over to the facility before practice. I parked my car. This was Mankato, I left my keys in the car," laughed Marinaro. "I come back out and my car's gone. I'm like, 'Holy shit.' I called the Mankato police. The police come and they're asking questions and meanwhile a walkie-talkie blurts, 'Is Ed Marinaro still there?' The police answered yes. 'We found his car.' I asked, 'Where?' The voice on the walkie-talkie says, 'It's down on the practice field, under the goalposts.' They stole my car. We would always get a couple thousand fans at practice and there's my purple Porsche, under the goalposts. I'm in the locker room getting dressed and I'm going, 'Hey, guys, I got to move the car, give me the keys.' Bud Grant comes out and says, 'Why's your car out there?' I told him I didn't know. Somebody stole it. Bud was different. We didn't straggle out to the practice field. We waited out by the door and went out together at exactly the time for practice. I'm like, 'Oh, God.' So just before we go out to practice, I go to my locker and my keys are sitting up on top of it. I run out there, with all those fans watching, in my full uniform. I get in the car and move it off the field. It was mortifying. I took a lot of crap for having a purple Porsche."

Marinaro played his scholastic ball at New Milford (New Jersey) High School. He got the opportunity to finish his career with the hometown Jets when he signed as a free agent in '76, and before an injury halted his season at six games, he had posted not only his best yards-per-rush total at 4.1 but also a pair of prolific rushing games.

"My career has been described as disappointing. But I proved when I went to the Jets I could gain yards," said Marinaro. "I had a two 100-yard-plus games, and then I got hurt. I averaged 40 carries a game in college. I got better as the game went along. I knew getting five carries a game wasn't going to work out for me in the NFL. When you get a little bit tired, you stop thinking as much and that's when running backs are at their best. But looking back, I know everything happens for a reason. I'm proud to say I played in two Super Bowls and played with some Hall of Famers. And when I left the Vikings, I held the record for most catches [11] in a game. I also had the [second] longest play [27-yard reception] of the game in the Super Bowl against the Dolphins."

Players like Marinaro finishing their careers with teams other than Minnesota became commonplace under Lynn's general managership.

"I don't think in the case of the players leaving it was on Bud," said defensive end Carl Eller. "I think a lot of it was because of [failed] negotiations with the general manager at the time [Lynn]. A lot of the guys were in the position to make more money, but it just didn't work out here. It just seemed like a lot of guys had a hard time coming to an agreement with the GM."

Marinaro still wonders what might have been.

"To have success in a sport at any level you must have 100 percent luck and 100 percent ability. I believe luck is more important than the ability. It's proven every year," said Marinaro. "You see examples of guys who get their break because somebody gets hurt. Tom Brady is the definitive example of that. This is how it works. You hear the expression 'Luck is when preparation meets opportunity.' The only thing you can be really sure of is preparedness because you may never get the opportunity.

"Who knows how many great athletes there are that never got a chance," he asked. "That's the reality of sports at almost any level. There are probably potential Hall of Famers out there who never played and got cut. You have to be with the right team and the right system that fits your abilities. I look at Franco Harris. He went to a system that was perfect for him and he flourished. People would laugh at me, but I'm not conceding that I couldn't have done what Franco did in Pittsburgh. But, then again, most people would have loved to have the career I had in the NFL."

Marinaro's up-and-down Vikings career ended that gloomy day in Minnesota. His teammates were left with no other choice but to move on, and in another remarkable show of resilience, an aging Minnesota team, led by a coach who was a veritable emotional Sahara, would gather itself during a painful postseason and right the ship in time to make one final single-minded run at the Super Bowl.

"In your career you got to learn how to lose before you learn how to win," said Grant. "You can't be devastated by losing. The world doesn't come to an end. What you're talking about is entertainment, sure it means something and goes into the record books, etc., but it's still entertainment. You have to learn to get over losing if you're going to continue in this business. You must learn to live with losing in order to keep your composure, your philosophy and approach."[5]

If a course for "Living with Losing" was ever offered, members of the 1975 Minnesota Vikings would have the opportunity to test out.

10

Sammy's Acrobatics

Minnesota Vikings 35, Washington Redskins 20
December 18, 1976, Metropolitan Stadium
Divisional-Round Playoff

Sammy White was just a softspoken rookie, but he let his play do the talking in his first-ever postseason game.

Surprisingly timed at a pedestrian by NFL standards 4.6 in the 40-yard dash, the fast-with-pads-on second-round pick out of Grambling made mincemeat of George Allen's vaunted secondary.

It was by no means an easy group to navigate as it featured the likes of Hall of Fame safety Ken Houston, two-time Super Bowl champ safety Jake Scott, long-armed and rangy corner Joe Lavender and his diminutive but indomitable sidekick Pat Fischer, who many believe should be enshrined in Canton after notching 56 career interceptions (tied with Lem Barney for 18th all-time) over his brilliant 17-year career with the St. Louis Cardinals and Redskins.

The soft-spoken White, who lasted until the 54th selection in the '76 NFL draft, finished with just four catches, but they accounted for 64 yards and a pair of TDs, the first of which was one of the top five scoring receptions in team playoff history given its level of difficulty.

Getting him the ball was Francis Tarkenton, who completed 12 of 21 aerials for 120 yards and three TDs as the Vikings dominated the wild-card entry Redskins by air and by land, winning 35–20.

The loss moved Allen to 0–7 in road playoff games, an unthinkable number for one of the greatest coaches of all time, a workaholic genius given the lion's share of the credit for Chicago winning the '63 NFL title with him as defensive coordinator. He also posted a remarkable 116–47–5 mark (.712) as head coach with both the Los Angeles Rams and Redskins but surprisingly went just 2–7 in the postseason, including a 14–7 loss to Miami in Super Bowl VII.

Missing the playoffs in '75 after finishing third in the NFC East at 8–6, Allen, with the Rozelle Rule no longer in effect, loaded up with veterans as only he truly knew in '76, signing as free agents not only former Cowboys Calvin Hill and Jean Fugett but also New York Jets halfback John Riggins. He also traded for Scott and Lavender. None of these players, thanks to White, were key factors in the loss to the high-flying Vikings.

"It looked like I was running in slow motion, but when the ball was in the air I shifted gears," laughed White with the mention of his 40 time. "I would have a

10. Sammy's Acrobatics

Minnesota Vikings wide receiver Sammy White (85) juggles the ball before making an acrobatic catch for a 27-yard touchdown in the first quarter of the Vikings' 35–20 divisional round playoff win over the Redskins on Saturday, Dec. 18, 1976, in Bloomington. Defending on the play is safety Ken Houston (27). White added another TD catch in the third quarter.

cornerback who was faster running with me side by side, but for some reason or another I would run past him when the ball was in the air."

He did just that on December 4, 1977, when he ran by San Francisco cornerback Tony Leonard with under two minutes left to catch a 69-yard scoring heave from Tommy Kramer to help the Vikings make the playoffs that season. It capped one of the greatest comebacks in team history as the Vikings trailed 24–0 in the third quarter before winning 28–27 on White's catch.

"He came up to press me and I got around him," said White on Leonard. "By the time the safety came over, it was too late."

While White had a huge outing versus the Redskins, it wasn't a bad day for the Minnesota offensive line either as both Chuck Foreman and Brent McClanahan rushed 20 times for better than 100 yards. Meanwhile, the swift Mike Thomas, the Redskins' Pro Bowl back who rushed for 1,100 yards during the regular season, was limited to just 45 yards by the Vikings.

The Vikings opened the scoring on an 18-yard catch and run by tight end Stu Voigt after McClanahan shocked Allen's defense when he broke off tackle for 41 yards on the first play from scrimmage.

McClanahan, starting alongside Foreman, took a handoff slanting left at his own 34 and broke clear down the sideline before Houston pushed him out of bounds at the Washington 25.

"That was an audible. We had worked on that play a lot in training camp," said

McClanahan, selected by the Vikings in the fifth round of the '73 draft after he rushed for nearly 1,000 yards and 12 TDs as a senior at Arizona State. "I was supposed to hit between guard and tackle and slant to the right. I ended up going left. You change your mind sometimes when you get through there."

"The play was what we call our 16," said Tarkenton. "We line up with two receivers to the right and we run left. Voigt and [Charles] Goodrum threw key blocks and McClanahan was off."[1]

Three plays later, on a third-and-three, Tarkenton rolled right and found Voigt, who made a nifty grab at the eight, then powered his way into the end zone over Fischer and linebacker Harold McLinton.

"Stu used to be a fullback," Grant told reporters. "If you hit him high, where's he strong, he'll take you with him."[2]

"I didn't feel anybody hanging on me," Voigt chimed in. "Most of the players forget to go for my legs. I just kept churning."[3]

Foreman definitely appreciated the tight end's effort.

"I have never seen anybody in my life who is there as consistently when you need him to be," said Foreman after the game. "When one of us gets 100 yards or more Stu Voigt has hit some people."[4]

It was after Voigt's bullish run that White, the deceptive speedster from Winnsboro, Louisiana, would make his presence known.

With the Vikings in possession with a third-and-nine from the Redskins' 28 after a Mark Moseley field goal made it 7–3, Tarkenton lofted the ball over the middle to White, who ran a skinny post out of his slot position. Guarded closely by Houston, White contended with the former Houston Oilers great for possession of the ball as he stumbled to the ground. Somehow, in an unbelievable display of concentration, will and desire, White was able to keep his eyes on the ball and gather in the pigskin as he rolled into the end zone with a minute left in the first quarter.

The Vikings led 14–3.

"Kenny had great position," said White. "He was about to intercept the ball, so I turned into a defensive back. The ball got batted around, and once I fell to the ground the ball pretty much just fell on me."

It wasn't lost on White how difficult it was to make a play like that against the likes of the rangy, long-armed Houston, whom Allen acquired by sending five players (Jim Snowden, Mack Alston, Clifton McNeil, Mike Fanucci and Jeff Severson) to the Oilers the May following the Redskins' loss to the Dolphins in Super Bowl VII. "He's the best strong safety in football," he said after the trade.[5]

"Sammy's catch was phenomenal," said Tarkenton. "Ken Houston had his hands in Sammy's face and was about to intercept the ball when Sammy caught it falling down. Then he had the presence of mind to get into the end zone."[6]

Despite being a 12-time Pro Bowler, Houston did not receive national acclaim until making a play for the ages his first year with the Redskins before 54,314 fans at RFK Stadium and millions more watching the Monday night game on national television against the 3–0 Dallas Cowboys.

The Redskins went up 14–7 after safety Brig Owens returned a Craig Morton pass 26 yards for a touchdown with two and a half minutes to play. The Cowboys then mounted a last-gasp drive that dramatically landed them on the Washington four and facing a fourth-and-goal with the clock running out.

Morton dumped a pass to Walt Garrison at the one and the roustabout fullback looked like a sure bet to score, but Houston grabbed him from behind around the waist and bulldogged him to the ground to preserve the win. It was the defining moment of his 14-year career and helped earn him a spot on the "NFL 100 Greatest" team announced in 2019, not to mention the Hall of Fame.

"We knew that he was pretty much All-Pro every year," said White of the gem the Oilers discovered in the ninth round of the 1967 draft out of Prairie View A&M. "Watching film on him, you just wanted to make sure you knew where he was located because you're going to try to run most of your stuff away from him. It was hard to get him out of position."

White had more rare skills to display.

Midway through the second quarter, Tarkenton faced a second-and-15 at his own 46. He scrambled to his right and found Ahmad Rashad, who had altered his pattern and worked his way free past Fischer near the sideline for a gain to the Redskins' 18.

After a five-yard penalty, White, running a corner route, then made yet another off-balance catch over Lavender at the Redskins' eight. Foreman scored two plays later, busting through tackles by Lavender and Brad Dusek, and it was 21–3 Vikings with 7:43 left in the half.

"Foreman's touchdown run from the 2-yard line was an example of how we played," said Vikings All-Pro right tackle Ron Yary. "He hit two Redskins, bounced off them, and scored a touchdown that most backs in the league wouldn't have made."[7]

Early in the third stanza, Foreman put the game away with a 30-yard skirting effort down the right sideline following a crushing block by Yary to make it 28–3.

"We didn't want another Dallas on our hands," said Foreman of the Hail Mary game. "We suffered all winter after losing in the final seconds to Dallas. Everybody was up for the game and we played like it."[8]

McClanahan, chosen in the same draft class as Foreman, didn't mind that the Vikings had a crowded running backs room.

"I wasn't worried about Foreman or any of the competition. I just wanted to do my job as a fullback and win. Winning took precedence with me," he said. "We had an awesome line. All the yardage we got between Foreman and I was due to them. They were for the most part tall, strong guys, with size 14, 15 shoes. Chuck and I clicked behind that line. All I was there for was to run, catch, block and win. And that's what we did."

Later in the third, White put the icing on the cake when he beat Lavender on another post-corner pattern for a nine-yard scoring reception to make it 35–6.

"I had told Francis that they were playing me man-to-man and trying to take away the inside. I was able to beat the defensive back. I liked misdirection patterns," said White, who played for the great Eddie Robinson at Grambling. "I thought that's what I could do well, trying to get them to think I was going to do one thing and then do another. The post-corner was one of my favorite routes."

Listed at 5-11, White didn't have problems with the taller corners and he showed it against the 6-4 Lavender, nicknamed "Big Bird."

"I actually preferred it," said White. "A smaller guy's tendency was to get up under you. A taller guy's idea was to get his hands on you. Then you could always fight the hands off and get by and get into your route. The shorter guy, like Pat Fischer, would wait for you to come to them and you don't get to separate right away. We watched a lot of film, and the Redskins and the Rams both had great defensive backs, but every one of them had a weakness. They're going to give you something, so that's what you got to take."

Tarkenton said the Rashad-and-White tandem gave him "the two best receivers I've had on one team."[9]

"Most of the time we were on the opposite sides of the field," said White of Rashad, whom he teamed with seven seasons. "Back then, we didn't run three or four receivers out there like they do now. The only time we were on the same side I would be in the slot. That was just the way our offense was designed."

There were doubts early on about White, who dropped several balls during preseason play as a rookie.

"I was focused so much on if I could beat a professional football defensive back and get open, I think I wasn't concentrating on catching the ball," he said. "I forgot the main thing was to catch the ball. In our last preseason game, Bud started me to get me some confidence, and sure enough I dropped a couple balls again. He took me out, but I came back in the game and caught a touchdown pass in the fourth quarter and my confidence rose from there."

His 10 TD catches as a rookie were the best of his brilliant 10-year career and earned him the NFL Rookie of the Year Award. He had nine TD catches each of the following two seasons.

"We threw the ball a lot to our backs. Most of the time I played on the same side of the field as Chuck, and they had to give him a lot of attention. I got a lot of one-on-one coverage," said White.

The Vikings were definitely a right-handed team, having the likes of Yary and Ed White at tackle and guard on that side, respectively. White said this gave his running mate a lot of room to operate on the opposite side.

"Ahmad ran a lot of sideline patterns. He didn't have the linebackers coming out to the flat like we did on the other side, which was the strong side with me, Chuck, Stu or whoever was at tight end," said Sammy White. "We had to run good combination routes on that side to pull people here or pull people there so we could get me, Chuck or Stu open."

Clicking on the opposite side of the formation were Tarkenton and Rashad, who joined the Vikings via a trade with Seattle in '76.

"We thought the same way. We were always looking at things the same way," said Rashad, who caught 53 passes for 671 yards despite missing the Vikings' first game. "When we'd run a play, he'd say, 'Give me something on the back [weakside].' Whenever I was running a route, if the defender was inside, I would run a route to go outside and Fran would throw the ball right where it was supposed to be. If the defender was outside, I would run a route inside and Fran would throw the ball right where it was supposed to be. The [defender] would always be wrong because we'd just go the opposite way."

Rashad, drafted fourth overall out of Oregon in the 1972 draft by the St. Louis Cardinals as Bobby Moore, was far and away the top running back in the country going into the selection process, but he made it clear to teams that he wanted to play receiver in the NFL.

His size, body lean and running style were strikingly similar to the great Lenny Moore, the 6–1, 191-pounder out of Reading, Pennsylvania, who excelled as both a back and flanker for the Baltimore Colts after being drafted ninth overall out of Penn State in 1956.

"I was a long, tall guy," said the 6–2, 205-pound Rashad, who wore No. 28 due to his admiration for the former Bears standout Willie Gallimore, a Gale Sayers clone who died in a car accident the summer after he helped Chicago win the NFL title in 1963. "Running backs didn't last long back then. As a receiver, I'm playing against guys who are not as big as me or as strong as me. Much easier position for me to play. You might be a great running back for a couple years and for the rest of your life not be able to walk."

Even with Rashad out of the mix, it was a solid class for running backs in '72. Most notable was Franco Harris, who went 13th overall to the Steelers, while joining him were standouts Jim Bertelsen (30th to Rams), Robert Newhouse (35th to Dallas), Lydell Mitchell (48th to Baltimore), and Lawrence McCutcheon (70th to Rams).

Rashad stepped into a St. Louis locker room that still had traces of the toxic element chronicled in Dave Meggyesy's 1971 groundbreaking book *Out of Their League*. The team was in the middle of three consecutive 4–9–1 seasons under former Vikings defensive coordinator Bob Hollway and then Don Coryell, who came out of San Diego State to lead the Cards in '73.

"I read the [Meggyesy] book and I was like, 'Please don't draft me,' and then they do," said Rashad. "I really wanted to be a receiver. I was vocal about it with teams who wanted to draft me. Don Coryell came in and tried to make me a running back. One of his assistants, Joe Gibbs, who was a dear friend, also lobbied for it. He said, 'Come on in, man. I'm going to make you the best running back you can be,' and this, that and the other, but I didn't want to play running back. I was determined to play wide receiver. The first year it wasn't a problem, but under Coryell they tried to move me to back."

Playing wingback at Oregon as a sophomore, Rashad had 54 catches for 786 yards and 10 TDs, while adding five TDs as a running back. He had another great all-purpose year as a junior, rushing for 824 yards and six scores and adding 45 receptions for 455 yards and five more TDs. Returning to a backfield that included quarterback Dan Fouts, he rushed for 1,211 yards and seven TDs as a senior and added 32 catches for 324 yards and three scores to earn All-American honors.

A frustrated Rashad had just 59 catches in two years with St. Louis, who were a year away from becoming the fabled "Cardiac Cardinals." He would be shuffling off to Buffalo by 1974.

"My second year I changed my name and I got booed out of the building every time a pass was intended for me," said Rashad, who now resides in Florida. "After my first year it was like I don't know if this is my life calling. I was just not going to play there. I asked for a trade and they sent me to Buffalo. They traded me there because they knew I hated the cold weather. None of that mattered to me, I just wanted to get out of there and Buffalo was an up-and-coming team at that point. St. Louis was just horrendous. It was just a tough time in my life. They had separate Black and White Bible meetings. I had a bonus if I started so many games and they began to start another receiver [Walker Gillette] and I'd go in the second play just so I wouldn't reach it. I'm like, 'This is not making any sense.'"

Given Rashad's abilities, the Cardinals got a laughable return in the subsequent trade to Buffalo in quarterback Dennis Shaw, who started just five games in two years with the Cardinals. That's because St. Louis already had a player named Jim Hart, who, along with NFL MVP runner-up Terry Metcalf, would lead the Big Red to the playoffs in 1974. Rashad, meanwhile, was enjoying a cathartic experience in Buffalo and a bridge to better things to come.

Riding the crest of Lou Saban's emotional exhortations—"If we die, we die together"—the Bills earned a wild-card playoff spot with a 9–5 record. With Joe Ferguson at quarterback and O.J. Simpson and Jim Braxton running the ball, Rashad, teaming with J.D. Hill, caught 36 balls for 433 yards and three TDs for a squad that was eliminated from postseason play with a 32–14 loss to Pittsburgh at Three Rivers Stadium.

In two short but eventful years, Rashad would be suiting up for the team the Steelers would go on to defeat in Super Bowl IX. After sitting out the '75 campaign with a knee injury suffered during a preseason game, Rashad became a free agent the following year.

"It went back and forth [in free agency] between Buffalo and Seattle. I went with Seattle's offer because I was from Washington and I thought it would be pretty cool to go back there to play professionally," recalled Rashad of joining the first-year franchise headed up by former Vikings defensive line coach Jack Patera. "I started doing my therapy in Seattle with the Seattle Supersonics trainer to get ready to play that next year. When the preseason started, I was getting better, but I wasn't right there yet. I think Patera realized I wasn't going to make a whole bunch of difference. Then Bud Grant asked for me. That's how I got to Minnesota."

It was a time in Rashad's journey where the human element of football came fully into play, because without the intervention of a singular, determined individual, the Portland, Oregon, native may have prematurely begun his second career as a top on-air talent at NBC Sports.

Before a deal was consummated between the two teams, Rashad flew to Minnesota for a workout. Desperate to replace John Gilliam, who left for Atlanta after a contract squabble, it was an critical time for the Vikings, whose only remaining receivers were fourth-year man Jim Lash and a pair of rookies in White and Leonard Willis, a fourth-round pick out of Ohio State.

Tarkenton recalled Rashad's workout.

"He stepped on that field and before long, I was like a kid in a candy store," he said. "He was coming up with everything I threw at him. He ran outs, ups, posts, hitches, quick outs, and he beat everybody on our team. I had never seen anyone like him before in my 15 years in the league."[10]

Tarkenton arrived to practice the next day still beaming over his early Christmas gift from the Seahawks. The only problem was he found Rashad sitting in the locker room in street clothes.

Rashad remembers the moment.

"Francis and I hit it off immediately," he said. "I knew him from before because I spent some time in Colorado with him after my first offseason in the league and we became very close guys. Once I got to Minnesota, I was like, 'Oh, man, we're going to burn it up now.' Then, all of a sudden, the general manager [Mike Lynn] comes in and said I failed my physical. I didn't even *take* a physical."

Lynn told Grant not to practice Rashad over concerns with his surgically repaired knee. Tarkenton didn't take the news well.

"I marched straight into Bud's office and asked him what was going on," recalled Tarkenton. "He said Lynn was worried we might have to pay him and then have him sit injured on the bench. I was wound up. 'Did you see what he did on the field? He beat every player we had out there.' I had never seen a receiver like him. I told Bud we needed to get Lynn on the phone."[11]

10. Sammy's Acrobatics

Tarkenton told Lynn if Rashad was not dressing for practice that he wasn't. "We've got to have this kid," he said.

"Fran Tarkenton, I love. He's one of my heroes. Without Francis, my career might have stopped that day in Minnesota," said Rashad. "They told me to get my stuff and go home, and Francis said, 'Don't get your stuff. If you go home, I'm going home.'"

Minnesota would send just a 1977 fourth-rounder to Seattle for a player who made the Pro Bowl four of his seven years in purple. Released to make room for Rashad was veteran backup Bob Berry, but it was worth it to acquire a receiver Grant described as a man with "fast feet, a good head and soft hands."[12]

"The only thing I know about the Vikings is that they win, and that they're a championship contender," Rashad said the day after the trade. "A guy has to be happy about that."[13]

Seattle general manager John Thompson, who said his team had "a surplus of receivers," a group that included eventual Hall of Famer Steve Largent and former Viking Sam McCullum, didn't seem too concerned over trading Rashad, telling Lynn after the deal, "We just put you back into the Super Bowl."[14]

Rashad, who virtually beat Minnesota single-handedly his rookie year when he caught a pair of 24-yard TD passes in the Cardinals' 19–17 win at Metropolitan Stadium, had to wait until the second week of the season to see his first action with the Vikings, a 10–10 overtime tie against Los Angeles on September 19 in a preview of the NFC championship game three months later. He had three catches for 20 yards in a game that saw Tarkenton throw for nearly 300 yards.

"Bud pulls me aside and said, 'I'm going to put you in the game and you're never going to come out. No one is taking you out unless it's me, so let's go,'" remembers Rashad. "He was just a dear man. When I first got to Minnesota, he said, 'How do you say your name so I can get it right every time?' He was the only one who called me [by the Arabic pronunciation] 'Akh-mad.' He and I were as close as any coach I had my whole career. I think he saw some of himself in me and he also expected a lot out of me. He knew I was capable. He'd always say, 'Come on, Ahmad.' That's all he had to say. As tough as guy as he was, he was like a father figure to me. Jim Marshall was also an exceptional man. He'd say the same thing to me, 'Come on, Ahmad.' They both expected me to perform."

Rashad, who wore No. 23 at Oregon because his favorite player growing up was Paul Lowe, San Diego's fluid runner of the AFL days, almost duplicated his first-year numbers with the Vikings in '77, catching 51 passes for 681 yards and two TDs.

With the new illegal contact rule that kept defensive backs from bludgeoning receivers after they were five yards from the line of scrimmage and the season moving to 16 games, Rashad flourished his last year together with Tarkenton in 1978, catching a then career-high 66 passes for 769 yards and eight scores to earn his first trip to the Pro Bowl.

"Fran and I were always on the same page. It was just a really good combination," he said. "We'd take Fridays and run routes for him. He would have us believing how things we're going to work so you ran your routes with conviction. Going into the game, I knew he'd put the ball perfectly where I needed to get it. He knew how to inspire everyone in that huddle. He was an inspirational leader."

Tarkenton didn't have a big arm, maxing out at about 55 yards following a shoulder injury in high school, but neither White nor Rashad worried about outrunning the quarterback's throwing range.

"Fran was very smart and he understood the law of averages of the game," said White, who, following his career with the Vikings, joined his old college quarterback and former Tampa Bay and Washington star Doug Williams on the Gambling coaching staff. "He was going to put that ball in the air in plenty of time. Most of the time the ball was in the air before I made my last break. All I had to do was look up and run under the ball. He always put the ball up in the air with a little height under it to allow me to run up under it."

"His anticipation was super," added Rashad. "It didn't matter how far he could throw it. You'd be 10 yards down the field and he'd throw it 40 yards, then you're running 30 yards to get it."

In 1979 with Tommy Kramer at quarterback, Rashad had his best year as a pro, catching 80 balls for 1,156 yards and nine TDs. He finished his 10-year career with 495 catches and 44 TDs.

White retired after the '85 campaign with an impressive total of 50 TDs (two more than Dallas Cowboys Hall of Famer Drew Pearson had in 28 more games) and 393 receptions.

"We have a long line of great, great receivers," said White. "I was just proud to be mentioned with some of them guys. I was a Vikings fan even before I got drafted here. I liked the receivers back then. I remember watching Gene [Washington] and John [Henderson] and Bob Grim. I just paid attention to them. For some reason I fell in love with the Vikings receivers. I was probably the only kid I knew from Louisiana who followed the Vikings."

White was assigned jersey No. 85 upon his arrival to Minnesota. Just as his speed rose when the ball was in the air, he raised the legacy of that number up a notch.

"I owe that to Stubby Eason, our equipment manager," said White. "He said he wouldn't give that number out to anyone unless he thought they were going to be great." That's because wearing No. 85 in the pre–Grant era was Northwestern product Paul Flatley, a Pro Bowl selection in 1966 who was undoubtedly Tarkenton's favorite target in the early years. A fluid route runner in the fashion of Fred Biletnikoff, Flatley had 306 receptions and 24 TDs in his eight years in the NFL, five coming with the Vikings. He had three seasons of 50 or better catches.

"I've spoken to him a few times over the years, and he said he's proud of what I did with that number," said White. "I think when Stubby gave me that number, he kind of had that in mind."

Rashad and White were both fluid and fearless, even when it came to the great defensive backfields they tangled with from perennial playoff contenders like the Redskins and Rams, who boasted All-Pro corners Monte Jackson and Rod Perry.

"I don't believe I ever played believing the defensive back was better than me," said Rashad. "They had to guard me. I didn't have to worry about them. That was my feeling every single game. I was a running back in college. I didn't give a shit about what a cornerback was going to do against me. I didn't care if they came up to try to tackle me. As a running back I was used to linebackers trying to tackle me, so this was a break. If you want to play bump and run against me, it's going to be bump and *run over*. That's what it's going to be. That's what my feeling was as a former running back. It was a plus for me to deal with defensive backs."

• • •

Rashad's fellow receiver Voigt also loved to run over defensive backs, but he was more known for opening holes. His nickname, "Chainsaw," was befitting, because he could routinely cut down would-be tacklers, paving the way for the likes of Foreman and McClanahan.

Despite possessing the strength of a power lifter, Voigt couldn't credit any of it to what equipment was made available to him.

"The Vikings had none of that stuff," said Voigt, who caught 17 touchdown passes during his 11-year Vikings career, mostly from his former roommate Tarkenton. "We basically had a universal gym that we shared with the Twins in the tiny locker room at Met Stadium. One year Jim Finks agreed to get us gym passes."

A former University of Wisconsin three-sport standout who didn't move full-time from running back to tight end until his senior year, Voigt made himself NFL ready by working out on his own.

"Wisconsin was a hotbed for power lifters," said Voigt, who remained in Minnesota following his retirement from football in 1980. "I was a weight event guy—shot put, discus—so I lifted, and I was kind of ahead of the curve in terms of supplements. Now everyone lifts weights."

Voigt said he maxed out at 375 in the bench and 590 in dead lift. So strong was the Madison (Wisconsin) West High School product that his 67–7 feet shot stood as a state record in Wisconsin for 39 years.

At nearly 6-2 and 230 pounds during his playing days, Voigt most likely couldn't play the same position in today's National Football League (Jim Kleinsasser with much better hands), but he was a perfect fit in a Minnesota passing offense fine-tuned under brilliant offensive coordinator Jerry Burns—a short-passing attack known today as the "West Coast offense."

"I'd catch a few passes here and there from Tarkenton, but I was the third or fourth option," understated Voigt, who nabbed 177 catches for 1,919 yards on his career. "I knew my role. You couldn't play on this team at tight end if you couldn't block. I mean, I never lined up more than three yards outside [tackles] Ron Yary, Grady Alderman or Steve Riley my whole career."

Voigt was certainly an underrated blocker on a team known for good ones such as Hall of Famers Mick Tingelhoff and Yary, along with wide-bodied White, et al.

"You had to block," said Voigt. "When I first came to the Vikings, in our division alone you had [Ray] Nitschke with the Packers, [Dick] Butkus with the Bears and [Joe] Schmidt with the Lions. And I had to go against ends like Claude Humphrey, Coy Bacon, Deacon Jones, Jack Youngblood, Fred Dryer and so on.

"I was pretty tenacious and pretty quick on my feet, and being undersized helped since the low man wins in football," added Voigt. "More than anything else, going against Jim Marshall and Carl Eller in practice every day got me ready. I had to block them, and they even knew what was coming! Some of the best action I saw was in our scrimmages. Of course, you hit a lot more in practice back then."

Primarily a running back in college, Voigt had a good enough senior season to draw the Vikings' attention. Almost mirroring his best season with the Vikings in 1975 when he grabbed 34 passes for 363 yards and four scores, Voigt rounded out his Badger career in '69 with 39 receptions for 439 yards and two TDs.

The Vikings, coming off a Super Bowl appearance against the Kansas City Chiefs, selected Voigt in 1970 with their 10th pick, 260th overall. It didn't hurt that Minnesota coach Bud Grant hailed from Superior, Wisconsin.

"I knew they had made the Super Bowl so I was pleasantly surprised when they selected me," said Voigt, "especially since I had not heard from the Vikings prior to the draft. I grew up a Green Bay Packers fan. And sure, I thought about playing for them. They had all those great teams under [Vince] Lombardi. It was just a great time to be a sports fan in Wisconsin in those days because you had the Packers winning every year, Henry Aaron with the Braves and Lew Alcindor [Kareem Abdul-Jabbar] and the 'Big O' [Oscar Robertson] with the Milwaukee Bucks."

Voigt played special teams as a rookie for the reigning National Football League champs and didn't mind it a bit.

"I was just glad to get on the field," he said. "Going in, I didn't know much about what the Vikings had at tight end, and I didn't know much about the position itself. I came from an era where a lot of teams were running the option. I was just glad to contribute out there. Back then with only a 40-man roster, you had to play specials teams. Guys like Fred McNeil and Matt Blair and Scott Studwell were great special team players before they became starters."

Voigt got his first big break in 1971. With starter John Beasley hurt in the final preseason contest, he started nine games and caught 15 passes for 214 yards. He also had his first NFL touchdown, that coming on a six-yard toss from Gary Cuozzo in a 20–12 playoff loss to the Dallas Cowboys at Met Stadium.

That devastating loss—which saw Bob Lee get benched after throwing two picks only to have Cuozzo come in and throw two more in a game the Vikings outgained the eventual world champion Cowboys 311–183 and out-first-downed them 17–10—prompted Finks to bring Tarkenton back to Minnesota.

Being drafted by the Vikings instead of the down-trending Packers was fortuitous for Voigt, and Tarkenton's return also proved to be a career maker for a tight end who now had a quarterback with no peer in executing off-schedule passes, plays that made Voigt's uncanny knack for finding soft spots in zone defenses invaluable during their seven seasons together.

"After [Joe] Kapp left," said Voigt, "there was a void there [at quarterback]. Cuozzo played well previously for Baltimore and Lee and Snead had NFL credentials, but Kapp was the fearless leader of the offense. Before Tarkenton, there were a lot of 7–3 games, 14–10 games where we would have [Bill] Brown and [Dave] Osborn slug it out on the ground and we'd get close enough in where Fred Cox could split the uprights. Our formula under Coach Grant was to play solid football and not make mistakes."

The initiation of Voigt's almost unspoken rapport with Tarkenton was temporarily delayed as Beasley returned to health in '72, a year that saw the team wrap up a dismal 7–7 campaign with a last-second loss in San Francisco, leading to a rare Grant tirade in the postgame locker room.

Things changed dramatically for Voigt and the Vikings in '73 with the draft-day addition of Foreman, a multiply talented dynamo who gave Tarkenton the playmaker he needed in the backfield. Tarkenton already had a game-breaking wide receiver in John Gilliam, whom the Vikings acquired from the St. Louis Cardinals the previous year in a trade in exchange for Cuozzo.

Voigt started all 13 of the regular-season games in which he played, catching 23 balls for 318 yards and a pair of TDs. He had eight catches in the Vikings' tremendous return to postseason play, which included impressive wins over Washington (27–20) and

Dallas (27–10) before finishing with a team-best three receptions for 46 yards in the 24–7 Super Bowl loss to the Dolphins.

"During the '73 playoff run, everyone wanted to redeem themselves after what happened the year before," said Voigt, who went into executive banking after his career. "We lost a lot of close games in '72. Losing close games was unthinkable under Grant."

Postseason money came in handy for players of the '70s, as the vast majority had to work jobs after the season to make ends meet.

"When we made the playoffs, I would stay with someone else because I didn't want to pay to extend my lease because I knew I was heading back up to Wisconsin for school. I was working on my MBA," said Voigt, who made $16,000 his first year with the Vikings with a $7,500 signing bonus. "In those three playoff games in '73, I think I got about $18,000 [$7,500 went to the Super Bowl loser], which was about your whole salary."

The Vikings did it again in 1974, returning to the Super Bowl with a hard-fought 14–10 victory over the Los Angeles Rams, a team they beat three times in four playoff games during Voigt's career, including a pair of NFC title games.

Following yet another division crown, the 10–4 Vikings defeated the St. Louis Cardinals 30–14 in the first round at home before meeting the Rams in the championship game at The Met. Voigt had a big game, catching four passes for 43 yards as the Vikings forged a 14–3 lead in the fourth and hung on for dear life after James Harris hit Harold Jackson with a TD pass midway through the stanza.

"Back then you knew you were always going to have to deal with the Redskins, Rams and Cowboys," said Voigt. "When we played the Redskins, we always felt we had the edge because they were an older team. They had some great defensive players, like [Chris] Hanburger, Jack Pardee, Myron Pottios and Ron McDole, but we had the edge on them physically. The Rams were a tough and physical team and we knew the scores would be close because they had a top-flight defense with guys like Youngblood and Dryer [and a great running game featuring Lawrence McCutcheon]. But they never had the top-flight quarterback, and we were able to slip by them."

In the Rams' three straight postseason losses to the Vikings in the '70s, their signal callers were the well-traveled Harris and the diminutive Pat Haden out of the University of Southern California. Neither were as awe-inspiring as the man the Cowboys had behind center, one Roger Staubach. The former Naval Academy star engineered three playoff wins over the Vikings during this stretch, losing to the Purple and White only in the '73 title game.

"The Cowboys played that [flex] defense where they were off the ball," said Voigt. "It gave us some challenges. They were more of a finesse team than the Rams, but they had the quarterback."

Staubach, while widely remembered for his last-second 50-yard TD pass to Drew Pearson to beat a shocked Minnesota team in the '75 Hail Mary game—"We had a really good team that year," said Voigt—didn't actually post huge numbers against the Vikings. In Cowboys playoff wins over Minnesota in '71, '75 and '78, he was 49 of 87 passing with just three TD passes and five interceptions and was sacked 12 times.

"That '75 game still haunts me," said Voigt. "Never should have lost that one. In our eyes it was an obvious push-off by Pearson. Paul [Krause] could have possibly made the tackle [Pearson caught the ball at the Vikings' four] but hesitated because he thought for sure there was going to be a flag."

Voigt's backup was Steve Craig, who came to the Vikings as a third-round pick out of the University of Northwestern in 1974.

Productive in college, he caught 30 balls as a senior for 479 yards and six TDs, averaging a sensational 16 yards per catch. He also had good numbers as a junior, with 39 catches for 362 yards and four scores.

With Voigt entrenched as the starter, and with Bob Tucker coming over from the New York Giants in '77 for a fifth-round draft pick, Craig finished his Vikings career with just 18 catches.

"Bud would always say you don't win a position—a person has to play himself out of a position," he recalled. "That was his philosophy, and I believe it may have kept some people around too long at some positions."

Craig boiled down the Vikings' success to a pair of elements.

"We were good because the defense was outstanding," said Craig. "The defense and Chuck Foreman took us to the Super Bowl. Especially his receiving out of the backfield."

Practicing against the Purple People Eaters, especially the ends, was a benefit to Craig.

"You had two of the best around," he said. "Marshall was fast off the ball. You had to be quick just to get a piece of him. And Eller was just strong. A specimen. As for Page, he was super quick and also very strong. There were seasons when we knew we were going to the Super Bowl because the defense was just dominating people."

Craig credits his pro career to his first college coach, former Browns star offensive lineman Alex Agase.

"Alex Agase was a force. I mean this, man. Look at the man's bio. He was an All-American at two different schools," Craig said. "He went to the service, then came back and was an All-American again. He and Doc [Tony] Adamle were the guards for the Browns on championship teams and his military experience was incredible. His whole life experience was incredible. He was a good teacher. The salt of the earth. He was one of my favorite people."

Even with a pair of brutal losses to the Cowboys in '71 and '75, Voigt said the rivalry never got ugly. But that was the Grant way.

"Although the Cowboys beat us in those games, we never really had a lot of animosity towards them," said Voigt. "There was mutual respect, but we did resent the whole 'America's Team' thing. In all, we never got chippy with teams. That's the way Bud coached us. He didn't want us talking during the game or fraternizing. He would tell us if we wanted to talk to the guys on the other teams do it in the parking lot after the game. We weren't a talkative team. We didn't go down that road because the teams in our division, especially the Bears, wanted us to get into that type of contest. We were always on guard against them because they had several cheap-shot guys. They wanted us out of our game, which was very methodical."

Viking players say the most difficult, hard-fought games were the contests in their own division.

"All the playoff games were physical, but the most physical games were in our division—Detroit, Chicago, Green Bay, regardless of their record," said Voigt. "You needed to wear your big pads for those games. When you talk about the Black and Blue Division, those were the toughest games we had. The other games were almost a delight compared to our divisional games. They came for it, they wanted to win, they wanted to knock us off."

While the Cowboys stung the Vikings in the playoffs four times in five games during the Grant regime (if you count the 17–13 Runner-up Bowl loss to Dallas on January 5, 1969), the Rams rarely did, finally getting to the Vikings in Tarkenton's last year and final game in '78, routing them 34–10 at home on New Year's Eve.

"By then we had gotten older," said Voigt. "We could commiserate with how the Redskins felt like when we played them. Plus, the Rams had built up so much frustration and angst. Them taking it out on us wasn't surprising after all those tough losses."

After the win over the Rams in the '74 title game, the Vikings faced the Steelers in Super Bowl IV, falling 16–6. Voigt had two catches for 31 yards as Pittsburgh held the Vikings to a meager 119 total yards of offense.

Following the heartbreak of the '75 loss to the Cowboys, Minnesota, always resilient under Grant's tutelage, won the Central Division again in '76 with an 11–2–1 record.

The Vikings would go on to lose to Oakland, 32–14, in Super Bowl XI, but Voigt turned in a nice contest with four catches for 49 yards and a TD.

"Our defense was getting older by the time we played the Raiders," said Voigt, who after his career also did color commentary on Vikings games on WCCO radio. "Especially our right side with Marshall [39] and Hilgenberg [34] going against the [Art] Shells and [Gene] Upshaws."

Voigt doesn't spend his time bemoaning the Super Bowl losses. He chooses rather to be positive, focusing on the greatness of a team that from 1968 through '78 won 10 division crowns and advanced to four Super Bowls.

"We were so good for so long because Bud had such a feel for the game," said Voigt, who was good enough in baseball to be drafted by the Angels. "He wasn't a great X's and O's guy, but he always had great coaches and he just had a good feel for game situations and what it took to win. He could watch how the ducks were flying and tell how the weather was going to be. It was remarkable."

Voigt's last season as a starter was in '77, as he posted 20 catches for 212 yards. By then, the Vikings had turned more and more to their wide receivers, with Rashad leading the team with 51 receptions and White with 41, including nine TDs.

Voigt had just one TD catch that season but it was one he still beams over.

It was October 17, 1977. You could throw out the records because the Bears were in town, and they always played the Vikings tough.

Minnesota by then was showing signs of wear and tear but was still good enough to have won three straight games following its 16–10 overtime loss at home to open the season against the eventual world-champion Cowboys.

The game was deadlocked at 16 when Matt Blair blocked a 41-yard field goal attempt by Bob Thomas to help send the game into overtime. The great linebacker had earlier blocked an extra point.

After stopping the Bears on their first OT possession on a Page sack, Tarkenton drove the Vikings 69 yards to the Bears' 11, a march aided by Foreman's four-yard run on third and three from the Chicago 15.

To Tarkenton's dismay, Grant sent the field goal unit onto the field. It was only first down. The Vikings QB called time-out, unaware of Grant's plans.

Cox, with still better than eight minutes left in OT, proceeded to step off seven yards and station himself in his customary position behind holder Paul Krause. But when the ball was snapped, Krause, a former star baseball player at Iowa, grabbed the ball and rolled right. He was supposed to look for either Craig, who lined up right, or Jeff Siemon, who lined up on the wing next to Craig.

Siemon was wide open, but Krause opted to throw to Voigt, who had crossed over from the left side and was also in the clear. Krause threw a tight spiral to Voigt to secure a 22–16 victory.

"He threw to me because he figured I would catch the ball," laughed Voigt. "Paul still talks about being a perfect one-for-one all-time as a passer in the NFL."

Unusual as it was, that victory was consequential because it helped the Vikings win the Central Division by tiebreaker as both they and the Bears finished 9–5.

It was time for playoff football yet again. Remarkably, even though Voigt admitted they "were better than we were by then," the Vikings upset the Rams at the Los Angeles Coliseum in the famous "Mud Bowl" game, 14–7.

"That was a crazy game," recalled Voigt of the contest, which saw Lee attempt only 10 passes. "They must have been thinking, 'What can we do to beat these guys?' You couldn't do anything out there. It was a deluge. We were just trying to survive."

The victory moved the Vikings to 4–0 all-time in playoff games with the Rams and allowed them to reach their third NFC title game in five years, where they lost 23–6 to the Cowboys.

"That game would have been different if we had Tarkenton," said Voigt of the star quarterback who broke his ankle in a 42–10 win over the Bengals on November 13 and missed the rest of the season. "We were in that game. [The Vikings trailed just 16–6 at halftime.]"

Voigt, as was commonplace with the collection of players Grant and Jim Finks assembled, was a remarkable team player.

"The only stat that mattered to us is if we had more points than the other team," he said. "Maybe we would have loved to be more flamboyant, but when we made a play or were lucky enough to get into the end zone, Bud told us to act like we had been there before. A lot of guys couldn't play here. We did ways a certain way and we won a lot of games because of it."

And helping pave the way for that success was the unheralded and brutish Voigt, a masterfully blocking tight end who, to Tarkenton's glee, always seemed to get open and catch everything thrown his way.

"I loved to throw the ball to Stu Voigt," said Tarkenton. "He was a smart and very disciplined player, a dependable tight end for the Vikings for 11 years. Stu was one of my roommates for a while, and he was always fun to be around. I bet there was no one who enjoyed putting on a Vikings uniform more than he did; he was always proud to wear the Purple colors."[15]

"Stu was a competitor," said the man who drafted him, player personnel director Jerry Reichow. "He wasn't your typical tight end. He might have been six foot tall, I'm not sure if he was or not. He was a solidly built guy. We're thinking, 'Where are we going to play this guy? Running back?' We took a stab and he turned out to be a heckuva player for us. He was another smart guy."

Joe Soucheray, who covered the team for the *Minneapolis Star*, may have said it best when describing Voigt after the impressive win over the Redskins:

"His catches will not be as acrobatic as Sammy White's and his cuts upfield not as slippery as Chuck Foreman's," he wrote. "But he will clear the path for the dancers and he will snatch the ball in that split second the seam opens. And if he ever catches the ball near the goal line, he will carry some monster on his back to get there."[16]

The next beast the team would face was the Los Angeles Rams.

11

Bobby's Big Day

Minnesota Vikings 24, Los Angeles Rams 13
December 26, 1976, Metropolitan Stadium
NFC Championship Game

Bobby Bryant was normally overlooked among the pantheon of stars that made December playoff games at Metropolitan Stadium a veritable rite of passage in the 1970s for CBS' *NFL Today* crew of Brent Musburger, Irv Cross and Phyllis George and eloquent sideline pontificator Jack Whitaker.

But it was the 6–1, 175-pound cornerback out of the University of South Carolina who came up with not only a game for the ages, but also a play that would be the envy of the team's three Hall of Fame defenders, one that all but sealed the Vikings' last National Football Conference championship game win nearly 50 years ago, a tension-packed 24–13 triumph over the Los Angeles Rams on December 26, 1976.

Vikings fans have endured a lot of pain since then, as the team has lost its last six NFC title game appearances, games that have come just about every 10 years—'78, '88, '99, '01, 2010 and 2018.

Bryant was not going to let this be another painful day for Minnesota as he posted a staggering game line—two interceptions and a special teams touchdown—that ranks with the all-time best in playoff history.

His biggest play came late in the fourth quarter.

The Rams, facing the Vikings for the second time in three years in the title game—it could have easily been three straight years if not for a guy named Drew Pearson—had come back from a 17–0 deficit to trail by just four points with 2:40 remaining.

They had driven to the Vikings' 39 and faced a fourth-and-long. Setting up the play, with tension at its zenith, former New York Giants star placekicker and CBS play-by-play man Pat Summerall said in the staccato parlance he became proficient in while working with announcing great Ray Scott, *"Fourth and 10, it might as well be fourth and goal. It might as well be anything. This is the play."*

Coming was what veteran Minnesota Vikings beat writer Jim Klobuchar later called "a clash of 22 desperate men."[1]

Stationed as always on the right side of the Vikings' stingy defense, the wiry Bryant backpedaled with his right eye on mercurial Harold Jackson and his left on Rams rookie quarterback Pat Haden. Bryant was, as Pearson described, "a cluer," the nomenclature for a defensive back who reads the QB more than the receiver.

Minnesota sent a rare all-out blitz, with Matt Blair and Wally Hilgenberg crashing from their outside linebacker spots, leaving both Bryant and Nate Wright, his

Bobby Bryant (20) moves from his right cornerback position to inside the hashmarks to intercept a fourth-down pass intended for Los Angeles Rams wide receiver Ron Jessie (81) as Nate Wright (43) looks on late in the fourth quarter of the NFC championship game on Sunday, Dec. 26, 1976, in Bloomington. Bryant had another interception and ran back a blocked field goal 90 yards for a touchdown as the Vikings won 24–13 to advance to the Super Bowl.

running mate on the left side, in single coverage. Wright was responsible for Ron Jessie.

"It was what we defensive backs called 'pucker time,'" said Bryant of the lonely feeling the island dwellers that are NFL cornerbacks feel sans backup.

Jackson ran a post, which led to Bryant drifting to his left.

"They both ran posts and as I turned to the middle of the field, I noticed Haden never looked my way. Whenever I was on my backpedal, I would always keep an eye on the quarterback to see which way he was looking. He never looked Jackson's way. When I saw him load up, I took off toward Jessie," said Bryant.

Jessie was running free of Wright and for a moment, as the ball was released on a high loft from the right hand of the diminutive former Trojan signal caller, time froze.

Joshua, when fighting one of Israel's enemies in the Old Testament, asked God that the sun stand still. He needed the daylight to help secure the victory for God's chosen people.

Bryant, who was playing in his ninth playoff game, six of them at The Met, just needed time.

It was less than a year removed, with Minnesota seeking its third straight trip to the Super Bowl, that Wright again found himself one-on-one in a game-deciding scenario.

Return to a winter's paled Met Stadium, December 28, 1975.

One-on-one this time with Wright was the rangy Pearson. Dallas trailed 14–10 with

32 seconds left when Roger Staubach launched the ball from his own 42 about as high and as far as he could throw it.

Bryant, as always, was on the opposite side, guarding Golden Richards—a good player, but not Pearson good. Richards's day to that point was two catches for 20 yards.

Staubach's pump fake Richards's way caused Paul Krause, one of those three Vikings defensive Hall of Famers, to get there a step and a half too late to help Wright, who was the recipient of what some believe to be probably the most subtle push-off in NFL history.

Pearson's touchdown catch off his right hip gave Dallas a 17–14 win. Had Minnesota won, they would have hosted the Rams the next week. Instead, they watched as the Cowboys defeated the Rams in the NFC title game en route to their third Super Bowl appearance.

"I wouldn't say we hated them, but they got a lot of press," said star running back Chuck Foreman. "They didn't become America's Team until they beat us on that doggone Drew Pearson crap."

Like Staubach's the year before, Haden's long heave hung seemingly forever in the air and Jessie, who spent time as a running back in the same University of Kansas backfield as John "The Diesel" Riggins, was about to conjure up Pearson.

"Not again. Not again," thought the God-fearing Bryant, sensational enough as a left-handed hurler to be drafted in consecutive years by the New York Yankees (1966) and Boston ('67).

Staubach's launch was fortuitously underthrown, causing Wright to stumble—an occurrence the Vikings say was aided by Pearson's slight right-handed basketball box-out push (he played basketball at South River, New Jersey, High School with Joe Theismann). Meanwhile, the average-armed Haden's toss was plenty out in front of Jessie.

Bryant was feeling safe with his risk. "I knew there was a chance he could come off Jessie and throw back to Jackson, but I had good position," said Bryant, who made like Krause and came from what seemed like the first-base dugout to make a range-roving, leaping interception in between the hash marks inside the 10.

"I tripped when I came down with it," said Bryant. "I got up and ran 10 to 15 yards with it and then got down. The last thing I wanted to have happen was to get tackled and fumble the ball."

In retrospect, it was not only one of the most athletic and improbable interceptions in NFL history but, given the game's magnitude, one of the timeliest, a combination that single-handedly belied Bryant's Hall of Fame detractors.

Bryant, who after his retirement lived five years in Minnesota before moving to Columbia, South Carolina, in 1985 to work in the auto glass industry, flew under the radar during his career in Minnesota, but his talents weren't lost on longtime Vikings scout Jerry Reichow.

"I just happened to be in South Carolina so I was able to see Bobby Bryant play," recalled Reichow. "He was not very big. He was tall enough but not a strongly built guy, but he had really good feet. He could run and made a lot of plays. I said that guy is a helluva player. He may not be big enough to hold up long, but he was a helluva player and getting him in the seventh round was a bargain."

"I got there right when the ball was there," said Bryant. "I have that picture at home. It may not have been my best game—I had a couple of three-interception games—but given the situation, it probably was. I'm thankful I got there in time. It probably would have been a touchdown. I was lucky he didn't come back the other way, but by that time our defensive line would have been all over him."

Bryant's otherworldly play against the Rams, who finished first in the NFC West at 10–3–1, left the young Haden shocked.

"I had no time to look at Harold and I threw one of my better passes of the day to Ron. That was it. I could see the points on the scoreboard: 19–17. Maybe 20–17," said Haden. "But then a purple shirt came flying across the field. Number 20, and he went high in the air on his own 8-yard line to take the ball away from Jessie, who didn't see him coming. Who was that?? And where did he come from? It was Bobby Bryant, their right cornerback, who should have been with Jackson. It was a super play, that's all I can say. I guess I should have given a look to Harold; when Bryant saw me concentrating on Jessie, he took a chance, a chance that paid off—big."[2]

It was the last of three game-changing plays Bryant was involved in, as earlier in the foray he not only ran a blocked field goal back 90 yards for a touchdown but also recorded a diving interception for the Vikings, who finished the regular season 11–2–1 en route to winning yet another NFC Central Division crown.

Bryant was more than glad to do Wright a solid against the Rams. He said his teammate deserves much more than being remembered as the one Pearson made his fateful catch against.

"He was a good corner, a good tackler who was real durable," said Bryant of Wright, who played for Atlanta and St. Louis before joining the Vikings in 1971. "He was a good guy, very articulate. We tried to help each other out and I was very glad to help him out. That's why it's the favorite play of my career."

Bryant had to be there because Krause, with the corners locked up in one-on-one coverage and both outside backers blitzing, was deployed in a middle zone in case McCutcheon or Cappelletti came out of the backfield. Safety Jeff Wright trailed tight end Bob Klein.

That was the Vikings way, having your teammate's back, said Hall of Fame defensive end Carl Eller. Much of that was due to the undisputed leadership of the man who wore No. 70 and played opposite Eller.

"There was a camaraderie among the players. I think a big part of this was Jim Marshall," said Eller. "Jim would play every game, every down. Jim was always there. He was our cheerleader, 'Come on, guys, let's do it!' Everybody who joined the team enjoyed the esprit de corps that was there. Jim is not given the credit he deserves and is even overlooked for the Hall of Fame. There's something in football you must have, and I don't have the name for it. But it's a commitment and it's a love for the game. It's a love you have and it's deeper than the love you would have for yourself—it's the love you have for one another. Like Nate [Wright], when he was on my left side and he would come up hard [to press the run], I didn't want to make things harder for him. The same thing with Roy Winston. That's the way everybody felt on the team."

Middle linebacker Jeff Siemon, who agreed with defensive coordinator Neill Armstrong's decision to blitz, knew the magnitude of the decision.

"Either you do it successfully or lose the game," said Siemon. "I thought it was the kind of hang-it-out call we needed. The blitz made Haden throw in a hurry. He got it out there, but with just enough loft so that Bobby was able to make that tremendous play to intercept.

"I guess you have to be a professional football player to appreciate what he did," he added. "When you're one-on-one against a great receiver like Harold Jackson, *that is your play*. But Bryant had one eye on Jackson and one eye on the quarterback. He is one of the finest big-play football players I ever saw. He's a ballplayer who created the situation for a big play. I don't think most of the crowd or the television audience really recognized all of the experience, finesse, timing and the guts that went into making a play like that."[3]

Siemon didn't start at middle linebacker after injuring his calf in the divisional-round game against the Redskins, resulting in Grant limiting him to the punt team. But he took over for backup Amos Martin in the first half as the Rams were gouging the Vikings with their powerful backs, Lawrence McCutcheon and John Cappelletti. McCutcheon rushed for 128 yards on 26 carries and a touchdown.

"We were leading 10–0, but the Rams had shown a lot of power on the ground," said Siemon. "I noticed on the punting team that my leg was relatively strong. As I was standing on the sideline near Bud Grant I leaned over and said, 'Bud, there's no way for me to know whether I can play unless I get in there and try to do something.' He suggested that if the Rams made another first down, I should go in. They did, and I went in."[4]

Siemon, unquestioned as both the team's tackling and spiritual leader, was drafted first by the Vikings in 1972 after a sensational career at the University of Stanford. Within both of those roles, his primary desire was to take hold of what he called "The Unreachable."

This was part of Siemon's nature.

The 6–2, 235-pounder's mission was not only to track down the NFL's many elusive ballcarriers but also those reluctant to share his steadfast faith in Jesus Christ.

One of the men Siemon prayed for daily was fellow linebacker Hilgenberg, a free spirit who came over to the Vikings after four years with Detroit and having been released by Pittsburgh. He is one of 11 players who was a member of each of Minnesota's four Super Bowl teams.

"Jeff came home one day all excited and said, 'Wally's wife came to know the Lord. I just know Wally will now,'" recalled Jeff's wife, Dawn. "And he did right after that. It was such a blessing."

Hilgenberg, who passed away in 2008 at age 66 after a two-year battle with ALS, wasn't too keen on the Vikings drafting Siemon because it put his buddy Lonnie Warwick's starting role in danger.

"We later became great friends," said Siemon, who spoke at Hilgenberg's funeral. "Wally trusted Christ as his savior and it was just a beautiful thing to watch."

Always on the attack, Siemon was all over the field against the Redskins before suffering his leg injury. His replacement, friend Amos Martin, held his own in Siemon's absence.

Siemon was a fixture in the Vikings' defense for 10 years after replacing Warwick, who was injured during a Monday night loss to the Bears in week six of Siemon's rookie campaign.

"It was a privilege playing for a team with that kind of football history and not hurt it, but help it," said Siemon. "It was special for me to be on that team."

Siemon was born in Rochester, Minnesota, but the family moved to Bakersfield, California, when his father, an eye doctor, accepted a practice there.

"I made a list prior to the draft of the top 10 teams I'd like to draft me," said Siemon, who ran an impressive 4.7 in the 40. "The Vikings weren't one of the teams I considered.

I was surprised when Jim Finks called me early the morning of the draft. I was thinking, 'Where on the list were the Minnesota Vikings?' I wasn't so sure how much I'd play there because I knew they were a veteran team, and I wasn't so fond of the cold. I grew up in California, following the 49ers. John Brodie was one of my favorite players."

It's safe to say things worked out well for the Vikings, although they finished just 7–7 Siemon's first year. A highlight for Siemon came in the last game of the season at Candlestick Park when he picked off a pass from Brodie, who had come off the bench in favor of Steve Spurrier to lead the 49ers to a last-second win.

"That was pretty cool having grown up a 49ers fan. The only time we got Vikings games out west was when they were in the playoffs," said Siemon.

• • •

It was truly Bryant's day, but this also was a game that showcased the considerable talents of Foreman, who Green Bay Packers great Paul Hornung once said "was the best draft choice the Vikings ever made."

Foreman, drafted 12th overall by the Vikings out of the University of Miami in 1973, finished the championship game one yard short of 200 total yards. He had 118 yards rushing on just 15 carries and another 81 yards receiving on five catches.

"He played all over at Miami and I liked an athlete like that," said Reichow. "First of all, he was a big guy. When he got into camp his first year, they ran sprints and he didn't time very good. Everybody's looking at me and saying, 'Oh, Jesus, what do we do with this guy?' I said let him play, and he was great out of the backfield catching the football. He was great running the football, too. He was such a big guy, defensive backs would get tired of trying to tackle him."

The graceful 6–2, 210-pounder from Frederick, Maryland, put his immense talents on full display in probably the most unforgettable 30 minutes of football in team history.

Leading 10–0 at intermission, the Vikings faced a second-and-seven on their own 36 on their first series of the third quarter.

Foreman exploded off the ball and took a handoff from Fran Tarkenton slanting right. The Vikings' two All-Pros on that side, Ed White and Ron Yary, cross-blocked. The result was devastation of the left side of the Rams' powerful front wall.

Yary got Merlin Olsen, White blew up Jim Youngblood and tight end Stu Voigt sealed off Jack Youngblood. Foreman broke a tackle by free safety Bill Simpson near the line and was—as fabled Vikings broadcaster Paul Allen would say—"Loose!" He was finally tripped up 62 yards downfield at the Rams' one-yard line by Rod Perry.

"I'm not a 100-yard-dash man. I can go like a sprinter for 40 or 50 yards, so when Rod Perry caught me, I wasn't running so fast. That was a great play he made," said Foreman. "It was a simple off-tackle play. We used to call it '34 lead,' with Yary and White cross-blocking. Strong formation and no split. We had good blocking on that strong side. I just got to that second level and that was it."[5]

Offensive line coach John Michels told the *Minneapolis Tribune* that Tarkenton changed the play at the line.

"As he was calling his cadence, he noticed the Rams switching into what we call an 'over' defense," Michels said. "Tackle Larry Brooks moved over our center. Tarkenton called the audible."[6]

Michels credited Yary, White, Tingelhoff and Voigt for making big blocks to pave the way for Foreman.

"The play was called a 34X," said White. "That meant Ron and I cross-blocked. He came down on the first lineman or linebacker in that spot. I would block out on the defensive end. If the linebacker was stacked up in the gap, I would take the Will linebacker. That would be an adjustment that I had to make. Because the end was wider, I would fold up and take the linebacker and that's exactly what happened. It was one of our bread-and-butter plays."

Three plays later, Foreman pounded into the line and bounced off a tackler to make it 17–0.

"The Rams defense is one of the best I've seen," Tarkenton told reporters. "They give you enormous problems. We knew that someplace in the game the Rams' aggressiveness would open a door for us. When they shifted into a different defense, I knew the play for it. It was a textbook response to the play they were in."[7]

Jack Youngblood's key fumble recovery after a Fred Dryer sack set up the Rams' second TD, which got them back into the game. Youngblood said he could only tip his cap after Foreman's huge run.

"Yary blocked down. That was a well-done play on their part," he said. "Foreman was very strong. He looked for that double team and he'd get behind it. That's going to give him three yards right there. He and Lawrence were both very good halfbacks. They had good linemen in front of them. They were both on the same page."

Foreman wasn't done.

Following Bryant's remarkable second pick, there was still more than two minutes to kill for the Vikings to go to a fourth Super Bowl.

The play that allowed them to do so was quintessential Foreman.

With the field in shadows, Minnesota stared down a daunting situation—third down and four from its own 30 with 2:09 left.

The Rams called their final time-out. A first down would likely seal the game. Were the Vikings thinking about their failure on third and two late in the dreaded Hail Mary game the year before, a play that could have sealed a win, a play call that still haunts Tarkenton?

This time, Foreman lined up wing left, with the dangerous duo of Ahmad Rashad and Sammy White to the right of the formation.

Tarkenton dropped straight back, then semi-rolled right, looking first for Robert Miller coming the same way out of the backfield. He instead opted to step toward the line of scrimmage, where he found the omnipresent Foreman slanting over the middle from left to right, a step ahead of speedy linebacker Isiah Robertson.

The throw was a little high and slightly out in front, but Foreman engulfed the ball with his huge hands, then broke a Robertson tackle at his own 45. With safety Dave Elmendorf trailing him near the massive and colorful NFL shield painted at midfield, Foreman adroitly sidestepped the oncoming Simpson, who proceeded to collide forcefully and fortuitously into Elmendorf. Foreman's pathway was now clear down the right sideline, where he eluded Perry before being brought down by Monte Jackson at the Rams' 12.

It was the kind of play legends are made of.

"Generally, that's what we did in those situations," said Foreman of lining up in a tight slot. "Either that or we'd be in a split backfield. We knew that normally I was going to be covered by a linebacker. I had different reads. I was going to read the middle linebacker or the weakside linebacker, whichever side I was on. I had to make moves depending on which way the middle linebacker was going to go, and it had to be a quick decision. No hesitation. These were option routes and it depended on what I saw out there. Of course, Fran was always on the job."

Sammy White, quiet in this one after a great game in the divisional round versus the Redskins, said he ran a clear-out route.

"I ran a post," he recalled. "They called an option route for Foreman, and he was great on reading where to go on those. He knew which way to go depending on where they played him."

It was one of the myriad Foreman highlight-reel skirmishes, but given its magnitude, the play may have been his greatest moment.

"It was probably one of my favorite plays," he said. "I did my little step back. I saw them both coming [Elmendorf and Simpson], so I stepped back and let them run into each other. That was like the first time I did that; it was kind of a weird situation. When I tried it and it worked, I was thinking, 'Damn!' Some of those things happen. I can't explain it, but it worked. I was just as surprised as everyone."

The play unfolded similarly to the Minneapolis Miracle, where Stefon Diggs, with seconds left, made a leaping catch on a pass from Casey Keenum near the right sideline as New Orleans defensive backs Marcus Williams and Ken Crawley slammed into each other to clear his way to the end zone and give the Vikings a 29–24 win and a spot in the 2018 NFC championship game.

Miller, who was playing in his first title game, detailed his role on the play.

"They were giving us certain things. The flare pattern I ran was routine from day one in training camp," he said. "The play was called for Chuck to run an 'over route.' We wanted to give them one picture and come right behind where they left. They think we're going to throw it out to me on the [right] flat and Chuck comes across the middle, from left to right. It's just to pull the defense over to that side and leave a hole up the middle."

Miller was adept at what the Vikings asked their backs to do—catch the ball. He had 56 catches in his three years in Kansas.

"They liked that I could block, run and catch the ball," he said. "That was the main reason I was drafted by the Vikings. I also played special teams every year. I was one of the two upbacks right next to center and I had outside containment on kickoff coverage."

The play was not a shocking development for one as skilled as Foreman, the Fred Astaire of football moves. His sidestep against Elmendorf and Simpson was so deftly executed, it brought to mind the hardcourt stylings of Earl "The Pearl" Monroe, the dazzling playmaker for Foreman's hometown Baltimore Bullets. Foreman's moniker, the "Spin Doctor," came from emulating Monroe's mastery of the spin dribble. Foreman not only used it on the basketball court, where he was so accomplished he received more scholarship offers for hoops than any other sport, but also repeatedly and expertly on the football field.

Fittingly, his first regular-season touchdown came via a spin move on opening day in '73 against the Oakland Raiders at The Met.

Foreman grabbed a pass in the left flat from Tarkenton at the Oakland five, then utilized his signature move on a bewildered Dan Conners and George Atkinson and waltzed untouched into the end zone in a 24–16 Vikings win. This same elegance enabled him to score 52 more TDs in his seven-year career in purple.

His flashy style would often be reflected in his choice of shoes. One year he got away with the closest any Viking came at that time to wearing white shoes under Grant (he allowed them in '85 after a year out of coaching). The shoes were something like the "spats" Lenny Moore wore playing for the Baltimore Colts, one of Foreman's beloved teams growing up along with the Redskins.

"Lenny Moore was special. He and my high school coach were teammates at Penn State. But these weren't Moore's spats. Actually, I used to work with a [shoe] company called Spot-Bilt," said Foreman. "I had them make me a shoe with a white stripe down the middle and I would have the trainer tape my ankles on the outside. I thought Bud might have said something, but they were mostly black."

Dennis Ryan, in addition to being a legendary coffee maker, knew just about everything that went on inside the Vikings' locker room. He said it was rare for a player to try to slip one past Grant, whom Reichow described as a "man who saw everything."

"What they would try to do is use white tape to spat their shoes," said Ryan. "Bud caught on to that, and he had the trainers order black tape. Before that, they'd put as much as that white tape on as they could. When Les Steckel took over [as head coach] in '84, he said, 'The players all want to wear white shoes, so we're going to wear white shoes.' We sold all of our stock of black shoes and put the white shoes on the shelf. The next year, Bud comes back and I assumed we would go back to black cleats, but when I asked him, he said, 'We'll just wear the white cleats, they're already on the shelf.' He always had a practical way of looking at things. We and the University of Michigan of all the major college and pro teams were the only teams still wearing black shoes at that time."

Grant, a stickler for even how players wore their socks (the purple nylon sock had to appear halfway up the calf), would sometimes look the other way for the five-time Pro Bowler.

"Once or twice, he would," chuckled Foreman.

Clinton Jones didn't try to get away with white shoes until after he left the Vikings.

"I was traded from the Vikings September 3, 1973, to the Chargers," he recalled. "We were going to play Minnesota the next week [in an exhibition game]. [Chargers coach] Harland Svare called me into the office to get a scouting report. My scouting report was, 'Shit, we don't have a chance against them.' Svare quickly said, 'That's enough.' For the game I spatted up because I thought it would look cool. Before the game, I go out to the middle of the field with Svare, like the coaches do before the game, to greet my old coach. I see Bud looking at me and looking down at my shoes, and he looks over to Harland and says, 'Tell him to take those off.'"

"Bud was kind of smart, too, now," Sammy White said with a grin. "On one guy he might see and another guy he might not see."

In other words, a player with Foreman's legendary résumé earned privileges not otherwise granted.

Ahmad Rashad, who had three catches for 28 yards against a stout Rams secondary (Tarkenton was just 12 of 27 passing for 143 yards and no touchdowns), enjoyed the same treatment.

"Bud never bothered me about nothing," laughed Rashad. "They used to call me 'Bud, Jr.,' just ask Ed White. I spatted my shoes. I had hand warmers in my pocket. He gave me hand warmers. I couldn't get long-sleeved shirts from the equipment manager so I went out and bought them, because I couldn't handle that cold weather. Bud never said a word. Not one word.

"There were times I wouldn't go out to warm up," he added. "It's like 70 degrees in this locker room and two degrees out there. I'm not going out there. He'd never say a word. I'd just go in the shower and hide somewhere. He'd let that go. When I'd come out, he'd give me a hand warmer. During a game, he'd call me over and say, 'Here's a hand warmer.' Never acknowledged it. He'd talk about guys not having hand warmers and I remember him walking over to me and handing me a hand warmer at least 10 times. When someone would ask, he'd say, 'No, I didn't.' Even at practice, it would be so damn cold outside and I could hardly stand it, my hands were frozen, my face was frozen. He would call me over from a drill, 'Hey, Ahmad, come over here a minute.' I go over to him and he'd start talking to me about some deer hunting trip he went on or deer licks or something like that. This would go on about 20 minutes, a half hour. Ed would say, 'There's Bud, Jr., again.' It was something."

There may never be a better manager of men, said Foreman.

"Bud Grant was the best coach to play for at that time," said Foreman, who finished his career in 1980 with the New England Patriots. "I don't know if he was ahead of his time or not, but he treated people the way they were supposed to be treated as far as the football field goes. Everybody was equal."

Unless, that is, you were a once-in-a-lifetime player who could beat you with both his running and receiving skills.

With the crowd still in a frenzy over Foreman's near supernatural pirouette, powerful Sammy Johnson found a gaping hole two plays later behind guard Charles Goodrum's block on Simpson and ran over the talkative Robertson at the goal line with under 40 seconds remaining to seal a fourth trip to the Super Bowl.

"Butch was always a talker," laughed Foreman. "He was an intense player on the field. For me, he did talk a lot of trash, but that was OK. Because while he was talking, I was beating him. Great player, too."

"I never liked the Rams," said Siemon. "I don't mean I have strong animosity toward all their people, or even toward most of them. I grew up in Bakersfield, where most of the football fans were obnoxious Rams rooters. I wasn't. Knowing what I knew as a player, I liked them even less. The Rams generally had some talkative people on their team."[8]

It was another playoff disappointment for Dryer, the Rams' great right defensive end.

"We reached the NFC title game for three years in a row. But we can't just show up," said Dryer, a teammate of Tarkenton's in New York. "We've got to take advantage of our chances. We knew we could shut down Tarkenton, and we did. But we made mistakes that let the Vikings get ahead. It was up to us to cash in. Championship teams do that, but we couldn't."[9]

• • •

Two great Vikings, Foreman and Bryant, came up big in situations others would shy from.

Bryant finished his 12-year career with 51 interceptions, just two behind Krause on the all-time Vikings list and good for 32nd all-time in the NFL. That number seems minimal in comparison with Krause's 81, but Bryant's tally compares favorably with Hall of Famers Mel Blount (57 picks), Willie Brown (54) and Mel Renfro (52).

He had more picks than Hall of Famers like Ken Houston (49), Willie Wood and Herb Adderley (48) and Mike Haynes (46).

"When you played with the Purple People Eaters, you only had to guard your guy about four seconds," said the humble Bryant, who would have piled up even more picks had he not lost to injury what amounted to three full seasons. "It made my job a lot easier."

Bryant played in a ton of big games and played well.

Three years earlier, Bryant picked off a Staubach pass intended for Bob Hayes near the right sideline and raced 63 yards unabated to the end zone in the third quarter to put Dallas to bed in the Vikings' 27–10 win in the 1973 NFC title game at Texas Stadium, sending the long-suffering Tarkenton to his first Super Bowl.

"Staubach took a two-step drop and cocked to throw," recalled Bryant, who had another pick in that championship game. "I took off toward [Bob] Hayes and made the play."

In the best Viking season of all time—the NFL championship year of 1969—Bryant opened the season with eight interceptions in 10 games before injuring a knee and going on to miss the playoffs and Super Bowl IV against Kansas City. That total put him on pace to break Night Train Lane's single-season record of 14 set in '52.

"I was on a pretty good clip that year," said Bryant, who if not run into by Krause would have had another interception in the waning moments of the team's season-opening loss at Yankee Stadium that season to the New York Giants. "I hurt my knee in the Pittsburgh game returning a punt and missed the rest of the season."

Of the corners of his era, only Krause, Blount and Brown played in more playoff games than Bryant's 14. Not winning a Super Bowl undoubtedly hurts Bryant's HOF chances, but it did not deter those who voted for Houston or Haynes.

"It's hard to say what criterion they use when they go into that room to vote," said Bryant, shaking his head.

What made Bryant special was not only his quick-twitch instincts with the ball in the air but his play on special teams. A solid return man early in his career, the Macon, Georgia, product's 90-yard scoop-and-score in the opening quarter after snaring off one bounce Nate Allen's block of Tom Dempsey's field goal attempt got the Vikings off on the right foot, so to speak, as they took a 7–0 lead.

The omnipresent Allen, after being acquired from San Francisco for Jim Lash, made a habit of blocking kicks with the Vikings. In the two teams' regular-season outing in September, Allen helped Minnesota salvage a 10–10 tie by blocking a kick in overtime.

"It comes from here," said Allen, tapping his heart. "Heart, character, whatever, this team makes you want to play hard."[10]

"We played a much better team than we played in September," added Grant. "We beat a great team. Our specials teams played exceptionally well, but it didn't surprise me."[11]

The rangy Blair blocked a punt in the first quarter to set up the 25-yard Fred Cox field goal that gave the Vikings a 10–0 lead.

Bryant's blocked-kick return was set up by yet another in a litany of Vikings goal-line stands. A defense playing at first without Siemon held the Rams for three downs, two of which came inches from the goal after end Mark Mullaney tackled Ron Jessie on a flanker reverse.

"Buddy Ryan said after the game if I don't make that play, we don't go to the Super Bowl," said Mullaney of the Vikings' defensive line coach. "He was a great coach. He was the best defensive coach I had. Look at what he did in Chicago. He was a genius."

Stationed at left end outside Eller with the Rams inside the Vikings' five on their second series of the contest, Mullaney read the play and held the edge, fighting off Rams tight end Terry Nelson. Getting support outside from Nate Wright, Mullaney brought down Jessie, whose right knee hit the ground before crossing the goal.

"We practiced short yardage all the time," said Mullaney. "We kept it simple. They wanted us to stay low and drive low and push the pile as far back as we could."

"I was sure I had scored," said Jessie, who was traded to the Lions for a fourth-round pick after being chosen by Dallas in the eighth round of the 1971 draft. He signed as a free agent with Los Angeles in 1975. "I could see the goal line under me."[12]

Two plays later, Hilgenberg stuffed Haden on a quarterback sneak and Rams head coach Chuck Knox, knowing in his mind his team's failures in short-yardage situations in the deadlocked game in September, opted for the field goal try and it terribly backfired.

"I wasn't a very good student. I learned by doing, a visual learner," said Mullaney. "Patera said you're built more like Eller, so watch how he plays. As a result, I become more of a strongside end. Eller and Marshall taught me by watching them play. As for techniques, I learned a lot from going against Ron Yary and Ed White. They, along with Mick Tingelhoff, were the best guys out there so I believed if I could beat them, I could play in the league. Eller and Yary would really go at it at practice. He and Marshall would point some things out to me, but I learned by doing. I eventually learned if I hit you before you hit me, I'm going to win."

Mullaney posted 41.5 sacks over his 12-year Vikings career, not bad for a man who had to learn on the fly.

"I got drafted to play a position I had never played before to try to beat out players who were the best in the NFL at that position in Eller and Marshall. Being put out of position was a normal role for me, though. It was certainly an interesting role," he said. "Going into college, I had played every position except for wide receiver."

Mullaney said he was probably more equipped to play offense.

"I came to Colorado State as a tight end but got moved to the offensive line. I had great hands and great speed. But I never got to play there. Following my senior year, I got invited at the last minute to play in the Senior Bowl as a replacement for Randy White [the No. 2 overall pick in '75 for the Cowboys]," he said.

Mullaney turned heads at Senior Bowl practices.

"I'm at Senior Bowl practice as an offensive tackle and I'm blocking a really good prospect who I didn't know at the time, who was like 6–8, 255 [Mack Mitchell, fifth pick overall in '75 out of Houston by Cleveland]," he recalled. "I drove him out of there pretty good. Our coach was [Denver Broncos coach] John Ralston and there's all these scouts on the sidelines. It really ticked Ralston off to see me do that. He told me to do it again. I did it again and he pulled me aside and he said, 'Son, what's your name?' I said, 'Mark Mullaney.' He asked me where I played. I said, 'Colorado State.'"

It was at that point Ralston decided he didn't want anyone else to take notice of the gem he had discovered.

"Ralston pointed to all the reporters and scouts on the field at the time and said I wasn't going to practice anymore. He told me he was going to draft me in the second round, so I went from a no-name to a second-rounder," laughed Mullaney. "He said the bad news was I was not going to play in the game. I told him OK, but I felt really bad because my family was looking forward to watching me play. I didn't practice another

11. Bobby's Big Day

day. I got dressed the day of the game, but that was about it. Toward the end of the game, we needed a touchdown and he put me in. I drove Mack Mitchell into the end zone and they followed me in for the score. There was one series left and they put me in at defensive end and I didn't even know where to line up. I got into the huddle and I ended up making a few plays and the Vikings ended up drafting me to play defense."

From not having played the position at all in college, Mullaney turned into a solid player, with his best stretch being his combined 17 sacks over a two-year period from '78–79.

"I didn't even know where Minnesota was and who the Purple People Eaters were," he laughed. "I loved playing, but I didn't know all the teams or the players. Minnesota called me and my brother Ed picked up and he said, 'Hey, it's the Vikings. Tell them no, you don't want to go up there!' My brother was like 6-10 and he was a great basketball player, and he went up to (the University of) Minnesota on a recruiting trip because they had offered him a scholarship. They brought him up in January. He said the snow was up over the stop signs and you couldn't see the streets. He said he had never been so cold in his whole life."

Ed Mullaney ended up playing for a junior college in Arizona before finishing his hoops career at nearby Colorado State. "He's the guy who motivated and pushed me to be my best," said Mullaney. "I guess it's good I didn't listen to him that time."

Against the Rams, Mullaney made the biggest play of his career, while Foreman defied the odds with his ballet-like moves, but it was a game for the ages for the unsung and soft-spoken Bryant, who wasn't about to let Nate Wright or Vikings fans down in that last glorious championship game triumph so long ago, on the frozen tundra at Met Stadium.

12

What Could Have Gone Wrong Did

The ball would never bounce in the Super Bowls for the Vikings the way it did for Bobby Bryant on December 26, 1976, at Metropolitan Stadium.

When Tom Dempsey's field goal attempt in the opening minutes of the NFC championship against the Los Angeles Rams was blocked, the Vikings cornerback easily corralled the ball off one hop and raced 90 yards for a touchdown. Minnesota never trailed and went on to win 24–13 to advance to meet the Oakland Raiders in Super Bowl XI in Pasadena, California.

Two weeks later, it was Fred McNeill, not Nate Allen, who came up with a huge block after Oakland failed on its third straight offensive series to open the game. Lining up at the Raiders' 34, McNeill charged in unscathed off the left side and did what no professional player had ever done: block a Ray Guy punt. The ball caromed crazily back to the Oakland seven. The speedy Bryant, bursting through from the opposite side, was once again poised to make the recovery and trot in for another euphoric, kick-starting, game-opening touchdown.

A lead in the Super Bowl? Could this be happening? Minnesota had never led in its three previous Super Bowl appearances. Hadn't Fran Tarkenton guaranteed a victory during a locker room interview following the Rams win?

McNeill's left-handed block created some insane spin, and just as Bryant was about to make the scoop, the ball took a kangaroo hop over his head to the Oakland 10 before spinning *back* inside the five, where McNeill fell on it.

"The ball was behind the punter going toward the goal line," said Bryant on Minnesota's 16th blocked kick of the season. "It was way up in the air and started coming down. I knew it was going to bounce, and I was trying to time it. I was going to catch it in the air and take it into the end zone. The ball hit the ground, and the turf at the Rose Bowl was really, really soft. The ball hit on the flat surface and bounced straight up in the air, like 12 feet up [and over his head]."[1]

"I blocked the punt clean because nobody really tried to block me," said the linebacker McNeill, the Vikings' first-round selection out of UCLA in the '74 draft. "I lined up right behind Windlan Hall on the flank, and I might have surprised Charlie Phillips, their outside guy, because he usually lines up pretty tight and he was even tighter because of where I positioned myself. Just before the snap I slipped out wide. Phillips couldn't get a shot at me, and neither could their up-man."[2]

Bryant not getting another perfect bounce wouldn't have mattered if Oakland linebacker Phil Villapiano and nose tackle Dave Rowe hadn't forced a Brent McClanahan fumble two plays later that Willie Hall recovered.

"After that, Oakland kind of ran over us," said Bryant. "That stands out more than any other play."

"We thought, 'These damn Vikings are doing it again,'" said Oakland fullback Mark van Eeghen, the upback in punt formation. "I mean we were dominating the game, but it looked like they were going to take the lead. I think that was the turning point of the game. It's funny, but a blocked punt turned things around for us. It made us mad, first of all. Then, for the Vikings not to get any points of it, well, that made us very happy."[3]

The Vikings still could have salvaged at least getting the ball back on a short field, maybe inside the 50, but Clarence Davis took a handoff on third down from his own five and raced 35 yards down the left sideline. Extracted from a deep hole, Oakland went on to kick a 24-yard field goal 48 seconds into the second quarter to take a 3–0 lead. By halftime, the lead would balloon to 16-zip.

"We blew a chance to get a touchdown after that blocked kick," said offensive coordinator Jerry Burns. "Really blew it. We almost never fail to score down there at the goal line. That's a sin. I think it shook us."[4]

Such was the story of each of the Vikings' four Super Bowl sojourns, games where they failed to capitalize on opponents' mistakes and made plenty of their own; never led; never controlled the line of scrimmage; tallied just four offensive touchdowns; were outscored 51–0 in first halves; and, of course, never won.

Oakland had a field day running behind its vaunted left side of Art Shell and Gene Upshaw, who combined to pave the way for a Super Bowl–record 266 yards rushing, getting a game-high 137 from the USC product Davis.

"It was the most daylight I have ever seen to the outside," said Davis. "The linemen did such a fantastic job of blocking. The holes were so big that my job was easy."[5]

"I knew the game was under control when we took the ball out of the hole on that play and then drove to the Vikings 7 [for a field goal]," said Upshaw. "That's what football is all about—a pit battle."[6]

Oakland certainly triumphed in the trenches. Vikings middle linebacker Jeff Siemon had a solid game with 15 tackles and two assists, but their vaunted front four combined for just 15 stops. Ten of those tackles were made by Alan Page. Jim Marshall was shut out by Shell and tight end Dave Casper, who double-teamed him on Davis's game-changing scamper.

Oakland scored a pair of touchdowns before the half on a catch by Casper and a short run by Pete Banaszak. After the Raiders tacked on a field goal in the third, the Vikings showed some signs of life when Sammy White caught an eight-yard TD pass from Fran Tarkenton late in the third stanza to make it 19–7.

Minnesota had a chance to make a game of it after driving from its own 22 to the Oakland 37 with 10:30 left, but Tarkenton's fourth-down desperation pass off a scramble was intercepted by Hall. Banaszak added another short scoring run to put the game out of reach at 26–7. Willie Brown followed with a 75-yard interception return for a score.

Backup quarterback Bob Lee's 13-yard pass to Stu Voigt gave Minnesota its first Super Bowl with two offensive TDs and made the final 32–14.

"I'm disappointed because we may never be in another Super Bowl," said a prophetic Siemon after the game.[7]

Siemon was right, but little did he know his prognostication would apply to Minnesota teams of the next half century.

• • •

The Vikings' best opportunity to win a Super Bowl came two years earlier, January 12, 1975, in gloomy New Orleans. Led by the front wall of Joe Greene, L.C. Greenwood, Ernie Holmes and Dwight White, and linebackers Jack Lambert, Jack Ham and Andy Russell, Pittsburgh had a dominating defense but was playing in its first Super Bowl and Minnesota its third.

As was the theme in all of its Super Bowl losses, Minnesota was dominated in the trenches, allowing a then-record 249 yards on the ground while gaining a measly 17. Franco Harris rushed 34 times for a record-setting 158 yards.

The Vikings were somehow still in the game with 10 minutes left, largely because backup safety Terry Brown was not plagued by the type of bad bounce that foiled Bryant's efforts against Oakland. Brown recovered a ball waist-high in the end zone after Matt Blair swooped in to block Bobby Walden's punt, and despite Fred Cox clanking the point after off the left upright, Minnesota trailed just 9–6. Alan Page set up the score by catching former Notre Dame teammate Rocky Bleier behind the line on a third-and-two run from the Pittsburgh 15.

On Pittsburgh's possession following the blocked punt, Terry Bradshaw, who had just six completions to that point, found tight end Larry Brown wide open at the Vikings' 40 on a third-and-two play from his own 42. Brown lumbered to the Minnesota 30, where he was slung down hard by rookie cornerback Jackie Wallace. Siemon, with Paul Krause right there, pounced on the loose ball and the Vikings jubilantly started racing off the field as the two officials near the play vehemently signaled Minnesota ball. But to their dismay, the side judge raced over and indicated that Brown was down at the 28 with 8:12 remaining.

"They gave us the ball. I started running off the field," said Krause. "The offense was coming on. Then this guy comes over from the other side and decides he saw it better."[8]

"I usually try to understand the officials' predicament on a play like that," said Siemon. "But it was simply called by the wrong person."[9]

"There's no way the ball could be ruled dead," said Wallace. "He was still on his way down when he lost the ball."[10]

"The official who called it was across the field and behind him [Brown]," said Vikings coach Bud Grant. "The official who ruled it was our ball was in front of the play."[11]

Seven plays later, after Harris was stopped on two runs in close, Bradshaw rolled right on a third-and-goal from the Vikings' four and found Brown open for a touchdown with 3:38 left. On Minnesota's first play from scrimmage following the kickoff, Tarkenton's pass intended for John Gilliam was intercepted by Mike Wagner to end any chances for a comeback as the Vikings fell 16–6.

It was a frustrating day for the Pro Bowler John Gilliam, who was pumped up about playing in his old stomping grounds with the Saints, Tulane Stadium.

"That's *my* stadium. I wanted the football," said Gilliam, who was limited to one catch for 16 yards and was unhappy about his usage versus the Steel Curtain.

"Put me all over the field. Put me at slot, put me at split end, put me in the backfield. I played running back some in college. I like to run the ball [after the catch], that's how I made my living," said Gilliam, who averaged a career-best 22.2 yards a catch during the regular season. "You got to find a way to get the ball to your special players. They told me Pittsburgh was going to use a zone against me and that they were going to use me as a decoy and try to get the ball to Foreman out of the backfield. We tried that and it didn't work."

Never afraid of contact, Gilliam played the game wearing a cast on his left wrist due to a fracture suffered during the regular season. This restriction came into play during a pivotal sequence with the Vikings down just 2–0 with under two minutes left in the first half.

It changed the course of the game.

Having done nothing offensively all game, the Vikings, after giving up a safety on a poor exchange between Tarkenton and Dave Osborn at their own 10, marched to the Pittsburgh 25 on their next possession thanks to a juggling 17-yard catch and run by Foreman and a key third-and-two reception for a first down by Osborn to the Steelers' 25. With 1:40 remaining in the second quarter, there was plenty of time to score and the Vikings had the benefit of receiving the second-half kickoff.

"Fran called 84 Divide," recalled Gilliam. "Stu Voigt would run a drag pattern and I would cut in [on a skinny post]. But he called the play from the 25. We were too close to the goal line. The safeties were in too close because they're backed up against the end zone. I pushed one corner [J.T. Thomas] back with my route, but the safety [Glen Edwards] was waiting on me. The ball was thrown high. I got my hands on it, but I couldn't lock it up because I couldn't bend my wrist. He hung me out to dry. I wanted the ball on my chest and I could've walked in the end zone."

Edwards clobbered Gilliam inside the five and the ball popped backward into the end zone, where cornerback Mel Blount gathered it in. It was another Vikings case of what could have been.

On the play, Minnesota lined up in a split backfield, with Jim Lash split left and Gilliam flanked right. The idea was for Gillam and Lash to cross over each other, with Lash running the deeper "over" route and Gilliam underneath. Both players were open, as Lash had a step and a half on Blount in the end zone. Voigt ran a drag from right to left, taking the other Steelers safety, Wagner, with him. That cleared room for Gilliam, who easily beat Thomas to the inside.

Instead of it being 7–2 or 3–2 in the Vikings' favor, it was soon 9–0 Pittsburgh. Fullback Bill Brown, by this stage in his career used primarily on special teams, failed to handle the second half's opening kickoff as the ball was inadvertently squibbed by a slipping Roy Gerela and spun crazily out of his hands. Four plays later, Harris swept left to the end zone from nine yards out.

Minnesota had a great chance to cut the lead to two after Krause recovered a fumble at the Pittsburgh 48 with 13:05 left in the contest. A pass interference call against Wagner on a deep ball to Gilliam got the ball to the Steelers' five, but Foreman coughed up the ball on the next play to end the threat.

The Vikings had an opportunity to chalk up the game's first score when defensive back Randy Poltl recovered a Bleier fumble at the Pittsburgh 24 two minutes into the second quarter. But a short gainer by Osborn was followed by two incomplete Tarkenton passes to Foreman (who was open near the sideline at the Pittsburgh five on the second throw), forcing the Vikings to bring on Fred Cox, who missed from 39 yards out. Pittsburgh's safety came five minutes later as defensive end White tapped down Tarkenton in the end zone.

Minnesota got a small degree of consolation when it beat Pittsburgh in a *Monday Night Football* game on October 4, 1976, in Bloomington.

Foreman, facing the same defense that held him to 18 yards rushing in the Super Bowl, had one of the top games of his carrier, gaining 148 yards and scoring both Vikings touchdowns in a 17–6 victory.

Foreman said Super Bowl IX weighed on his mind.

"I was definitely thinking about that," he said. "But what we did on that *Monday Night* game is what we should have done in the Super Bowl. And that is run our natural offense we used the entire season. We used to change up our offense in those big games. They were damn good football players, but we had some damn good football players up front, too. Instead of respecting what the players had done all season, we'd go into those games thinking, 'I don't think we can do that.' That's just my thinking. Sure, they had Joe Greene, but we had Yary and White, the arm-wrestling champ, and while Tingelhoff was a little undersized, we could play. Charles Goodrum was tough as well."

The final score would have been worse had a Lee connection in the end zone not been called back.

"I threw a touchdown pass to [Ahmad] Rashad on a post corner. I got the hell knocked out of me and it was a heckuva throw," said Lee, who started for an injured Tarkenton. "Then I see a flag. They call [left tackle Steve] Riley for holding. I was like, 'Oh man!' He felt so bad. He said, 'General, I didn't do it!' The next day we look at the film. What happened was L.C. Greenwood, their one defensive end, went down and he ended up catching his foot in Steve's face mask and they call holding. That would have put the game out of reach. Luckily, we still won."

The loss dropped the Steelers to 1–3, but they won nine of their last 10 games to make the playoffs for the fifth straight season.

Minnesota made a habit of defeating teams soon after losing to them in Super Bowl play. On opening day in 1970, nine months after their Super Bowl IV loss to Kansas, the Vikings routed the Chiefs 27–10 in a game played September 20 at Metropolitan Stadium. Playing against the same Kansas City defense that throttled them earlier and fired up after watching the NFL Films coverage of the game where a wired-for-sound head coach Hank Stram repeatedly mocked the Vikings, the hosts recorded 17 first downs to the Chiefs' eight and out-rushed them 132 to 63, with Brown leading the way with 55 yards.

The Vikings picked off Lenny Dawson twice and Roy Winston ran a fumble back 36 yards to make it a 10–0 game in the second quarter.

"It's always an advantage to get the lead," said Grant after the game. "They've been shoving it down our throats for eight months. What can you say when you get beat. It's sour grapes then. Today we proved the defense of the 1960s could beat the offense of the 1970s. Our game plan was almost exactly the same as the one we used in losing the Super Bowl."[12]

• • •

Jake Scott didn't make it two straight Super Bowl MVP performances, but the star safety was involved in a pair of plays that made a long day even longer for the Minnesota Vikings.

Scott recovered a pair of first-half fumbles, including one of his own, to pave the way for the Dolphins garnering their second-straight Vince Lombardi Trophy as they throttled the Vikings 24–7 in Super Bowl VIII in Houston. The year before, he picked off a pair of Billy Kilmer passes and was named MVP as Miami completed a 17–0 campaign with a 14–7 win over Washington.

A sensational return man, Scott returned the opening kickoff against the Vikings 31 yards to the Miami 38. The Dolphins' offense took it from there, seizing immediate control with a 10-play drive covering 62 yards, with the final five coming when a lumbering Larry Csonka crashed into the end zone to make it 7–0.

The Vikings went three and out on their next possession, forcing a Mike Eischeid punt. The sure-handed Scott fumbled, but instead of Minnesota getting the ball at the Miami 44, it was Scott who pounced on the ball. The Dolphins then launched another 10-play drive, culminated by Jim Kiick's one-yard plunge. In two possessions, Miami churned out 11 minutes of clock and scored twice.

With Miami up 17–0 late in the first half after a 28-yard field goal by Garo Yepremian, the Vikings mounted their best offensive drive of the game on the strength of four Tarkenton completions, moving 74 yards to the Miami six, where they faced a fourth-and-one with a minute left. With the Vikings receiving the second-half kickoff, a touchdown would be a huge momentum boost going into the locker room. Tarkenton handed the ball to Oscar Reed, who had a hot hand in the playoffs, but he fumbled after being hit by middle linebacker Nick Buoniconti. Falling on the ball was none other than Scott, whom Miami selected in the seventh round of the 1970 draft out of Georgia.

"I feel bad about the fumble," said Reed after the game. "I can't say for sure whether I would have made the first down if I didn't fumble. I didn't just drop the ball. He [Buoniconti] really delivered a blow."[13]

"If they score a touchdown, they would have come out in the last half with the momentum favoring them," said Buoniconti. "When you get all the way down there and get stopped for zero points on the board it has to hurt."[14]

Fitting considering Minnesota's bad fortune, Gilliam ran the second-half kickoff back 65 yards, but the effort was called back due to a clipping penalty.

After another Minnesota punt, Csonka added the final nail in the coffin with a three-yard TD run to make it 24–0. The Vikings scored early in the fourth on a four-yard keeper by Tarkenton, but Terry Brown's recovery of the ensuing onsides kick was nullified due to an offsides penalty, ending any notions of a serious comeback.

Csonka was the game's MVP, rushing 33 times for a record 145 yards.

"He's 6-foot-3 and I don't know what they list him at, but he's got to be 245 pounds," said Krause, who was in on eight tackles. "It starts to hurt when he's 5 yards away. I don't know anybody who hits harder."[15]

Miami's running game was so overwhelming behind the line of Jim Langer, Larry Little, Bob Kuechenberg, Norm Evans and Wayne Morris that quarterback Bob Griese threw only seven passes. He threw only *six* passes in the 27–10 win over Oakland in the AFC championship game.

Vikings beat writer Jim Klobuchar summarized Miami's total domination:

"To the losers go the post-mortems," he wrote. "The difference between the Vikings' post-mortems and the ordinary loser is that the Vikings don't want to replay the Super Bowl's first half, the second half or the goal line fumble. The Vikings want to replay the coin flip."[16]

In a nationally televised tilt at Metropolitan Stadium on September 1, 1975,

Minnesota took out nearly two years' worth of frustration when it defeated the Dolphins 20–7 in an exhibition game that had the intensity of a playoff contest.

"These are two of the finest teams in football," said Tarkenton, who was 15 of 21 passing for 214 yards and two scores. "Give or take a few people, they are the same one that played in the Super Bowl a couple years ago and Miami really took it to us. We dominated them tonight. It's satisfying of course, but still a preseason game."[17]

"There wasn't any doubt that the Vikings were the better team," said Langer, a native of Minnesota. "There's no comparison between the way they played against us in this game and the way they played against us in the Super Bowl."[18]

Miami was adjusting to an offense that would not include Paul Warfield, Csonka and Kiick, all who defected to the World Football League. Other star players followed, such as the Vikings' Gilliam. That didn't change Minnesota's desire to show the world it could compete with the Dolphins.

"When you're playing the Miami Dolphins who beat your brains out in the Super Bowl and the game is on national television, it's only natural that you're up a little higher than normal," said Voigt.[19]

It was a coming-out game for third-year man McClanahan, who had 105 yards of total offense. Both teams used their starters in the first half, which saw Minnesota outgain the Dolphins 207–40 and grab a 13–0 lead on Tarkenton TD passes to Steve Craig and Lash. Griese was just one of eight passing and sat the final two quarters. Norm Bulaich, brought in from the Colts to help in Csonka's absence, put Miami on the board in the fourth quarter on a 53-yard run.

"Their No. 1 team beat our No. 1 team and their subs beat our subs," said Miami coach Don Shula, whose team finished regular-season play 10–4.[20]

• • •

The only Super Bowl the Vikings entered as a favorite was Super Bowl IV versus the Kansas City Chiefs. It was the final NFL-AFL championship game.

The 23–7 loss was a frustrating day all around, said Osborn, who accounted for all the Vikings' scoring when he twisted in from four yards out to cap a 10-play, 69-yard drive on the team's first series of the second half. He was limited to 15 yards rushing on seven carries after posting 108 yards in the 27–7 NFL championship game win over Cleveland.

Kansas City, which scored on four of its first five possessions, got three field goals from Jan Stenerud and a five-yard TD run on third and goal by Mike Garrett on the famous "65 Toss Power Trap" play late in the first half to gain a 16–0 halftime lead. The Chiefs outrushed the Vikings 151–67.

"They played a five-man line and that threw us off," said Osborn. "Brown and I were getting hit as soon as we touched the ball. Everyone then was playing a 4–3 defense. We adjusted at halftime, but it was too late."

What looked like a five-man front to Osborn was actually Stram's fabled "Triple Stack Defense," which saw linebackers Bobby Bell, Willie Lanier and Jim Lynch play directly over the down linemen instead of in the gaps.

Defensive end Jerry Mays, who opted to play for the AFL's Chiefs after the Vikings selected him in the 11th round of the 1961 draft out of Southern Methodist, described what made the defense so unique.

"In our Triple Stack Defense, we have our weakside tackle playing head-on against the center. We over-shift our three linebackers to the left side, with one playing up close between the tackle and defensive end," said Mays, a six-time AFL All-Star. "It gives us what amounts to a 5–3 defense instead of a 4–3."[21]

Following Osborn's scoring run, Minnesota had a ray of hope after pinning Kansas City down at its own 18 on the ensuing kickoff. That hope turned quickly to despair as the Chiefs answered with an 82-yard scoring march.

Wide receiver Frank Pitts got it rolling with a key run for a first down to the Chiefs' 39 on a third-down play. Pitts burned the Vikings for 36 yards on three reverses and, in doing so, stymied the aggressiveness of defensive ends Jim Marshall and Carl Eller. On the next play, Vikings linebacker Wally Hilgenberg was whistled for a 15-yard personal foul call to advance the ball into Minnesota territory. Dawson then cashed in when he tossed a short hitch to the right flat to Otis Taylor, who broke tackles by Earsell Mackbee and Karl Kassulke and high-stepped down the sideline for the game-clinching touchdown.

The Norwegian Stenerud, who went to Montana State College on a ski jump scholarship, dominated the first half with a powerful right leg that enabled him to go 33 for 41 for the season on field goal tries. He recorded a pair of touchbacks on kickoffs in addition to splitting the uprights from 48, 32 and 25 yards. Ironically, the Chiefs' first touchdown came following a *short* kickoff that an on-charging Charlie West fumbled away inside his own 20.

"Stenerud had been hitting them out of the end zone," said West. "But this one wasn't that far. I saw it all the way. I just dropped it."[22]

"There isn't any doubt that the fumble by Charlie West that led up to the second-quarter touchdown hurt our chances," said Grant. "Had we gone to the dressing room at halftime down 9–0 instead of 16–0 it might have been different. All year we won because we didn't make mistakes. We beat the Rams and the Cleveland Browns without really making any errors. We made as many against Kansas City as we've made all year."[23]

"Unfortunately, we didn't win a Super Bowl, but we won a lot of tough games to get there," said Osborn, who rushed for 643 yards and a career best seven TDs in 1969. "We had a lot of great teams and I thought we were good enough to win any of those [Super Bowl] games."

Minnesota, a team whose weekly regimen under the stoic Grant was Spartan-esque, could not overcome the circus atmosphere of a Super Bowl.

"In Grant's carefully arranged universe, routine guarded against the deadly intrusion of surprise," wrote Klobuchar. "And routine meant doing on Friday before the game what you did last Friday before the game, and the Friday before that, and the Fridays of last year. And when you lump the Fridays, with the Thursdays and the Wednesdays and the Saturdays, you get an awful lot of days that look familiar. So you were very comfortable on those days, and therefore almost always on Sundays."[24]

"We never played up to our abilities in the Super Bowl games," said right tackle Ron Yary. "I believe strongly we were a better team than our performances. When Bud would travel, we could get to the opposing city on the afternoon the day before the game. We would do our walkthroughs on Saturday at Met Stadium. Spending 10 days on-site and being in a hotel, that different schedule for Super Bowls was disruptive for us. We couldn't stay in Minnesota to practice for the Super Bowl games. I think that had a lot to do with maybe not the outcome of the games but certainly our performances. It affected our rhythm. There's an itinerary rhythm to each team."

Safety Dale Hackbart's still frustrated over Super Bowl IV.

"It was a devastating loss," said Hackbart. "Going into the game, Kansas City had an outstanding offense and defense and it was the first time we played against that style defense. The Chiefs' offense had a lot of motion. They used what was called the Tight I, both ends in tight with the quarterback lined up with the fullback, tight end and halfback. Then before the play, they moved to different positions and then went into motion. They had multiple sets with multiple plays off these sets. It confused us. We were underprepared. A lot of the players were overconfident, and the Chiefs were just absolutely ready to kick our butts. We just weren't ready to play, but that changed when we played them the next year."

Kansas City's motion on offense troubled the Vikings, but so did its usage of tight end Fred Arbanas, said middle linebacker Lonnie Warwick.

"They would switch their tight end from one side of the field to another. Our defensive coaches wanted us to switch with him. We were switching Karl Kassulke all the way across the field [to play over Arbanas]. I told them we don't have to do that," said Warwick, who was famously captured by NFL Films raising his hands in the air in the huddle and looking over to the Vikings' sideline in frustration. "Just move our [weakside] linebacker up. We tried to switch everybody around. Karl Kassulke, our strong safety, couldn't adjust to that. They were saying, 'Paul Krause can't play strong safety.' I said, 'Yes, he can.' Karl Kassulke could play free safety. But they said, 'No, no.' I argued with them and argued with them. That's why you hear Hank Stram saying [in game audio], 'Look at Kassulke, he's running around like he's on a Chinese fire drill.' We didn't have to do that. I never could understand that."

As great as the Vikings' defense was, one can only imagine the level it may have attained had a man who played outside linebacker against them in New Orleans opted to stay in Minnesota.

Bobby Bell would have looked nice in purple.

"Not long before his death, Bud Grant told me, 'Dammit, Bell, if you would have come here, we would have kicked the shit out of everybody,'" laughed the Hall of Famer. "[Dallas Texans owner] Lamar [Hunt] just wanted me more."

Bell, who hails from Carl Eller's native North Carolina, was selected 16th overall by the Vikings in the second round of the '63 draft out of the University of Minnesota. He came out a year before Eller, whom he deftly teamed with under the tutelage of head coach Murray Warmath to help the Golden Gophers to Big Ten titles in '61 and '62. The 1962 Outland Trophy winner led Minnesota to a national title in '60.

The expectations were that Bell would stay in Minnesota; the only problem was the Dallas Texans of the AFL (who would soon become the Kansas City Chiefs) had chosen the versatile Bell at 56th overall in the seventh round of the AFL draft. He eventually signed with the Chiefs.

Don Klosterman, whom Hunt hired away from the San Diego Chargers in 1962 to become his director of player personnel, was the key man in Bell's decision to not play locally, said Michael MacCambridge in his remarkable book *America's Game.*

"Klosterman was the quintessential closer," he wrote. "Flying from Dallas to Minneapolis in November of 1962, he found himself seated next to Minnesota senator Hubert Humphrey, who after introductions asked him what he was going to the Twin Cities for."[25]

"I'm going up to talk to Bobby Bell," said Klosterman.

"You'll never sign Bobby Bell," said Humphrey flatly. "He's going to be our first black mayor; he's the most important player we've ever had."[26]

Klosterman spent a week in Minneapolis with Bell and signed him away largely due to offering a five-year, no-cut contract. One of the best athletes to ever play pro ball, Bell would go on to a career that saw him selected to the NFL's 100th Anniversary All-Time team.

"The Vikings and Norm Van Brocklin just sort of had this attitude like, 'Oh, don't worry about it, he'll come here,'" said Bell, who had four tackles against the Vikings in the Super Bowl. "But Don Klosterman was a salesman. He said, 'Bobby, we really want you with us, what's it going to take?'"

Bell remembers little if any contact with Vikings GM Bert Rose or chief of scouting Joe Thomas.

"I didn't really talk to them. They didn't think it was going to be a big deal, that I was going to stay there," he recalled. "I talked to Van Brocklin two or three times. Coach Warmath wanted me to be protected, to get a guaranteed contract. I asked Van Brocklin if he'd give me three years and he said yes. I then asked him if he'd guarantee that and he said, 'We can't do that.'"

"Moneywise, we lost him," said Vikings scout and later player personnel director Jerry Reichow. "It was terrible keeping up with the AFL's money. You'd have to draft lesser players who you knew would sign. We knew Bell wasn't going to sign."

Bell, Eller, Page and Marshall on the same team—Reichow could only sigh, "Bell and Eller, you'd think that would have been good?"

Klosterman played a key role in the signing, but Bell credits Hunt for his decision to choose the Chiefs.

"He didn't want me to go to the Vikings because originally they were going to be in the AFL," said Bell. "He gave me a long-term contract and the NFL didn't like that. Lamar wanted me. Almost all my communications were with Lamar. I met Klosterman but he was just bringing me the contract. Lamar came over to my house and I said, 'Let's go get some ice cream' and we did. He said he wanted me to be part of his family and I've been a part of it for 60 years."

To add insult to injury, the Vikings' first-round pick that year, a round ahead of Bell, was defensive tackle Jim Dunaway out of Mississippi. The AFL also lured him away, and he became a four-time Pro Bowl selection for the Buffalo Bills, teaming up with Ron McDole to give the team a rock-solid interior defense.

"They probably would have outlawed that," laughed Eller on the prospects of Bell flanking him at the outside linebacker position he mastered upon joining the Chiefs. "It would have been great, but it wasn't to be. Bobby was a great athlete. Bobby started off as a lineman in college before moving to linebacker. I think it would have been great to have him. He was a great player with the Chiefs. But I think I had a reliable and great teammate in Roy Winston. We were together for a long time, and I liked the way he played. Very seldom would people get outside of Roy. We played our assignments well, I thought."

While fully aware of what it would have meant to have an athlete such as Bell in the Vikings' front seven, Warwick was happy to play with Winston, who leaped over Robert Holmes to record one of his team's three sacks against Dawson, who was 12 of 17 passing for 142 yards and a TD.

"I think it would have been really neat to play with Bobby Bell, who was an unbelievable player, but I don't know if he would have had a job with Roy Winston there," said Warwick with a smile.

Bell started his career as a quarterback on Cleveland High School's six-man football team. With Minnesota already boasting Sandy Stephens, its first Black to start at quarterback, Warmath moved the versatile Bell to tackle.

"I just wanted to play," said Bell, who Stram once said could have "played all 22 positions." "When Coach Warmath said I was switching to tackle, I said, 'Coach, I've never played tackle before.' He said he wanted his best players on the field so I said just teach me how to play and I'd do it."

With Bell inside and Eller at end wearing No. 76, the duo become a force, leading the Golden Gophers to a 21–3 win over UCLA in the 1962 Rose Bowl.

"I never regretted my decision to go to the Chiefs," said Bell. "We ended up having a pretty good defense, the best in the world in 1969–70. We handled the Vikings. We were just stronger. We had the first strength coach, Alvin Roy, and it made a huge difference. Teams just didn't lift weights back then. Everybody was in the weight room, backs, receivers, everybody. Joe Kapp didn't talk to anyone for months after the Super Bowl. I finally talked to him, and he said he couldn't believe how physical we were."

As talented as Bell was, it was a challenge for a Black man to break into the NFL. Otto Graham, Bell's coach for the 1963 College All-Star game against the Green Bay Packers at Chicago's Soldier Field, was less than enamored with his abilities.

"He told me I couldn't play," said Bell. "He called up Coach Warmath and Coach Stram and he told them I couldn't play. He told Stram he was wasting his money. Otto Graham put me and Dave Robinson at linebacker for the All-Star game. Robinson was an All-American tight end at Penn State. The NFL wouldn't put Black players at linebacker. He figured we would be sitting on the bench, but we beat out all the other guys and got to play in the game and we kicked the Packers' butts. I was talking with Jim Brown, Bobby Mitchell and Leroy Kelly at the Pro Football Hall of Fame once and they didn't even get to play in the All-Star game. It got to the point where NFL teams started saying, 'Where are they [the AFL] getting these Black players?' They started looking at more Black players."

The AFL was light-years ahead of the NFL in terms of its recruitment of Black players. Lloyd Wells became Hunt's kingpin in this arena as pro football's first full-time Black scout. Wells, using his vast contacts among Black colleges, was instrumental in the Chiefs selecting behemoth defensive end Buck Buchanan first overall in '63, the first Black player to earn this distinction.

"We got Buck in the first round, [guard] Ed Budde in the second and me in the seventh," said Bell of the '63 draft. "I didn't think I was going to be drafted. I was told I was too little. I played at 210, 215 pounds. Also, in the early '60s you didn't have very many Blacks playing in the NFL. How many Blacks were on a team? You could hardly name three Black players on any NFL team at the time."

More connected than astute, Wells helped bring to Kansas City three Hall of Famers from historically Black colleges who started on defense on the '69–'70 championship team—Willie Lanier (Morgan State), Buchanan (Grambling) and Emmitt Thomas (Bishop), not to mention the great wideout Taylor of Prairie View A&M.

Reichow, after taking over for Joe Thomas in '65, remarkably was the Vikings' only scout until Frank Gilliam joined the staff in 1970 after the team's first trip to the Super Bowl. Gilliam, an African American, made it easier for the team to get inroads in the Black college circuit. During this era, Reichow said it was a struggle to get into any colleges, let alone Black colleges.

"A lot of coaches weren't happy with you coming there," he said. "Like [Joe] Paterno, for instance. We couldn't even get into Penn State, and the guy at Washington [Jim Owens], too. Michigan was tough as well, but I was a Detroit [Lions] guy, so [Bo] Schembechler let me in. But he said you've got to do this, and you can't do that, etcetera. There were guys like that. Texas Tech was like that. You travel across the country to Lubbock and the coach says, 'You can watch the guys warm up.' We had a helluva time getting into Alabama, too. I don't know why they were so hesitant. A lot of guys we couldn't see at all.

"Back then we had to carry our own projectors into schools to watch film," he added. "A lot of schools didn't have them. It was a different time. During those days, pro football was pretty much nothing and now we're talking to their best players and God forbid if you try to talk to a junior. Nebraska didn't want us in there and their coach [Tom Osborne] played pro football."

Black schools were even more of a challenge.

"I remember going to one in Arkansas [Pine Bluff]. I wanted to see a really good defensive lineman. No film and the defensive lineman didn't play," shrugged Reichow, who drafted Sammy White and Jake Reed out of Grambling State. "He was sitting under a tree watching the game. It was L.C. Greenwood. Times were different. A lot of times we simply couldn't get in. And if you went down to Mississippi, you'd better watch it. You had to be careful. I was going to Delta State [Cleveland, Mississippi] and [Deacon] Dan Towler was a scout with the Rams then. He said let's go together. We were at practice and it was getting late and he said, 'Let's go.' I said I wanted to stay and look at this running back and he said, 'Let's go, you don't want to be here when it's dark.' Sure enough, we're driving out of there and there's a man lying dead in the road. You had to be awfully careful in the South then. Frank Gilliam came on and he helped us with the Black schools. I worked with him 37 years. He was good at breaking guys down: Does he do this or does he do that? Frank grew up in Steubenville, Ohio, and Iowa got three Black kids off that team. All three [the Steubenville Trio, Gilliam, Calvin Jones and Eddie Vincent] came in as freshmen and started as sophomores."

Eleven years after the Vikings selected Bell, Reichow drafted a player similar in style to the Kansas City great in Blair, the rangy 6–5, 235-pound linebacker out of Iowa State. Chosen 51st overall, he played special teams his first two years before taking over for Winston as a full-time starter in 1976.

"He was a heckuva athlete," said Reichow. "He had a bad knee. That's the only reason he lasted as long as he did. He turned out to be a great linebacker for us. I'm standing there one day with Bud. We still had Roy Winston. He was a good player. But he's barely six foot and you have Matt Blair, a good athlete, about 6–4, 6–5, backing him up. I said to Bud, pointing at Blair, 'I think that guy right there is better than Roy.' He looked at me said, 'It may be, but I know what Roy's going to do.' It was rough to start as a rookie with Bud. He didn't like turnover. It was a little different with Alan Page. He knew this guy was going to be special. Ed White played his rookie year, but that was due to an injury [to Jim Vellone]. Yary didn't even start his rookie year and he was twice as big as our right tackle [Doug Davis]. That was Grant's way. He took his time with players, but you just knew that Yary was going to be a helluva player for us."

Yet another devastating Super Bowl loss didn't prevent a resilient Vikings team from picking up the pieces in time to claim another Central Division championship the next season, its ninth in 10 years, and prepare to face a familiar postseason foe in the mud and muck at the Los Angeles Coliseum.

13

One More Time for the Master

Minnesota Vikings 14, Los Angeles Rams 7
December 26, 1977, Los Angeles Coliseum
NFC Divisional Playoff

The rousing soundtrack *One More Time for the Master* was fittingly composed by the great Sam Spence.

That's because the rain-drenched and cavernous Los Angeles Coliseum, the stately showcase that remains the football home of the legendary NFL Films musical composer's alma mater, the University of Southern California, was where the foundational players who carried the Minnesota Vikings to 10 division championships in 11 seasons gave their legendary coach his last true playoff hurrah and his final trip to a title game.

While Bud Grant would enjoy one more playoff victory five years later when the Vikings defeated Atlanta 30–24 on January 9, 1983, at the Hubert H. Humphrey Metrodome, gone by then were the likes of the famous warriors of the past, the Marshalls, the Pages, the Ellers, et al., not to mention the idea of playing football in the elements.

Having also moved on by 1982 were rangy free safety Paul Krause, tackle Ron Yary and his sidekick, guard Ed White, each of whom played significant roles in an unlikely 14–7 victory over the Los Angeles Rams.

It would go down for the ages as the "Mud Bowl."

Krause would grab his final playoff interception and it would prove critical in one of the craziest weather games in NFL playoff history. It would also be White's final shining moment in purple, as he was honored with a game ball that he didn't know about until after as he was traded in the offseason to San Diego.

It was truly "One More Time for the Master."

The victory was particularly sweet since Los Angeles had thoroughly punished the Vikings 35–3 in week-six play on *Monday Night Football*.

"They should have saved some of those points for tonight," Page smilingly told reporters after the game. "But they don't carry over."[1]

"What happened in the regular season didn't matter," said Yary. "What matters is the team's intensity the week of the game and how you prepared for it personally. You live this game day to day; you never look behind your shoulder. There was no difference in my psychology or my effort. The condition of the field had nothing to do with me. I wasn't a running back. Everything my whole football life happened within four feet of my position. My whole life was spent four feet to 10 feet away from my space."

If the Rams were ever going to beat the Vikings, it would be this year. Not only had they trounced them at the Coliseum in October, but the Vikings would be playing without Fran Tarkenton, whose season ended with a broken leg suffered in a week-nine win over Cincinnati.

Making Minnesota's prospects even more bleak was the fact the Rams had allowed just 146 points for the 14-game season, second fewest in the NFL, and had not lost yet at home.

Due to the NFL's avoidance of having playoff games contested on Christmas Day, the divisional-round games were held over a span of three days. The AFC playoff games were played on Christmas Eve, while the NFC games were held on Monday, December 26.

It marked the only year since the AFL-NFL merger in 1970 that one conference held both of its divisional playoff games on one day and the other conference held both of its on another day. This ensured the teams in each conference championship game had the same amount of rest (eight days for the AFC and six days for NFC).

It rained and rained and rained in Los Angeles Monday afternoon, and the expansive Coliseum playing field quickly turned into a quagmire. "The conditions were more suited to us than to them," admitted Grant.[2]

Most Vikings players thought Grant could walk on water. Little did they know he seemingly controlled the elements, too.

The Vikings brought the rain with them. Searching for warmth, Grant flew his team from frosty Minnesota to Tucson, Arizona, for four days of workouts before the game. It had hardly rained in Tucson since September, but it rained two of the four days the Vikings were in town. Minnesota practiced anyway.

"I remember the emotional feeling we had when it started pouring rain in Los Angeles," said White, who played his college ball at the University of California. "I think it never rained before there like that. I saw how uncomfortable they were and how suited we were to bad weather and what an advantage it was. We had such a positive attitude about that, and it was contagious. We loved it."

The Vikings essentially won the game in the first quarter.

On their opening drive, the Rams drove the ball to the Vikings' 31, where they had it fourth and one. Everyone knew the ball was going to Rams 1,200-yard rusher Lawrence McCutcheon, and it did. But Page and Mark Mullaney stonewalled him for a yard loss.

Mullaney, who entered the game for Doug Sutherland, was positioned to the right of Page, who was shading veteran Rams center Rich Saul. The athletic Mullaney beat Rams offensive tackle Doug France inside and got a piece of McCutcheon, who left Colorado State the year Mullaney arrived there, and Page beat Rams right guard Greg Horton as the two combined to stuff the play.

"Doug France was a big man," said Mullaney of the former Ohio State All-American. "I used to look at the scouting report. I saw France was 300 pounds. The bigger the better for me. I would beat them with one move. I used to look at their weight. [Five-time Pro Bowler] Mike Kenn for Atlanta only played at 255, 260 but he was the best tackle I went against because he was an athlete. He could stay with me."

After stymying McCutcheon, the Vikings responded with a 70-yard drive culminated by Chuck Foreman's five-yard TD surge. Bob Lee, starting for Tarkenton, went five-for-five on the drive. They would be his only pass completions on the contest.

Offensive coordinator Jerry Burns, in an interview with the *Minneapolis Star* after the game, was bubbling over with praise for Lee, who started his college career under Frank Kush at Arizona State prior to transferring to the City College of San Francisco, where he played with O.J. Simpson.

"I think you could watch football for a whole generation and never find more perfect offensive execution when you factor in all the conditions: big game, terrible weather, a gumbo field, a great defensive pass rush, and the fact our offense was operating without two of the people who were in it most of the season: Fran Tarkenton and Brent McClanahan," said Burns. "I told Bob Lee after the game he was good all game, but he was just super on that drive. It was the best I've ever seen."[3]

"Bobby Lee was a good backup quarterback. He always had his head in the game," said Ahmad Rashad, who had a pair of key receptions on the opening drive. "You knew when he came into the game for Francis or whoever, he was always aggressive. He was trying to take that team up the field and he was going to wing it. He had a strong arm, a very strong arm that he was proud of."

Starting out throwing was another example of the Grant genius.

"If you play on bad fields, they're going to get worse," said Grant, who became an expert on bad fields when he coached in Canada. "We wanted to throw early and get any passing advantages we could, because late in the game we knew it would be difficult to throw the ball. On a good field, a seven- or 14-point lead isn't very much, but on a bad field it gets to be monumental."[4]

The game was a triumphant moment for the well-spoken Lee, who saw and experienced about everything a man could encounter in his eventful 12 years in the league.

"We were practicing in Tucson, which we had done before for playoff games. Burns and I talked about throwing early, and, of course, Bud was in on it, too," said Lee. "In those days we called our own plays and Jerry would send in a play or two. I spotted a couple things with the way they were lining up. We got a good drive going and they looked confused. Everything was working, we didn't have any negative plays and we score. The big thing was the team that scores first has the advantage.

"The Rams would always say, 'We're going to get you when we get you in LA.' They hated the frozen tundra," added Lee. "Then we play that game at their place and go right down there and score. Sammy White and I just missed out on a post corner that would have really made it out of reach later, but I had to throw the ball a little earlier than I wanted to."

Losing to the Vikings again was almost too much to bear for Fred Dryer.

"Weather like that is always an advantage if you score first," said the right defensive end. "They did and sat on the lead. They deserved the touchdowns they got. They kept the ball away from our offense, although our offense wasn't doing anything. The field was a terrible mess. I rely on quickness, and I couldn't get any traction on that slop."[5]

"It was frightening. You had no traction whatsoever," said Jack Youngblood, Dryer's sidekick. "We were all running flat-footed, trying to stay on our feet. There's not much power when you're slipping. The ball's snapped and it's like being a kid again with all the slipping and sliding."

Lee had two solid games to end the season to help the Vikings capture their ninth NFC Central Division championship in 10 years with a 9–5 mark. The University of Pacific grad was 11 of 19 passing in a 28–27 win over the 49ers in week 12, a game in which Tommy Kramer came in for the save. Then, in one of the best games of his career, he was 11 for 16 for 203 yards and a pair of TDs in the 30–21 division clincher, a Saturday night edition of *MNF* in the final week at the Pontiac Silverdome against the Lions, who stayed in the game due to a pair of kick-return TDs by Eddie Payton.

The Vikings' opening scoring drive gained some steam on third and 10 when Lee hit Ahmad Rashad near the left sideline for a first down to the Vikings' 41 in front of cornerback Monte Jackson.

The sensational Rashad, who caught 51 balls during regular-season play, good for sixth in the NFL, then beat Jackson deep for 27 yards to the Rams' 31. Lee's throw was right on the money.

Facing another key third-down play from the Los Angeles 14, Lee rolled right, then dumped the ball in the flat to a wide-open Robert Miller. In a sign of good things to come for the Vikings, Miller, just as he was crossing the sticks for a first down, had the ball squirt out of his hands only to have wideout Sammy White make a sliding recovery at the Rams' six.

"He had Ahmad on the break, he called the little running passes at the right time," added Burns. "He handled the ball without a slip. Young (Pat) Haden is a fine young quarterback. But Bob here was a real master, a real master of his trade who had to convince a lot of people. Well, there were millions of them watching on television."[6]

Foreman finished the drive by slashing over from the five behind White and Yary with 5:33 left in the first. It was Foreman's 66th TD in 67 career games.

"When I got up here and I got to experience the type of weather they had, I was told how to run in it," Foreman said of his transition to Nordic conditions. "You never ran on your toes—you had to run flat-footed [having nearly size-14 shoes didn't hurt]. You learn to do that, and that's basically what we did out in LA. We kept it simple and direct. They had a cattle show out there the day before and you could tell the field was going to get nasty."

The Rams had a chance to knot the game at 7–7 early in the second quarter but Pat Haden's second-and-goal pass from the Vikings' five intended for tight end Charle Young, another USC product, was easily intercepted by Nate Allen.

"I thought Charle was going to the corner, but he hooked up, which is what he's supposed to do if he's not open," said Haden. "He did the right thing, and I did the wrong thing. To me, that was the key play of the game. I should never have thrown it."[7]

Rafael Septien could have cut the Vikings' lead to four with four minutes left in the half, but the Rams kicker missed from 33 yards out. The Vikings went to the locker room up 7–0.

Both teams went scoreless in the third quarter, but Manfred Moore's 18-yard punt return early in the fourth put the Vikings in good shape at the Rams' 40.

In what would amount to their last great pressure drive under Grant in postseason action, the Vikings used 10 straight running plays to take a 14–0 lead when Sammy Johnson bulled over from the one.

The reliable Miller, who contributed a steady 52 yards on 12 carries, converted a first down on the drive with a determined three-yard run on a third-and-two from the Rams' 32. Then, on the first play of the fourth quarter, Foreman almost crossed the goal line on a third-and-four from the Rams' 12. On the play, Miller went in motion right to draw the defense that way before Foreman brilliantly slashed left off guard and tackle.

Banged up on the play, Foreman, who had a career playoff-high 31 carries for 101 yards, was replaced by Johnson, who pounded over two plays later to make it a virtually unsurmountable 14–0 Vikings advantage.

Made for weather games was Miller, a sturdy 5-11, 204-pounder who defied the odds by putting together an under-the-radar six-year career with the Vikings despite being drafted in the fifth round in '75 out of Kansas.

Miller said his first training camp in Minnesota was trying mentally and physically until he had what he described as "an encounter with God," an occurrence that completely changed his mindset and approach.

"I knew the Vikings had lost to Pittsburgh in the Super Bowl and the first thing I heard when I got to rookie camp was that we were going back. I was thinking, 'Wow! What a mindset,'" said Miller, a football star at Yates High School in Houston. "It was just miserable the first training camp. I was just totally shocked. I was wondering why God would put me in the lions' den, so to speak, so early. I had one perception, and my heavenly father gave me a reality check. I had to spend time with him to deal with my heart and my attitude because I didn't like the way things were.

"The Lord told me, 'This [mindset] is where people choose to go when they don't trust me or obey me,'" added Miller. "That woke me up and put me on a path that said, 'I yield to you.' From that point on, he didn't have a problem with me. I was wanting things my way and he was saying, 'I have a plan for you.' I realized later that he had a plan and a purpose for me being in Minnesota."

What Miller didn't know during those struggles was that devout Christian teammate Jeff Siemon was praying for him.

"Jeff was praying that other believers would come to Minnesota so that we would have a revival on the team," said Miller, who noted that before long, the Vikings had a steady flow of players attending their weekly prayer group. "I found all this out later. When you have a guy who loves the Lord like Jeff Siemon, it's not surprising this happened. His heart was to evangelize teammates. The trajectory of my life changed. I could have gone to Atlanta or to New York. There was a reason my heavenly father wanted me in Minnesota. Like he said with [the apostle] Philip, your life is good, but I want something better. The Lord wanted something bigger for me. He wanted me to be in the right place at the right time. I'm still learning that his plan is always the best plan. It's God's journey for me, one that he has designed specifically for me."

Miller was married with a child by the time he arrived in Minnesota. He had to mature quickly because both of his parents died prior to his arriving at the University of Kansas.

"My dad passed away in 1968 and it changed my whole world. My mom had already passed. I was being offered scholarships all over the country. Those next couple of years were difficult for me and I just wanted to get out of Houston," said Miller on becoming a Jayhawk. "The emphasis was to have all four of the Miller boys go to college. I had my mind on a certain area of study. Lawrence, Kansas, was my first visit and I asked them if they had a business degree. It was exactly what I needed. My dad had a business and I respected how he ran it. But I needed to get away. I had just lost my world."

Miller's biggest fan was his roommate Mullaney.

"He was my best friend on the team. He was the one who brought me to Christ," said Mullaney, a devout Christian who joined the Vikings along with Miller in '75. "The Vikings were notorious for cutting their draft picks, even guys as high as the second round, even the first round. It was a tough team to make, a veteran team which had already played in three Super Bowls. Rookies weren't expected to make the team. Here's a guy [Miller] that was a fifth-round draft choice. Autry Beamon also made it as a 12th-round pick. I didn't think my roommate was going to make it because of his draft position and the Vikings had a great backfield. You had to earn the right to be there. It was scary for me, too, because they only kept six defensive linemen."

The quagmire at the Coliseum didn't faze Miller one bit.

"That was fun," he recalled. "It's amazing, my brother-in-law was living out in Los Angeles at that time, and he told me they hadn't had rain in two years! I wondered why it had to rain when we are coming to town. He said it was 'just time, just time.' I loved playing in the mud. I grew up in Houston, Texas, and I always loved playing in the rain. I learned how to run in the mud by watching Gale Sayers."

Miller remembers watching fellow Kansas alum Sayers's six-touchdown game against the 49ers in the mud and slosh at Wrigley Field on December 12, 1965.

"Gale Sayers would run flat-footed, never on his toes. Everyone else would be slipping all over the place," he noted. "I would use longer cleats. It was just fun playing in the mud, just like on the schoolyard. That came to memory when we got to the field to play the Rams. I said, 'Oh, man, it's going to be one of those nights.' It turned out to be one of those exciting mud games."

In week 13 of the '76 season, Miller had a game at home against the Packers that would have made Sayers proud.

"The weather was sunshine, blue skies. It was beautiful. Toward the end of the first quarter, it got cloudy and started raining," he said. "We come out for the third quarter and there was snow all over the place. Bud put me in because the field was bad. He said go in and have some fun. I ended up having a fun game against Green Bay."

Playing just the final 30 minutes, Miller finished the contest with 15 carries for 95 yards as the Vikings came back from a 6–3 halftime deficit to win 20–9 to improve to 10–2–1.

The Mud Bowl was a boon for Miller and Foreman as the Vikings threw just three passes in the second half (Lee finished five-of-10) and ran the ball on each of their last 25 plays. In the third quarter alone, thanks to players like All-Pro right guard White, Minnesota's ground game ate up nearly 12:30 minutes of the clock, leaving the Rams just two minutes and 30 seconds to play catch-up.

For his efforts, White was awarded a game ball.

"After we played the Rams and after I left to go down to San Diego [White was traded to the Chargers for Rickey Young on July 28, 1978], I was with the equipment man there," recalled White. "He said, 'Hey, something came for you from Minnesota.' I opened it up and it was a game ball. Apparently, Bud had awarded me a game ball for the Mud Bowl. I was amazed. It unfortunately got burnt up years later in a house fire we had. I believe it was my first game ball with the Vikings. It was incredible.

"The last time I talked to Bud, it was on a Zoom call," said White. "Bud said, 'The worst decision I ever made was letting you go.' All I could say was, 'Wow, thank you.' It was a great game and a great feeling and I was just shocked when that game ball arrived."

With the Rams looking to cut the lead in half, Krause came up big with 5:38 remaining when he picked off a Haden pass intended for Billy Waddy near the goal line and returned it 19 yards. The hosts would not get on the scoreboard until a one-yard Haden pass in the left corner of the end zone to Harold Jackson made it 14–7 with 56 seconds remaining.

The Rams gave the Vikings a scare when Jim Jodat recovered the ensuing onsides kick at midfield. The Rams would get to the Vikings' 30, but Jeff Wright grabbed Haden's desperation heave near the goal line with seven ticks left, sending Minnesota to yet another NFC championship game.

Remarkably, Lee said neither the Mud Bowl nor beating an undefeated Minnesota team on *Monday Night Football* in '73 when he was with Atlanta rank as the top games of his career.

"The game that ranks up there because of the opponent was when we [Atlanta] played the Steelers on *Monday Night Football* at Three Rivers not more than a year later [from the '73 game against Minnesota]. The game against the Steelers was a famous *MNF* game for another reason," he said of the Falcons' 24–17 loss to the eventual Super Bowl champs on October 28, 1974. "That was the night a Muhammed Ali impersonator got on air to supposedly promote the 'Rumble in the Jungle' [heavyweight championship fight two days later against George Foreman]. It was a phony deal. There was a lot going on. Terry Bradshaw was struggling to keep his job. Chuck Noll wasn't a fan of his. He said this was his last shot. We lost, but I threw at least two touchdown passes which I never saw caught. I think Pittsburgh set the record at that time for most sacks in a *MNF* game [Steelers ended with seven]. We had fallen apart in '74 with the Falcons. We weren't the team we were the year before. Based on what we had and the team they had, it was one of the top games I had. That defense was unbelievable."

Lee's scoring passes against the vaunted Steelers were to wide receivers Al Dodd and Ken Burrow. He completed six other passes against a defense that garnered his utmost respect.

"The thing that was unbelievable about their four championships is that they stayed healthy," said Lee of the Chuck Noll era. "When artificial turf first came out, places like Cincinnati, Pittsburgh, San Francisco, Houston, which was the worst one of all, and Philadelphia, etcetera, guys became leg weary because of those fields and they ended up getting hurt. The baseball clubs didn't want padding under the carpet, so it was like playing on concrete. It also made everyone a half step quicker, thus the impacts were more severe."

Foreman said the Vikings-Rams rivalry was intense but not hatred-filled.

"We had a lot of respect for them," he commented. "These were tough players, and it was always a tough game between us. At that time, we were the two best teams in the NFC, along with Dallas. There were a lot of Hall of Famers out there. They were always memorable games, and fortunately we came out on top most of the time."

The Vikings had the Rams' number, and the Cowboys had Minnesota's. In the playoffs, whom you play and when you play them means everything, said Lee.

"You get down to the final eight teams and for the most part any of the teams can win it. It depends on who is playing the best and who is the healthiest," he noted. "Look at how many playoff games the Raiders lost before they won the Super Bowl. Anything can happen. When they beat Miami [in the Sea of Hands] game, Stabler threw a wobbler that Clarence Davis somehow catches. How the hell does that happen? Kenny could have easily thrown an interception there that would have gone back 100 yards."

The Raiders beat the Houston Oilers 40–7 in the '67 AFL title game to advance to play Green Bay in Super Bowl II, but the postseason was a house of horrors for them in ensuing years. Raw playoff brutality is what they endured prior to winning the 1976 AFC title game 24–7 over Pittsburgh:

1968: Lost 27–23 to Jets in AFL championship.
1969: Lost 17–7 to Chiefs in AFL championship.
1970: Lost 27–17 to Colts in AFC championship game.
1972: Lost 13–7 to Steelers in divisional round.
1973: Lost 27–10 to Miami in AFC championship.
1974: Lost 24–13 to Steelers in AFC championship.
1975: Lost 16–10 to Steelers in AFC championship.

The Vikings and Raiders knew as well as anyone that playoff football was not for the faint of heart.

• • •

Playoff football is brutal in its finality.

Thanks partially to Krause's ability to track the ball from his free safety position, skills honed during his baseball career, Minnesota won four of the five NFL/NFC title games it played under Grant.

"I loved baseball," said Krause, who remarkably had to wait nearly 20 years after retirement to be selected for the Hall of Fame. "I had some pretty significant offers from teams like Detroit, Cleveland and the Yankees. I had a really good arm. I switch-hit and could run. I loved to drag bunt and they rarely got me at first. But then I injured my shoulder."

Twenty-some years before the so-called "Mud Bowl," a rare, albeit fledgling, athlete would give the sports world a glimpse of the enjoyment that would come from watching him play pro football:

It's the late 1950s in the car manufacturing capital of the world. You stride up a musty upper-deck ramp at Detroit's Briggs Stadium, which opened in 1912 as Navin Field. You reach its concrete summit and are captivated by the sounds of the ushers' booming voices and the chattering of arriving fans and the color and smell of freshly cut grass. The lush sod serves as a stark backdrop to the Tigers' deep navy blue caps and the crisp white home uniforms with the familiar Old English script *D* stitched across their chests.

Upstaging these sensatory eruptions is the sight of a graceful and angular scholastic athlete from Flint, Michigan, roaming the outfield below. Along with other top Tiger hopefuls—strapping youngsters like Willie Horton and Dave DeBusschere—he was invited to shag fly balls during pregame, thus showcasing his fluid outfield movements at the hallowed ballyard located on the corner of Michigan and Trumbull avenues.

It was Paul Krause of Bendle High School. It might as well have been the Yankee Clipper, Joe DiMaggio. Witnessed was an athlete of elegance, one who could roam a radius that would make his childhood hero, Mickey Mantle, proud.

For sure, the Tigers boasted outfielders such as Harvey Kuenn and Al Kaline, and would soon employ Rocky Colavito, but Krause was an otherworldly athlete, one explosive enough as a prep star to run down a fly ball in the gap and proceed to easily bound like a deer over the outfield fence after the putout.

So strong was Krause's arm that playing for Iowa he once threw out four runners at home plate in a game against Bradley University.

He also had power, often reaching the stands during batting practice made available

13. One More Time for the Master

to the region's top prospects on the Briggs Stadium diamond while the Tigers were on the road.

"Horton was the only one of the guys who could reach the upper deck," said Krause, who once scored 54 points in a high school basketball game and was both an all-American and all-state selection in football, baseball and track.

But as providence would have it, Krause would not join the power-hitting Horton (Tigers) and DeBusschere (two years with the White Sox before starting an NBA career) in the "Show." There was another plan for one of the greatest all-around athletes ever. Major League Baseball's loss would be the Vikings' gain.

We will never know if Krause would have beaten out Mickey Stanley to start in centerfield on the Tigers' 1968 championship team. His path would take him on a different route, one that saw the 6–3, 200-pounder finish his 16-year NFL career as the all-time interception leader with 81. The season following the Mud Bowl, he would go without an interception, but he recorded three his final year in '79—the last two coming at the Los Angeles Coliseum—to pass New York Giants great Emlen Tunnell on the all-time list.

A natural centerfielder made for a natural NFL free safety. Krause, who could easily dunk a basketball with two hands, was an athlete who just happened to be good at football. And contrary to the thought that defensive backs were just failed receivers, the eight-time Pro Bowler had the kind of hands that rarely let him down when a ball was up for grabs.

"You played both games with the same approach," said Krause. "No matter if the ball was coming off the bat or coming off some quarterback's hand, you still reacted. You react differently on line drives than you do on deep fly balls. You have to be able to adjust and locate the ball."

"Paul Krause was a centerfielder—he played that zone as good as anyone I had ever seen," said Terry Brown, who had the luxury of playing alongside two Hall of Famers in Krause and Larry Wilson of the St. Louis Cardinals. "Larry Wilson was a master at the safety blitz, and he could cover a lot better. He was a big hitter. Paul didn't do a lot of hitting because he played so deep, but both on their own were great in the way they played."

Krause would accept a full-ride scholarship to the University of Iowa, which was open to letting him play multiple sports. But after making All-American in baseball his sophomore season, he would see his diamond career come to an end when he dislocated his shoulder in a football game against Michigan.

"They didn't have the medical capabilities that they have today," said Krause. "We didn't know what Tommy John surgery was yet."

He finished his collegiate career concentrating on football, where he played both free safety and receiver for the Hawkeyes. As a senior, he led the Big Ten in three receiving categories—TDs (six), yards (442) and yards per catch (23.3).

His play landed him spots in the East-West Shrine Bowl and Collegiate All-Star Game in Chicago before he was drafted in the second round (18th overall) in 1964 by the Washington Redskins.

It didn't take the Redskins long to know they had a generational talent. And they certainly needed athletes after going 3–11 in '63.

Immediately upon entering the lineup in his first exhibition game with the Skins, Krause intercepted a ball thrown by Chicago quarterback Billy Wade, who had led the Bears to the NFL title over the New York Giants the previous year.

In a further portent of excellent things to come, he snared two interceptions in his first regular-season game against a Cleveland Browns team that would go on to win the NFL championship game over the Baltimore Colts.

"They had Frank Ryan at quarterback, with guys like Paul Warfield and Gary Collins at receiver," recalled Krause. "I was starting to think that maybe this was going to be easy."

Krause would go on to notch the highest single-season interception total of his career, posting 12 picks, just two shy of the season mark Dick "Night Train" Lane set in 1952 with the Rams.

One would think that all was hunky-dory and "Hail to the Redskins" for Krause in Washington, but there was trouble brewing.

Bill McPeak, a former lineman with the Pittsburgh Steelers, was head coach during Krause's first two years in Washington. He posted a dismal 21–46–3 mark in his five years as coach, but McPeak did know how to accumulate talent.

Doubling as general manager, he brought in many Hall of Fame–caliber players, including Sonny Jurgensen, Bobby Mitchell, Jerry Smith, Charley Taylor, Len Hauss, Sam Huff and Chris Hanburger.

"Chris and I were roommates at Washington and we both made the HOF," said Krause. "But it just didn't work out for me there."

It didn't work out because defensive backs coach Ed Hughes miscalculated the kind of player he had in Krause. "He just didn't like my style of play," said Krause. "I'm not sure what it was. They let me roam but he just didn't like me for some reason."

The situation worsened Krause's last two years in Washington. That's when Otto Graham took over for McPeak. For a football coach, he made a great quarterback. Although the Redskins climbed to 7-7 in Graham's first year in '66, players began to realize why Paul Brown signaled in the plays in Cleveland.

A ball-hawking free safety was on Grant's wish list following his first year at the helm of the Vikings in 1967. The squad went 3-8-3 and finished next to last in the 16-team league with just 15 interceptions. Cornerback Ed Sharockman led the team with three. Krause didn't know it yet, but he would soon prove to be the vital final piece of a secondary that already had a trio of solid corners in Earsell Mackbee, Bobby Bryant and Sharockman to go with the hard-nosed Karl Kassulke and equally wild Dale "Crazy Crane" Hackbart at the safety position.

It would take a lot of behind-the-scenes work to get him to Minnesota, where Krause would help lead the Vikings to four Super Bowls and 10 division titles in his 12 years in purple.

Graham would last three tumultuous years in Washington, but before he was replaced by the great Vince Lombardi in '69, he would make one of the most historically awful trades in NFL history, sending Krause to Minnesota after the 1967 campaign for tight end Marlin McKeever and a seventh-round pick.

McKeever was a solid player in his own right. The fourth overall pick out of the University of Southern California in the 1961 draft by the Los Angeles Rams made the Pro Bowl in 1966 as a tight end and played 12 years in the league, also spending time in Philadelphia.

McKeever was no Paul Krause, but Graham believed the 6-1, 235-pounder could contribute both as a blocker and receiver. He deemed Krause as expendable after picking up defensive backs Jimmy Burson and Pat Fischer in offseason moves from the Cardinals and signing the team's No. 1 pick, Oregon free safety Jim "Yazoo" Smith.

13. One More Time for the Master

Fischer played well for the Redskins, but otherwise the transactions met with meager results. Smith lasted just 14 games in Washington as a return man and never played again, Burson was released before the season started and McKeever failed to start a game, although he lasted three years in the nation's capital before being shipped back to the Rams by George Allen.

Grant and the man who pulled off the trade, brilliant general manager Jim Finks, were overjoyed to have a player the Redskins took for granted.

"I wasn't insulted by the trade," said Krause, who had a whopping 28 interceptions in his four years in Washington. "I just looked at it as I was getting away from a guy who didn't like me."

What were the inner workings of a trade that became so lopsided? There's a theory.

Jimmy Carr, a starting defensive back on the Eagles' 1960 NFL championship team, was playing out the string in Washington, where he was Krause's teammate in 1964 and '65. By then, the man known affectionately as "Gummy" had moved to linebacker.

"I had Sam Huff in front of me and Jimmy Carr was the right outside linebacker," said Krause. "Jimmy knew the game. He had a knack for where to be positioned. Just a brilliant guy."

The quarterback in Philadelphia was Norm Van Brocklin, who just happened to be the head coach of the Vikings in 1966. Van Brocklin, knowing full well Carr's keen defensive mind, brought the defensive genius onto his staff and Grant retained him the next year.

"I'm not sure, but Gummy knew I wasn't happy in Washington, and he probably told the Vikings," Krause surmised.

Krause would work only one year in Minnesota with Carr, who left after the '68 season to become the defensive coordinator with the Bears. But their time together made an impact.

"Carr played a long time and was a mastermind of defensive back play," said Krause, who has three children and five grandchildren, including Maggie Malecha, formerly a star ice hockey goalie at Northfield High School. "He helped me all the time. It was a picnic in Minnesota. Bud never tried to tell me how to play. It was my belief that he knew I could play it."

Another contributing factor to the trade was that Grant had wisely brought Jerry Burns in from Green Bay to join him in Minnesota as offensive coordinator. Burns happened to be Krause's head coach at Iowa.

"One reason we wanted to recruit Krause was because he was such a great athlete," Burns said after the trade. "We played him at halfback his first year then moved him to receiver and free safety. As a sophomore at Iowa, he hit .325 in the Big Ten and impressed the New York Mets so much he was offered a contract. As a junior he took up golf for the first time and was shooting in the low 70s at the end of the year. I recall the day he had at Michigan when he returned a punt 80 yards just before the half, then in the final minutes he caught a pass surrounded by three or four men and ran 25 yards for the tying TD. He could help us on offense or defense."[8]

Krause took over for Dale Hackbart, who still saw a lot of playing time as a fifth defensive back before being traded in '71 to the St. Louis Cardinals. Hackbart said he never resented Krause for changing the trajectory of his career because he respected the man for the generational player he was.

"Paul Krause was a top draft pick. He was highly regarded. That was my competition," he said. "Paul was not one of those guys who was going to knock your head off. When he came to the Vikings, he was used as a hanger-back. That's the way the coaches wanted him to play. They knew he had a lot of speed, a lot of moxie. He could cover to his left, cover to his right, so our defense was set up for him to be our deep safety. We were similar athletes. When a back had the ball, I was always eager to come up and meet them. Paul was not an aggressive person, but he read the quarterback and the formations and excelled at it. They knew Paul could handle it. They put him in position to intercept balls. That was his gig."

Grant's instructions to Krause were simple. "Don't get beat deep." And he rarely did.

"Paul Krause had good instincts and great hands," Grant said in a 2021 interview. "He was a tremendous athlete who could have played pro baseball had he not hurt his shoulder."

"Bud never played the position, so he just let me play," said Krause, whose best year in Minnesota was '75, when he had 12 interceptions in his final Pro Bowl season. "I took it as my job to be the last line of defense and do what I was supposed to do, which was play the deep middle. I would figure out what was going on and help who needed help."

Grant may never have played safety full-time, but he shared Krause's knack for interceptions. Playing both offense and defense after leaving the Philadelphia Eagles to play in Winnipeg, Grant once had five interceptions in a CFL playoff game against former Washington Redskins and Giants quarterback Frank Filchock. "That's one record Krause doesn't have," laughed Grant. "It's still the best single-game total in North American pro football.

"I knew Filchock's tendencies from playing against him while I was in Philadelphia," Grant added. "I normally played left corner but I asked our coach if I could move to safety so I could get a better look at the whole field. I knew Filchock liked to throw deep, and that he always tried to look off defenders."[9]

"Bud's idea was he was going to give them the short ball," noted Krause, a co-captain at Iowa along with Vikings teammate Wally Hilgenberg, who joined the Vikings the same year. "He always figured if we make them go 14 plays that somewhere down the line they would make a mistake. They often did."

It was all coming together for the Vikings in 1968. Krause was added to a talented secondary; Page, in his second year was becoming the inside pass-rushing force the team needed to balance out of the play of quicksilver defensive ends Jim Marshall and Carl Eller; and there was a terrifying gauntlet of linebackers in, from left, Roy Winston, Lonnie Warwick and Hilgenberg.

Krause had seven interceptions his first year with the Vikings and helped lead the team to the Central Division title with an 8–6 mark. The team qualified for its first-ever playoff game, a 24–14 loss to the eventual NFL champion Baltimore Colts. Nevertheless, the tide had turned and a team that had not won a playoff game before Krause's arrival would win nine before he retired following the 1979 season.

"You had to fit into want Bud wanted," commented Krause. "His mold became the Viking mold. Bud's hands were strong on this team. You had to play his way and not make mistakes, or you were going to get let go.

"It was just going to be that way," added Krause. "We played as a team, and we had a great blend of guys who loved playing together. Bud made sure everyone was on the same page. Playing on that defense was something special. We were all proud to be a part of it and we loved picking each other up."

Krause missed just two games in his 16 seasons and played in 19 playoff games with the Vikings. Playoff encounters would repeatedly see the Vikings meet the Rams, Cowboys or Redskins, but the teams that drew most of their ire were the divisional opponents.

"We always wanted to win our division, and we did the majority of the time," said Krause. "No matter the record, the games with the Bears, the Packers and the Lions were always tough, even though I think we went 22–2 against Detroit during my career in Minnesota. It was the familiarity between the teams. That was some tough football. We didn't want to get beat by anybody, but we certainly wanted to control that division."

Krause had the luxury of having to guard for only around four seconds thanks to the Purple People Eaters.

"It was just a staggering defense," he beamed. "Jim Marshall was one of the greatest leaders you're going to see in football. I mean, he didn't miss a game in 20 years and he's not in the Hall of Fame? That defensive line never stopped.

"We got to a point where we trusted each other so well," Krause added. "Bobby turned into one of the best cornerbacks I'd ever seen, and we had Nate [Wright] on the other side and he was a good one. I think Karl Kassulke was the best strong safety in the game before he got hurt. He was just a terror. Then Jeff Wright came in and was so smart it was unreal. Our linebackers were tough. All three guys—Lonnie, Roy and Wally and then later Jeff Siemon—were nasty."

Krause doesn't lament over the lost Super Bowls. He just looks at it as part of the game.

"One game didn't stand out over the other," said Krause, a member of the Vikings' Ring of Honor. "We just played a steady brand of football and kept coming back every year and being competitive. That was part of the Vikings way. We didn't get too up or too down. Everyone did their job, and that's what Bud preached."

Minnesota has retired six numbers—10 (Fran Tarkenton), 53 (Mick Tingelhoff), 70 (Jim Marshall), 77 (Korey Stringer), 80 (Cris Carter) and 88 (Alan Page). While Harrison Smith has been a sensational player since joining the Vikings in 2012, should anyone else have worn Krause's fabled No. 22 jersey?

"It hurts," said Krause of not having his number retired. "But that's someone else's decision. I'm just glad the good Lord gave me the ability to play and the health to make it 16 years."

How glorious would it be for Vikings fans to once again witness on Met's Stadium's painted and icy sod Page, Eller, Marshall and Gary Larsen clamoring after the quarterback with Krause behind them, piloting the back third like no other.

A Mickey Mantle of the gridiron.

• • •

While Krause was a Vikings legend on the deep third, White was an indomitable force in the trenches.

When the opposition put ball in the air, Marshall would turn and yell, "*Krause!!*" When the Vikings needed a big first down, it was time to run behind the twin, purple-clad behemoths—right tackle Yary and right guard White.

The strongest player in the National Football League to not lift weights doesn't mind that he hasn't gotten a call from Canton. While the seven-time Pro Bowler Yary was elected to the HOF in 2001, it's enough for White to know that in the minds of his peers, he undoubtedly deserves to be there, too.

As much, if not more, they say, than any offensive lineman of his time. Just ask legendary quarterback Dan Fouts.

"He was the first of his time to make the Pro Bowl in both conferences," said Fouts, who played behind White for eight seasons. "And he played in 241 games, a record at the time of his retirement. No doubt he should be in the Hall. He was equally effective as a pass and run blocker."

Untold other former teammates and coaches emphatically say his likeness should be cast in bronze alongside Yary and Tingelhoff. He's an obvious Hall of Famer to all who watched the 6–1, 280-pounder terrorize opposing defenses for 17 years. White played with a unique, marauding style, bringing an aggressive Alex Karras–like approach to offensive line play.

"I played offensive guard like a defensive player," said the 1968 University of California consensus All-American. "I wanted to get there first, with a quick first step and a quick punch. I probably broke some ribs along the way and didn't know it."

"He was good player," said Youngblood. "Very, very good player. We respected him very much, too. He would come my way sometimes."

In New Testament scripture, Peter described Satan in the same manner defensive coordinators may have pictured White, as *"a roaring lion roaming about, seeking whom he may devour."*

He was that ferocious.

He was powerful, but also the possessor of nimble feet during a time when offensive linemen could not extend their arms and had to use everything within their abilities to ward off a would-be tackler.

"I was naturally strong," said White, who won the NFLPA's first and only arm-wrestling championship in 1975. "I could bench 400, but Coach Grant didn't like us lifting weights. We got into shape by playing other sports such as racquetball."

It would take more than a HOF snub to steer White from his positive approach. He's a man of depth; a remarkable individual, one loved by both his teammates and coaches, a gentle giant who possesses a rare artistic ability to capture things on canvas, a skill honed sketching hot rods as a daydreaming youngster in Indio, California.

"I just don't think about it," said White, who remarkably played almost the identical number of games in his nine years with the Vikings (122) that he did in eight years with the San Diego Chargers (119). "I know not winning a Super Bowl has probably been a hinderance to some of our guys not making it, but knowing a lot of people I played with believe I should be there makes me feel good."

White, who made four Pro Bowls during an illustrious career spent mostly as a right guard, knows life is too precious to be bitter.

That's what perspective brings.

He lost his 21-year-old daughter, Amy Joe, three years after she fell from a moving car in 1994. In 2003, he and his high school sweetheart Joan's home burned to the ground due to wildfires, and just a few years ago he underwent heart valve replacement surgery.

"I'm in a lot of Hall of Fames as it is," said White, a member of, among others, the NCAA, University of California and East-West Shrine Bowl football halls. "It's not something I dwell on."

This is a man who knows he has been truly blessed.

13. One More Time for the Master

After he was drafted in the second round in 1969 by Minnesota and 39th overall, the Vikings were about to set out on a meteoric rise, making four Super Bowls and winning eight division titles during his near decade in purple. Playoff football at Metropolitan Stadium in December was as sure as Rod Carew batting .300.

It was a beautiful existence.

And just when the Vikings were starting a downswing after a series of poor drafts following the irrepressible Fink's departure to Chicago, White was fortuitously traded in '78 to the Chargers. All San Diego did was advance to a pair of AFC championship games and capture three division titles in his eight seasons there.

Along the way, he played in two of the most famous games in NFL history, both in the playoffs following the 1981 season—the wild 41–38 overtime divisional-round win at Miami's Orange Bowl over the Dolphins (the Kellen Winslow game) and the 27–7 loss to Cincinnati in the AFC championship game known as the "Freezer Bowl."

"Ironically the coldest game I ever played in was after I got traded to San Diego," laughed White, who was allowed by San Diego coaches to play at 280, some 20 pounds heavier than his days with the Vikings. "Not too many people know that the NFL wanted to move the game [from Riverfront Stadium] to Dallas but [Bengals coach] Paul Brown said no."

Former Rams coach Tommy Prothro was the head man during White's first year in San Diego, but the next year saw the arrival of Don "Air" Coryell. Oh, what changes were in store.

"I was fortunate to go from one Hall of Fame coach to the other," added White of going from Grant to Coryell. "They were amazing. Coryell was so innovative in the passing game—we led the league in offense for six straight years. In Minnesota it was three yards and a cloud of dust. Bud was so great with his players. He had a great football mind. He played the game, so he knew how to take care of us. We were always the last team to come into training camp, and it paid off in December."

Consider the timing again of who drafted White.

Although White was a rock-solid nose tackle on a tremendous defensive unit at Cal known as the "Bear Minimum," Vikings director of player personnel Jerry Reichow, an astute talent evaluator, viewed White as an offensive guard. It was not only great foresight by the Vikings, who were loaded on defense, but eventually proved to be great for White's career.

"I looked at him and he was playing defensive tackle," said Reichow. "I said, this is just a strong dude here. I just didn't think he had quite the movements of a defensive tackle, but I was convinced he'd be a heckuva offensive player and he was, and he was a great guy. We also had Yary on the right side and Tingelhoff was right next to them so that wasn't a bad group."

"I doubt I would have played 17 years as a defensive tackle," said White, who relished every opportunity he had to make a hard tackle after an interception. "I wanted to play defense, but it certainly turned out to be a blessing in disguise for me."

In 1969 Minnesota already had the great Page, whom they drafted in the first round out of Notre Dame in 1967, as well as Larsen, who took over the starting role from Paul Dickson in 1968.

White was talented enough to have given Larsen a run for his money at the tackle spot opposite Page, but the man Vikings offensive line coach John Michels lovingly called his "huge elephant" most likely would not have been satisfied playing defense.

"The Vikings pretty much let the other three guys [Page, Carl Eller and Jim Marshall] go after the passer," said White. "Gary was used in a different role. More of a maintain-the-line-of-scrimmage, stay-at-home type of player. In college, I was more of a quick, penetrating-type tackle. I wouldn't have been a good fit."

White had to wait only a year before becoming a starter on the offensive line, moving in at left guard in game four of the 1970 season after veteran Jim Vellone suffered an appendicitis attack.

"The first game I started was against Bob Lilly," said White of the Dallas Cowboys great. "It was scary. Lilly was bigger than I was and really quick. What a great player. He co-signed on what you were doing. He knew ahead of time. Always a step ahead."

The Vikings won White's starting debut, blasting the eventual NFC champion Cowboys, 54–13. Not a surprise since virtually all the teams White played on excelled, including the 1968 Cal team that went 7–3–1 and went on the road to defeat Michigan 21–7 in the season opener.

"You got used to playing against guys like Lilly, players like Charlie Krueger, Merlin Olsen, Alex Karras and Joe Greene," said White. "But lining up against Alan Page every day made it a lot easier."

The Vikings went on to win the Central Division with a 12–2 mark but their season ended with an unexpected 17–14 playoff loss to San Francisco in the divisional round at Met Stadium.

White became the full-time starter in 1971 as Vellone was sadly diagnosed with leukemia and never returned to football. The season was almost a mirror image of the previous campaign as the Vikings finished 11–3, won the division and lost another home playoff divisional-round game, this time by a 20–12 score to Dallas.

What was missing in '70 and '71 was one Joe Kapp, a fellow Cal grad who left the Vikings due to a contract squabble after leading the team to a historic NFL championship game win (the last before the merger) and a Super Bowl appearance against the Kansas City Chiefs.

"I loved Joe Kapp," said White. "Finks was a tough guy to negotiate with, but he was fair. Joe didn't think he was making what he was worth. Finks believed in 'payroll integrity.' In other words, one guy couldn't make so much more than the other. What we missed most in Joe was his leadership. He was half part great football talent and half part great leadership and toughness. He was a defensive lineman in a quarterback's body. He was just a great and dynamic leader. If he asked you to run through a brick wall, you would do it and he'd be the first one to go."

With Kapp's departure, Grant tried Norm Snead, Gary Cuozzo and Lee at quarterback, many times using two in the same game, but it never was the same without the former Canadian League star.

"Sometimes you have to see beyond the playing talent," said White. "That was a big mistake letting him get away. For a team which did so well keeping its nucleus together [the Vikings had virtually the same defense for almost 10 years], it was amazing that we didn't do that at the most important position of all."

Nevertheless, a savior was on the way as Tarkenton was brought back into the fold in '72 following a trade with the New York Giants. But a team projected to win the Super Bowl finished 7–7. "It wasn't a good feeling, but it was nothing to do with Francis," said White. "He had a good year but it was just a matter of everything not jibing. We had a lot of parts coming together and it was an adjustment."

13. One More Time for the Master

A golden era in team history started the next year with the addition of Foreman out of Miami with the 12th overall pick.

"Foreman was a jewel," said White, who moved over to right guard in 1975 and made his first Pro Bowl. "He was impossible to tackle one-on-one and he just changed the game for us with his receiving skills."

It was during Foreman's great Minnesota career that White would go nose to nose in the playoffs with the vastly talented front fours of Dallas, Los Angeles and Washington. Facing the likes of Bob Lilly and Merlin Olsen and the Redskins' Diron Talbert and Dave Butz, White more than held his own.

"Diron was a tough one as well," said White. "He was very much like Lilly and Olsen. His brother [Don] played in the league as an offensive tackle. The Talberts were tough guys from Texas. As a matter of fact, one Texas establishment was known to have a sign saying, 'No shirts, No shoes, No Talberts...'"

A shot-putter at Cal, White played four playoff games against the Cowboys, including NFC championship games in '73 and '78; four playoff games versus the Rams, all wins in '69, '74, '76 and '77; and two against the Redskins in '73 and '76, both victories. He helped the Vikings to a 4–1 mark in conference championships.

"I look back at those teams we had, and I don't think about what could have been. In all those years, we were one of the top teams in all of football," said White, one of just 11 Vikings to play in all four of their Super Bowl appearances. "I look at this as a success story. This was a story of success and not of failure. On any given day, anything could have gone differently that would have enabled us to come out victoriously in some of those Super Bowls. For my nine years there, we were always one of the best."

After the 32–14 Super Bowl loss to the Oakland Raiders following the '76 season, the underpaid White, coming off a second straight Pro Bowl selection, opted to hold out.

"I didn't return to the team until the fourth game," he recalled. "My salary was out of line with other players of my caliber. My whole career I had been doing my own contract negotiations and I found out I was doing a horrible job and that I was being taken advantage of. [General Manager Mike] Lynn said if I came back, he would take care of me, so I did. But he never did take care of my situation."

Showing signs of age by then, the Vikings managed to win the Central Division crown 'in 77 but fell to Dallas 23–6 in the NFC title game without Tarkenton, who had broken his ankle in a November game against Cincy.

"I never reported the next year, and they traded me to San Diego for Rickey Young," said White. "What I was asking for wasn't out of line for a Pro Bowl player and I ended up making almost double in San Diego. It was tough to leave there. My whole family was in Minnesota and we embraced the lifestyle there. We loved snowmobiling. Every Friday we would go out and then have dinner with the Osborns. It was a great experience."

The trade to the Chargers turned out to be a great move for White, but it was painful at the time.

"I loved Coach Grant but you never felt that closeness with him," said White. "He wasn't a warm-and-fuzzy kind of guy. What bothered me the most was Bud was the first NFL player to play out his option [after the 1952 season with the Philadelphia Eagles]. It was surprising, but Bud and I got along great in the years removed."

The upside of the move was twofold. Not only did Big Ed get to go back home to Southern California, but by the second year he was gone the Vikings had slipped to 7–9, while the Chargers in '79 were going 12–4 in their first season under the masterful

Coryell to win the first of three straight West Division titles. The Chargers, with skill players like Winslow, Charlie Joiner, John Jefferson, Fouts and Chuck Muncie, were a force to be reckoned with.

"At the time of the trade [at age 31], I was one of the younger players in Minnesota," said White. "In San Diego, I was one of the oldest so I was sure to share the info people like Marshall and Eller taught me."

After retiring as a player, White coached in the NFL for several years. Today, he can concentrate on his art and reflect on a career that saw him become a lineman who could have played in any era, and at the same time being what his former San Diego line coach Jim Hanifan called "a beautiful man."

• • •

It didn't take long for the Vikings' white road uniforms with the UCLA shoulder stripe and purple numbers to turn a murky brown playing on the same fabled USC turf where the likes of Yary, Frank Gifford, Mike Garrett, Simpson, Sam "Bam" Cunningham and Marcus Allen once performed. With the notable exception of the always dapper Rashad, players on the field were virtually indiscernible to CBS announcers Vin Scully and Alex Hawkins.

"My uniform wasn't muddy," Rashad said with a smile. "I played the whole game with no dirt on me. I would get tackled, and I would turn so the defender hit the ground and I didn't. No matter which defensive back it was, they were going to get dirty."

The deluge presented challenges for equipment man Dennis Ryan, who took over for Jim "Stubby" Eason in 1981. He was just 21 years old.

"We changed jerseys and T-shirts at halftime as the guys got into some dry clothes," said Ryan. "Everybody had a backup jersey except for Chuck Foreman. Foreman's was not in the bags Stubby had packed. We had practiced in Tucson for four days so Stubby told me to go to the truck and find his practice jersey. It did not have a nameplate on the back. We put that in his locker and Chuck was pretty upset about it. He said, 'Hey, this isn't my game jersey!' Stubby was quick on his feet and said, 'Chuck, you are so popular, of all the players in here yours was the only one they stole.' Chuck was proud of that. 'It was just mine they stole?' he asked. By early in the third quarter, you couldn't tell the difference anyway."

In an unusual twist, Minnesota almost wore purple jerseys.

"When we went out to Tucson to practice before the game, we got word from the Rams that they were going to wear their blue jerseys and we would wear white," said Ryan. "They changed their minds on Thursday of that week and wanted us to wear purple. Stubby told them, 'Hey, we're in Tucson and we just packed our white jerseys.' The league got involved and they told us we could do whatever we wanted. Stubby asked me if I wanted to fly home and get the jerseys and I told him I was enjoying the weather too much out there. I don't know why the Rams changed their minds. Maybe they wanted to beat us in purple because we had beaten them so many games wearing purple in Met Stadium."

Wearing purple or white didn't matter that night at the Los Angeles Coliseum because no color other than a murky brown could be seen as the battle-tested Minnesota Vikings not only slung mud at their longtime rivals' collective face but gave a generational coach his last true postseason hurrah.

Epilogue

There was a reason this team, these players, this coach came together, and it wasn't for their fans to lament over the loss of four Super Bowls.

It went deeper than that. There seemed to be something greater at work here. This team. These players. This place.

"It was a magical time," said Bob Hagan, who saw it all during his 32 years as the Vikings' director of public relations, and before that as a wide-eyed youngster captivated by his hometown team. "The players hung around so long back in that era. That will never be repeated. The same guys were back year after year. It was so fun to follow and it didn't hurt that the team was very good, too."

Starting with the 1968 season, there was for the Minnesota Vikings a coming together of undeniable forces that led to a decade of dominance rarely seen in the National Football League.

It was then that Alan Page, in his second year, became the last piece of the Purple People Eaters front wall; the acquisition of Paul Krause completed the secondary; a No. 1 pick garnered from the trade of Fran Tarkenton to the Giants produced Ron Yary; and the team learned enough from the mistakes made in Bud Grant's first year to win the franchise's first playoff-clinching game in Philadelphia.

For the Minnesota Vikings, it was the fullness of time.

None of this should have happened. Ten division championships in 11 years should never have become a reality.

That's because many of the team's players believe that it was an act of God, a virtual implausibility, how this epochal period came to be.

It's inconceivable 13-year-old Bud Grant would survive the Armistice Day Blizzard of 1940 when he stepped out of a snow-trapped car in Yellow Lake, Wisconsin, and volunteered to seek help for him and his two hunting buddies, having no clue where he was going in the face of a rampaging storm that killed 154 people, including 42 in his native northern Wisconsin.

It's beyond belief Bud Grant, a star receiver for Winnipeg, would make it home from the 1956 Canadian Football League East-West All-Star Game since the Trans Canada Air Flight 810 he was scheduled to be on crashed into Mount Slesse in British Columbia, killing all 62 passengers, including five CFL players.

It's unimaginable Jim Marshall would survive a 1960 bout with encephalitis, contracted while training at Fort Leonard Wood in Missouri, leaving him in Cleveland Marymount Hospital for a month so close to death doctors chose to place him in a coma.

It's by no means likely 10 years later Jim Marshall would survive a 1970 snowmobile expedition cutting through Beartooth Pass in Montana, when a blizzard nearly blew his vehicle off a cliff.

There was no way Jim Marshall would outlast a self-inflicted gunshot wound, a carotid artery hemorrhage, two plane crashes and a serious car wreck.

It's unfathomable Francis Tarkenton would even step foot on a pro football gridiron after he and three teammates decided they were going to leave the University of Georgia due to mounting frustration with their strong-willed and stubborn coach, Wally Butts.

It's ludicrous to believe that religiously steeped Francis Tarkenton would survive six years of haranguing from a vulgar coach, his diametric opposite in Norm Van Brocklin, who once said, "Tarkenton, you're sure not strong enough to make that throw, but you're dumb enough to attempt it."[1]

It's incomprehensible Francis Tarkenton would make it through five years of physical beatings playing behind a lilliputian New York Giants offensive line and still be a Pro Bowl–caliber player.

Grant, Marshall and Tarkenton each miraculously endured.

Grant, following the sound of a distant train horn, worked his way to shelter at a gas station to survive the blizzard that produced two feet of snow; his friends back at the car were rescued by a farmer. Sixteen years later, in 1956, his lifelong yearning to be close to home and with his family prompted him to move to an earlier flight out of Vancouver following the all-star game, saving his life. "I was a minute away from being on that airplane," he later said.[2]

Grant's Winnipeg teammate Calvin Jones, the first African American to win the Outland Trophy, died on that flight. Jones, who was said to have stayed out late the night before and opted to stick with the later flight, played guard on University of Iowa gridiron teams that included Vikings scouts Jerry Reichow and Frank Gilliam. The Hawkeyes retired his jersey.

Marshall outlasted encephalitis after his first year in pro football with the Browns, and after being traded to the Vikings in 1961 dodged several near-death experiences and played 19 seasons.

"Up in the mountains it seemed so easy to just go to sleep and die. But I decided my body had to make it. Driving to the hospital when that artery broke, I felt my body beginning to die several times. I made it stop. I went into shock when I walked into the emergency room," said Marshall of two of his nearly half dozen near-death experiences.[3]

Tarkenton, talked out of leaving the University of Georgia by his beloved freshman coach, Quentin Lumpkin, returned to lead the Bulldogs to an SEC title as a junior and made it through six abusive years with Van Brocklin and five frustrating seasons in the Big Apple in time to lead the Vikings to three Super Bowls in six years.

The mind-boggling convergence of the team's coach and both his offensive and defensive leaders ushered in a span that will never be duplicated given the parity of today's National Football League.

"I am proud of our team. The thing about football is that it's the ultimate team sport," said Tarkenton. "We had a chance. We knocked on the door. We knocked on the door every year, and that was fun and that was great. But not being able to push it across the line, I feel like I let myself down, the team down, the people of Minnesota down that I couldn't deliver a Super Bowl championship. It was probably the only time in my life I couldn't deliver what I wanted to deliver."[4]

Tarkenton is troubled that he was unable to accomplish this feat, the first time in his life he had fallen short in a football endeavor. He had led Athens High School to a state championship, the Georgia Bulldogs to an SEC title over Auburn and an Orange Bowl victory over Missouri and the Vikings to six straight Central Division crowns starting in 1973, but a Super Bowl win eluded him.

"It is what it is," said Marshall. "We worked very hard to win a Super Bowl but sometimes you just don't get over that hump. We kept thinking that we were going to be better each of the Super Bowl games we played, but we didn't come away with the most points. That will always be someplace in the back of my mind, that we didn't achieve our goal. The life lesson is you have to put forth the best effort that you can, to leave it out there on the field. If you don't win, you have to accept that and try to get better next time. Unfortunately, our guys won't get another chance."

"It's a shame in football," said safety Terry Brown. "Baseball you get two or three chances. Football it's just one game. If we played those same teams again, we'd probably beat them. On that particular day we didn't do that."

Drafts no longer produced the likes of Carl Eller and Page. First-round selections Mark Mullaney ('75), James "Duck" White ('76) and Randy Holloway ('78), while solid, weren't the Purple People Eaters.

"Good situational players, that's about all they were," said Reichow. "Randy never did show what you thought he might show. Duck White was a solid guy and Mullaney, too. But he was banged up a lot. Big, good-looking athlete. If you drew up a defensive end, you'd say that's him right there. He wasn't quite what we thought he'd be but injuries played a role."

Prior to the cup running dry in the late '70s, these great players from all over the United States and from all walks of life and backgrounds came together in one singular place. In the tumultuous '60s, the Minnesota Vikings displayed no signs of racial tension or social misgivings and came together as a body jointly fitted together.

Credit Grant.

"Bud was an amazing person," said Hagan. "I was with him so much inside and outside of the building and I was close to [Grant's longtime best friend] Sid Hartman. We had hundreds of meals together. As Fran Tarkenton said, Bud Grant had more common sense than any man he ever knew. I felt the same way. He knew how to deal with different types of people. He had his own way of doing things. That's why his book is called *I Did It My Way*. He tried to do things how he wanted them done but if he found out someone else had a better way, he'd copy that. He'd say, 'You don't have to reinvent the wheel.' He had his own way of doing things and it just fit with every type of player that was out there. He had all these guys from different walks of life and different regions of the country: big towns, small towns. He just had a way of being able to connect with all different types of players and coaches."

There Grant was, amid it all. A picture of poise amid the chaos that is an NFL sideline, as Jim Klobuchar wrote: "Grant had become sanity's fixed beacon at Metropolitan Stadium, nerveless and impregnable, an emotional Sahara."[5]

It is believed he was Vikings ownership's first choice to be the coach when the franchise debuted in 1961. One can only speculate how things would have changed if that scenario had played out.

"I was in consideration, but I understood new coaches don't do too well in expansion situations," Grant said. "It's usually the guy who comes behind him who fares better. I didn't want to be a one-and-done kind of guy. I'm a football coach, but most of all

I'm a husband and a father and a family guy. That's my No. 1 job. A football coach is what I did but it was not who I was."[6]

"I didn't classify Bud as a coach," added wide receiver John Henderson. "I saw him as a manager of people. One of the first things I noticed was that Black and White players roomed together with the Vikings. And that was not my experience with [another] team back in the mid–'60s."

Duane Thomas said he would have loved to play for the Vikings because the team "wasn't as plasticky as the Cowboys." He said he noticed their esprit de corps. He said their players weren't "robots."

"It's all about the team," said Clinton Jones, who kept in touch with Thomas until his untimely death in August 2024. "And there was something spiritual about ours."

Many of the Vikings are men of faith, and the shared hope that was in them developed a bond greater than football.

"I started the Fellowship of Christian Athletes in Georgia," said Tarkenton. "I was a very religious kid. My dad was a pastor. It was a good atmosphere to grow up in. I'm a religious person, a Christian, and I have a deeper faith now than I did then."

These Vikings were a collection of colorful individuals who, under Grant's leadership, still managed to play as a team.

Clinton Jones arrived out of Michigan State as firecracker running back. He got a measly 13 carries his rookie year in '67.

Gene Washington, his college teammate, was bothered more by the Vikings' dismal record his first pro season in '67—a lowly 3–8–3—than catching just 13 passes, ironically the same number of carries logged by Jones, drafted by Minnesota the same year.

Yet neither of these former college stars issued complaints.

Ed Marinaro was all-world at Cornell as a running back, as prolific as one can be, but pride didn't get in the way of his becoming a standout receiver out of the backfield for a quarterback in Tarkenton who seemingly preferred other backs.

"I did two things in Minnesota I never had to do in college—block and catch," Marinaro said with a smile.

In a not-so-simple time, the Vikings were all about simplicity.

"Coach Grant expected you to do your job," said Brown. "Of course, during hunting season he wanted to get out of there as much as we did. We didn't leave our games on the practice field. We came in late for training camp. He treated everyone the same. From Fran Tarkenton all the way down to the last player.

"There was total respect for this guy. He was as good of a coach I've ever been around. You never had to guess what he thought about you. He'd come up and tell you. He was in total control. We had a receiver who was supposed to be pretty good from Oakland. We traded a third-round pick for him. But he wouldn't get his haircut, so Bud traded him. He just wouldn't follow the rules."

The team showed no signs of division. Roles were understood.

"The role Bud had for me was standing next to him and taking the next play in. I did that for my entire career," said running back Robert Miller. "My role was completely decided by Coach Grant. He trusted me to take the play in and make the call and do what was necessary. I came off the bench, but that was my role."

And when Miller was called upon, like the time he started for Brent McClanahan in the famous "Mud Bowl" game, he thrived.

Grant was a players' coach in the respect that he knew players won ball games, not coaches.

When asked why Paul Brown, his football coach in the navy who would go on to lead the Cleveland Browns to 10 straight championship game appearances, was such a great coach, he replied:

"He had the best players," said Grant, who also played basketball at the Great Lakes Naval Academy under Weeb Ewbank. "Coaches are a dime a dozen. You get all kinds of coaches that know X's and O's. You gotta accumulate [players], manage and put them in the right places and recognize their talents. That's what wins football games, not coaches. Lots of great coaches out there."[7]

Grant admired coach Brown's ability to accumulate talent.

"He was ahead of his time in that regard," he added. "He knew when he was at Great Lakes [during World War II] that he was going to be coaching the Browns. He had great attention to detail and the ability to compile information about players from his network of fellow coaches."[8]

And this Brown trait was something Grant emulated.

"I was out recruiting, or looking, and talking, getting an idea of players, and analyzing," he said. "[For instance] Paul Krause. We got him for almost nothing from Washington, but I had seen him play in college and I followed him and I knew him. We got players that played great for us but were not recognized by other teams. We didn't have one player who went to another team who had any great success. We didn't miss on any of those and that was just because we [the coaches] spent a lot of time analyzing the best players."[9]

As Vikings players looked back at their careers, they had a common theme. While the team had a great coach whom they unquestionably and undeniably followed in Grant, a man who Mullaney said "talked to you with his eyes," the straw that stirred the drink, to repeat the phrase Yankees legend Reggie Jackson once used to describe himself, was undoubtedly Jim Marshall.

"Bud Grant once said there would be no Vikings success if it weren't for Jim Marshall," said Jones.

Marshall was, as Jones said, "an iconic man."

"By the testimony of his teammates, Marshall has a special quality, and they speak of it with awe, as though the man were mildly superhuman," wrote *New York Times* columnist Peter Range the week leading up to the Vikings' 1973 NFC championship game showdown with the Cowboys.[10]

So revered was Marshall that after his retirement, longtime Vikings equipment man Stubby Eason confiscated all of his No. 70 jerseys and refused to give out the number until it was retired.

One can gain a window into Marshall's soul by reading what he told the *Minneapolis Star* after the Mud Bowl, a 14–7 Vikings win.

"You can't be a faint-hearted, man. You got to seek. You got to strive. You got to climb mountains and turn corners and swim upstream. It keeps you young," said Marshall, then 39 years old.[11]

"Jim was a funny guy. A happy guy," said Dennis Ryan, who took over for Eason. "A welcoming person. He was the guy who welcomed me in and made me feel comfortable. He did that for a little kid working part-time for Stubby. He did that with everybody. I saw it in the South and in some of the major cities, but I didn't grow up around any racial problems in our area. When I started working with the Vikings, I never saw anything that indicated any racial divide. They all got along and they always loved each other."

Quarterback Bob Lee teared up when talking about the efforts Marshall made on his behalf during his rookie campaign with the Vikings. This is the type of love the players displayed for a man who owns NFL career records for most consecutive starts (270) and most games played (282) by a defensive player.

"There's no doubt he was the centerpiece," said Brown. "He was a great leader. He's the most unbelievable person I've ever been around. He never missed a game all those years and I don't know how he did it, especially at his age. He wasn't a big specimen, but he could sure play."

It's sadly fitting the most respected player on a team that dropped four Super Bowls doesn't have the last jewel in his NFL crown. How the Hall of Fame voters have continued to ignore Marshall is beyond the imagination of his Vikings teammates, as well as those whom he played against.

"I wish I would have known him earlier. Just on his longevity alone he should be elected," said Jack Youngblood, who was inducted into the HOF in 2001. "I always thought that he was just as good as Eller. They were a great pair. They knew how to work together. They were great athletes. It's a shame he's not in. He was both wiry strong and quick. He was a tremendous athlete and he knew what he was doing. He wasn't out there trying to beat up the offensive tackle. His perspective was 'get away from the big, ol' ugly guy in front of me and I'm going to go hit this little quarterback over here.' He deserves to be in the Hall. It's like [Denver Broncos linebacking great Randy] Gradishar. It took 35 years with him [to make the HOF]."

Arriving to the Vikings by way of Canada, and then Cleveland, Marshall had a career that is a microcosm of the team's journey: steadfast, determined, indomitable, long-suffering and exceedingly successful, but always one step short of total completion, total fulfillment.

"He was just the heart and soul of the team," Hagan added. "You cannot tell the history of the Minnesota Vikings without Jim Marshall. He just meant so much in terms of what he stood for. His longevity streak for one thing was great, especially given the position he played. With all the different injuries and the different personal accidents he was involved in, it was amazing that he still answered the bell each time. Bud Grant would always say, 'Durability is an ability.' It's a trait you want to have, and he had it."

Minnesota also enjoyed during this era five players—nearly double any other team—who ranked in the top 50 in the NFL in "Approximate Value," a player tenure value statistic created by Pro Football Reference founder Doug Drinen that boils down a player's overall value to a single number. For example, according to Drinen's tabulations, the top all-time AV number for a career is Tom Brady at 326. In Tarkenton (No. 6, 233), Page (No. 17, 197), Eller (No. 24, 180), Marshall (No. 29, 168) and Krause (No. 43, 162), the Vikings remarkably had five franchise-altering players on one team, in one era.

For example, the great Dallas Cowboy teams of the 1990s enjoyed just two top 50 players on the AV career leaders list in Emmitt Smith (No. 27, 169) and Deion Sanders (No. 38, 163).

Results in the ultimate game weren't there, but the Vikings enjoyed an unprecedented confluence of both leadership and talent to go 104–67–1 from 1968 to 1977 for a plus-.600 winning percentage.

Remember the note Jim Finks carried in his wallet?

"It's the journey, not the arrival that counts. Does the road wind uphill all the way? Yes, to the very end."

"I always tell people in my 32 years with the Vikings we had less than 10 losing seasons [eight]," said Hagan. "How many other teams would leap over backwards for those results? We have been a very successful franchise for a long time, but you have to believe that on the horizon is a Vince Lombardi Trophy. We've had a long, storied history and when we finally get the cherry on top, it will be an unbelievable parade. I went to both Twins' World Series parades. When those happened, it just captivated the town."

This era of Vikings football was "the coming of age of young football fans across the country," said Pat Duncan in *The Last Kings of the Old NFL*.[12]

During this time, playoff football meant winters in Minnesota.

"The TV ratings were super high," said Hagan of this unprecedented period. "The Vikings have always been one of the top teams in terms of the percentage of fans in our region watching games. It was a ritual for families. Church would get done at 11:15 or whatever and we'd be listening to the pregame on the way home. At our house, my mom, one of the nicest persons around, a true church lady, if somebody called our house during the game she'd pick up and say, 'Don't you know the Vikings are playing?'"

Jon Bois, a journalist for Secret Base, an SB Nation website, released a remarkable seven-part YouTube series on the history of the Vikings. The series covers the team from its inception in 1961 and continues a Bois theme of chronicling teams that have gone through heartbreaking pasts.

"We call the Vikings the 'Great American Storytellers,'" said Bois. "Not only are they a factory of so many fascinating stories, but they also pull on so many threads of Americana and what it means to be American in modern times.

"When you dive into the Vikings' story, there's a lot of themes related to Minnesotans' geographical place in America, their relationship to the cold and so many questions of identity that we found really fascinating," he added.[13]

Some say the Vikings are cursed. Bois does not agree.

"Comparatively, the Vikings are a thoroughly pleasant story," he said. "Obviously, there's no shortage of heartbreak. But it's all temporary with the Vikings, because unlike any other franchise, they pick themselves up and return to competitiveness."[14]

That's why the Vikings have the third-most wins of the Super Bowl era. Les Steckel's 3–13 team in '84 was a rare exception.

Even so, it's as if time has stood still since Sammy Johnson's rousing run gave the Vikings an insurmountable 24–13 lead over the Rams in the '76 NFC championship game. Tarkenton's subsequent leap of exuberance, jumping with his arms thrust in the air, celebrated the team's last qualification for the Super Bowl.

"Stubby [Eason] pleaded with me to stay for the whole '76 season, but I left in November because wrestling started," recalled Ryan, then a senior in high school. "He said if I finished the season, he would take me to the Super Bowl. I figured I'll just go next year. We always go. The Vikings have never been back."

Nevertheless, none of the players interviewed seem depressed over their careers, over not winning a Super Bowl.

The Purple-Clad Boys of Winter may not have been "America's Team," but they captivated the American spirit.

The players of this era, this team, have withstood the test of time, forging in the hearts of their fans a steely will.

Would Roger Kahn have stopped loving his beloved Brooklyn Dodgers had they not finally broken through and beaten the New York Yankees for a World Series title in 1955?

Prior to that, they fell in World Series play to the Yankees in 1941, 1947, 1949, 1952 and 1953.

Vikings fans keep hoping that one day an elusive Super Bowl win will come. But will they stop loving them if this is not the case?

There's something more than the wins and the brutal losses with this team.

In the fullness of time, these players came together under one great coach and one iconic leader to captivate our hearts and minds.

For they were the "Purple-Clad Boys of Winter."

Chapter Notes

Introduction

1. Pro Football Reference (pro-football-reference.com) Bud Grant Memorial Service, May 21, 2023.
2. Jack Whitaker, CBS Sports *NFL Today* Show. Dec. 28, 1975.
3. Franklin D. Roosevelt, Democratic National Convention. Philadelphia, June 27, 1936.
4. Sid Hartman, "Vikings Salute Nitschke for 'Bear-Killing.'" *Minneapolis Tribune*, Dec. 16, 1968.
5. Stan Hochman, "Philly Fans Set Record Straight on Philly Fans." *Philadelphia Inquirer*, Nov. 25, 2021.
6. Stan Hochman, "Philly Fans Set Record Straight on Philly Fans." *Philadelphia Inquirer*, Nov. 25, 2021.
7. Sid Hartman, "Vikings Salute Nitschke for 'Bear-Killing.'" *Minneapolis Tribune*, Dec. 16, 1968.
8. Sid Hartman, "Vikings Salute Nitschke for 'Bear-Killing.'" *Minneapolis Tribune*, Dec. 16, 1968.
9. Staff Writer, "Early Vikings Christmas: Come on Packers, Come to Me Santa.'" *Minneapolis Star*, Dec. 16, 1968.
10. Staff Writer, "Early Vikings Christmas: Come on Packers, Come to Me Santa.'" *Minneapolis Star*, Dec. 16, 1968.
11. Staff Writer, "Early Vikings Christmas: Come on Packers, Come to Me Santa.'" *Minneapolis Star*, Dec. 16, 1968.
12. Staff Writer, "Early Vikings Christmas: Come on Packers, Come to Me Santa.'" *Minneapolis Star*, Dec. 16, 1968.

Chapter 1

1. Michael MacCambridge, *America's Game: The Epic Story of How Pro Football Captured a Nation*. New York: Anchor Books, 2005.
2. Mike Richman, *George Allen: A Football Life*. Lincoln: University of Nebraska Press, 2023.
3. Metropolitan Stadium: Ballparksofbaseball.com.
4. Fran Tarkenton, *No Time for Losing*. Westwood, NJ: Fleming Revell. Jan. 1, 1967.
5. Sabr.org/journal/article/twin-cities-ball parks-of-the-20th-century-and-beyond.
6. Sabr.org/journal/article/twin-cities-ball parks-of-the-20th-century-and-beyond.
7. Paul Lukas, "The Untold Story of Minnesota's Uniforms." ESPN.com, Nov. 22, 2017.
8. Paul Lukas, "The Untold Story of Minnesota's Uniforms." ESPN.com, Nov. 22, 2017.
9. Paul Lukas, "The Untold Story of Minnesota's Uniforms." ESPN.com, Nov. 22, 2017.
10. Paul Lukas, "The Untold Story of Minnesota's Uniforms." ESPN.com, Nov. 22, 2017.
11. Paul Lukas, "The Untold Story of Minnesota's Uniforms." ESPN.com, Nov. 22, 2017.
12. Paul Lukas, "The Untold Story of Minnesota's Uniforms." ESPN.com, Nov. 22, 2017.
13. Paul Lukas, "The Untold Story of Minnesota's Uniforms." ESPN.com, Nov. 22, 2017.
14. Jim Finks, Jr., *It's Been a Pleasure: The Jim Finks Story*. Newport Beach, CA: AMO Productions, 2003.
15. Bud Grant Interview. David Spada, Feb. 13, 2021.
16. Charles Johnson. "Bauer Admires Twins, But Won't Concede." *Minneapolis Star*, Sept. 22, 1965.
17. Johnson, Charles. "Bauer Admires Twins, But Won't Concede." *Minneapolis Star*, Sept. 22, 1965.
18. Jim Finks, Jr., *It's Been a Pleasure: The Jim Finks Story*. Newport Beach, CA: AMO Productions, 2003.

Chapter 2

1. Tex Maule, *The Game*. New York: Random House, 1963.
2. Sid Hartman, "'Page's Vision' Becomes Vikings Title Reality." *Minneapolis Star*, Dec. 28, 1969.
3. Sid Hartman, "'Page's Vision' Becomes Vikings Title Reality." *Minneapolis Star*, Dec. 28, 1969.
4. Sid Hartman, "'Page's Vision' Becomes Vikings Title Reality." *Minneapolis Star*, Dec. 28, 1969.
5. Tex Maule, "On Saturday a Battle, On Sunday a Breeze." *Sports Illustrated*, Jan. 5, 1970.
6. Sid Hartman, "'Page's Vision' Becomes Vikings Title Reality." *Minneapolis Star*, Dec. 28, 1969.

7. Tex Maule, "On Saturday a Battle, On Sunday a Breeze." *Sports Illustrated*, Jan. 5, 1970.
8. Peter Range, "A Team Within a Team Within a Team." *New York Times*, Dec. 23, 1973.
9. Sid Hartman, "'Page's Vision' Becomes Vikings Title Reality." *Minneapolis Star*, Dec. 28, 1969.
10. Carl Eller Interview. Tdb8420 YouTube Channel, Oct. 6, 2011.
11. Sid Hartman, "'Page's Vision' Becomes Vikings Title Reality." *Minneapolis Star*, Dec. 28, 1969.
12. Curry Kirkpatrick, "A Man for 20 Seasons." *Sports Illustrated*, Dec. 24, 1979.
13. Carl Eller Interview. Tdb8420 YouTube Channel, Oct. 6, 2011.
14. Mike Richman, *George Allen: A Football Life*. Lincoln: University of Nebraska Press, 2023.
15. Mike Richman, *George Allen: A Football Life*. Lincoln: University of Nebraska Press, 2023.
16. Bud Grant Interview. David Spada, Feb. 13, 2021.
17. Bud Grant Interview. David Spada, Feb. 13, 2021.
18. Dick Gordon. "'8 New Vikings Fill Needs'—Grant." *Minneapolis Star*, March 14, 1967.

Chapter 3

1. Dwayne Netland, "For Collier, Being Prophet Not Profitable." *Minneapolis Star*, Jan. 5, 1970.
2. Jim Kaplan, "Back to Back 'Thing' Proves Browns' Undoing." *Minneapolis Star*, Jan. 5, 1970.
3. Dick Cullum, Vikings Column. *Minneapolis Star*, Jan. 5, 1970.
4. Dwayne Netland, "For Collier, Being Prophet Not Profitable." *Minneapolis Star*, Jan. 5, 1970.
5. Dwayne Netland, "For Collier, Being Prophet Not Profitable." *Minneapolis Star*, Jan. 5, 1970.
6. Dwayne Netland, "For Collier, Being Prophet Not Profitable." *Minneapolis Star*, Jan. 5, 1970.
7. Merrill Swanson, "'Super' Vikings NFL Champs." *Minneapolis Star*, Jan. 5, 1970.
8. Paul Lukas, "The Untold Story of Minnesota's Uniforms." ESPN.com, Nov. 22, 2017.
9. Paul Lukas, "The Untold Story of Minnesota's Uniforms." ESPN.com, Nov. 22, 2017.
10. Ross Bernstein, *Pigskin Pride: Celebrating a Century of Minnesota Football*. Cambridge, MN: Nodin Press, 2019.
11. Bud Grant Interview. David Spada, Feb. 13, 2021.
12. Sid Hartman. Vikings Column. *Star Tribune*, Jan. 5, 1970.

Chapter 4

1. Dick Cullum, Vikings Column. *Minneapolis Star*, Jan. 5, 1970.
2. Dick Cullum, Vikings Column. *Minneapolis Star*, Jan. 5, 1970.
3. Bill Hengen, "Could-Have-Been Vikings Year Ends." *Minneapolis Star*, Dec. 28, 1970.
4. Bud Grant Interview. David Spada, Feb. 13, 2021.
5. Peter Range, "A Team Within a Team Within a Team." *New York Times*, Dec. 23, 1973.
6. Jim Klobuchar, *Tarkenton*. New York: Harper and Row, 1976.
7. Associated Press, NY. "Five Vikings for One Giant—Tarkenton." *The Reporter Dispatch*, Jan. 28, 1972.
8. Dick Gordon, "Tarkenton Return Opens More Deals." *Minneapolis Star*, Jan. 28, 1972.
9. Dick Gordon, "Tarkenton Return Opens More Deals." *Minneapolis Star*, Jan. 28, 1972.
10. Merrill Swanson, "Vikings 'Sold' Tark, Now They 'Buy' Back." *Minneapolis Star*, Jan. 28, 1972.
11. Bill Hengen, "Vikings Change Offense." *Minneapolis Star*, Jan. 28, 1972.

Chapter 5

1. Dwayne Netland, "Reed Sparks Vikings Victory." *Minneapolis Star*, Dec. 23, 1973.
2. Dwayne Netland, "Reed Sparks Vikings Victory." *Minneapolis Star*, Dec. 23, 1973.
3. Pat Duncan, *Last Kings of the Old NFL: The 1969 Minnesota Vikings*. Lexington, KY: CreateSpace, 2014.
4. Dwayne Netland, "Reed Sparks Vikings Victory." *Minneapolis Star*, Dec. 23, 1973.
5. Sid Hartman, Vikings Column. *Star Tribune*, Dec. 23, 1973.
6. Sid Hartman, Vikings Column. *Star Tribune*, Dec. 23, 1973.
7. NFL Films. *They Call It Pro Football*. 1966.
8. Dwayne Netland, "Reed Sparks Vikings Victory." *Minneapolis Star*, Dec. 23, 1973.
9. Fran Tarkenton, *No Time for Losing*. Westwood, NJ: Fleming Revell, 1967.
10. Jim Bruton, *Every Day Is Game Day*. Chicago: Triumph Books, 2009.
11. Jim Bruton, *Every Day Is Game Day*. Chicago: Triumph Books, 2009.
12. Jim Klobuchar, *Tarkenton*. New York: Harper and Row, 1976.
13. Jim Klobuchar, *Tarkenton*. New York: Harper and Row, 1976.

Chapter 6

1. Thomas Paine, "The Crisis." *Common Sense*. Dec. 23, 1776.
2. Dwayne Netland, "Vikings Roar into Super Bowl." *Minneapolis Star*, Dec. 31, 1973.
3. Jim Klobuchar, "Vikings Out of Pits Together." *Minneapolis Star*, Dec. 31, 1973.
4. Bill Hengen, "Cowboys Adjusted Too Late." *Minneapolis Star*, Dec. 31, 1973.
5. Jim Klobuchar, "Vikings Out of Pits Together." *Minneapolis Star*, Dec. 31, 1973.
6. Thomas Paine, "The Crisis." *Common Sense*. Dec. 23, 1776.

7. Jim Bruton, *Every Day Is Game Day*. Chicago: Triumph Books, 2009.
8. Jim Bruton, *Every Day Is Game Day*. Chicago: Triumph Books, 2009.
9. Fran Tarkenton, *No Time for Losing*. Westwood, NJ: Fleming Revell, 1967.
10. Jim Bruton, *Every Day Is Game Day*. Chicago: Triumph Books, 2009.
11. Jim Bruton, *Every Day Is Game Day*. Chicago: Triumph Books, 2009.
12. Gregory Lane, "'Sapp All-Time FB,' Says Georgia's Butts." *Atlanta Journal*, Sept. 22, 1958.
13. Cecil Darby, "Puts Bite into Bulldogs." *Columbus Ledger*, Sept. 22, 1958.
14. Mickey Logue, "Young Bulldog Came of Age Under Eyes of Longhorns." *Atlanta Constitution*, Sept, 22, 1958.
15. Dwayne Netland, "Vikings Roar into Super Bowl." *Minneapolis Star*, Dec. 31, 1973.
16. Jim Klobuchar, "Did Dallas' Staubach Try to Do Too Much?" *Minneapolis Star*, Dec. 31, 1973.
17. Jim Klobuchar, "Vikings Out of Pits Together." *Minneapolis Star*, Dec. 31, 1973.
18. Dwayne Netland, "Vikings Roar into Super Bowl." *Minneapolis Star*, Dec. 31, 1973
19. Dick Young, "Greenest Rookie in the Bowl." *N.Y. Daily News*, Jan. 10, 1974.
20. Thomas Paine, "The Crisis." *Common Sense*, Dec. 23, 1776.

Chapter 7

1. Sid Hartman, Vikings Column. *Minneapolis Tribune*, Dec. 22, 1974.
2. Larry Baston, "Vikings Stomp Cardinals 30–14." *Minneapolis Star*, Dec. 22, 1974.
3. Doug Grow, "Tie at Half Aided Vikings." *St. Louis Dispatch*, Dec. 22, 1974.
4. Tom Barnidge, "Big Red Point to Tough Breaks in Defeat." *St. Louis Dispatch*, Dec. 22, 1974.
5. Tom Barnidge, "Big Red Point to Tough Breaks in Defeat." *St. Louis Dispatch*, Dec. 22, 1974.
6. Joe Soucheray, "Cards Praise the Vikings." *Minneapolis Star*, Dec. 22, 1974.
7. Sid Hartman, Vikings Column. *Minneapolis Tribune*, Dec. 22, 1974.
8. Larry Baston, "Vikings Stomp Cardinals 30–14." *Minneapolis Star*, Dec. 22, 1974.
9. Larry Baston, "Vikings Stomp Cardinals 30–14." *Minneapolis Star*, Dec. 22, 1974.
10. Sid Hartman, Vikings Column. *Minneapolis Tribune*, Dec. 22, 1974.
11. Bud Grant Interview. David Spada, Feb. 13, 2021.
12. Bud Grant Interview. David Spada, Feb. 13, 2021.
13. Bud Grant Interview. David Spada, Feb. 13, 2021.

Chapter 8

1. Allan Holbert, "Vikings Defeat Rams for NFC Title." *Minneapolis Star*, Dec. 30, 1974.
2. Allan Holbert, "Vikings Defeat Rams for NFC Title." *Minneapolis Star*, Dec. 30, 1974.
3. Allan Holbert, "Vikings Defeat Rams for NFC Title." *Minneapolis Star*, Dec. 30, 1974.
4. Dick Gordon, "Getting Even Didn't Worry Vikings' Wallace." *Minneapolis Star*, Dec. 30, 1974.
5. Jim Klobuchar, "Vikings Wright Finds the Right Angle." *Minneapolis Star*, Dec. 30, 1974.
6. Jim Klobuchar, "Vikings Wright Finds the Right Angle." *Minneapolis Star*, Dec. 30, 1974.
7. Jim Klobuchar, "Vikings Wright Finds the Right Angle." *Minneapolis Star*, Dec. 30, 1974.
8. Sid Hartman, "Page Gambles on Preventing Rams TD, Wins." *Minneapolis Tribune*, Dec. 30, 1974.
9. Sid Hartman, "Page Gambles on Preventing Rams TD, Wins." *Minneapolis Tribune*, Dec. 30, 1974.
10. Sid Hartman, "Page Gambles on Preventing Rams TD, Wins." *Minneapolis Tribune*, Dec. 30, 1974.
11. Allan Holbert, "Vikings Defeat Rams for NFC Title." *Minneapolis Star*, Dec. 30, 1974.
12. Jim Klobuchar, "Vikings Wright Finds the Right Angle." *Minneapolis Star*, Dec. 30, 1974.

Chapter 9

1. Jim Klobuchar, "Vikings Shocked by Dallas." *Minneapolis Star*, Dec. 29, 1975.
2. Jim Bruton, *Every Day Is Game Day*. Chicago: Triumph Books, 2009.
3. Jim Bruton, *Every Day Is Game Day*. Chicago: Triumph Books, 2009.
4. Jim Bruton, *Every Day Is Game Day*. Chicago: Triumph Books, 2009.
5. Bud Grant Interview. David Spada, Feb. 13, 2021.

Chapter 10

1. Sid Hartman, Vikings Column. *Minneapolis Star*, Dec. 19, 1976.
2. Jim Soucheray, Vikings Column. *Minneapolis Tribune*, Dec. 19, 1976.
3. Jim Soucheray, Vikings Column. *Minneapolis Tribune*, Dec. 19, 1976.
4. Jim Soucheray, Vikings Column. *Minneapolis Tribune*, Dec. 19, 1976.
5. Mike Richman, *George Allen: A Football Life*. Lincoln: University of Nebraska Press, 2023.
6. Sid Hartman, Vikings Column. *Minneapolis Star*, Dec. 19, 1976.
7. Sid Hartman, Vikings Column. *Minneapolis Star*, Dec. 19, 1976.
8. Sid Hartman, Vikings Column. *Minneapolis Star*, Dec. 19, 1976.

9. Jim Bruton, *Every Day Is Game Day*. Chicago: Triumph Books, 2009.
10. Jim Bruton, *Every Day Is Game Day*. Chicago: Triumph Books, 2009.
11. Jim Bruton, *Every Day Is Game Day*. Chicago: Triumph Books, 2009.
12. Jim Klobuchar, "New Vike Rashad What Grant Ordered." *Minneapolis Star*, Sept. 8, 1976.
13. Jim Klobuchar, "New Vike Rashad What Grant Ordered." *Minneapolis Star*, Sept. 8, 1976.
14. Associated Press, NY. "Rashad Goes as Seahawks Clean House." *Bellingham Herald*, Sept. 8, 1976
15. Jim Bruton, *Vikings 50: All-Time Greatest Players in Franchise History*. Chicago: Triumph Books, 2012.
16. Jim Soucheray, Vikings Column. *Minneapolis Tribune*, Dec. 19, 1976.

Chapter 11

1. Jim Klobuchar and Jeff Siemon, *Will the Vikings Ever Win the Super Bowl?: An Inside Look at the Minnesota Vikings of 1976*. New York: Harper and Row, 1977.
2. Robert Kaiser and Pat Haden, *Pat Haden: My Rookie Season with the Los Angeles Rams*. New York: William Morrow and Company, 1977.
3. Jim Klobuchar and Jeff Siemon, *Will the Vikings Ever Win the Super Bowl? An Inside Look at the Minnesota Vikings of 1976*. New York: Harper and Row, 1977.
4. Jim Klobuchar and Jeff Siemon, *Will the Vikings Ever Win the Super Bowl? An Inside Look at the Minnesota Vikings of 1976*. New York: Harper and Row, 1977.
5. Max Nichols, "Almost Every Play Was Big." *Minneapolis Star*, Dec. 27, 1976.
6. Jim Klobuchar, "No Pain-Killer Shot for Injured Siemon." *Minneapolis Star*, Dec. 27, 1976.
7. Jim Klobuchar, "No Pain-Killer Shot for Injured Siemon." *Minneapolis Star*, Dec. 27, 1976.
8. Jim Klobuchar and Jeff Siemon, *Will the Vikings Ever Win the Super Bowl? An Inside Look at the Minnesota Vikings of 1976*. New York: Harper and Row, 1977.
9. Chan Smith, "Knox's Memory Plays Trick on Rams." *Minneapolis Star*, Dec. 27, 1976.
10. Jim Soucheray, Vikings Column. *Minneapolis Star*, Dec. 27, 1976.
11. Jim Soucheray, Vikings Column. *Minneapolis Star*, Dec. 27, 1976.
12. Chan Smith, "Knox's Memory Plays Trick on Rams." *Minneapolis Star*, Dec. 27, 1976.

Chapter 12

1. Bob Sansavere, "1970s Vikings Remember Four Trips to Super Bowl." *Pioneer Press*, Feb. 1, 2018.
2. Jim Klobuchar, "Grant Won't Dwell on Hindsight." *Minneapolis Star*, Jan. 10, 1977.
3. Bob Fowler, "Vikings Made Oakland Nervous." *Minneapolis Star*, Jan. 10, 1977.
4. Jim Klobuchar, Vikings Column. *Minneapolis Star*, Jan. 10, 1977.
5. Max Nichols, "5 Blocks Made Key Play Go." *Minneapolis Star*, Jan. 10, 1977.
6. Max Nichols, "5 Blocks Made Key Play Go." *Minneapolis Star*, Jan. 10, 1977.
7. Associated Press. "Super Bowl Quotes." *Saint Cloud Times*, Jan. 10, 1977.
8. Jim Klobuchar, "Siemon, Brown Disagree on Key Fumble Call." *Minneapolis Star*, Jan. 13, 1975.
9. Jim Klobuchar, "Siemon, Brown Disagree on Key Fumble Call." *Minneapolis Star*, Jan. 13, 1975.
10. Jim Klobuchar, "Siemon, Brown Disagree on Key Fumble Call." *Minneapolis Star*, Jan. 13, 1975.
11. Jim Klobuchar, "Siemon, Brown Disagree on Key Fumble Call." *Minneapolis Star*, Jan. 13, 1975.
12. Sid Hartman, Vikings Column. *Minneapolis Tribune*, Sept. 21, 1970.
13. Jim Klobuchar, "TD Oasis Vanished at the Dolphins' 6." *Minneapolis Star*, Jan. 14, 1974.
14. Dick Gordon, "Buoniconti Saw What Was Coming." *Minneapolis Star*, Jan. 14, 1974.
15. Jim Klobuchar, "Vikings End Came at the Beginning." *Minneapolis Star*, Jan. 14, 1974.
16. Jim Klobuchar, "Vikings End Came at the Beginning." *Minneapolis Star*, Jan. 14, 1974.
17. Jim Klobuchar, "McClanahan 'Rivets' Spot on Vikings." *Minneapolis Star*, Sept. 2, 1975.
18. Sid Hartman, Vikings Column. *Minneapolis Tribune*, Sept. 2, 1975.
19. Sid Hartman, Vikings Column. *Minneapolis Tribune*, Sept. 2, 1975.
20. Bob Fowler, "Griese: Vikings Ruined Miami's Running Game." *Minneapolis Star*, Sept. 2, 1975.
21. Staff Writer. "KC Triple Stack Stymied Vikings." *Minneapolis Star*, Jan. 12, 1970.
22. Pat Thompson, "Interceptions, Fumbles, Penalties All Prove Costly." *Austin Daily Herald*, Jan. 12, 1970.
23. Sid Hartman, Vikings Column. *Minneapolis Tribune*, Jan. 12, 1970.
24. Jim Klobuchar, *Tarkenton*. New York: Harper and Row, 1976.
25. Michael MacCambridge, *America's Game: The Epic Story of How Pro Football Captured a Nation*. New York: Anchor Books, 2005.
26. Michael MacCambridge, *America's Game: The Epic Story of How Pro Football Captured a Nation*. New York: Anchor Books, 2005.

Chapter 13

1. Jim Klobuchar and Dan Stoneking, "The Greatest Football Drive I Ever Saw." *Minneapolis Star*, Dec. 27, 1977.
2. Joe Marshall, "Bud Thrives in the Mud." *Sports Illustrated*, Jan. 2, 1978.
3. Jim Klobuchar and Dan Stoneking, "The Greatest Football Drive I Ever Saw." *Minneapolis Star*, Dec. 27, 1977.

4. Joe Marshall, "Bud Thrives in the Mud." *Sports Illustrated*, Jan. 2, 1978.

5. Jim Klobuchar and Dan Stoneking, "The Greatest Football Drive I Ever Saw." *Minneapolis Star*, Dec. 27, 1977.

6. Jim Klobuchar and Dan Stoneking, "The Greatest Football Drive I Ever Saw." *Minneapolis Star*, Dec. 27, 1977.

7. Jim Klobuchar and Dan Stoneking, "The Greatest Football Drive I Ever Saw." *Minneapolis Star*, Dec. 27, 1977.

8. Sid Hartman, Vikings Column. *Minneapolis Tribune*, July 14, 1968.

9. Bud Grant Interview. David Spada, Feb. 13, 2021.

Epilogue

1. Jerry Byrd, "The Dutchman." *Shreveport Journal*, May 2, 1983.

2. Bud Grant Interview. David Spada, Feb. 13, 2021.

3. Peter Range, "A Team Within a Team Within a Team." *New York Times*, Dec. 23, 1973.

4. Fran Tarkenton Interview. Rena Sarigianopoulos, KARE 11 News. Nov. 16, 2017.

5. Jim Klobuchar, *Tarkenton*. New York: Harper and Row, 1976.

6. Bud Grant Interview. David Spada, Feb. 13, 2021.

7. Bud Grant Interview. David Spada, Feb. 13, 2021.

8. Bud Grant Interview. David Spada, Feb. 13, 2021.

9. Bud Grant Interview. David Spada, Feb. 13, 2021.

10. Peter Range, "A Team Within a Team Within a Team." *New York Times*, Dec. 23, 1973.

11. Jim Klobuchar and Dan Stoneking, "The Greatest Football Drive I Ever Saw." *Minneapolis Star*, Dec. 27, 1977.

12. Pat Duncan, *Last Kings of the Old NFL: The 1969 Minnesota Vikings*. Lexington, KY: CreateSpace, 2014.

13. Abby Sliva, "The Vikings Will Win a Super Bowl." *Star Tribune*, Sept. 8, 2023.

14. Abby Sliva, "The Vikings Will Win a Super Bowl." *Star Tribune*, Sept. 8, 2023.

Bibliography

Interviews

QB: Fran Tarkenton, Gary Cuozzo, Bob Lee
RB: Clinton Jones, Dave Osborn, Ed Marinaro, Chuck Foreman, Oscar Reed, Brent McClanahan, Robert Miller
OL: Ed White, Ron Yary
TE: Stu Voigt, Steve Craig
WR: John Gilliam, Ahmad Rashad, Gene Washington, John Henderson, Sammy White, Jerry Reichow
DL: Jim Marshall, Carl Eller, Gary Larsen, Bob Lurtsema, Mark Mullaney
LB: Jeff Siemon, Lonnie Warwick
DB: Paul Krause, Bobby Bryant, Nate Wright, Jeff Wright, Dale Hackbart, Terry Brown, Randy Poltl
Other: Bob Hagan (public relations), Jerry Reichow (scout, player personnel), Dennis Ryan (equipment), Dave Finks (son of GM), Dick Jonckowski (sideline worker), Paul Lukas (uniform watch)
Non-Vikings: Bobby Bell (Kansas City Chiefs), Drew Pearson (Dallas Cowboys), Duane Thomas (Dallas Cowboys), Jackie Smith (St. Louis Cardinals), Jack Youngblood (Los Angeles Rams), Dave Robinson (Green Bay Packers)

Website

Pro Football Reference (pro-football-reference.com)

Books and Articles

Associated Press. "Five Vikings for One Giant—Tarkenton." *Reporter Dispatch*, Jan. 28, 1972.
_____. "Rashad Goes as Seahawks Clean House." *Bellingham Herald*, Sept. 8, 1976.
Baston, Larry. "Vikings Stomp Cardinals 30–14." *Star Tribune*, Dec. 22, 1974.
Bernstein, Ross. *Pigskin Pride: Celebrating a Century of Minnesota Football*. Cambridge, MN: Nodin Press, 2000.
Brownlee, David. "Architectural Masterpieces at Penn." A virtual walking tour. June 3, 2020. https://giving.upenn.edu/architectural-masterpieces-at-penn/.
Burton, Jim. *Every Day Is Game Day*. Chicago: Triumph, 2009.
CBS Sports. *NFL Today*. Dec. 28, 1975.
Duncan, Pat. *Last Kings of the Old NFL: The 1969 Minnesota Vikings*. Lexington, KY: Create Space, 2014.
"Early Vikings Christmas: Come on Packers, Come to Me Santa." *Minneapolis Star*, Dec. 16, 1968.
Finks, Jim, Jr. *It's Been a Pleasure: The Jim Finks Story*. Newport Beach, CA: AMO, 2003.
Gordon, Dick. "'8 New Vikings Fill Needs'—Grant." *Minneapolis Star*, March 14, 1967.
_____. "Getting Even Didn't Worry Vikings' Wallace." *Minneapolis Star*, Dec. 30, 1974.
_____. "Tarkenton Return Opens More Deals." *Minneapolis Star*, Jan. 28, 1972.
Hartman, Sid. "Page Gambles on Preventing Rams TD, Wins." *Star Tribune*, Dec. 30, 1974.
_____. Vikings Column. *Star Tribune*. Jan. 5, 1970. Dec. 22, 1974. Dec. 23, 1973.
_____. "Vikings Salute Nitschke for 'Bear-Killing.'" *Minneapolis Tribune*, Dec. 16, 1968.
Hengen, Bill. "Could-Have-Been Vikings Year Ends." *Minneapolis Star*, Dec. 28, 1970.
_____. "Cowboys Adjusted Too Late." *Minneapolis Star*, Dec. 31, 1973.
_____. "Vikings Change Offense." *Minneapolis Star*, Jan. 28, 1972.
Hochman, Stan. "Philly Fans Set Record Straight on Philly Fans." *Philadelphia Inquirer*, Nov. 25, 2021.
Johnson, Charles. "Bauer Admires Twins, But Won't Concede." *Minneapolis Star*, Sept. 22, 1965.
Kaiser, Robert, and Pat Haden. *Pat Haden: My Rookie Season with the Los Angeles Rams*. New York: William Morrow, 1977.
Kaplan, Jim. "Back to Back 'Thing' Proves Browns' Undoing." *Minneapolis Star*, Jan. 5, 1970.
Klobuchar, Jim. "Did Dallas' Staubach Try to Do Too Much?" *Minneapolis Star*, Dec. 31, 1973.
_____. "New Vike Rashad What Grant Ordered." *Minneapolis Star*, Sept. 8, 1976.
_____. "No Pain-Killer Shot for Injured Siemon." *Minneapolis Star*, Dec. 27, 1976.
_____. *Tarkenton*. New York: Harper and Row, 1976.
_____. "Vikings Out of Pits Together." *Minneapolis Star*, Dec. 31, 1973.
_____. "Vikings Wright Finds the Right Angle." *Minneapolis Star*, Dec. 30, 1974.

Bibliography

Klobuchar, Jim, and Dan Stoneking. "The Greatest Football Drive I Ever Saw." *Minneapolis Star*, Dec. 27, 1977.

Klobuchar, Jim, and Jeff Siemon. *Will the Vikings Ever Win the Super Bowl? An Inside Look at the Minnesota Vikings of 1976*. New York: Harper and Row, 1977.

Lukas, Paul. "The Untold Story of Minnesota's Uniforms." ESPN.com, Nov. 22, 2017.

MacCambridge, Michael. *America's Game: The Epic Story of How Pro Football Captured a Nation*. New York: Anchor, 2005.

Maraniss, David. *When Pride Still Mattered: A Life of Vince Lombardi*. New York: Simon & Schuster, 2000.

Marshall, Joe. "Bud Thrives in the Mud." *Sports Illustrated*, Jan. 2, 1978.

Maule, Tex. *The Game*. New York: Random House, 1963.

———. "On Saturday a Battle, on Sunday a Breeze." *Sports Illustrated*, Jan. 5, 1970.

Netland, Dwayne. "For Collier, Being Prophet Not Profitable." *Minneapolis Star*, Jan. 5, 1970.

———. "Reed Sparks Vikings Victory." *Minneapolis Star*, Dec. 23, 1973.

Nichols, Max. "Almost Every Play Was Big." *Minneapolis Star*, Dec. 27, 1976.

Richman, Mike. *George Allen: A Football Life*. Lincoln: University of Nebraska Press, 2023.

Sliva, Abby. "The Vikings Will Win a Super Bowl." *Star Tribune*, Sept. 8, 2023.

Smith, Chan. "Knox's Memory Plays Trick on Rams." *Minneapolis Star*, Dec. 27, 1976.

Spada, David. Bud Grant Interview, YouTube, Feb. 13, 2021, https://www.youtube.com/watch?v=iNRx4tWapsQ.

Swanson, Merrill. "'Super' Vikings NFL Champs." *Minneapolis Star*, Jan. 5, 1970.

———. "Vikings 'Sold' Tark, Now They 'Buy' Back." *Minneapolis Star*, Jan. 28, 1972.

Index

Adderley, Herb 39, 72, 158, 172
Alderman, Grady 21, 35, 40, 46, 85, 89, 143

Beasley, John 24, 29, 42, 47, 72, 97, 144
Bell, Bobby 168, 170–173
Brodie, John 57, 63, 114, 154
Brown, Bill 6, 29, 31, 36, 38–39, 58, 65, 75, 77, 85, 131, 144, 165–166, 168
Brown, Bob 2, 5, 7, 29–30
Brown, Jim 40, 76, 119, 172
Brown, Larry 164
Brown, Paul 23, 40–41, 184, 189, 197
Brown, Terry 77, 89–90, 93, 110, 115, 119, 121, 123, 126, 164, 183, 195–196, 198
Brown, Willie 158–159, 163
Bryant, Bobby 2, 24, 42, 47, 86, 100–101, 104–105, 110, 116–117, 120–123, 126, 149–153, 158–159, 161–163, 184
Burns, Jerry 52, 59, 65, 84, 86, 128, 143, 163, 177, 185

Cappelletti, John 107, 153
Carr, Jimmy "Gummy" 118, 120, 185
Chicago Bears 4, 6, 10, 12, 24, 25, 36, 55, 59, 63, 65, 68, 75, 91–92, 102, 116, 118, 139, 143, 146–148, 153, 183, 185, 187
Cox, Fred 11, 46, 66, 74, 85, 99, 128, 144, 159, 164–165
Craig, Steve 107, 128–130, 146–147, 168
Cuozzo, Gary 21, 49, 53, 58–66, 87–90, 99, 113, 144, 190

Dallas Cowboys 6, 10, 12, 14, 33, 38–39, 46, 65–67, 73, 80, 84–89, 92, 94, 102–104, 110, 113–116, 118, 120–122, 124, 120–130, 134, 136, 142, 144–148, 151, 160, 172, 181, 187, 190–191, 196–197
Detroit Lions 10, 18, 21, 23, 25, 38, 51–52, 78, 118, 120, 126, 143, 160, 173, 178–179, 187

Eason, Jim "Stubby" 15, 18, 77, 94, 142, 192, 197, 199
electric football 11–14
Eller, Carl 2, 11, 25, 28–35, 42, 51, 53–54, 57, 59, 77, 93, 97–101, 105, 107, 109, 122, 124, 133, 143, 146, 150, 152, 160, 169–172, 175, 186–187, 190–192, 195, 198–199

Finks, Jim 21–25, 48, 58, 61–62, 67, 91–92, 114, 116, 143–144, 148, 154, 185, 190, 199
Foreman, Chuck 37–38, 45, 54, 58, 66, 68, 71, 74, 77, 84–87, 94, 100–101, 108–110, 115, 121, 127–130, 132, 135–137, 143–144, 146, 151, 154–158, 161, 165–166, 178, 180–181, 191–192
Franklin Field 1–2, 4, 6, 12, 23, 119

Gilliam, Frank 173, 194
Gilliam, John 2, 14, 44, 47, 54, 61, 69–74, 80–81, 84, 86–91, 85, 97, 99, 106–108, 114, 127–128, 131, 140, 144, 164–165, 167–168, 173
Graham, Otto 172, 184
Grant, Harry "Bud" 1, 3–7, 9, 15, 22, 24–25, 28–29, 32–36, 38–42, 47–50, 52–54, 65–67, 71, 76–77, 81, 84, 86, 90, 92, 94, 96–97, 99–102, 105, 108–111, 113–116, 132–133, 136, 140–148, 153, 156–159, 164, 166, 169, 170, 175–178, 182, 185–186, 188–198
Green Bay Packers 4, 6, 10, 12, 33–35, 37, 39, 50, 52, 61–63, 68, 119, 129, 131, 143–144, 154, 172, 180, 187

Hackbart, Dale 4, 7, 33–35, 42, 97, 118, 120, 170, 184
Haden, Pat 101, 145, 149
Hagan, Bob 14, 193, 195, 198–199
Hail Mary 2, 9, 38, 91, 96–97, 100, 116, 118–129, 131, 133, 137, 145, 155
Hayes, Bob 66, 86, 120, 129, 159
Henderson, John 51–55, 62–64, 142, 196
Henderson, Thomas "Hollywood" 121, 130
Hilgenberg, Wally 6, 51–53, 64, 98, 105, 107, 116, 118, 120, 147, 149, 153, 160, 169, 186
Hollway, Bob 52, 90, 97, 118, 139
Houston, Ken 74, 134–136, 158

Jackson, Harold 2, 101, 106, 145, 149, 153, 180
Jessie, Ron 101, 150, 159
Jonckowski, Dick 16, 126–127
Jones, Calvin 173, 194
Jones, Clinton 2, 21, 24–25, 29, 38–42, 47–48, 54, 58, 64, 66, 77, 90, 131, 157, 196–197
Jones, David "Deacon" 33, 82, 88, 112–113, 143
Jones, Ed "Too Tall" 128
Jones, Homer 69

Kapp, Joe 1, 5–6, 18, 29, 31, 40, 44–46, 53–54, 56, 58–59, 61–63, 67–68, 95, 113–114, 144, 172, 184
Klobuchar, Jim 21, 67, 86, 149, 167, 195
Krause, Paul 2, 34–35, 42, 62, 64, 100, 105, 108, 111, 116–117, 119–122, 145, 147–148, 151–152, 158–159, 164–165, 167, 170, 175, 180, 182–187, 193, 197–198

Landry, Tom 15, 81, 84, 129
Larsen, Gary 5, 30–32, 86, 92–84, 105, 109, 187, 189
Lee, Bob 1, 4–5, 7, 32, 40, 46, 48, 53, 58–59, 61–63, 65–66, 113, 125–126, 144, 148, 166, 176–178, 180–181, 190, 198
Lilly, Bob 12, 85, 120, 190

Index

Lombardi, Vince 129, 144, 184
Los Angeles Rams 1–3, 9–10, 12, 18–20, 22, 27–33, 36–38, 40–42, 48, 53, 59, 61, 64, 73–74, 82, 85, 91–93, 98, 100–101, 105–113, 116, 119, 123, 125, 128, 130, 134, 137, 139, 142, 145, 147–155, 157–162, 169, 173, 175–178, 180–181, 184–185, 187, 189, 191–192, 199
Lukas, Paul 19–21, 37, 49–50, 94–95
Lurtsema, Bob 32, 109, 111–112, 119, 122–124, 126

Marinaro, Ed 58, 77, 123, 128–133, 196
Marshall, Jim 2–3, 6–7, 11, 15, 21, 24, 28, 31–32, 35, 40, 48–51, 54, 59, 90, 93, 96–97, 103–105, 109, 115, 122–124, 127, 141, 143, 146–147, 152, 160, 163, 169, 171, 186–187, 190, 192–195, 197–198
Mason, Tommy 3, 21, 24, 38, 48, 58, 93
McClanahan, Brent 58, 125, 127–129, 135–137, 143, 163, 168, 177, 196
McKeever, Marlin 42, 93, 184
Metropolitan Stadium 2, 4, 7, 12, 15, 17, 25, 27–28, 43, 45, 63, 65, 69, 78, 96, 105, 113, 118, 134, 141, 149, 162, 166–167, 189, 195
Michels, John 154, 189
Miller, Robert 58, 123, 128, 155–156, 178–180, 196
Moore, Lenny 60, 137, 157
Morton, Craig 66, 136
Mullaney, Mark 9, 76, 122, 124, 159–161, 176, 179, 195, 197

Oakland Raiders 30, 33, 68, 147, 156, 162–163, 181–182, 191
Osborn, Dave 28–29, 32, 35–40, 46, 51, 54, 58, 64, 66, 71, 77, 85, 95, 108–109, 131, 144, 165, 168–169

Page, Alan 2–3, 6, 11, 14, 22, 24–25, 30–32, 35, 40, 42, 47–50, 54, 66–67, 93–94, 97–99, 105, 107, 109–110, 120, 122–124, 127, 141, 146–147, 155, 163–164, 171, 173, 175–176, 186–187, 189–190, 193, 195, 198

Patera, Jack 29, 31, 93, 109, 124, 140
Pearson, Drew 9, 15, 88, 96, 104, 118, 121–123, 125–127, 142, 145, 149–152
Pearson, Preston 104, 118, 130
Pittsburgh Steelers 10, 21, 25, 38, 58, 68, 79, 91, 102–104, 130, 139–140, 147, 165–166, 181–182, 184
Poltl, Randy 110, 119, 165
Pugh, Jethro 86, 128

Rashad, Ahmad 44, 71, 87, 137–142, 147, 155, 157, 166, 177–178, 193
Reed, Oscar 38, 58, 69–70, 74–77, 85–87, 90, 131, 167, 173
Reichow, Jerry 2, 22–25, 38, 58–59, 61, 67, 76, 82, 89, 115, 119, 131–132, 148, 151, 154, 157, 171–173, 189, 194–195
Richards, Golden 120, 151
Robinson, Dave 74–75, 129, 172
Rose, Bert 17, 19, 27, 49, 130, 171
Ryan, Buddy 159
Ryan, Dennis 15, 17–18, 77–78, 94–95, 157, 192

Scott, Jake 134, 166
Siemon, Jeff 59, 94, 105, 107, 114, 116, 118, 120, 147–148, 152–154, 158–159, 163–164, 179, 187
Smith, Charles "Bubba" 39, 42, 44, 48, 60
Smith, Harrison 187
Smith, Jackie 10–11, 17, 73, 89–90, 101–104
Smith, Jim "Yazoo" 184–185
Snead, Norm 6, 30, 53, 58, 64–65, 67, 79, 114, 144
Sunde, Milt 29, 46, 78

Tarkenton, Francis 1–3, 10, 13, 16, 18, 21–22, 24, 35, 48, 52–53, 55–56, 58–59, 65, 67–71, 73–76, 78–84, 95–96, 99–100, 103, 105–108, 110, 114, 116. 121. 126, 128–130, 134, 136–138, 140–141, 143–144, 147–148, 154–159, 162–163, 165–168, 176–177, 187, 190–191, 193, 196, 198
Thomas, Duane 12, 17, 66, 196
Thomas, Joe 21–23, 27, 38, 171–172
Thomas, J.T. 165

Tingelhoff, Mick 46, 128, 143, 160, 187

uniforms (Vikings) 18–19, 21, 94

Van Brocklin, Norm 4, 12, 18–19, 21–24, 27, 35–36, 38, 49, 51, 60, 65, 80, 82, 94, 97, 119, 171, 185, 184
Vellone, Jim 28–29, 46, 173, 190
Voigt, Stu 34, 66, 72, 74–75, 77–78, 85–86, 101, 108, 127–128, 135–136, 143–148, 154, 163, 165, 168

Warwick, Lonnie 25, 30–31, 34, 48, 51–54, 58–60, 63, 65, 120, 153, 110–112, 186
Washington, Gene 2, 6, 10–13, 16–19, 22–25, 27, 32–35, 38, 43–49, 51–55, 58, 62, 64, 68, 72, 87–88, 142, 196
Washington Redskins 12, 33, 69–70, 78, 97, 114, 119, 134, 183, 186
Waters, Charlie 128–129
White, Dwight 164–165
White, Ed 21, 42, 58, 70, 75, 85–86, 93, 154–155, 157, 160, 166, 173, 175–176, 178, 180, 187–192
White, James "Duck" 195
White, Randy 120, 160
White, Sammy 44, 71, 134–140, 142, 147, 156–157. 163, 173, 177–178
Winston, Roy 31, 51–52, 89, 105, 107, 110, 116, 120, 152, 166, 171–173, 186
Winter, Max 41
Wright, Jeff 2, 99–101, 105–117, 119, 152, 181
Wright, Nate 71, 75, 90, 96–101, 103–105, 107, 117, 119, 121, 125–127, 149–150, 154, 152, 160–161
Wright, Rayfield 124

Yary, Ron 7, 21, 29–30, 42, 46, 52, 54–55, 58, 74–75, 85–86, 92–93, 112–114, 137–138, 143, 154–155, 160, 166, 169, 173–175, 178, 187–189, 192, 193
Youngblood, Jack 73–74, 106, 111–113, 143, 145, 154–155, 177, 188, 198
Youngblood, Jim 154

www.ingramcontent.com/pod-product-compliance
Lightning Source LLC
Chambersburg PA
CBHW060343010526
44117CB00017B/2946